A FOREST OF PEARLS
FROM THE DHARMA GARDEN
VOLUME V

BDK English Tripiṭaka Series

A FOREST OF PEARLS FROM THE DHARMA GARDEN

VOLUME V

(Taishō Volume 53, Number 2122)

Translated

by

Harumi Hirano Ziegler

BDK America, Inc.
2022

First Printing, 2022
ISBN: 978-1-886439-87-0
Library of Congress Catalog Card Number: 2019935629

Published by
BDK America, Inc.
1675 School Street
Moraga, California 94556

Printed in the United States of America

A Message on the Publication of the English Tripiṭaka

The Buddhist canon is said to contain eighty-four thousand different teachings. I believe that this is because the Buddha's basic approach was to prescribe a different treatment for every spiritual ailment, much as a doctor prescribes a different medicine for every medical ailment. Thus his teachings were always appropriate for the particular suffering individual and for the time at which the teaching was given, and over the ages not one of his prescriptions has failed to relieve the suffering to which it was addressed.

Ever since the Buddha's Great Demise over twenty-five hundred years ago, his message of wisdom and compassion has spread throughout the world. Yet no one has ever attempted to translate the entire Buddhist canon into English throughout the history of Japan. It is my greatest wish to see this done and to make the translations available to the many English-speaking people who have never had the opportunity to learn about the Buddha's teachings.

Of course, it would be impossible to translate all of the Buddha's eighty-four thousand teachings in a few years. I have, therefore, had one hundred thirty-nine of the scriptural texts in the prodigious Taishō edition of the Chinese Buddhist canon selected for inclusion in the First Series of this translation project.

It is in the nature of this undertaking that the results are bound to be criticized. Nonetheless, I am convinced that unless someone takes it upon himself or herself to initiate this project, it will never be done. At the same time, I hope that an improved, revised edition will appear in the future.

It is most gratifying that, thanks to the efforts of more than a hundred Buddhist scholars from the East and the West, this monumental project has finally gotten off the ground. May the rays of the Wisdom of the Compassionate One reach each and every person in the world.

NUMATA Yehan
Founder of the English
Tripiṭaka Project

August 7, 1991

Editorial Foreword

In the long history of Buddhist transmission throughout East Asia, translations of Buddhist texts were often carried out as national projects supported and funded by emperors and political leaders. The BDK English Tripiṭaka project, on the other hand, began as a result of the dream and commitment of one man. In January 1982 Dr. NUMATA Yehan, founder of Bukkyō Dendō Kyōkai (Society for the Promotion of Buddhism), initiated the monumental task of translating the complete Taishō shinshū daizōkyō edition of the Chinese Tripiṭaka (Buddhist canon) into the English language. Under his leadership, a special preparatory committee was organized in April 1982. By July of the same year the Translation Committee of the English Tripiṭaka was officially convened.

The initial Committee included the following members: (late) HANAYAMA Shōyū (Chairperson), (late) BANDŌ Shōjun, (late) ISHIGAMI Zennō, (late) KAMATA Shigeo, (late) KANAOKA Shūyū, MAYEDA Sengaku, (late) NARA Yasuaki, (late) SAYEKI Shinkō, (late) SHIOIRI Ryōtatsu, (late) TAMARU Noriyoshi, (late) TAMURA Kwansei, (late) URYŪZU Ryūshin, and (late) YUYAMA Akira. Assistant members of the Committee were as follows: KANAZAWA Atsushi, WATANABE Shōgo, Rolf Giebel of New Zealand, and Rudy Smet of Belgium.

After holding planning meetings on a monthly basis, the Committee selected one hundred and thirty-nine texts for the First Series of the project, estimated to be one hundred printed volumes in all. The texts selected were not limited to those originally written in India but also included works composed in China and Japan. While the publication of the First Series proceeds, the texts for the Second Series will be selected from among the remaining works; this process will continue until all the texts, in Japanese as well as in Chinese, have been published. Given the huge scope of this project, accomplishing the English translations of all the Chinese and Japanese texts in the Taishō canon may take as long as one hundred years or more. Nevertheless, as Dr. NUMATA wished, it is the sincere hope of the Committee that this project will continue until completion, even after all the present members have passed away.

Dr. NUMATA passed away on May 5, 1994, at the age of ninety-seven. He entrusted his son, Mr. NUMATA Toshihide with the continuation and completion of the English Tripiṭaka project. Mr. Numata served for twenty-three years, leading the project forward with enormous progress before his sudden passing on February 16, 2017, at the age of eighty-four. The Committee previously lost its able and devoted first Chairperson, Professor HANAYAMA Shōyū, on June 16, 1995, at the age of sixty-three. In October 1995 the Committee elected Professor MAYEDA Sengaku (then Vice President of Musashino Women's College) as Chairperson, and upon the retirement of Professor Mayeda in July 2016, the torch was passed to me to serve as the third Chairperson. Despite these losses and changes we, the Editorial Committee members, have renewed our determination to carry out the noble ideals set by Dr. NUMATA. Present members of the Committee are Kenneth K. Tanaka (Chairperson), MAYEDA Sengaku, ICHISHIMA Shōshin, KATSURA Shōryū, MINOWA Kenryō, SAITŌ Akira, SHIMODA Masahiro, WATANABE Shōgo, and YONEZAWA Yoshiyasu.

The Numata Center for Buddhist Translation and Research was established in November 1984, in Berkeley, California, U.S.A., to assist in the publication of the translated texts. The Publication Committee was organized at the Numata Center in December 1991. In 2010, the Numata Center's operations were merged with Bukkyō Dendō Kyōkai America, Inc. (BDK America), and BDK America continues to oversee the publication side of the English Tripiṭaka project in close cooperation with the Editorial Committee in Tokyo.

At the time of this writing, in July 2017, the project has completed about sixty-five percent of the seven thousand one hundred and eighty-five Taishō pages of texts selected for the First Series. Much work still lies ahead of us but we are committed to the completion of the remaining texts in order to realize the grand vision of Dr. Numata, shared by Mr. Numata and Professor Hanayama, to make the Buddhist canon more readily accessible to the English-speaking world.

Kenneth K. Tanaka
Chairperson
Editorial Committee of
the BDK English Tripiṭaka

Publisher's Foreword

On behalf of the members of the Publication Committee, I am happy to present this volume as the latest contribution to the BDK English Tripiṭaka Series. The Publication Committee members have worked to ensure that this volume, as all other volumes in the series, has gone through a rigorous process of editorial efforts.

The initial translation and editing of the Buddhist scriptures found in this and other BDK English Tripiṭaka volumes are performed under the direction of the Editorial Committee in Tokyo, Japan. Both the Editorial Committee in Tokyo and the Publication Committee, headquartered in Moraga, California, are dedicated to the production of accurate and readable English translations of the Buddhist canon. In doing so, the members of both committees and associated staff work to honor the deep faith, spirit, and concern of the late Reverend Dr. Yehan Numata, who founded the BDK English Tripiṭaka Series in order to disseminate the Buddhist teachings throughout the world.

The long-term goal of our project is the translation and publication of the texts in the one hundred-volume Taishō edition of the Chinese Buddhist canon, along with a number of influential extracanonical Japanese Buddhist texts. The list of texts selected for the First Series of this translation project may be found at the end of each volume in the series.

As Chair of the Publication Committee, I am deeply honored to serve as the fifth person in a post previously held by leading figures in the field of Buddhist studies, most recently by my predecessor, John R. McRae.

In conclusion, I wish to thank the members of the Publication Committee for their dedicated and expert work undertaken in the course of preparing this volume for publication: Managing Editor Marianne Dresser, Dr. Hudaya Kandahjaya, Dr. Carl Bielefeldt, Dr. Robert Sharf, and Rev. Brian Kensho Nagata, Director of the BDK English Tripiṭaka Project.

A. Charles Muller
Chairperson
Publication Committee

Contents

Translator's Introduction

The *Fayuan zhulin* (*A Forest of Pearls from the Dharma Garden*), compiled by Shi Daoshi at Ximing Monastery, belongs to the category of *leishu* (reference books with entries arranged according to subjects) in the classification of Chinese literature.[1] As such, this work can be considered an encyclopedia of Buddhism.

As for *leishu* of Buddhism prior to the *Fayuan zhulin,* catalogues of Buddhist scriptures list several titles, including the *Fayuan jing* (*Sutras in the Dharma Garden*), in one hundred and eighty-nine fascicles,[2] and the *Neidian boyao* (*Extensive Essential Points of Buddhist Scriptures*), in thirty fascicles, compiled by Yu Xiaojing of the Liang dynasty,[3] which was one model for the *Fayuan zhulin.*[4] However, only the *Jinglü yixiang* (*Various Phases of the Sutras and Vinayas,* T. 2121), in fifty fascicles, compiled by Baochang in 516 C.E., and the *Zhujing yaoji* (*Collected Summaries of All Scriptures,* T. 2123), in twenty fascicles, by Shi Daoshi are currently extant.

Regarding the completion date of the *Fayuan zhulin,* two different dates are found in Li Yan's preface to the text: "In the first year of the Zongzhang period (668 C.E.), on the thirtieth day of the third month, the compilation was completed."[5] Yet another preface to the *Fayuan zhulin* by Li Yan, found in Daoxuan's *Guang hongming ji,* says, "The compilation was completed in the third year of the Linde period of the Great Tang dynasty, the Year of the Tiger (666 C.E.), on the tenth day of the third month."[6] While the former date is most commonly used,[7] the completion date for this compilation remains controversial. Ichirō Kominami agrees with Yoshiteru Kawaguchi's theory that the compilation was first completed in 666 C.E. and a new edition was brought out in 668.[8]

According to Shi Daoshi's biography in the *Song gaoseng zhuan,*[9] Daoshi was also known as Xuanyun (pseudonym). He was from the Han family whose ancestors had emigrated from Yique (present-day southern suburbs of Luoyang) to Chang'an. His birth and death dates are unknown. Daoshi renounced the world at the age of twelve at the Qinglong (Blue Dragon) Monastery in Chang'an, where he studied vinaya texts. Later he joined Xuanzang's scripture translation group and moved to Ximing Monastery where he promoted Buddhism with his senior, the monk Daoxuan.

The *Fayuan zhulin* is composed of one hundred chapters starting with "The Measurement of the World Age" (*jieliang*) and closing with "Biographies" (*zhuanji*). Each chapter is divided into several sections (*bu*). In some cases, sections are further subdivided, forming a complicated structure. In the twenty-eight chapters, from Chapter Ten to Chapter Thirty-seven, that I have translated, the basic framework of each chapter is that it begins with an introduction (*shuyi*), followed by quotations from sutras, vinayas, or *śāstra*s, and miracle stories (*ganying yuan*) about events that took place in China, related to the theme of the chapter, serve as the conclusion.[10] The adoption of miracle stories is the most significant distinction of the *Fayuan zhulin,* and is not a feature found in the other extant *leishu,* the *Jinglü yixiang* and the *Zhujing yaoji.*

Following the *Jinglü yixiang,* Daoshi indicates the sources of all quotations from Buddhist scriptures in both the *Fayuan zhulin* and the *Zhujing yaoji.* In the *Jinglü yixiang* the source of an explanation or description quoted from Buddhist scriptures is given after the quotation, while in the *Fayuan zhulin* and the *Zhujing yaoji* the title of the source scripture comes before the quotation. Similarly, Daoshi provides a source for every miracle story, and these sources are various and extensive, including official histories, monks' biographies, local gazetteers, travel records and journals, and narrative literature. It is particularly remarkable that many stories of *zhiguai* (literary works of mysterious stories), mostly compiled during the Six Dynasties period (222–589 C.E.), such as the *Mingxiang ji* (*Records of the Profound and Auspicious*) and the *Mingbao ji* (*Records of Rewards and Retributions from the Unseen World*), are quoted.

Thanks to Daoshi's indication of the sources of the quotations from Buddhist scriptures and miracle stories, we can see what Buddhist texts were circulated and how Buddhism was accepted by Chinese people from the Six Dynasties period through the early Tang dynasty (third century to mid-seventh century). We also find many texts, both Buddhist and non-Buddhist, cited in the *Fayuan zhulin* that are no longer extant. Kawaguchi's study shows that one hundred and four Buddhist scriptures (sutras, vinayas, and *śāstra*s) among those quoted in the *Fayuan zhulin* are not included in the Taishō canon. Of these, forty-four texts have never been listed in any Buddhist catalogue.[11] Outside of Buddhist scriptures, there are various miracle stories from lost literary works in the *Fayuan zhulin.* It is well known that Lu Xun compiled the *Guxiaoshuo gouchen* by collecting major stories from this encyclopedia of Buddhism.[12] In addition to these lost texts, the *Fayuan zhulin* provides a good corpus of material for the study of Sinitic Buddhism.[13]

A FOREST OF PEARLS FROM THE DHARMA GARDEN

VOLUME V

Fascicle 28

Chapter Twenty

Wonders

(This chapter consists of five parts:) (1) Introduction, (2) Competition of Supernatural Powers, (3) Subduing Demons, (4) Conception [of Life], and (5) Miscellaneous Wonders.

1. Introduction

Regarding the Way of the Spirit that stands as edification, it is likely intended to restrain arrogance and violence, to smash haughtiness and rudeness, to quell excessiveness and vigorousness, and to remove worldly troubles. As for the sun and the imperial seal, people have good faith and surrender to them. In case of being suffocated by smoke among towering rocks, even a strongman would conceal himself [to avoid it]. We must know that perfect good order is detachment, and toughness and gentleness consist in edification.

Therefore, some [monks] conceal their abilities and intentions and stoop to be the same as deluded secular people. Some [monks] manifest miracles and from a distance account for divination based on directions. Some [monks] die and are reborn. Some [monks] meditate and annihilate themselves later. There is nothing to survey the condition of their spiritual trances and strange and rare conduct.

Those who are valued in truth agree with the [Buddhist] Way and those who are valued in phenomena relieve people. Therefore an incarnation of a buddha or bodhisattva goes against the ordinary way and yet agrees with the [Buddhist] Way, benefiting and encouraging people in order to accomplish their task.There is nothing in historical records, however, to examine this in detail. It is either the Dharma body's response to [sentient beings'] feelings or a reclusive transcendent's lofty and outstanding [manifestation]. He merely divides one [body into multiple bodies; one of the divided bodies] has the capacity of two persons combined and is then sufficiently lofty.

If someone brags about his divination or medical skill, disorders the times by means of corrupt ways, flies high owing to medicines, or seeks for a long life relying on a fragrant mushroom, is it any different from cocks crowing above heaven and dogs barking in the clouds (i.e., ascending to heaven by taking medicine), snakes and cranes being immortal, or turtles living a thousand years? These cannot be compared with the sacred transformations.

What are collected now are just the records of *śrāvaka*s' three or five miracles. If we try to talk about all the buddhas' and bodhisattvas' sacred virtues and freedom, it is impossible to know them by means of language or to speculate about them by means of mind. As I enumerate them throughout this compilation in every possible way, I am not concerned with them in this chapter.

2. Competition of Supernatural Powers

Just as the *Dafangdeng daji nianfo sanmei jing* says:[14]

> Mahāmaudgalyāyana said to Ānanda, "I recollect that I formerly took this trichiliocosm entirely into my mouth in a short time. At that time sentient beings were consequently astonished, and they did not have a thought of the transmigration of birth and death even for a moment.
>
> "Moreover, I remember that in former times I expounded the Dharma before the World-honored One as powerfully as a lion roars. I could put Mount Sumeru into my mouth and pass through for a *kalpa* or a *hāni-kalpa*
> 487b (*jianjie*).[15] I did things like this regularly. I further recall that in former days I reached the east and resided in the trichiliocosm there. There was a big city called Treasure Gate. In that place there were six million upon a billion households. In each household I manifested myself and expounded the Dharma for them and caused them to peacefully abide in the true Dharma."
>
> At that time Śāriputra said to Ānanda, "I remember that in olden days I took a *kaṣāya* [robe] and threw it on the ground. Mahāmaudgalyāyana, the greatest among the monks of the upper seats, was awesome and marvelous like this. Yet he was unable to take up [the *kaṣāya*] at all. He could not lift it up and cause it to part from the earth. Why coulddn't he lift it with his hands?
>
> "Ānanda, I further remember that I formerly expounded the Dharma before the World-honored One as powerfully as a lion roars. At that time

various non-Buddhists intended to compete with me by making themselves invisible and preaching the Dharma. Except for the World-honored One who sees with all-knowing wisdom (Skt. *sarvajña-jñāna*) and bodhisattvas who have great powers, all the other *śrāvaka*s and Buddha's disciples including non-Buddhists asked where I had been during the whole time I had disappeared. In the end they could not know where I had been."

At that time, Mahākāśyapa said to Ānanda, "I recollect that one time I expounded the Dharma before the World-honored One as powerfully as a lion roars. I was able to break and scatter Mount Sumeru and all kinds of mountains in this trichiliocosm by blowing a wind from my mouth. Consequently there was nothing left, not even anything as small as fine dust. Some sentient beings who dwelled in those mountains were not harmed nor were they aware of it, either. In this way all the mountains were entirely wiped out.

"In addition, one time I caused all the water of all the great seas, rivers, and ponds including the immeasurable water pools in this trichiliocosm all to dry up by blowing a wind from my mouth, but the sentient beings [who lived] there did not know it and they were not aware of anything.[16]

"Moreover, I once expounded the Dharma before the masses as powerfully as a lion roars. In the trichiliocosm I could cause a conflagration to burn vigorously throughout, just like the fire *kalpa* (Skt. *kalpa-dāha*), by blowing a wind from my mouth. Not a single sentient being was injured at all, either. They went through the whole course being unaware of it."

At that time, various great bodhisattvas such as Maitreya and Mañjuśrī heard Mahākāśyapa's expounding the Dharma as powerfully as a lion roars. Consequently they immediately scattered transformed flowers as massive as Mount Sumeru over Kāśyapa repeatedly. Furthermore, by supernatural power they made a large seven-treasure canopy, which hovered in the air and covered the crown of Mahākāśyapa's head as well as all of the *śrāvaka*s and the sangha.

At that time, Pūrṇa said to Ānanda, "I remember that in the past, among sentient beings, there were those who had to be edified with supernatural powers. For their sakes I then took up the trichiliocosm, rolled it in my hands, and showed it to them. Just at that moment not even a single sentient being had a thought of fear. They were not aware of [what had happened], either. Only those sentient beings who had to be given the edification saw that I had rolled up this world in my hands.

"Again, I can take the trichiliocosm and turn it in my hands. I do not think it is difficult to do so. Furthermore, before the World-honored One, I took up all the pools of water in this trichiliocosm with one of my knuckles
487c and placed them between my knuckles. There was not even a single sentient being who had a thought of loss.

"Moreover, in the early night (7:00–9:00 P.M.), I once observed with my pure heavenly eyes that in this trichiliocosm all immeasurable sentient beings [give rise to] doubts. Without coming out of meditation, I [thought that I] should entirely remove their doubts for them. I caused each of those sentient beings to give rise to the thought, 'I am favored by the Venerable One who alone stays before me and explains for me.' In accordance with each one's faculty, they attained a benefit. No one had obstruction and hindrance."

At that time Rāhula said to Ānanda, "I remember that in the past I kept all kinds of mountains in this trichiliocosm within a pore of my skin. My body was as before and sentient beings had nothing unusual. Furthermore, I once put all the pools of water, the great seas, rivers, and ponds in this trichiliocosm entirely into the pores of my skin, yet my body was not damaged and no sentient beings were harmed. All of the pools of water [in my body] were just like the original.

"Moreover, I once entered meditation at this place and then reached a buddha land in the northeast. The buddha there is called Nansheng.[17] After revealing my body and bowing to [that buddha], I immediately returned to this world. I sought sandalwood incense, brought it back, and offered it to [Nansheng] Buddha. The incense perfumed everywhere. I made all immeasurable various transformations."

At that time Subhūti said to Ānanda, "I recall that I once entered *samādhi.* This trichiliocosm, as great and broad as this, I placed on a tip of my hair and turned it round and round just like a potter's wheel. Just at that time there was not even a single sentient being who had fear. [Sentient beings] did not realize that they were [on a tip of my hair], either.

"Furthermore, I formerly expounded the Dharma before the Tathāgata as powerfully as a lion roars. I said, 'O World-honored One! If I can blow a slight wind from my mouth to the trichiliocosm like this and cause it to entirely scatter and vanish, I will cause the sentient beings in it to not be surprised or frightened and to have no thought of this change.'

"What is more, [I said] before the Buddha, 'I can place all sentient beings of the trichiliocosm entirely on a tip of my finger, go to Akaniṣṭha Heaven, return to my original place, and cause those sentient beings to have no thought of going and returning.'

"Again, I remember that I once easily sat in *samādhi.* I saw all the buddhas in the ten directions. In each of all sorts of immeasurable and vast worlds there were sixty thousand various buddhas. I had not seen them previously but I recognize them all now. On this account I manifested supernatural power by the mind of meditative concentration, came to the summit of Mount Sumeru, took a handful of the sandalwood incense powder at Śakra-devendra's side, and went to those all immeasurable worlds where I made an offering to some tathāgatas of former times. All the sentient beings of those worlds clearly saw that I had remained [all the time] in this Jambudvīpa, and made offerings to and served [those tathāgatas]."

3. Subduing Demons

Just as the *Ayuwang jing* says:[18]

In ancient times King Aśoka deeply believed in the Three Treasures, to
which he frequently made offerings. All the brahmans and non-Buddhists 488a
became jealous. They got together, selected seniors, and chose five hundred people, who all recited the four kinds of the sacred books of the Vedas. They had broad knowledge of astronomy, geography, and other things. They met and discussed together, [saying,] "King Aśoka offers everything completely to the tonsured people. We, senior [brahmans], have not received anything from him. We must set up some expedient means to cause his intention to turn to us." There was a brahman who was good at making spells. He said, "All virtuous ones! Just follow me! In seven days I will transform into Maheśvara (i.e., Śiva) by means of the power of a spell and fly to the palace gate. You should all follow me on foot. I can cause [King Aśoka] to make great offerings, which you will all obtain." All the brahmans consented to do so.

At the beginning of the seventh day the brahman who was good at making spells chanted a spell and transformed himself into Maheśvara. He flew in the air and approached the imperial gate. All the brahmans accompanied him, drawing near to the imperial gate. They sent a messenger to address to the king, "Maheśvara is there in the air. He leads four hundred ninety-nine brahmans. He descended from the sky and is now outside the gate. Other brahmans are on the ground below. He wishes to be granted an audience with you."

King Aśoka summoned them and had them come before [him]. Those who were summoned came in and sat on couches on either side of the state chamber. The king said, "Be seated and at ease!" [The king and the brahmans] questioned one another, and then [the king] said to [the brahmans], "O Maheśvara! Why did you oblige yourself to come to see me? What do you want?" Maheśvara replied, "I want food and drink." [The king] immediately ordered them to a kitchen. [Servants] carried five hundred tables of food and drink and placed them before [the brahmans]. Maheśvara and the others all pushed them away with their hands and said, "We have never had food like this since the time we were born." King Aśoka responded, "I ordered [this food] without a previous agreement. I do not know what kind of food you wish to eat." Maheśvara and all others said with one voice, "What we wish to eat are the tonsured people."

King Aśoka promptly ordered a vassal, "You! Go to Kurkuṭārāma Monastery and tell Venerable Yaśa that there are five hundred brahmans in the imperial palace. One of them calls himself Maheśvara but I do not know whether this is a person or an evil *rākṣasa*— please tell me the cause of this. I beg the *ācārya* to come and send them away, to make them leave for my sake!"

The man who was sent with the message was a disciple of a brahman of wrong views. When he came to the sangha his intention was not to tell what the king had really said. [The messenger said,] "King Aśoka has five hundred brahmans, whose features look like those of human beings and whose language sounds like that of the *rākṣasa*s. They said only these words, 'We want to get the *śramaṇa*s in order to make a meal of them.'"

Yaśa, the senior monk of the monastery, talked to a monk in charge of clerical work, "Make a sound by beating with a hammer to call the monks

to assemble!" He stood up and said to the sangha, "Since I am extremely old, I would like to deal with things like this for the sake of the sangha. The sangha peacefully protects and maintains the Buddhist Dharma. Listen 488b
to me and let me go!" The second senior monk said, "You should not go. I am not skillful in anything. I think I should go." The third [senior monk] said, "The second senior monk should not go. You just need me to go." In this way the issue was turned round and round, reaching even to the novices.

A seven-year-old novice, the lowest rank among a hundred and sixty eight thousand sangha members, stood up and came into the midst of the sangha. He kneeled upright with his hands joined in prayer and said, "All great monks do not deserve to be agitated. Since I am a child, I am unable to be competent in the task of protecting and maintaining the Buddhist Dharma. I pray only that the sangha will certainly let me go." The senior monk Yaśa was extremely delighted. He said, patting the novice on the head, "Boy, you are suitable to go."

The messenger did not wait for [the novice] and left first. Aśoka asked him, "Is anyone coming?" He answered, "They shifted [responsibility] from one to another and a novice of the lowest rank is coming now." The king said, "Since adults have a sense of shame, they made a child come deal with [the brahmans]." King Aśoka heard that the novice had arrived. He went out of the gate to meet [the novice]. He took a seat and bade the novice to sit next to him. All the brahmans were in great dudgeon, [saying,] "King Aśoka seriously failed to discern [people]. We are virtuous old masters yet he did not stand up to meet us, while he went out in person to greet this young boy."

The novice asked the king, "Why did you summon me?" The king answered, "This Maheśvara wants to get an *ācārya* to eat as food. I will let the *ācārya* ponder whether or not he wants to be eaten." The novice said, "I am a child. I have not had a meal yet since this morning. O king, please give me food first. Later I will give [myself] to be eaten." The king then ordered a cook [to prepare some food] and [a servant] came with a meal and gave it to [the novice]. [The novice] ate all the food on the table; everything was completely consumed. In this way [servants] brought five hundred sets of meals and gave them to [the boy], and yet he was still not full. The king again ordered the cook, "Bring all the remaining food and give it to him." All the food brought to the novice was completely consumed in an instant. [The king] asked, "Are you full?" [The novice] replied, "No, not yet. I am as hungry and thirsty as I was at the beginning." A kitchen supervisor addressed the king, "All the food and drink are gone." The king said, "Bring all the dried wheat, dried meat, and all other dried foods from my storehouse!" [Again,] it was all instantly consumed. The king asked, "Are you full?" [The novice] replied, "No, not yet." The king said to him, "All the food and drink are now completely gone. There is no more food." The novice said, "Please bring the brahmans of the low rank! I would like to eat them. I will consume them in an instant." In this way he consumed all four hundred and ninety-nine brahmans. Only Maheśvara remained, and he was struck with intense fear. He flew into the sky, intending to escape. From his seat the novice promptly raised his hands, grasped Maheśvara's head with his fingers from the sky, and consumed him completely.

The king was immediately very frightened. He saw that [the novice] had eaten all brahmans up [and thought,] "Is he going to eat me, too?"
488c The novice knew the king's thought. So, he said to the king, "O king! You are a donor for the Buddhist Dharma. You will have no loss after all. Do not fear indeed!" Then he said to the king, "Could you come to Kurkuṭārāma Monastery with me?" The king replied, "You, *ācārya*, lead me. I must follow you to go up to heaven or to enter the earth."

The novice quickly arrived at Kurkuṭārāma Monastery along with the king. The king saw all the food the novice had eaten in the morning. All the sangha members shared the food and ate together. All of the five hundred brahmans that had been consumed by [the novice] had shaved their beards and hair and put on Dharma robes. They were in the lowest seats of the bottom row among all the sangha members. The one who ate first was the head monk, who sat on the upper seat, while Maheśvara stayed at the end of the row. When the five hundred people saw the king and the novice they were extremely ashamed of themselves. [They said,] "We are still unable to contend with this novice, much less compete with all the sangha members in power. We are just like the tail of a crane that awaits at a fireplace, like a mosquito that competes in the speed of flight with a *garuḍa* bird, or like a small rabbit that competes with a lion king in destructive force. Just as in these comparisons, we overrated our own abilities." The five hundred brahmans felt ashamed in their minds. They attained the path of the *srota-āpatti-phala.*

4. Conception [of Life]

Just as the *Za baozang jing* (T. 203) says:

> The Buddha said to the *bhikṣus*, "In the immeasurable remotest past there was a mountain called Mount Ṛṣi (Xianshan; Mount Immortal) in Vārāṇasī. A brahman resided on that mountain. He often relieved himself on a rock. Afterward he emitted semen, which fell into the place where he had discharged urine. A doe came and licked it. At that moment [the doe] became pregnant. When her full term came she went to the [brahman] hermit's place and gave birth to a girl. [The girl] was well-featured and extremely good, but her feet looked like a doe's hooves. The brahman accepted her and brought her up.
>
> "This brahman worshiped fire; he tended the fire and kept it alive. The girl kept the all-night vigil for the fire but she was slightly careless and allowed the fire to die out. She was frightened, afraid of the brahman's anger. There was another brahman who lived apart from this residence. The girl went to him and begged him for a fire.[19] The brahman saw the path she had tread and lotus flowers [had sprung up] on the course. He requested the girl, saying, 'Go around my house seven times and I will give you a fire. When you leave here, go around [the house] seven more times. Do not walk on your original pathway. Go home using a different path.' She did so, following his instruction, took the fire, and left.
>
> "At that time King Brahmadatta went out hunting. He saw the brahman circumambulating his house surrounded by fourteenfold lotus flowers. [The king] also saw two paths on which there were two lines of [lotus] flowers. He wondered about this and asked the brahman, 'There is no water pond here at all. Why are there such wonderful flowers?' [The brahman] explained [what had occurred] in detail to him.
>
> "Looking around on the trail of the flowers, the king came to the [first] brahman's place. He accordingly sought the girl and found her. [The king] saw that she was well-featured and she suited his fancy. He immediately

489a asked the brahman for the girl, and the brahman gave her to the king. The king then installed her as his second wife.

"Later she became pregnant. A physiognomist divined and said, "She will give birth to a thousand children.' The king's legitimate wife (i.e., the queen) heard about this and became jealous. She schemed little by little against [the second wife]. With great favors she summoned the doe girl's servants, instructed them in person, and gave them many valuables.

"[The girl's] full time came and she gave birth to thousand-leaved lotus flowers. When they were about to be born, the queen covered [the girl's] eyes and did not allow her to see for herself.[20] [The queen] took some rotten and stinking horse's lungs, and put them under [the girl]. Then she took the thousand-leaved lotus flowers, piled them up in a basket, and threw them into a river. She came back, unwound the bandage from [the girl's eyes], and said to her, 'Look at what you gave birth to! There is only a gobbet of rotten and stinking horse's lungs.'

"The king sent his man to ask, 'What did you give birth to?' [The girl] replied to the king, 'I gave birth only to a stinking lung.' The queen said to the king, 'O king! Are you happy about this embarrassment of what this animal gave birth to? She who was raised by the hermit gave birth to this inauspicious stinking and filthy thing.' The king promptly deposed [the girl] from the position of [second] wife and no longer allowed her to see him.

"At that time King Udayana (Wuqiyan), along with various attendants, followers, wives, and court ladies, was playing downstream [in the river]. He saw something covered by a yellow cloud come floating down toward him, following the current from the upper stream. He thought, 'There must be supernatural beings under this cloud.' [The king] sent someone to go and see this. [This person] saw a basket under the yellow cloud and promptly took it. [The king] opened it and found the thousand-leaved lotus flowers; each leaf contained an infant boy. He took [the boys] under his charge and raised them. Whent they eventually grew up they all had enormous strength.

"King Udayana usually made an annual tribute to King Brahmadatta. He collected all the articles for presentation and dispatched a messenger, who was about to leave. All the boys asked, 'What are you going to do?' The king replied, 'I would like to pay a tribute to King Brahmadatta of that [state].' All of the boys said, 'If one has a boy he still wishes to be able to prostrate the world and cause others to come and pay tribute to him, much more if you have a thousand boys. Yet you are going to pay tribute to that [king]!' His thousand boys immediately led the military forces and conquered various countries. Eventually they reached Brahmadatta's state.

"King [Brahmadatta] heard that the army had come so he recruited soldiers from all over the country. [He asked,] 'Who can repel enemies like this?' None, however, could repel them at all. [The king's former] second wife came by [the king's] invitation and said, 'I can drive them away.' She was asked, 'How can you drive them away?' [The king's former] wife replied, 'Just make a platform a hundred *zhang* high for me. If I sit upon it, I will certainly be able to repel them.' After the platform was completed [the king's former] wife sat on it.

"At that time the thousand sons were about to lift up their bows to shoot, but spontaneously they could not raise their hands. [The king's former] wife said, 'You, be cautious! Do not raise your hands against your parents! I am your mother.' The thousand sons asked her, 'With what can you prove it?' The mother answered her sons, 'When I massage my breasts each breast will emit five hundred streams of milk, which will go into your mouths. This is [proof that I am] your mother. If this does not come to pass then I am not your mother.' She immediately massaged her breasts
with both hands. Each breast poured out five hundred streams of milk, 489b
which entered the mouths of her thousand sons. None of other soldiers received [the milk]. The thousand sons surrendered. Facing their parents, they repented. They all thereupon harmonized with [their parents] and there was no enmity between the two countries. They spontaneously exhorted and led each other to give five hundred sons to the biological parents and the other five hundred sons to the foster parents. At that time the two kings shared Jambudvīpa and each raised five hundred sons."

The Buddha said, "If you want to know about a thousand sons of that time, they are a thousand buddhas of the auspicious *kalpa.* The jealous queen who deceived the others at that time is the blind dragon Mucilinda. The father of that time is King Śuddhodana, and the mother of that time is Lady Māyā.

All the *bhikṣus* addressed the Buddha, "Through what cause and condition did this girl come to be reborn in a doe's womb and to produce lotus flowers under her feet? Moreover, by what cause did she become a king's wife?"

The Buddha said, "This girl was reborn in a impoverished family in her former existence, and both she and her mother hoed the fields for grains. They saw a *pratyekabuddha* holding a bowl and begging for alms. The mother said to her daughter, 'I would like to take my portion of food from our house and give it to this good fellow.' The girl said, 'I will also take my share and give it [to him].' The mother then went home, took their share of food, and started back to give it to the *pratyekabuddha.*

"[In the meantime,] the girl picked grasses and collected flowers and for [the *pratyekabuddha*] she spread out a seat mat of grasses, scattered flowers on [the mat], and waited for the *pratyekabuddha* to be seated.

"The girl wondered why her mother was taking so long. She ascended to an elevated spot and saw her mother in the distance. After meeting her mother she said to her, 'Why did you not hasten? Even a deer comes more swiftly.' [Although] the mother had already come, [the girl] was not happy about her mother's delay, and subsequently said in resentment, 'I was reborn at my mother's side but it is not as good as being reborn to a doe.'

"The mother then gave their food to the *pratyekabuddha,* and the mother and daughter together ate the leftovers. After the *pratyekabuddha* ate, he threw his bowl up into the air and made eighteen kinds of transformations. At that time the mother was greatly delighted and vowed, 'Please let me be always reborn in the future as a sage just like this saint here today.' For this karmic condition, she later gave birth to five hundred sons, who all attained the state of a *pratyekabuddha.* One [group of the five hundred sons] became the foster mother's and the other became the biological mother's. Because [the daughter] had said to her mother, 'Even a deer comes more swiftly,' she was reborn in a doe's womb and her feet looked like a doe's hooves. Because she had collected flowers and scattered them over the *pratyekabuddha,* she produced a hundred flowers wherever she left her footprints. Because she had spread [a mat of] grasses [for the *pratyekabuddha*], she was continually able to become a king's wife. The mother became King Brahmadatta in a later rebirth and the daughter became

Lady Lotus Flowers in a later rebirth. By this karmic condition she later gave birth to the thousand sages of the auspicious *kalpa.* By the power of her vow [the mother] was continually reborn as a worthy or a sage."

After hearing this, all the *bhikṣu*s rejoiced. They upheld and practiced the teaching.

Moreover, the *Fenbie gongde jing* (i.e., *Fenbie gongde lun,* T. 1507) says:

In the past there was a wealthy man called Sudatta. In his family there was a daughter who had not yet gone out of the gate (i.e., engaged with the outside world). At home, as she sat in front of the fire, a warm vapor entered her body and she thereupon became pregnant. Her parents were surprised and asked her the cause of this situation. The daughter answered that she 489c
really had no idea of the cause. The parents repeatedly asked her and beat her with a cane or whipped her, but she had no other answer. Consequently they reported [the event] to the king. The king also pressed [the girl] for an answer, yet her answer was the same. The king then sentenced her to atone for it with death. She said resentfully, "In this world there is such an unreasonable king as you! You are wrongly killing an innocent person. If I did something bad I should have been responsible to examine myself. [Nevertheless, as a matter of fact] I will be wrongly [killed for having suffered] like this." The king examined [the matter] further and verified it was just as the girl had said. There was nothing added or left out [of her account]. The king said to the parents, "I would like to take her in marriage." The mother replied, "Please take her in marriage as you please! What will you do with this condemned girl?" The king admitted her into the palace and supported her at all times. When her full term came she gave birth to a boy who was well-featured and extremely wonderful. When he grew up he renounced the world and attained the [Buddhist] Way. He was bright and erudite. He practiced diligently and quickly attained the path of arhatship. He also liberated his father [the king] and his mother.

Furthermore, the *Piyu jing* (*Sutra of Allegories*) says:[21]

Formerly there was a married couple who had no child. They worshiped the heavenly god and offered sacrifices seeking a son to succeed them. The god heard them and subsequently the wife became pregnant. She gave birth to four kinds of objects. First was uncooked rice in a large sandalwood container; second was a bottle of nectar; third was a bag of treasures; and fourth was a supernatural cane with seven knots. The man lamented, "I prayed to the god for a son, who was reborn as other objects." Then, he went to the god's place and repeatedly prayed for what he wished. The god said, "You wish to obtain a son. What beneficial things can you say?" The man answered, "My son should give support to us." The god said, "Eat the rice! This peck [of rice] is inexhaustible even if you eat it all. The bottle of nectar and honey will not decrease when you drink it, and it removes all sorts of diseases. There will be no less of the jewels and valuables in the bag if you use them. You can defend against atrocious beings with the supernatural cane with seven knots. How could a son better these?" The man was greatly happy, returned home, and tried the objects. As he had been told, it was not false. He consequently made a great fortune that could not be calculated. Hearing of this, the king immediately sent many soldiers to go attack him and take [the four objects] by force. The man lifted the cane and flew about, attacking his enemies. He destroyed the powerful soldiers and they all completely dispersed. The man was greatly delighted and there was no further touble.

5. Miscellaneous Wonders

Just as the *Piyu jing* says:[22]

In former times there was a rich and influential family of long standing. They buried a thousand *hu* of collected grain in the ground.[23] A warm spring came and they opened the cellar in order to take some seeds of the grain but they could not find them at all. There was, however, an insect as large as a cow.[24] [The insect] had neither hands nor feet, and no head or eyes, either. It was just an insensible piece of flesh. Everyone, the master of the family, the adults, and the children, was surprised at it. [The insect] came out onto the flatland. [The people] asked it, "What are you?" Consistently it said nothing. [The insect] then stabbed one hole with an iron awl and said, "If you want to know what I am, take me and place me on the side of a wide road. There will naturally be someone who knows me." So they carried the insect and placed it on the side of a wide road.

In three days no one could name [the insect]. On the next day there were several hundred yellow carriages and the attendants' clothes were 490a
[also] all yellow. They halted the carriages and [one] cried out, "The grain thief! Why are you here?" [The insect] replied, "I ate the grain of these people and they brought me and placed me here." They talked for an extremely long time and then said goodbye. [The group of carriages] left. The master of the family asked the grain thief, "Who is the person [you talked with] some time ago?" [The insect] replied, "It is the spirit of gold treasures, who dwells under a big tree located more than three hundred paces west from here. He has a hundred stone jars filled with gold." The master of the family immediately led several tens of people and went to dig there. They found jars filled with gold. His dependents were very happy. They put [the jars] on handcarts and returned. [The master of the family] bowed his head to the ground and said, facing the grain thief, "Today I acquired gold. Thanks to your favors, great god! We would like to ask you, god, to stay here. Let us return home together and I will further arrange to make an offering to you." The grain thief said, "Regarding the fact that I previously ate your grain and did not give my name, I wanted you to obtain this reward of gold. Now I must spread happiness around in the world. I can no longer stay here." After saying this, [the grain thief] suddenly disappeared.

Again, the *Piyu jing* says:[25]

In the southeast corner of Rājagṛha there was a deep water pond. The water channels in the city were filthy, full of excrement and urine. [The pond] was stinking and unapproachable.

A large insect lived in the pond. It was several *zhang* long and had neither hands nor feet. [The insect] slowly floated around or up and down, playing in the pond. Several thousands of spectators saw it. Ānanda was out begging for alms when he saw [the crowd] and went to look at [the insect]. The insect then jumped about, stirring up waves. [Ānanda] fully related this to the Buddha.

The Buddha went to the pond together with all *bhikṣu*s. When the people saw the Buddha [coming], everyone thought and said, "Today the

Tathāgata will explain the cause and effect of the insect for the assembly in order to disperse people's doubts. Shouldn't we be happy?"

The Buddha said, "In the past, after Vipaśyin Buddha's nirvana, there was a stupa. Five hundred *bhikṣu*s passed through the monastery. The head monk of the monastery saw them and was greatly delighted. He entreated them to stay in order to make offerings to them for three months. The *bhikṣu* sangha all accepted his invitation. The head monk of the monastery devoted all his energies and provided food and drink exhaustively.

"Later five hundred merchants entered the sea and collected treasures. On their way back when they passed by the stupa, they saw five hundred *bhikṣu*s dedicatedly and diligently practicing the [Buddhist] Way. Every [merchant] then simultaneously awaked the aspiration [for enlightenment]. Everyone took responsibility for making a small offering. Each of the five hundred merchants gave a *maṇi* gem. The five hundred *maṇi* gems thus obtained were entrusted to the head monk of the monastery. On giving the head monk of the monastery [the gems, the merchants] said, 'Our *maṇi* gems are enough to offer the sangha.' The *bhikṣu* (i.e., head monk) replied, 'Certainly!' and accepted them.

"Later [this monk] gave rise to a malicious thought and schemed and intended to monopolize [the gems]. He did not offer them to the sangha. The sangha asked him, 'The *maṇi* gems previously donated by the merchants should be set up for an offering. Has this been done?' The head monk of the monastery replied, 'Those were donated only to me. If you try to take them from me by force I will give you dung. If you do not leave now, I will cut off your hands and feet and throw them into a night-soil reservoir.' The sangha had pity on his ignorance and everyone departed in silence."

Therefore it is known that an evil wish should be restrained.
Moreover, the [*Da*] *zhidu lun* (T. 1509) says:

When the Buddha resided in this world, there was a person who traveled
490b some distance and who lodged alone in a vacant house. At midnight an ogre came, carrying on its shoulder a corpse, and it placed the body in front of the traveler. Then another ogre chased the [first] ogre and reviled him angrily, "The corpse is mine. You carelessly carried it here on your

shoulder." The first ogre said, "It is mine. I personally brought it here." The other ogre said, "This corpse was really carried here by me on my shoulder." The two ogres fought over [the corpse,] grasping a foot and hand [of the body]. The first ogre said, "There is a person here. We should ask him." The other ogre then asked, "Who carried this corpse here on his shoulder?" The traveler pondered. "These two ogres have great strength. Even if I say either the truth or a falsehood, I will not avoid death in either case." He then said, "The first ogre carried this here on his shoulder." The other ogre, enraged, grabbed the traveler's hand, pulled it off, and placed it on the ground. The first ogre felt pity for him, so it quickly took the corpse's arm and attached it to [the traveler]. In this way, the arms, feet, head, and torso, the entire body [of the traveler] was completely replaced with [that of the corpse]. Thereafter, the two ogres together ate the traveler's body [parts] that they had replaced with the corpse's body, wiped their mouths, and left.

That traveler thought, "I saw with my own eyes that the body begotten by my parents was completely eaten by the two ogres. Now my current body is entirely made of the other's (i.e., the corpse's) flesh. Do I now really have a body or not?" He went to a Buddhist stupa, asked questions to all the *bhikṣus*, and extensively explained the preceding incident. The *bhikṣus* said, "From the beginning you are spontaneously and continually non-self. Since the four great elements have just united [and formed themselves into a body], you consider it to be your own body. There is no difference between your original body and your current body." The *bhikṣus* liberated him. He practiced the [Buddhist] Way and attained the fruit of arhatship.

Furthermore, the *Shanxin jing* (*Sutra of Good Faith*) says:[26]

There are marvelous medicinal trees called *madana*.[27] The god of the earth detests all poisons of the world that must not recklessly prevail.

There was a huge mysterious serpent, a hundred and twenty *chi* long. The serpent traveled about searching for food. An insect with a black head, five *zhang* tall, while on its way came across the serpent. [The serpent] wanted it, raised his head, stepped forward, and bit the big insect. The serpent then smelled the scent of medicine, so it bent its head and intended to run away, but the serpent's body was in a *madana* tree. The body was then broken apart and divided into two parts. The head part was alive and could run away, but the tail part was rotten and stinking. All poisons were smelled and the serpent stank. [Later] all the evil poisonous vapors completely died out.

Again, the [*Da*] *zhidu lun* says:

A *maṇi* gem that glows in the dark is often in the brain of a dragon. Some meritorious sentient beings naturally obtain it. It is also called the wish-fulfilling gem (*ruyi zhu;* Skt. *cintāmaṇi*). It regularly produces all treasures, clothes, food, and drink. [With it,] one may obtain everything at will.

Those who acquire this gem cannot be killed by poison or burned by a fire. [It is also said that] when Śakra-devendra wielding a *vajra* fought against *asura*s, [the *vajra*] was broken and [its pieces] fell to Jambudvīpa and changed into these gems. Again, it is said that relics of the Buddha of the remotest past, when the Dharma had already been completely exterminated, changed into these gems in order to benefit [sentient beings].

What is more, the *Garland Sutra* (*Huayan jing,* T. 278) says:[28]

There are four treasure gems in the ocean. All various treasures are born
490c from them. If these four treasure gems were not existent, all treasures would gradually disappear. The minor dragon deities cannot see them. Only the dragon king Sāgara secretly places them in a deep treasury. There are four kinds of names for this deep treasury. First, it is called the storage of numerous treasures. Second, it is called the inexhaustible treasury. Third, it is called the flaming in the distance, and finally it is called the collection of all adornments.

In addition, there are four vigorously bright great treasures in the great sea. The first one is called the great treasure of the light stored in the sun. The second is called the great treasure of the light of leaving behind the dampness [of defilement]. The third is called the great treasure of the light of a fire pearl. The fourth is called the great treasure of the ultimate light without remainder. If these four treasures are not in the ocean, the four continents [around Mount Sumeru], Cakravāḍa, and even the abode of neither thought nor non-thought (Skt. *naiva-saṃjñā-nāsaṃjñāyatana*) will entirely drift away and sink. [The great treasure of] the light stored in the sun can change seawater into milk. [The great treasure of] the light of leaving behind the dampness [of defilement] can change the sea milk into *koumiss*.[29] [The great treasure of] the light of a fire pearl can burn the sea *koumiss,* and [the great treasure of] the ultimate light without remainder can burn the sea *koumiss* eternally and completely without remainder.

Verses say:

The Ultimate Sage (i.e., the Buddha) imperceptibly moves about.
You neither think it nor recognize it.
A prodigious feat covers the sunlight.
[The difference between] the wise and the ignorant is hard to speculate about.
Good and bad reside together.
Ups and downs are the same state of things.
Facing something, you think of it and realize it.
If you know of it, the supernatural being hides himself.
Being defiled by afflictions, he is not blocked up.
To abandon afflictions is the place where he rests.
If this is not his abstruse and subtle view,
Who stirs up its apex?
I examine myself and see that I am ignorant and lazy.
I highly admire virtue to be equal to [the Ultimate Sage].
He wins fame eternally and
The power of merit and wealth for a thousand years.

Miracle Stories

(Eighteen stories are briefly cited.)

[Shi Tansui, a *Śramaṇa* of the Jin Dynasty]

In the Jin dynasty there was Shi Tansui at White Horse Temple (Baimasi) of Heyin (in present-day Henan province). His original domicile is unknown. He renounced the world when he was very young and stayed in White Horse Temple of Heyin. Eating only coarse food and wearing simple clothing, he recited the *Lotus Sutra* (*Zheng fahua jing*), regularly once a day.

491a Furthermore, he was well versed in the tenets of the sutras and also explained them for the people.

One night, he suddenly heard someone knocking at the door. [The person] said, "I would like you, Dharma teacher, to preach the Dharma for ninety days." [Tansui] declined but the person insisted. So [Tansui] proceeded. Yet in fact [Tansui] was still asleep. Then he woke up and found himself in a small shrine in the village of Baimawu along with one of his disciples. From that day on, [Tansui] secretly went out every day. No one else knew about it.

Later, when a monk of [White Horse] Temple passed by the front of the shrine, he saw a couple of raised seats. Tansui sat on the northern seat and Tansui's disciple on the southern seat. [The passing monk] heard voices just as [Tansui] preached [the Dharma] and also smelled the wonderful aroma of incense. Thereafter both clergy and laypeople talked about this incident, saying that it was miraculous. When summer came and [the ninety-day preaching] was completed, the god [of the shrine] donated a white horse, five white sheep, and ninety rolls of silk fabric [to the temple]. The [god's] vow was thus fulfilled. Thereupon, interchanges [between the god of the shrine and monks of White Horse Temple] ceased.[30] It is unknown where Tansui went after that.

[Shi Faxiang, a *Śramaṇa* of the Jin Dynasty]

In the time of the Jin dynasty, there was Shi Faxiang in Yuecheng Temple. His secular family name was Liang. His homeland is unknown. He always resided on a mountain and practiced religious austerities diligently. He recited sutras of more than a hundred thousand syllables. Birds and beasts gathered around him, tame as if they were domestic animals.

In a shrine on Mount Tai was a big stone container in which money and jewels were deposited. One time Faxiang traveled to Mount Tai and stayed overnight near the shrine. Suddenly a person in dark clothing with a military officer's cap appeared and ordered Faxiang to open the container. After speaking, the person disappeared. The cover of the stone container weighed more than a thousand *jun* (30,000 catties), yet when Faxiang went to lift it, it easily came up. [Faxiang] then took the money and jewels and disributed them to poor people. He passed away in the last year of the Yuanxing era of the Jin dynasty (404) when he was eighty years old.

(These two stories are found in the *Biographies of Eminent Monks* compiled in the Liang dynasty [*Liang Gaoseng zhuan*]).

[Shi Shixing, a *Śramaṇa* of the Jin Dynasty]

Śramaṇa Shixing of the Jin dynasty was from Yingchuan (in present-day Henan province). His secular family name was Zhu. He had a lofty aspiration and a deep and virtuous nature. His actions accorded with his mind and he could not be swayed by honor and dishonor. At that time the sutras had not yet been thoroughly transmitted [to China]. Only the short version [of the *Prajñāpāramitā*] (i.e., *Daoxing bore jing,* T. 224), missing some chapters and verses, was available but the meaning was not clear.

In the fifth year of the Ganlu era of the Wei kingdom (260), [Shixing] left Yongzhou (part of present-day Shaanxi and Gansu provinces) for the west and arrived at Kustana (present-day Khotan). He traveled around various countries seeking the Buddhist canon. Buddhist monks of the Western Region (i.e., Central Asia) were mostly scholars of Hinayana Buddhism. When they heard that Shixing sought various sutras of Mahayana Buddhism, they were all astonished and would not give [the sutras] to him. They said, "People from a frontier region do not know the true Dharma. So they will be more confused [by these Mahayana sutras]." Shixing replied, "A sutra says that a thousand years [after the Buddha's time] the Dharma will be transmitted to the east. If you doubt that this is not what the Buddha said, please allow me to testify to it with utmost sincerity." He then burned some firewood and poured oil over it. The wood burned briskly, producing volumes of smoke. Shixing lifted up a sutra, bowed his head to the ground, weeping, and vowed, "If [this sutra] truly came from [the Buddha's] golden mouth, it should be circulated in the land of China. All buddhas and bodhisattvas should certify it!" Thereupon, he threw the sutra into the fire. The fire blazed up and after awhile they saw a pile of ashes but the text of the sutra was undamaged and its leather binding was just as it had been before. All the nation joyfully respected [Shixing]. Because of this they bade him to stay and made an offering to him.

[Shixing] sent his disciple Farao [back to China] to offer Sanskrit texts, which were delivered to all the temples in Chenliu, Junyi, and Cangyuan.[31] They took out [the sutras,] which consisted of ninety chapters in two hundred
thousand syllables in total. Zhu Shulan, a layman of Henan, was skilled in 491b
many customs [including the languages] of the Western Region and was also well versed in Buddhist doctrines. So he personally worked together [with Wuluocha] in the translation work.[32] This is the present *Faguang shoupin* (i.e., *Faguang bore jing,* T. 221).

Shixing passed away at the age of eighty. Accordingly, he was cremated. For many days after the cremation fire was extinguished [Shixing's] body still remained intact. Amazed, the people all said, "If [Shixing] really attained the Buddhist Way his body must be destroyed." Responding to their voices, the body broke into pieces and scattered. His bones were collected and a stupa was built for him.

[This story] was transmitted to the Buddhist monk Huizhi from his master monk. Master Shi also fully recorded this matter.[33]

[Shi Jīvaka, a *Śramaṇa* of the Jin Dynasty]

Śramaṇa Jīvaka (Qiyu) of the Jin dynasty was Indian. He came from the Western Region by the sea route. He was traveling to Luoyang, Guanzhong (present-day Shaanxi province), but arrived at the former Xiangyang (in present-day Hubei province). He intended to board a boat to cross to the north. The boatmen, seeing that he was an Indian *śramaṇa* with worn and ugly clothes, slighted him and would not take him on board. [Yet] when the boat reached the north bank Jīvaka had also already arrived there. All the people on board were amazed.

As Jīvaka moved forward, a couple of tigers came out to greet him; they lowered their ears and wagged their tails. Jīvaka patted them on the head. The tigers then disappeared into the grass. Those on the south and north banks [who had witnessed this] ran to [Jīvaka], asking about it. Jīvaka, [however,] said, "I have nothing to say," and departed. Several hundreds of people chased after him. Jīvaka appeared to move slowly yet the people still could not overtake him even when they ran after him.

Around the final year of Emperor Hui's reign (306), Jīvaka arrived in Luoyang. The Buddhist monks of Luoyang all came together to him to extend their greetings. Jīvaka, [however,] did not stand up [to return their compliments]. Through an interpreter, he ridiculed the ornamentation on their garments, saying, "You monks distribute the Buddhist Dharma but you do not do so with sincerity. You only seek offerings for superficial beauty." When he saw the Imperial Palace of Luoyang he commented, "This looks like the palace of Trāyastriṃśa. It should be accomplished through the power of the Buddhist Way, but instead it was made by the efforts of [sentient beings who experience] birth and death. Did they work diligently in defiance of hardships?"

When the young *śramaṇa*s Zhi Fayuan and Zhu Faxing arrived late [to greet Jīvaka], Jīvaka stood up for them. After Fayuan had bowed to [Jīvaka], Jīvaka patted him on the head and said, "Good bodhisattva, you were reborn from the realm of sheep." When Jīvaka saw Faxing coming through the gate, he smiled in great joy. He went out to greet and bow to Faxing, held Faxing's hands, lifted them to his head, and said, "Good bodhisattva, you were reborn from the realm of heavenly beings."

A person from the Directorate for Imperial Manufactories had suffered from an incurable disease for several years and was about to die. Jīvaka went to see him and said, "Why did you indulge in evil ways and produce this distress?" [Jīvaka] had the ill person get down on the ground, laid him out on a single-layer mat, put a monks' iron bowl on his belly, and covered him with linen cloth. Jīvaka then chanted three Indian hymns, and after that he intoned *dhāraṇī*s of several thousands of syllables. An offensive odor soon filled the room. The ill person said, "I have recovered my strength!" Jīvaka ordered him to take off the linen cloth, and they saw in the iron bowl something abhorrent that looked like mud. The ill person was thus cured.

The Governor of Changsha, Teng Yongwen, [practiced Buddhism] very diligently from his early days. At that time he resided in Luoyang. Both of his legs were crooked because of paralysis for years. Jīvaka chanted *dhāraṇī*s for him. Immediately [Yongwen] could straighten [his legs] and after several days he stood up and walked.

In Yushui Temple there was a *bodhi* tree that had withered. Jīvaka chanted *dhāraṇī*s facing the tree. In ten days the tree revived and produced verdant foliage. 491c

At that time in that temple resided Zhu Faxing, who was good at speaking and discussion. In those days he was compared to Yue Ling (i.e., Yue Guang).[34] When he met Jīvaka he bowed his head to the ground and said, "I have already attained the testimony in the Buddhist Way. I wish to receive the Dharma (i.e., certification of spiritual achievement) from you." Jīvaka replied, "Bridle your tongue, control your intentions, and do not commit bodily offense. Those who practice these points will transcend the world." Faxing replied, "Those who attained the Buddhist Way should be given what they have not yet heard. What you told me now can be recited even by an eight year-old novice; it is not what those who have attained the Buddhist Way expect to hear." Jīvaka said, laughing, "It is indeed as you said! It is what an eight year-old [novice] can recite, yet it is something that even a one hundred-year-old man cannot practice. People all know to respect those who have attained the Buddhist Way, yet they do not know that to practice these points is precisely to attain the Buddhist Way oneself. From my viewpoint, it is easy. Subtlety simply lies in oneself. How can you be resentful for not hearing the Dharma you have not yet heard?"

People of all ranks and classes in the capital city sent Jīvaka gifts of clothes and other things, which were counted as several tens of millions or hundred millions. Jīvaka accepted all of them, but on leaving the capital city he sealed them and left them behind. He made eight hundred streamers, which were carried on the backs of camels. [Jīvaka] sent them in advance, and they followed merchants to return to India in the west. Furthermore, he had a *kaṣāya* robe belonging to Faxing [who had been reborn from the realm of heavenly beings] and carried it himself. He told Faxing, "This region greatly commits the offense of making new things. How pitiful it is!"

When Jīvaka took his departure, several thousand people came to see him off. He left after taking a meal at a temple in Luoyang. There was a monk who had departed Chang'an on that day to travel to [Luoyang]. He saw Jīvaka at a temple in Chang'an [even though Jīvaka was then in Luoyang]. Moreover, when the merchants and camel drivers that Jīvaka had sent in advance approached a river in Dunhuang, they met a younger brother of one of the merchants who had come from India. The brother said that he had seen Jīvaka at a temple in Dunhuang just a little while before. The brother's son, Shideng, said that he had met Jīvaka north of the desert and they had talked heartily. When they calculated for that day, it had been ten days before, the same day that Jīvaka had departed from Luoyang. In short, the distance [Jīvaka] had traveled was then already ten thousand *li*.

[Shi Fotiao, a *Śramaṇa* of the Jin Dynasty]

It is unknown what country the *śramaṇa* Fotiao of the Jin dynasty came from. He went to Changshan [prefecture] (in present-day Hebei province) and strove in religious practice for years. He esteemed simplicity and did not use refined language. People of the time valued him because of his manner.

In Changshan [prefecture] there were two brothers who believed in the Dharma. They lived a hundred *li* away from [Fotiao's] temple. The elder brother's wife fell seriously ill. So they moved near the temple in order to keep medical services and medicines handy. The elder brother admired Fotiao as his teacher. He sought advice and practiced the Buddhist Way in the temple, always in daytime hours.

One day Fotiao unexpectedly visited their house. The younger brother asked about the condition of his elder brother's wife in detail and inquired after his elder brother. Fotiao replied, "The ill lady is almost well. Your brother is as usual." After Fotiao left, the younger brother followed him, whipping his horse [to make speed]. He told his elder brother that Fotiao had visited their house early that morning. The elder brother said in surprise, "The *upādhyāya* has not gone out of the temple from early this morning. How could you have seen him?" The brothers vied with each other in asking questions [about this matter] to Fotiao, but Fotiao just smiled and never gave an answer. They all considered it to be strange.

Furthermore Fotiao went deep into the mountains alone. He brought only several *sheng* of dried grain for a year or a half-year, but when he returned he always had some left over.

Someone once followed Fotiao and traveled several tens of *li* in the mountains. The sun went down and it snowed heavily. Fotiao went into a rock cave
and stayed overnight in a tiger's den. When the tiger returned and lay down 492a
in front of the den, Fotiao said, "I have deprived you of your den. How can I deal with this shame?" The tiger lowered its ears and descended the mountain. The person who had been following [Fotiao] was surprised and fearful.

Fotiao personally announced beforehand what would be his last day. All the people from far and near came to see him. Fotiao then gave a farewell statement. "Even though the universe lasts a very long time, it still arrives at the day of collapse. How could human beings intend to live eternally? If you are able to wash away the three major evil passions and concentrate your whole mind upon true purity, even though the body leaves you, your spirit certainly remains in the same way." All the people wept. Fotiao returned to his room and sat upright. He covered his head with his robe and suddenly passed away.

Several years after [Fotiao's] death, eight of his lay disciples entered the Western Mountains. As they were cutting wood, they unexpectedly saw Fotiao appear on a high rock. His clothing was distinct and he looked cheerful and exuberant. They were all pleasantly surprised and bowed to him. They asked, "O *upādhyāya!* Are you still here [in this world]?" [Fotiao] replied, "I am always free." He asked for news of his friends in detail. Shortly he departed. The eight people then stopped their work and returned to their homes. They told the story to those who practiced the Buddhist teaching together with them, but the others said, "There is nothing to prove your story." So, they dug up [Fotiao's] grave together and opened his coffin. [Fotiao's] body had disappeared.

[Shi Jiantuole, a *Śramaṇa* of the Jin Dynasty]

The home country of Jiantuole of the Jin dynasty is unknown. He once traveled to Luoyang and went all over the city for several years. While the people respected him for his character and behavior, no one knew of his profound abilities.

Afterward [Jiantuole] said to the people, "On Mount Panchi there is an old stupa. If it can be repaired the merit [from this] will be immeasurable." Many people approved of this and went to the mountain with him, and when they arrived there were trees and plants growing densely and luxuriantly. No one knew where the trace [of the stupa] was. Jiantuole, pointing to a place, said, "This is the foundation of the temple." Some people dug there and sure enough they discovered the stone base of the stupa. [Jiantuole] furthermore pointed out the sites of the lecture hall, the resident monks' quarters, a well, and a kitchen. When the sites were dug everything was where [Jiantuole] had said they would be. Only then did the people wonder if [Jiantuole] was extraordinary.

After the temple was repaired Jiantuole became the chief priest. [The temple] was located a hundred *li* from Luoyang. [Jiantuole] went to Luoyang every morning. After attending a Buddhist service and hearing lectures, he then begged for a bowl of oil and carried it back to the temple. Although the time it took to go and return varied, he never failed to return by noon. A person who could travel several hundreds of *li* in a day intended to follow [Jiantuole] and testify [if Jiantuole could walk that fast]. He departed at the same time as [Jiantuole], but even though he ran he could not catch up with [Jiantuole]. [Jiantuole] turned his head and said, smiling, "Hold on to my *kaṣāya* and you will not get tired." When he held onto the back of [Jiantuole's] *kaṣāya* he promptly arrived at the temple. The man rested for several days [at the temple] and then returned home. The people realized that [Jiantuole] was a supernatural person. It is unknown when and where he passed away.

[Di Shichang, a Layman of the Jin Dynasty]

Di Shichang of the Jin dynasty was from Zhongshan (in present-day Hebei province), from a wealthy family. During the Taikang era (280–289) Chinese people were prohibited from becoming *śramaṇa*s. Shichang believed in the Dharma and diligently practiced it. He secretly built a monastery at his premises, where he made offerings to *śramaṇa*s. Yu Falan was among them. No monk who came to [Shichang] was rejected.

There was a *bhikṣu* with a stupid and vile appearance, wearing worn-out clothes covered in dust. It looked like he had traveled through mud to come [to Shichang]. Shichang went out, bowed to him, and ordered a servant to go and get water so that he could wash the *bhikṣu*'s feet. The *bhikṣu* said, 492b
"O Shichang! You should yourself wash my feet." Shichang replied, "I am old, weary, and feeble. I will let my servant [do it] instead of me." The *bhikṣu* would not listen to him. Shichang called him names under his breath and left. The *bhikṣu* then revealed his supernatural power, transformed himself into a giant eight *chi* tall with a fabulous and extraordinary countenance, and flew away. Shichang beat his breast, regretted [his actions], lamented, and threw himself down onto the mud.

At that time, the monks and nuns of Di's [monastery] along with some passersby, fifty or sixty people, all could see clearly and distinctly [the *bhikṣu*] floating several tens of *zhang* high in the air. The extraordinary vapor of wonderful fragrance [emitted during this event] did not dissipate even after a month. [Yu] Falan was revered as the Dharma master of logic. (His biography appears in the latter part of this writing.) Falan related this story to his disciple Fajie, who told it to other people, both monks and laypeople, on many occasions.

[Cheng Dedu, Administrator of the Song Dynasty]

Cheng Dedu of the Song dynasty was from Wuchang (in present-day Hubei province). His father Daohui was Regional Inspector of Guangzhou. Dedu became the Acting Administrator of the General of the Guards, the king of Linchuan (403–444). At that time [Dedu] resided in Xunyang (in present-day Jiangxi province). In his room there was a swallow's nest. One night the room suddenly became bright spontaneously and a young boy came out of the nest. He was more than one *chi* tall, with a clean and clear appearance. He came to the front of Dedu's bed and said, "You will attain the way of longevity in two years." The boy suddenly disappeared. Dedu felt that this was very mysterious and peculiar.

In the seventeenth year of the Yuanjia era (440), Dedu followed the king and guarded the area of Guangling, where he met the meditation master Shi Daogong. Accordingly, Dedu learned meditation from [Daogong] and his understanding was very good. In the spring of the nineteenth year [of the Yuanjia era] (442), the unoccupied study of his house in Wuchang suddenly filled with a distinguished fragrance. The fragrance reached the thoroughfare. All the people in the area went and inspected [the room]. [The fragrance] dissipated after three days.

(These six stories are found in the *Mingxiang ji* [*Records of the Profound and Auspicious*]).

[Shi Hongming, a *Śramaṇa* of the Qi Dynasty]

During the Qi dynasty there was Shi Hongming at Bolin Temple in Yongxing [village]. His original family name was Ying. He was from Shanyin in Guiji (in present-day Zhejiang province). He renounced the world when young and virtuously and diligently observed the precepts and principles. He resided at Yunmen Temple in Shanyin, where he recited the *Lotus Sutra,* received training in meditation, and industriously devoted himself to worship and repentance. He did [the practices] at all six times a day.[35]

Every day at dawn a water jar spontaneously filled up. [Hongming] truly impressed various heavenly youths, who thereby became sextons. Once [Hong]ming was sitting in meditation at Yunmen [Temple] when a tiger came into his room and lay down in front of his [meditation] couch. [The tiger], seeing that [Hong]ming sat upright and never moved, left after awhile. Moreover, on one occasion [Hongming] saw a young boy who came to listen to his chanting of a sutra. [Hong]ming asked him, "Who are you?" [The boy] replied, "Formerly I was a novice at this temple. After I stole food that had been [offered] under the canopy, I fell into a pit toilet and now I am [trapped] there. I heard about your practice of the [Buddhist] Way, holy priest. Therefore I came to listen to the sutra [you chant]. I pray that you will help me and with expedient means cause me to escape from this nuisance." [Hong]ming promptly expounded on the Dharma, exhorting and edifying [the boy]. Having received and understood [the teachings the boy] [suddenly] disappeared.

[Hongming] later entered into meditation in the Shilao cave in Yongxing. A mountain spirit came and disturbed [Hong]ming. So he seized [the spirit] and tied it up with a cord [from his robe]. The spirit surrendered and apologized to him and then asked to be released, saying, "I dare not come back again!" [Hong]ming released it and it then vanished completely.

[Hongming] passed away in the fourth year of the Yongming era (486) of the Qi dynasty at Bolin Temple, at the age of eighty-four. 492c

[Shi Faxian, a *Śramaṇa* of the Qi Dynasty]

In the Qi dynasty there was Shi Faxian on Mount Jing in Nanhai. He was from Guangzhou. He first resided at North Temple (Beisi). When the temple became old and fell into disrepair, [Fa]xian led and solicited people who were related [to the Buddha in their former existences] (*youyuan*), and [the temple] was repaired to a great extent. The name was changed and it was called Prolonging Auspiciousness (Yanxiang) [Temple].

Later [Faxian] went to Mount Zangwei, where he established a temple. After the completion of the temple, a couple of boys came hand in hand, singing a song:

There is the virtue of the Buddhist Way in Zangwei.
Happiness is not yet halfway through.

After singing this song they suddenly disappeared. All the people of the temple exclaimed and sighed in wonderment at this miraculous occurence.

Afterward [Fa]xian entered into meditation and suddenly saw someone come, who said, "A string of the *qing* (a sonorous stone) has snapped. Why don't you repair it quickly?" [Fa]xian was surprised, got up [from meditation], and went to see it. [The broken string] hung down, nearly touching the ground. He reconnected [the string]; it was undamaged. It is unknown where he died.

[Shi Puan, a *Śramaṇa* of the Sui Dynasty]

In the Sui dynasty there was Shi Puan (530–609) in Pianzi Valley on Mount Zhongnan (in present-day Shaanxi province). His secular family name was Guo. He was from north Jingyang in Yongzhou (in present-day Shaanxi province). As for his manual of rituals and method of practices, he [practiced] alone in forests and fields, did not participate in the human world, and solely esteemed meditation until the end of his life. He settled in the dangerous wilderness and did not avoid wolves and tigers. He always read the *Garland Sutra* (*Huayan* [*jing*]); he would not let go of the scroll [of the *Garland Sutra*]. He cultivated asceticism, ignoring his own comfort for the sake of others. He often wandered about in the mountains and fields, and while doing so he offered [his body] to birds and beasts. Even though tigers and leopards approached him, they only sniffed him and did not attack him. He had a pure mind, was incompatible with abiding in the secular world, and never broke his sincere vow.

During the persecution of Buddhism [carried out by Emperor Wu of the Northern] Zhou dynasty, more than thirty great virtuous monks took shelter in [Mount] Zhongnan. [Pu]an settled them in a dark ravine, and himself practiced almsbegging [to support them]. [So] they were well fed and clothed. Even though they heard that [the persecution] was thorough, they were all able to escape from hardship.

At that time Dharma teacher [Jing]'ai (534–578) avoided the disasters and stayed at Du Yingshi's house in Yiyu. [The Du family] dug a kiln in which they hid him. [Pu]an was released and on his return [to his place] he passed by [Du Yingshi's house], paid his respects to [Jing'ai], and had an audience with him. [Jing]'ai said, "You, Eminent [Pu]an, clearly understand the Buddhist Dharma. Your knowledge is not very extensive but your spirit and determination are matchless. You are aware of the fact that evil guards strongly against the good. It is probably difficult to reach [that stage]." [Pu]an replied, "I have now escaped from hardship and this is solely due to the power of the *Garland Sutra*."

When the new era of Emperor Wen (r. 581–604) of the Sui dynasty began, Buddhism greatly flourished. Former monks were called back from at large and settled down in accordance with the old system. At that time, more than thirty monks [who had hidden] in the ravine of Pianzi [publicly] renounced the world, responding to the imperial decree, and they all went to live in an official temple. [Pu]an alone enjoyed the mountain dwelling with which he had familiarized himself. He maintained simplicity and enjoyed the tranquility of the trees and valleys. While he sometimes went to a village or town and benefited the people, he continued to abide in nature and did not join the superficial secular world.

Later, a person cut into a wall and made a small shrine beside a mountain stream where the two valleys of Zihuo and Hulin met. He built a hermitage

and invited [Puan] to live there. On the first day [Puan] went to live near the small shrine, there was a large rock above [the small shrine], hanging right over it. Afraid that the rock might fall, [the man] wanted to dig it out and move it away from the high place by dropping it down [the mountain. Pu]an prayed, "Would that the big rock be moved somewhere else without damaging the small shrine cave!" Consequently, the rock, complying with [Puan's] words, cracked apart and shifted to another place. The people were all surprised at this. [Pu]an said, "This is due to the power of the *Garland Sutra*. 493a
It is not anything peculiar."

Furthermore, on the left side of the mountain stream near the east stone wall of the small shrine lived Suo Tuo, a notorious villain from the rural community along the river. He forced his way in numerous things. He was secretly jealous of [Pu]an's virtue and always plotted to denounce him for his faults and ruin him. Accompanied by three cohorts, he carried a bow in his hand and a knife under his arm. He lifted his arms and drew the bow, but when he was about to let loose an arrow, it would not leave the string [of the bow] and he could not stop his hands from opening. He glared, his tongue was frozen, he was rooted [to the spot], and he stayed like that all night. As for the aspect of his voice, it vibrated. People from far and near gathered like clouds. Villagers bowed their heads to the ground and sincerely took refuge in [Puan]. They asked him to help [Suo Tuo]. [Pu]an said to them, "Originally I did not understand clearly [what was going on]. Isn't his predicament due to the power of the *Garland Sutra*? If he wishes to be released from [these conditions], you should simply cause him to repent." They taught [Suo Tuo] just as [Puan had] said and he was rescued [from the difficulty].

Moreover, there was Zhang Hui in Wei village to the west of the small shrine. From early in life he conceived evil thoughts and considered thievery his occupation. He went to [Pu]an's place in the night and secretly took some oil [used for] Buddhist rites. He put five *dou* [of oil] in a pot[36] and went out, carrying it on his back. He had already reached the gate of the courtyard when he became confused and got lost. He could not move, as if he was bound by something. His entire family and the people of his community came to [Puan] and apologized for [Zhang Hui's] sake. [Pu]an said, "I do not know anything about it. It is probably due to the power of the *Garland Sutra*. You should tell him [about the power of the *Garland Sutra*] and cause him to repent. Help him return the pot of oil." [They did] as [Puan] said and [Zhang Hui] was delivered.

Furthermore, there was Zhang Qing, who lived to the south of the small shrine. He stole [Puan's] money, carrying it away in his sleeve. When he was back in his house he shook [his sleeve] but [no money] came out. His mouth remained shut [against his will] and he had to remain silent. [Zhang] Qing soon took refuge [in Puan], repented, admitted his fault, and left.

Another time, in Chengguo village there was Cheng Huihe, who greatly embraced faith [in Buddhism] without doubt. He often came to [Pu]an's place, listened to him, and received the essence of the Dharma. He died of an illness. After two nights had passed his corpse lay shrouded on the ground. The mourners were getting ready to put the body in a coffin. [Pu]an had gone to Hu county (in present-day Shaanxi province) before [Huihe's death] and was on his way back [to his place]. He arrived at Dexing Temple in the southwest, five *li* west from Hui[he]'s village. From far away [Puan] called out, "Cheng Huihe, why don't you come out to meet me?" He called out repeatedly. A farmer told him, "[Hui]he died a long while ago. There is no way he can come to meet you." [Pu]an replied, "This is a nonsensical joke! I do not believe it." [Puan] soon arrived at Huihe's village, and he shouted angrily and called out [to Huihe] loudly. [Hui]he's body then moved. His distant relatives cut off the rope holding the shroud around his body. [Pu]an entered [Huihe's] yard and again called out to him loudly. [Hui]he immediately got up and crawled to [Pu]an. [Pu]an ordered [the people] to remove the coffin and cover all the bamboo baskets and mats in order to make [a place] for the Buddha's seat. He ordered [Hui]he to circumambulate [the Buddha's seat]. [Huihe] was soon restored to health; he was as healthy as he had been before and lived for twenty more years. Later, when he became seriously ill, he came to [Puan] begging for help. [Pu]an said, "To let you fall into dissipation is no concern of mine." [Cheng Huihe] then died.

At that time [Pu]an's fame ascended rapidly. Both clergy and laypeople revered and admired him. Many people gathered around him, asking to have an audience with him. He initiated the meritorious assembly (*fuhui*), in which many people experienced communication with buddhas and bodhisattvas.

Formerly in Bai village, northeast of Kunmingchi (in present-day Shaanxi province), there was an old lady who was ill in bed and who lost her hearing

for more than a hundred days. She informed her children about her intention to see [Pu]an. [Puan] understood the mother's intention to ask him to visit her. When he arrived at her house, the ill mother saw him, unconsciously descended [from her bed], and came out to meet him. [Puan] asked her about 493b
her daily life. Suddenly she returned to her former [healthy condition] as before and the suffering from the disease was gone. Because of this, [Puan's] reputation increased even more. The villagers assembled and wanted to set up a great purification ceremony.

In Dawan village there was Tian Yisheng. His family was poverty-stricken. He had four daughters. His wife had only worn-out clothes that covered only to above her knees. His four daughters went around naked and cold; they had nothing to cover their bodies at all. The oldest daughter, who was already twenty years old, was called Huayan. [The family] had only two *chi* of coarse fabric, which they intended to give as a donation. [Pu]an, leading the villagers [on mendicant rounds], arrived at the gate [of Tian's house]. He had compassion for their hardship of poverty, and so he walked past [their house] and did not go in [to receive the offering].

The oldest daughter thought, "Because I am tormented by poverty I cannot join the meritorious assembly. If I do not study now, how can I be saved in the future?" She looked around for something [to donate] but there was nothing at all. Looking up, she wept sadly. Then she saw a bright hole in the roof tiles and saw a bundle of mixed grain. She pulled [down the bundle] and shook it, and was able to obtain ten grains. She crumbled them and they became rice. At the same time, she took the coarse fabric and decided to use it for participating in the Buddhist ceremony. Since she wore nothing on her body, she waited for the darkness of night to go and then crawled to the site of the religious offering. She threw the donation mentioned above toward numerous people from a distance. She separately offered more than ten grains of rice to cook.

Accordingly she made a vow, "I, a woman, am beset by poverty because of former parsimonious acts. Now I have received the retribution of poverty. My hardship is just like this. Today I do my best in poverty and make a donation in order to hope for a reward in the future." After making this prayer she put the ten grains of coarse rice into an earthenware pot to cook them. "If through utmost sincerity my karma of poverty is exhausted, I pray that the cooked rice will turn to a yellow color. If I receive no response from you, it is my fate. What else can I do?" After making this oath, she returned to her home, covering her face and weeping. Thereafter, the five *dan* of rice in the earthenware pot turned yellow.[37] All the people were surprised and exclaimed about this, but they did not know why it had happened. Seeking for the reason, they found [the answer] and thereupon said, "This is due to the power of Tian Yisheng's daughter's vow." The assembly of purification was carried out in an orderly way, and the ten *dan* of grain was obtained. [The people] quickly gave [Huayan the grain to relieve her hunger]. [Pu]an purchased a Dharma robe for Huayan, initiated her into [the Buddhist Way], and sent her to a temple in the metropolis. After this, his reputation became even greater. His lofty awakening is difficult to explain.

Even though [Pu]an's dwelling place was hidden, he performed merciful acts of salvation every day. Many people offered animal sacrifices to the god of the land regularly two times a year. [Puan] went around [the towns and villages] and saved [the sacrificial animals] from death by paying for them. He exhorted [the people] to practice the meaning of the Dharma. The number of towns that no longer killed living things [as offerings] was more than a few.

In the village near [Puan's] small shrine, there were three hogs tied up, which were going to be butchered and cooked [as an offering] for the god of the land. [Pu]an heard about this and went to buy their freedom. The villagers who served the god were afraid that they would not be able to kill [the hogs to make the offering]. So they increased the price and demanded ten thousand in cash from him. [Pu]an said, "I think I have three thousand in cash, which is already ten times more than the original price. We can come to an agreement." The people had different opinions and angrily contested with one another.

Suddenly a boy, whose torso was covered with a sheepskin, came to the assembly for the god of the land. He helped [Pu]an purchase the hogs' freedom. Having seen that the people were competing with [one another], he ingratiated himself to them and asked for some wine. He drank and danced, turning around and around, shining brightly. Then both old and young who had gathered for the god of the land offering all lost their eyesight; they were in darkness for a brief moment and did not know where they were. [Pu]an
493c promptly drew a knife, cut some flesh from his own buttocks, and said, "Both this and that are simply all flesh. Hogs eat dung and filth and you still eat

them. Needless to say, human beings eat rice. [Therefore,] by this reasoning [human flesh] is more precious." When the people who served the god of the land heard and saw this they immediately freed [the hogs]. The [young] hogs, having escaped from [the danger], circumambulated [Pu]an three times and rubbed their noses against his body as if showing affection and respect for him. Hence, [this incident] caused the villages within fifty *li* south and west [from this community] to stop the practice of [sacrificing] chickens and hogs [for offerings].[38] It has continued to the present time. The way [Puan] felt and expressed benevolence was entirely in this manner.

[Puan] had a very sincere and faithful nature. He delighted in chanting the *Garland Sutra*. With an [alms]bowl and the three kinds of robes, he exerted himself more year after year. In the eighth year of the Kaihuang era (588), he entered the metropolis responding to a repeated imperial decree and became Palace Mentor of the Heir Apparent. A princess built Jingfa Temple and invited [Puan] to reside there. Even though [the temple] was called Imperial Palace (Diyu), [Puan] still continued to sleep in a mountain cave. On the fifth day of the eleventh month of the fifth year of the Daye era (609), he passed away at Jingfa Chan Temple at the age of eighty.

[Shi Faan, a *Śramaṇa* of the Sui Dynasty]

In the Sui dynasty there was Shi Faan (518–615) at Baoyang Temple in the Eastern Capital (i.e., Luoyang). His [secular] family name was Peng. He was from Chungu in Anding (present-day Gansu province). He renounced the world when he was young and resided at Jiulong Monastery on Mount Taibo (in present-day Shaanxi province). He revered meditation and made it his specialty. He had only coarse food and worn-out clothes throughout his life until he died from old age.

In the mid-Kaihuang era (581–600) [Faan] came to Jiangdu (in present-day Jiangdu county of Jiangsu province). He ordered [the gatekeepers] to report the reason for his visit to the king of Jin, [who later became Emperor Yang of the Sui dynasty (r. 605–617)]. The gatekeepers did not think his visit was worthy of reporting [to the king], since he was short and ugly in appearance and spoke and laughed carelessly. He came to the gate every day[39] and was always told to go away, but he would not leave. [The gatekeepers] tried to convey [Faan's intention to the king] for his sake. The king [of Jin] heard this and called him into a room. When they saw each other it was as if they had known each other for a long time. [Faan] then resided at Huiri [Monastery] and offered to attend [the king] wherever the king traveled. When [the king] made an honorable visit to Mount Tai (in present-day Shandong province), [his group] became thirsty. They looked around in every direction but there were only rocks; there was no place from which water could be obtained. [Fa]an slashed open a rock with a knife and drew water, which poured out with a rush. [The water] was given to the king, who greatly marveled at [Faan's skill] at that time. He asked him, "With what kind of power did you cause this?" [Faan] replied, "With Your Majesty's power I caused this." Following the king, [Faan] went into a desert. The party arrived in the middle of a sea of silt, where they encountered extraordinary and strange affairs. They all avoided [difficulties] ahead of time and suffered no damage or defeat.

Later, [the king and his attendants] went to Mount Tai. The monks of Shentong Temple came to them and invited them as donors. [Fa]an arrived there on behalf of [the monks]. The king handwrote an inscription, "Great Protection (*honghu*)," on the wall of the temple.

At the beginning [of the journey] when [Faan] entered a valley with the king, he saw a monk wearing worn-out clothes and riding on a white donkey approach. The king asked, "What is he?" [Fa]an answered, "He is Eminent [Fa]lang (507–581)." [Falang] had built Shentong [Temple], so he came out to greet and guide them.

When they reached the temple, they again saw a deity of extraordinary appearance. [The deity] was up on [the roof of] the lecture hall, leaning on a roof ornament and observing the people below. Again, the king asked [Faan about him] and [Faan] replied, "This is the god of Mount Taibo and he obeys you, Your Majesty." It is impossible to extensively record all the wonderful events that happened after that.

By the beginning of the Daye era (605) the emperor valued [Faan] even more. [Faan] was more powerful than princes. Those who saw him all kneeled down before him. He was continuously attended by the Three Capital Guards (i.e., members of the Bodyguard Garrison, the two Distinguished Garrisons, and the two Standby Garrisons), who served [Faan] just as they would a deity. Furthermore [Faan] went to famous mountains and invited various recluses. Once Guo Zhibian, Eminent Shi [Bao]zhi, Eminent [Fa]deng, and

Beidu all gathered at the same time at Huiri Monastery. More than two thousand virtuous and learned people supplied them with the four kinds of necessities, and they served [Fa]an as their leader. Moreover, Baoyang Monastery was built for [Faan] in the Eastern Capital. Only [Fa]an's group resided and cultivated practice there. 494a

In the spring of the eleventh year [of the Daye era] (615), at time when there were many hardships in every direction, [Faan] died without having fallen ill. He was ninety-eight years old.

Before he was about to die, he told the emperor, "A hundred days after my death a fire will break out in the palace. You must be careful about this." On the *hanshi* seasonal day[40] oil bubbled up and caught fire. During the night the gate was closed [so] all the courtiers of the Three Bureaus of the Censorate burned to death. At the time the emperor did not think this was strange.

[Faan's] coffin was sent to [Mount] Taibo and government funds were provided to support [the maintenance of his tomb]. Nevertheless, [Fa]an's virtue lay hidden and he was externally [treated] in the same way as various of his associates were. He did not use a pillow when he slept so his neck was not bent at all. He laid with his head extended to the edge of the bed[41] and drooled from his mouth. Every night he drooled more than a *sheng*. Whatever he manifested, we can see mysterious signs there.

[Shi Huikan, a *Śramaṇa* of the Sui Dynasty]

In the Sui dynasty there was Shi Huikan (524–605) at Daguishan Temple in Jiangzhou (in present-day Jiangsu province). His [secular] family name was Yang. He was from Qua in Jinling (in present-day Wujin county, Jiangsu province). [When young he studied with an eminent monk. This monk] was able to discern good omens of this world as well as from the other world. No one in the world knew [whether his learning was shallow or deep].[42] He highly respected a venerable [buddha] image and served it in the same manner as one would serve the actual Buddha. Whenever he saw the standing [buddha] statue he would not venture to sit [in front of it]. He urged [other people] to make another image [of the Buddha] in a seated posture. If he was out on a street and encountered others having difficulties, he saved them without concern for his own life.

Later Huikan went to Lingnan (present-day Guangdong and Guangxi provinces), where he took refuge in Zhendi (Paramārtha, 499–569), and exclusively interpreted the teaching of meditation. He was greatly and deeply awakened. In his closing years he resided at Qixia [Temple near present-day Nanjing in Jiangsu province]. He was calm and had an open and peaceful mind. He would come and go [between the temple and regular domicles]; his life was not restricted to the mountains.

He once went to the place of the Dharma teacher Si in Yangdu (in present-day Hongdong county, Shanxi province). Si knew in advance that [Huikan] was coming and received him with exceptional courtesy. As [Huikan] was leaving to return to the mountain temple, he was asked to show his supernatural power. [Hui]kan said, "Certainly! How could it be difficult?" Then he immediately stuck out his arm from a window and it extended to several tens of *zhang* long, then he removed the horizontal tablet of the upper side of the Buddha Hall of Qixia Temple and retracted his arm back into the room. [Huikan] said to Si, "Common people have no profound knowledge. When they see [my supernatural power] they are simply surprised. This is the reason I do not perform it."

In the first year of the Daye era (605) [Huikan] died at Daguishan Temple in Jiangzhou, at the age of eighty-two. In the morning of the day [Hui]kan died, he threw his three robes and hood away into the hall, saying, "I am returning the three robes to the sangha. I am now departing this world. Everyone, good luck!" Then he returned into his room. All the people got up, frightened, and went after him. They found a full set of white bones in a seated posture with legs crossed on a couch. When they touched [the bones] they rattled yet did not scatter.

[Shi Zhuanming, a *Śramaṇa* of the Tang Dynasty]

In the Tang dynasty there was Shi Zhuanming at Huadu Temple in the western capital city (i.e., Chang'an). His secular family name was Lu. His original domicile is unknown. His appearance and clothing followed the monastic standard. His facial appearance was mediocre; his countenance was merely indifferent and there was neither pleasure nor displeasure in his gaze.

In the eighth year of the Daye era (612) of the Sui dynasty, [Zhuanming] arrived from nowhere apparent to take up residence in Luoyang. He warned, "Rebels will arise!" [People] went to investigate but they did not see [any evidence of] the original [threat warned of by Zhuanming]. At that time the

emperor (i.e., Emperor Yang, r. 605–617) felt misled by him but could not sentence him. So he ordered that Zhuanming be temporarily taken into custody. At that time [the emperor] did not infer that [Zhuanming] was like that (i.e., that he could make predictions). In the sixth month of the following year, just as [Zhuanming had warned, the emperor] was confronted by the rebellion 494b
raised by Xiao Gan (i.e., Yang Xuangan). Violent men approached the Eastern Capital (Luoyang) and filled [the city]. They killed people in extreme and exceedingly awful ways. [The emperor] acceded [Zhuanming's] words and issued an imperial decree to release him. [Zhuan]ming was released from custody and his mental state was as usual.

[Zhuanming] had discussions with various people, and no one had ever been a match for him. It happened that the emperor went to Jiangdu (present-day Jiangsu province). [On the way] he stopped at Yanshi (present-day Heluodao in Henan province). At that time in the prison there were fifty convicts who had been sentenced to death. On a set date they were to be beheaded. [Zhuanming thought,] "Tomorrow I should release them from this distress of death." He went to the prison and bribed [the wardens]. Seeing all the convicts he announced, "Tomorrow His Majesty will pass by here. You should all cry out loudly and shout all together, 'Rebels are coming!' If you are asked the reason for this, just say that it is what I have ascertained. Then you will certainly escape from death." When the time came, [the convicts did] just as they had been told. An imperial decree was issued and all the convicts were released, but [Zhuan]ming was seized and imprisoned. Bursting out in laughter, he accepted it and had no anxiety or fear at all. At that time bandits throughout the land had a pessimistic view of life. It was just as [Zhuan]ming had predicted.

In the final year of the Daye era (617) [Zhuanming] was still imprisoned. When the king of Yue succeeded to the throne and [became Emperor Gong, Zhuanming] was released. Even though he could then freely come and go, he always lived inside the Qianyang gate. He was given a branch temple. [The emperor] was afraid that [Zhuanming] would secretly escape, so he confidentially sent the Three Capital Guards to privately protect him. In the Huangtai era (618),[43] when a strategy to militarize the nation was proposed, [Zhuanming] was put in charge of the strategic planning staff to plan and assess the advantages and disadvantages. [Wang] Shichong, [founder] of the illegitimate Zheng dynasty, redoubled his trust in [Zhuanming]. The guard was strictly established. [Zhuanming] concurrently served in ordinary rules.

The second year of the Kaiming era (620) [of the Zheng dynasty] is exactly the third year of the Wude era of the Tang dynasty. [Zhuan]ming moved out peacefully from the palace of Luo[yang], which was surrounded on five sides [by enemy troops.] At first he found no vestiges of the city and discerned that the metropolis of the illegitimate [dynasty] had gone into decline. He headed west and arrived at the capital [Chang'an]. From his early days Emperor Taiwu had received news about [Zhuanming] with respect and deeply understood the miraculous events [carried out by Zhuanming]. [The emperor] made a special bow to him cordially and issued an imperial decree to allow [Zhuanming] to reside at Huadu Temple. [Zhuanming] was often brought to the palace where he explained omens and [divine] responses in detail. Later, when these events manifested, they all tallied with [what Zhuanming had foretold].

In the eighth month of that year [Zhuanming] suddenly disappeared. His clothes, property, and miscellaneous goods were left neatly in his room. [The people] looked for him; they traveled around all over the country but ended up obtaining no news [of him].

Whenever someone inquired about learning, [Zhuanming said,][44] "I usually make up my mind with the single Dharma, equality, and follow it." On the other hand, what [Zhuanming] predicted about monks and laymen, such as past and future events and their joys and sorrows as reward and retribution, all had mystic efficacy.

He went to Zongchi [Temple] and said, addressing the monks, "Before long, there will be bloodshed in this temple. You should all be cautious." At the time monks such as Chairman of the Lecture Assembly Fagai were self-ordained and the world was full of their descendants. They were sought, listed in the record, and then killed in a metropolis. [The monks of Zongchi Temple] repented of their past faults but it was no use crying over spilt milk.

[Shi Jiayi, a *Śramaṇa* of the Tang Dynasty]

In the Tang dynasty there was the *śramaṇa* Jiayi in Anzhou (in present-day Hubei province). His original domicile is unknown. At the beginning of the Renshou era (601) of the Sui dynasty he traveled in Anlu (present-day Dean county in Hubei province). In making a joke, he appeared and disappeared.

[His joking] was more than omens and prophecies. His apperance and clothing changed [variously], and he wandered about without settling down. One time 494c
he was a monk and another time he was a layman. He could manifest himself in many bodies in various counties [at the same time]. As he was examined and investigated, his virtue garnered respect. He did not complete [the practices as a monk] and he felt ashamed of his lack of knowledge.

Śramaṇa Huigao at Fangdeng Temple was extensively versed in learning and practices. [Jiayi] accordingly went to see him. He gave [Huigao] fifty pages of writings and said, "Dharma teacher, you will simply be able to understand [my intention] from this." At the beginning [Huigao] could not surmise from where [Jiayi's words] came. Later, a dispute arose and [Hui]gao was imprisoned. Government officials blamed [Huigao] and demanded he give an explanation. Arranging [the evidence written in the papers, Huigao] clarified [the circumstances] and answered, "When the paper runs out, the affair becomes clear." Just as two pieces of a tally match as perfectly as in their original condition, the omens and [divine] responses [completely] matched [Jiayi's prophecies]. [Other] examples were all just like this.

Afterward [Jiayi] came to one family and said, "I have heard that you have a daughter. I would like to marry her." The family initially accepted [his proposal]. So [Jiayi] went to a marketplace and made a public announcement, saying, "The family must obtain [wedding] presents in order to give to my [future] wife." He widely demanded money and rice and on a set day they married. [Jiayi] often went to the gate of that family's house and spoke aloud. The family of his wife was ashamed of this. Consequently, they killed him secretly and buried his corpse under nightsoil. [Jiayi's body] remained there for three days. Then he was seen walking around the marketplace, where he met people and told them about the incident of his murder.

In the fifth year of the Daye era (609) the world was clean and peaceful. [Jia]yi played with various groups of children at the shore; he would climb up onto the railings of a bridge and hang from the railings by his hands. He said, "Lower the head of sheep (*yang*)! Twist with your hands the head of the sheep!" The people saw him sitting on [the railings] and laughed at his antics. When the disasters of the Yang [royal] family of Jiangdu (in present-day Jiangsu province) occured, [the incident] completely matched what [Jiayi] had said previously. It is unknown where he died.

[Shi Fashun, a *Śramaṇa* of the Tang Dynasty]

In the Tang dynasty there was Shi Fashun (557–640) at Yishan Temple in Yongzhou (present-day Shaanxi province). His secular family name was Du and he was from Wannian county in Yongzhou. His natural disposition was gentle and he determinedly practiced austerity.

The small hill area east of Jingshi [county] was called Matou ("Horse's Head"). The sky and precipices deeply met one another, and it was a place suitable for making a miraculous cave.

Chan Master Sengzhen at Yinsheng Temple was originally a teacher from whom [Fa]shun had received [instructions in] practice. [Seng]zhen had begun to make the [temple] foundation [in the cave] and now exhorted the laymen to repair it. He sat upright and directed [the workers for the construction]; he instructed them in its rules.

Suddenly a dog was seen and no one knew where it had come from. [The dog had] white legs and a yellow body, and was natural, tame, and submissive. [The dog] directly entered the cave and came out with some soil in its mouth. It went back and forth for a short while, working hard, but it did not become tired. It ate in the same way as monks did; it did not drink after noon. [The dog] had strange [behavior] like this. The news [of the strange dog] spread to every remote place, and was eventually heard by Emperor Gao (i.e., Emperor Wen, r. 581–604) of the Sui dynasty. The emperor honored [the dog], granting three *sheng* of rice per day, and accordingly the offering became a regular stipulation. Subsequently, after the small shrine was completed [the dog] died for no apparent reason. This is the present-day Yinsheng Temple.

[Fa]shun, at that time, personally witnessed this matter and took refuge in [the Buddhist Way] more and more. He did his best to help [the people] with the construction, and exhorted them to set up an assembly. [The number of people] for whom provisions were offered was limited to five hundred, but when the time came twice as many people arrived. The host [of the assembly for] offering provisions was afraid that they did not have enough. [Fa]shun said, "Nevermind! If you offer [provisions] to a thousand people, your offering is sufficient. There might still be a surplus."

Formerly Zhang Hongchang in Qinghe (present-day Qinghe county in Hebei province)[45] raised oxen and horses in his house. His nature was originally evil and everyone was troubled by him. Even if he tried to sell [his oxen and horses], no one would buy them. [Fa]shun spoke to him about benevolence. [Hongchang] appeared to listen and follow [Fashun]. After that, [Hongchang] attended to wholesomeness and no longer turned on other people.

Furthermore, during the summer every year, [Fashun] led the people to Mount Li (in present-day Linzhang county in Shaanxi province) and he remained there in tranquility. There were numerous insects and ants on the 495a
ground and [the soil] was too poor for planting vegetables. [Fa]shun was afraid to harm [the insects and ants,] so on the spot he instructed [the people] to move the insects somewhere else. Shortly afterward he went to [the place] and it was just as if there had never been any insects.

Once [Fa]shun suffered from a [infected] swelling that burst and [pus] flowed out. Someone respectfully sucked out the pus, another wiped it off with silk fabric. Soon it was healed. The remaining pus emitted fragrance and its auspicious vapor was dificult to compare with anything else. The silk fabric with which [the pus] had been wiped still held fragrance that did not dissipate.

In addition, Tian Saduo, from Sanyuan county (present-day Shaanxi province), suffered from deafness since his birth, and there was also Zhang Su, who suffered from dumbness.[46] [Fa]shun heard [heaven's] decree and went to them and discussed together with them. Consequently they regained their health and permanently recovered from their disabilities.

Furthermore, in Wugong county (in present-day Shaanxi province) there was a monk who had been spellbound by a venomous dragon. Because of this, the people submitted themselves to [the monk]. [Fa]shun made an upright bow, joining his hands before his chest, and sat across from [the monk]. The venomous [dragon] consequently said, through the mouth of the ill monk, "You, Chan Master, have already come. There is no point for me to stay here any longer." They were both tired and extremely weak. Soon [Fashun] released [the venomous dragon] but there were some others who suffered from disease attributed to miasma and demonic evil. They all submitted to [Fashun] and recovered from their disease. [Fashun] did not apply incantation but the power of his merit worked in this way. Those who were unable to understand him said, "[Fashun] has something added by hidden virtue. Therefore, he moves numinous beings and makes them solely pay respect to him." What he taught through his words was to restrain from groundless expressions and clearly reveal right principles. He held sincerity in mind.

When he saw sacred trees and the shrines of popular (i.e., non-Buddhist) religions, he burned them down and removed them. He extensively loved monks and laypeople. The eminent and the humble all submitted to him. There were two ways, to praise him or to slander him. When he opened his mind, it was singlehearted. He appeared not to be affected [by either praise or slander even if he heard it]. He suddenly spoke of [the time after his departure] and then went to Nanye.

Just as he was about to cross the Huangqu [River], the water level rose. No one ventured to cross it; the bank was steep and slippery. Even if someone tried to climb up on the bank he would fall into the water. Suddenly [Fashun] broke apart the stream and went on just as if he were traveling on land. When he went up on the bank [on the other side], the water quickly rushed back and flowed over [his path]. [Fashun's] disciples saw this but they could not fathom this reality. Regarding cases where [Fashun] perceived communication with the unseen world, such events were numerous.

[Fashun] was not stingy with valuables, which were distributed and used without his officiating. He took only coarse [food] and wore [worn-out] clothes. He had no change [of clothing] throughout his life. The government and the people knew of him very well, and conveyed thorough [information about him] to the emperor. [The emperor] invited [Fashun] to the palace, revered him, and extended every courtesy to him. All the palace people submitted to him in reverence and asked him to bestow on them the precepts and the Dharma.

In the fourteenth year of the Zhenguan era (640) [Fashun], who was not suffering from any disease, repeatedly told his disciples and followers his constitutional method of practice, and later had them receive and employ it. After doing this, he sat down crossed-legged as usual. He passed away at Yishan Temple in the southern suburb at the age of eighty-four.

At the moment of his death a pair of birds suddenly appeared and flew into his room. They were dismayed with heavy sorrow. Accordingly, his body in a sitting position was sent to the northern graveyard in Fanchuan (in present-day Chang'an county in Shaanxi province). A grave was dug and [his body] was placed there. The monks and laypeople of the metropolis all lamented [his death]. People in mourning dress and their horses gathered all over the fields. Their mournful cries and extreme grieving filled the earth. The color of [Fashun's] flesh did not change and became brighter as time went by. [Fashun's upright body] remained stable for three years; the bones of his skeleton did not scatter. From the time of his death until today there is always rare fragrance that flows into the place where his corpse was placed. Those who go there all smell it. [Fashun's] associates in learning, his disciples, and followers were concerned that there might be invaders from outside, so they hid [Fashun's remains] in a small shrine. Then they were not afraid that it would be stolen [or disturbed]. The four categories of Buddhists (monks nuns, laymen, and laywomen) went there to make offerings on pleasant days. [The crowd of people who gathered at Fashun's grave] grew larger and larger.

(These eight stories are found in the *Biographies of Eminent Monks Compiled in the Tang Dynasty* [*Tang Gaoseng zhuan,* i.e., *Xu Gaoseng zhuan*]).

[Zhang, a Man from Zou County in Yan Province in the Tang Dynasty]

In the Tang dynasty there was a man from Zou county in Yan province 495b
(in present-day Shandong province) whose family name was Zhang but his pseudonym is forgotten. He was once appointed District Defender.

In the sixteenth year of the Zhenguan era (642) [Zhang] intended to go to the capital city to take a selective examination for official posts. On his way [to the capital] he traveled along the base of Mount Tai. Accordingly he visited the shrine to pray for good fortune. In the shrine the Magistrate of Mount Tai, his lady, and their sons all appeared as images. Zhang worshiped each image in turn. When he came to the image of the fourth son, he saw that its appearance was exceptionally graceful. He was with five traveling companions, but only Zhang said a prayer to [the image of the fourth son], "If I could associate with you, Silang (i.e., fourth son), compose poems together, and drink a toast together, my lifelong wishes would be fulfilled. How is it useful to serve as a government official?"

As he proceeded several *li* [from the shrine], suddenly several tens of horsemen whipping their horses caught up with Zhang. An attendant among them said, "Here is Silang." Silang said, "I know that a little while ago you showed me your courteous feeling. Therefore, I came to see you with respect." He continued, "You would like to take the selective examination for official posts but this year you will not be able to attain a position. Moreover, I am afraid that you have calamities ahead of you. You do not have to go any further."

Zhang did not take [the son's advice] and persisted in leaving there and proceeding [to the capital]. Traveling by night, after going more than a hundred *li* Zhang and his companions were robbed by burglars and stripped of all the equipment they had. Zhang then prayed, "Silang, won't you help me?"

After a while, Silang arrived, along with all his vehicles and horses. He was surprised [by what had befallen Zhang] and grieved for a very long time. He then ordered his retinue to chase after the burglars and arrest them. [The burglars] fell, confused, and were brought back to the place [where they had robbed Zhang's group]. Silang ordered his people to punish them by caning them several tens of times. The burglars were smeared with blood all over their hips and shoulders. After this punishment Silang said goodbye to Zhang and, pointing to a large tree, said, "The day when you return, please call me here."

That year, as had been expected, Zhang came back without attaining an official position. When he came to the appointed place, he called out for Silang. In an instant [Silang] arrived. He guided Zhang, saying, "Let's go to my house!" Promptly high towers and magnificent buildings were laid out far in the air. Parapets with complicated patterns of embrasures stretched around the perimeter. It was all extraordinarily splendid. The manner in which the bodyguards solemnly stood erect like mountains was the same as in king's palace. Not long after Zhang entered, Silang said, "We must visit the Magistrate of Mount Tai before we can take our ease." Then, leading Zhang, he went into [the mansion]. They passed through ten-odd double gates at a trot. They arrived at the base of a large hall where Zhang had an audience with the Magistrate of Mount Tai. [The Magistrate] was extraordinarily dignified. Zhang trembled with fear and dared not gaze at him. Fierce-looking judges [sitting beside the Magistrate] seemed to write in red ink and the Chinese characters were very large. The magistrate ordered his attendant to pass his words on to [Zhang], "You are suitable to associate with my son. You cordially follow the proper path. You must stay here for a couple of days enjoying food and drink at ease, and leave whenever you like." He then ordered [his attendant] to lead [Zhang] out.

[Zhang] came to another large building where an abundance of rare delicacies were set out; dainties of land and sea were all prepared. String and bamboo instruments were played. Music and song filled his ears. Accordingly, Zhang slept in the same room with Silang for one night.

The next morning, Zhang walked around in the courtyard. As he strolled about he looked in on a side yard, where he saw his wife standing in the pillory in front of many officials. He went back into the hall but he was very unhappy. Silang felt strange and asked Zhang the reason for his unhappiness. Zhang told Silang in detail what he had seen. Silang was very surprised and 495c said, "I did not know your wife was here."

Immediately [Silang] personally went to the judicial offices. There were dozens of officials in the offices. When they saw Silang coming, they all rushed down to the lower floor and stood at attention. [Silang] beckoned a judicial official with his hand. The official approached closer and Silang told him all about the incident. The judicial official replied, "Not that I am against your order but I must report it to my office manager." Thereupon the office manager was summoned and he consented [to release Zhang's wife]. He said, "I must then put this case with some other cases and expediently judge them as a group. Only then will it be possible [to release her]." So, the judicial official made his ruling and said, "This lady was investigated for another case. She once earned merit by copying sutras and observing various precepts. It is not appropriate to let her die now." Consequently she was released and ordered to return [to the world].

Zhang said goodbye to Silang, weeping. At the time of Zhang's departure, [Silang] instructed him, "Solely make merit and you will be able to prolong your life." Zhang rode his own horse, his wife borrowed a horse from Silang, and they returned home together. Even though his wife was a spiritual being [without a corporeal body], everything she did was the same as usual. They traveled and were approaching their home, but about a hundred paces away from the house his wife suddenly disappeared. Zhang felt great fear and ran into the house, where he found the men and women [of his family] wailing, and he then knew that they had just finished a burial. Zhang promptly called his children, hurriedly went [to the burial place], and dug the grave open. When the coffin was opened, they saw that Zhang's wife abruptly raised herself and sat up straight. With a sweet smile on her face she said, "[I disappeared] because I yearned for my sons and daughters. Please do not blame me for coming home before you." At that time, six or seven days had passed since the time of her death but she was brought back to life.

An educated person in Yan province related this story.

(This story is found in the *Mingbao ji* [*Records of Rewards and Retributions from the Unseen World*]).

[Various Transmissions and Miscellaneous Records to Clarify Wonders]

The *Shuzhengji* (*Records of Expeditions*) says:

Huan Chong was Regional Inspector of Jiangzhou (in present-day Jiangxi province). He dispatched people to tour Mount Lu and record mysterious things. In the meantime they advanced to the peak of Mount Chong. There was a lake around which mulberry trees grew. There was also a flock of swans. In the lake was a broken barge and red-scaled fishes. The messengers were extremely thirsty and wanted to drink water [from the lake]. The red-scaled fishes spread their fins and rushed at them. The messengers dared not drink [the water].

The *Shenyi jing* (*Scripture on Miracles*) says:

In a very remote place of the north there is a lake, one side of which measures a thousand *li.* [The lake] is flat and completely level. There is a fish seven or eight *chi* long, which in appearance is like a big catfish with red eyes. In the daytime [the fish] stays in the lake, but at night it transforms into a human being. Even if [the fish] is harpooned, [the harpoon] does not penetrate [the fish]. Even if it is boiled, it does not die; however if it is boiled along with fourteen dried plums, then it will be cooked. If you eat this you can recover from evil diseases.

The *Linhai ji* (*Records of Linhai County*) says:

Ren Cengyi's house, located twenty-five *li* northeast from the county seat, has a stone well that is a product of nature, not human-constructed. The well is four *zhang* deep and has a continually bubbling fountain. Even if there is a flood [the well] does not overflow, and if there is a serious drought it does not dry up. In summertime [its water] is absolutely tasty and cold, and in wintertime it is very sweet and warm.

Elders say from generation to generation, "Formerly there was a woodcutter. He was washing tableware close to a stream when a wine cup was carried away by the stream. Later it came out from a well."

The *Dijing tu* (*Charts of the Earthly Mirror*) says:

Treasures are found in the inner and outer city walls, hillocks, or walls. Regarding wonders made by trees, you see that the branches incline to one side, or that there are broken and withered branches. These are signs 496a [that indicate where to hunt for treasure]; when you see broken and withered branch faces, a treasure can be found in that direction. Generally, wherever there is gold or treasure, wonders always make numerous snakes. When you see this sort of thing, you should take off one of your shoes. If you throw the shoe at them, and if you can drown them, then you will obtain [the treasure]. Generally, treasures are hidden and then forgotten. [The people] do not know where [the treasure has been hidden]. If you fill a bronze basin with water, place it on the ground in question, and shine light on it, if you see the shadow of a person [on the water] the treasure will be found below it.

The *Dijing tu* also says, "If you see a place without hoarfrost on the roof tiles, there is a collection of treasures below it."

The *Yanzi chunqiu* (*Annals of Yan Ying*) says:

He's *bi* (a precious piece of jade obtained by Bian He) was originally an unwrought gem found in a village. When an expert craftsman worked on it, it became a treasure of the state.

The *Kong Xiangzi* says, "The stone *jue* in a village" [instead of "an unwrought gem found in a village]." It also says, "When Wangren polished [the *jue*] it became the treasure of the world."

The *Shuyi ji* (*Records to Give Accounts of Extraordinary Things*) says:

Yudu county in Nankang prefecture (present-day Jiangxi province) is located along the Yangzi River. A place three *li* west, far from the county seat, is called Mengkou ("Mouth of a Dream"), and there is a cave that looks like a stone chamber. It has been handed down from former days that there is a supernatural fowl [in this cave]; its color is just like that of good-quality gold. [The fowl] comes out from within this cave, spreads its wings, and soars up, turning round and round; its long cry resounds through the area and if someone sees it, it flies back into the cave. Accordingly, [the people] designated this stone [cave] the "Gold Fowl Stone [cave]."

Once someone was tilling on the side of this mountain and saw the fowl come out and play about. There was an extremely tall person who shot at it using a pellet bow. The fowl saw this from a distance and flew back into the cave. The pellet struck just above the cave [entrance]. The diameter of the pellet was about six *chi,* and it hung down and covered the cave entrance. There was still a crevice but it was not large enough for anyone [to pass through].

Moreover, some people were returning to the county by boat from downstream. Several *li* away, before reaching this cliff, someone wearing yellow clothes, covering his body, and carrying a couple of baskets of yellow melons on his shoulders requested [the boat] to approach and take him on board. The person in yellow clothing begged for food and the ship owner gave some to him. He finished eating just as the boat arrived at the foot of the cliff. The ship owner begged for a melon. The person, however, would not give one to him. Then [the person in yellow clothing] spit onto a basin and climbed up the cliff, and straightaway went into the stone [cave]. At first the ship owner was quite furious about this. He did not know [that the person in yellow clothing] was a spiritual being until he saw him enter the stone [cave]. He looked at the tableware and found that the spit on the basin had completely turned into gold.

The *Wu lu* (*Records of Wu*) says:

In Bijing county in Rinan prefecture (in present-day Vietnam) there are fire mice (*huoshu*).[47] Their fur is collected to make textiles, which are cleaned by burning. [Hence,] this is called the textiles cleansed in fire (*huohuan bu*).

The *Jin yangqiu* (*Annals of the Jin Dynasty*) says:

There was a person who was in charge of reporting to the throne. He tried to mix fine cloth woven loosely with [the textiles cleansed in fire] in the usual manner, but Emperor Wu did not approve of it.

The *Soushen ji* (*Records of Inquiries of the Spirits*) says:

On the high peaks of the Kunlun Mountains, there is a flaming mountain, on which there are birds, animals, trees, and plants. They all live amid the flames. Therefore, there are the textiles cleansed in fire. [The textiles] are not made out of the bark or skins of trees and plants of this mountain but from animal fur.

Ruler Wen (i.e., Cao Pi; r. 220–226) of the Wei kingdom [of the Three Kingdoms period] thought that the nature of fire was atrocious and contained no energy of nutrition. He wrote this in his book *Dian lun* (*Discourse on Laws*), which was [later] engraved on [a stone monument] outside of his mausoleum. At that time a messenger from the Central Asia presented *kaṣāya* robes made of the textiles cleansed in fire. Thereupon this statement was blotted out. 496b

The *Dijing tu* says, "There are scallions on a mountain. Below them there is gold."

The *Bowu zhi* (*Records of Natural Studies*) says, "Pregnant women cannot eat ginger, beause it causes their babies to have more fingers than nomal."

The *Baopuzi* says:

> If [you hear that] a tree in the mountains can speak, it is not that the tree speaks. It is the spirit [of that tree,] called Yunyang ("Clouds and Sun") that speaks. If you see the glow of fire in the mountains at night, this is what all old withered trees make. Do not be surprised by it! If [you see] a person who calls himself a hermit on the *huori* day (fifth day of the fifth month) in the mountains, he is an aged tree.

The *Sun Chuozi* (*Book of Sun Chuozi*) says:

> A fisherman and a mountain dweller debated things about their localities. The fisherman said, "We have a fish in the wide sea. Its forehead is as large as the peak of Mount Hua, and it sucks in all the waves from a vast area all at once." The mountain dweller said, "We have a tree in the Deng Grove[48] whose circumference is equivalent to thirty thousand fathoms, and it rises straight up a thousand *li* high. It shelters several nearby states." Someone said, "There is a giant in the far east. He cuts down a tree to fashion a whip. It is too short and cannot be used as a cane. He catches fresh fish but they are not fresh enough for dried and seasoned fish."

The *Xuanzhong ji* (*Records of the Profound Within*) says:

The sap of a hundred-year-old tree is as red as blood. The spirit of a thousand-year-old tree becomes a blue sheep. The spirit of a ten thousand-year-old tree becomes a cow.

[End of] Fascicle Twenty-eight of *A Forest of Pearls from the Dharma Garden*

Fascicle 29

Chapter Twenty-one

Feeling Auspicious Omens

(This chapter consists of two parts:) (1) Introduction and (2) Sacred Vestiges.

1. Introduction

I respectfully ponder Śākyamuni's teaching. Starting from [the reign of Emperor] Ming (57–75) of the Han dynasty up to the brilliant Tang dynasty, political situations have flowed on from time to time throughout the ages, for nearly six hundred years. Light carriages for imperial emissaries go on one after another, completely inspecting all regions. More than a thousand states have entirely turned to [Chinese] customs and influence. Everyone scales mountains and offers tribute [to China]. It is seen that every day they come to our sovereign, but there are discrepancies in the biographies and records before and after; [their descriptions] differ from one another. [Historical] vestiges are seldom explained and there is a lot of confusion about the names of people and places. Even though we have been granted an abundance of benefits from them, their profound purposes are not perfectly understood. Between foreign regions and China there are differences in pronunciation, and the meanings of passages were often incorrect. In investigating sacred traces [those biographies and records] have difficulties in conveying [information on foreign regions] completely. Therefore, all the monks of this land felt bitter and discontented.

At that time Dharma Master Xuanzang, a *śramaṇa* of the great Tang
dynasty, deplored the inarticulateness of the Great Way and regretted the fact 496c
that [the transmission of] Śākyamuni's teaching was restrained and muted. Consequently, in late spring, in the third month of the third year of the Zhenguan era (629), he set out completely alone to go in search of sacred vestiges in the west.

First he departed the capital city and eventually reached Shazhou (present-day Dunhuang county in Gansu province). He alone went on through precipitous and dangerous places. He passed through a dangerous area to Yiwu (present-day Hami) and Gaochang (Karakhoja, near present-day Turfan). At that time he met the king of Gaochang of the Qu [royal family], who granted material and financial help to him. [Xuan]zang was delivered to the place governed by [Tong] Yehu [Khan] of the Turks. Furthermore, he was sent to all the foreign states north of the Snowcapped Mountains. He fully witnessed the Buddhist edification [there]. Again he went southeast and came out of the great Snowcapped Mountains. The ancient people said, "Snow stays on the Pamirs, that is to say, the Snowcapped Mountains." [Xuan]zang personally witnessed these scenes. After passing the area of the Snowcapped Mountains, he reached India. Later, after ten years had passed, he returned [to this land]. He went through all the states from north of the southern Snowcapped Mountains in the Pamirs. When he returned east, he passed through more than a hundred and fifty states, including Kustana and Loulan [south of Lobnor]. He experienced every difficulty [in those places where] there is no human habitation.

Right at the beginning of the winter of the nineteenth year of the Zhenguan era (645) he arrived at the capital city. He received an imperial decree to translate sutras [into the Chinese language]. Concurrently he was ordered to compose twelve fascicles of the record of [Xuanzang's] travels to the Western region (i.e., *Da Tang xiyuji,* T. 2087). Now, in the third year of the Longshuo era (663), the translations of the sutras and discourses have been completed.

There has been no case similar to that of Master [Xuan]zang; he traveled around [many] states, learned extensively, and translated more sutras than anyone else [during the transmission of Buddhism to China].

According to the record of Master [Xuan]zang's travels *(Da Tang xiyuji*), the *Wang Xuance zhuan* (*Record of Wang Xuance's Travels*), and Buddhist monks and laymen of the Western Region, places suitable for a Chinese government office have wonderful and extraordinary features.

Following an imperial decree, educational officials and others compiled [Xuanzang's] complete works in detail. They arranged [the length of the compilation] and completed the sixty fascicles entitled the *Xiguo zhi* (*Record of the Western States*), in a hundred fascicles, with forty fascicles of drawings [in addition to the sixty fascicles of the text]. From the region between the state of Kustana and the state of Pārasya (present-day Persia) to the east, the great Tang dynasty has Area Command, Provincial, or District Offices, and an Assault Resisting Garrison at three hundred and seventy-eight locations in total; the Area Command in nine locations, Provincial Offices in eighty locations, District Offices in a hundred and thirty-three locations, and Assault Resisting Garrisons in a hundred and forty-seven locations. What is appropriate in the four continents and distinguished and extraordinary personages were all briefly prepared.

All the chapters are not clarified here. What is recorded now are simply citations about the Buddhist Dharma. Regarding the preservation of sacred vestiges, one fascicle is separately completed. The remaining items that are not mentioned all exist in the larger [original] version. I hope that future generations will take these lacunae as a lesson and be aware that [my work on this] is broad and rough.

2. Sacred Vestiges

The *Xiyu zhuan* (*Exposition of the Western Regions*) relates that Master [Xuan]zang left Chang'an and finally reached Gaochang, where he received hospitable treatment. From Gaochang he was given transportation to the eastern border of the state of Kustana, which is precisely the state of Yutian mentioned in the history of the Han dynasty. The local people call this state Yudun.

The city of Bhīmā (Pimo) is two hundred-some *li* east of [Kustana].[49] In
the city there is a standing [buddha] statue [carved from] sandalwood, more 497a
than two *zhang* tall. The statue has extremely marvelous efficacy and emits light. If anyone who suffers [from pain] pastes gold leaf on the statue corresponding to the area of his pain, then the pain is immediately alleviated. This statue was originally in the state of Kauśāṃbī (Jiaoshangmi); it was made by King Udayana. It flew through the sky and arrived at the city of Roruka (the capital city of Sovīra) in the north of this state. There was a strange arhat who went to worship [the statue] every day. The king at first did not believe in [the buddha statue]. [He ordered people to] cover [the arhat] with sandy soil. The arhat then told someone who respected and believed in [Buddhism], "For the next seven days sandy soil will fill the city. On the day after tomorrow treasures will fall [from the sky] and fill the streets." In

fact, on the night of the seventh day the [sandy] soil that had fallen [from the sky] filled up [the city]. Almost no one survived. The person to whom [the arhat] had previously spoken dug an underground passage beforehand, through which he escaped [from the city].

At that time, in the middle of the road a hundred and sixty *li* west from the capital city, there was a large pile of gravel, simply a mound of earth created by some rats [when they dug up the ground]. [The rats'] bodies were as large as that of a hedgehog and their fur was gold and silver in color. In the past, when the Xiongnu had invaded [this area], the king prayed to the spiritual power of rats [for help]. During the night [the rats] gnawed on [the Xiongnu] people and their horses, and damaged their weapons and arrows. [The Xiongnu] withdrew on the run of their own accord.

The temple located about five *li* west from the capital city has a stupa that is a hundred-plus *chi* high. It frequently emits light. The king obtained several hundred pieces of relics through his receptivity [to the Buddha's power]. An arhat lifted up the stupa with his right hand and [the relics] placed in a box [were buried in the ground]. Then [the arhat] set [the stupa] back down [on the ground], with no collapse or damage.

To the southwest ten-plus *li* away from the capital city is Mount Gośriṅga (Qushilingqieshan). It is called Mount Ox Horn (Niujiaoshan). There is a temple in which a [buddha] image emits light. The Buddha once traveled here and expounded the Dharma for heavenly beings. An arhat lives in a stone chamber within the mountain cave. He enters the meditation in which mental functions are completely exhausted (Skt. *nirodha-samāpatti*), waiting for Maitreya [to descend] as a buddha. The southern border of that county is contiguous with Suvarṇa (Dongnüguo, "East State of Women").

Furthermore, going west from the capital city, crossing over mountains and valleys, and traveling more than eight hundred *li,* we reach the state of Cakoka (Zhejujia, present-day Karghalik), which is precisely the territory of the Juqu [family]. In the south of the state there is a mountain on which many stupas of arhats stand. The pine forest is dense and the stone chamber is deep and pure. [In the chamber] three arhats enter the meditation in which mental functions are completely exhausted. Their beards and hair are constantly long. Monks often shave them. Five Indian monks among them have attained fruition. They frequently stay in this chamber.

Moreover, northwest from the state we go up to a great ridge of gravel, cross over the Śīta River (i.e., Yārkand River; Tuduo he, formerly called Xintou he [in China]), and travel five hundred *li* to reach the state of Khāṣa (present-day Kashgar; Qusha guo, formally called Shule guo [in China]). According to the customs of the people of this region, when a baby is born his or her head is pressed to become a flattened shape.

Going south five hundred *li* from here, we arrive at the state of Uṣā [or Och] (Wusha). To the west, two hundred-plus *li* from the capital city, we reach the great mountain range in which there is a stupa. Several hundreds of years ago a precipice of the mountain spontaneously collapsed. Inside [of the collapsed precipice] there was a *bhikṣu* who sat with closed eyes. His body was very large, and his beard and hair hung down and covered his shoulders and face. The king poured ghee over him and struck a Buddhist gong (Skt. *ghaṇṭā*) [in order to summon the *bhikṣu* out of meditation]. The *bhikṣu*, with uncommon dignity, looked at [the king] and asked, "Where is my teacher Kāśyapa Buddha?" [The king] replied to him, "Nowhere. You must be hearing this for the first time now. He has already entered nirvana." Again [the *bhikṣu*] asked, "Has Śākyamuni Buddha risen in the world?" He was told, "He already passed away." [The *bhikṣu*] then ascended into the sky, transformed into fire, and burned up his own body.

Furthermore, crossing to the southwest over the great Pamirs, in eight hun- 497b
dred-plus *li* we reach the state of Kharbanda (Qiepantuo; i.e., present-day Tashkurghan). In the southeastern part of this state there are two large stone chambers. In each of them an arhat has entered the meditation in which mental functions are completely exhausted. They have already passed through seven hundred years. Their beards and hair are long, and they are shaved annually.

Again going beyond three states, after traveling four thousand-plus *li* we arrive at the state of Damo Tiexidi.[50] In a temple in the capital city there is a stone statue, over which a bronze cupola is suspended. [The cupola] is ornamented with various kinds of gems. Whenever someone circumambulates [the stone statue] the cupola also revolves, following [the person]. When they stop, it stops as well. All sides [of the temple building] are stone walls, so no one can determine how it works. Someone [once] said that it is due to sacred power.

From Gaochang to the Iron Gate we pass through sixteen states altogether.[51] The evaluations of the people and their degrees of faith [in Buddhism] are fully described in the *Zhuguo zhuan* (*Exposition on Various Countries*).

Regarding the Iron Gate, this is precisely the western outpost of the Han dynasty and the frontier pass with an iron gate. The two parts of the Han gate, one of which is upright and the other prone, are made of wood covered with iron, on which various bells are hung. When this frontier pass is firmly closed it truly achieves natural security.

Going out of this gate, and traveling south more than a thousand *li,* we come to a place the eastern side of which the Pamirs occupies, the western side is adjacent to Persia, on its southern side are the great Snowcapped Mountains, and on its northern side is the Iron Gate. The great Vakṣu River (Fuchu; i.e., Oxus River) runs west in the central area [of this place]. This river is what is called the Bocha River in sutras. This area is naturally divided into twenty states; it is impossible to list all of the names [of these twenty states]. In each state there is a ruler who seriously believes in Buddhism. The monks go into retreat (Skt. *vārṣika*) on the sixteenth day of the twelfth month[52] and keep on until the spring equinox. This is because [during that period of time] there are high temperatures and much rain.

Again, following a path to the north and crossing through thirteen states from the state of Termez (Demi), we reach the state of Bactria (Fuhe, present-day Balkh). This region is gorgeous and rich. The common people of that time called it the "small Rājagṛha." This state is close to the South Command of [Si] Yehu [Khan of the Turks]. A temple to the southwest outside of the capital city has the Buddha's water bottle, which can contain about a *sheng* [of water] and which is bright and brilliant in multiple colors. It is hard to say if [the bottle is made of] gold or precious stone. Furthermore, there is the Buddha's tooth [relic], which is one-plus *cun* long and eight or nine *fen* wide.[53] Its color is yellowish-white and it is bright and clean.

There is also the Buddha's broom made from *kāśa* (a kind of eulalia), two-plus *chi* in length and about seven *chi* around. The broomstick is decorated with miscellaneous jewels. Buddhist monks and laymen perceive that these three items emit light on the days of purification.

Fifty-plus *li* northwest from the capital city is Trapusa's town, and forty-plus *li* to the north from the capital city is Bhallika's town. In each of these towns there is a stupa about three *zhang* tall, and [these stupas] indicate [Śākyamuni Buddha's] wonderful traces. These are precisely the stupas for Śākyamuni's hair and nails in the domiciles of the virtuous men who first offered a cake (Skt. *tarpaṇa*) to Śākyamuni when he attained buddhahood. Moreover, [Trapusa and Bhallika] built stupas [following the Buddha's instruction that] his *saṃghāṭī, uttara-āsaṅga,* and *saṃkakṣikā* robes [are folded and stacked], over which his upended almsbowl is placed, and his staff with metal rings is set [on the very top].

Again, crossing a couple of states to the southeast and entering the great Snowcapped Mountains, we arrive at the state of Bāmiyān (Fanyanna). Crossing over the great Snowcapped Mountains to the east, [we come to] a temple that has the Buddha's tooth [relic] and the tooth of a *pratyekabuddha* at the time of the formation of this world. It is five *cun* long and four *cun* wide. 497c
Moreover there is the tooth of the golden-wheel king (Skt. *suvarṇa-cakravartin*), which is three *cun* long and two *cun* wide.

In addition, there is an iron almsbowl of the great arhat Śānakavāsa (Shangnuojiafupo, formally called Shangnahexiu [in China], who is the third patriarch of Indian Buddhism). [The bowl] holds nine *sheng* [of food]. There is also his *saṃghāṭī* robe made out of nine pieces of cloth, deep red in color and made from thread spun from the bark of the *śānaka* plant. In a former existence [Śānakavāsa] had donated [garments made from] this plant to monks on the day the [monks] come out from the summer retreat. Due to the power of this meritorious act, he continually wore [a garment made out of the *śānaka* plant] during his intermediate state between death and the next life (Skt. *antarābhava*), as well as at the moment of his rebirth, for five hundred existences. [At his final birth] he emerged from the womb with [the garment], which became larger as his body grew. When Ānanda ordained [Śānakavāsa, the garment] turned into a Dharma robe. After he had received the complete set of [two hundred and fifty] precepts, it again changed into [a monk's formal robe made of] nine pieces [of cloth, the *saṃghāṭī* robe]. His teeth, almsbowl, and other items are all sealed with gold. From the meditation in which he testified to his extinction, this arhat entered [the meditation of] ultimate wisdom (*bianji zhi*). Because of the power of his vow, he left his *kaṣāya* [in this world]. Later, when the Dharma bequeathed [by the Buddha] becomes exhausted, [his *kaṣāya*] will disintegrate. Today [the robe] shows only minor damage and [it] truly has efficacious power.

Furthermore, going east we enter the Snowcapped Mountains and cross over the Black Ridge (i.e., mountains without snow during the summertime), to arrive in the state of Kāpiśī (Jiabishi). [The people here] are more distinctive in their respectful belief in Buddhism. Every year the king commissions a silver statue [of Buddha], one *zhang* and eight *chi* tall. He cultivates himself by offering worship to it.

At the foot of the northern mountain, three *li* east from the capital city, is a large temple. To the south of its eastern gate is a statue of a great divine king. [Under the ground] beneath its right foot is a large treasure storehouse. Recently the king of another state drove off the monks [of this temple], intending to dig up and take [the treasures]. The figure of a parrot in the divine [king's] cap flapped its wings and cried out, and the earth quaked. The king's troops all fell down. [Then] they got up, apologized, and returned [to their country].

On the mountain ridge north of the temple are several stone chambers in which a number of treasures are stored. If someone tries to open it secretly, the *yakṣa* (*yuecha,* formally called *yecha* [in China]), transforms into a lion, a snake, or a [vicious] insect that is greatly infuriated at [the interloper].

On the great ridge of the mountain three *li* west from the [stone] chambers is an image of Avalokiteśvara. To those who sincerely pray, the image manifests the wondrous body [of Avalokiteśvara] and speaks to the practitioners, pacifying them.

Forty-plus *li* southeast from the city is Rāhula Temple, built by a state minister [called Rāhula]; [the temple] was named after him. A stupa [in this temple] is more than a hundred *chi* high. In the past, one night the state minister had a dream in which he was ordered to build a stupa and beg the king for the relics. The [next] morning he went to the palace, where someone was holding a bottle of the relics. The minister took the relics and ordered that person to go in first. He then ascended the stupa carrying the bottle of relics. The top part (*fubo*) [of the stupa] spontaneously opened. After he placed the relics [in the stupa], the king's messengers caught up with him. The stone [top part] had already closed again. On the days of purification [the stupa] emits light and black [fragrant] oil flows out [of the stupa], and during the night music is heard.

On the summit of the great Snowcapped Mountains more than two hundred *li* northwest from the capital city is the dragon pond. At the foot of the mountain is Longli (Standing Dragon) Temple. In the stupa [of the temple] there are more than one *sheng* of the Buddha's relics of flesh and bone. Once, smoke arose [from the stupa] and it violently blazed as if on fire. When [the flames and smoke] gradually abated, [the people] saw the relics that looked like white pearls went around a pillar, entered the clouds, and returned into the stupa.

On the south bank of a large river northwest of the city is a temple of the former king in which there is a milk tooth from the Buddha's childhood, one-plus *cun* long. Moreover, southeast of this [temple] there is a temple of an ancient king, which has a piece of the Buddha's parietal bones, two-plus *cun* wide and yellowish-white in color. The pores [of the bone] are clear. In early 498a
spring of the first year of the Longshuo era (661) of the great Tang dynasty, the envoy Wang Xuance brought [the Buddha's parietal bone] back from a western state. Today it is offered in worship in the palace.

Moreover this temple has a hair of the Buddha, blue in color, which spirals clockwise. When [the hair] is extended, it is more than a *chi* long, and when curled up, it is about a *cun* long.

In addition, southwest [of the temple of the Buddha's parietal bone] is a temple of the former queen. Its bronze stupa is more than a hundred *chi* high. [In the stupa] are one-plus *sheng* of relics of the Buddha. On the night of the fifteenth day of every [month, the relics] emit a halo that revolves around the dew plate (Skt. *chattra*) [of the stupa] and returns into the stupa at daybreak.

Southwest of the city is Mount Beiluopolu.[54] On a huge circular stone on the top of the mountain a stupa stands, more than a hundred *chi* high, which contains one-plus *sheng* of relics [of the Buddha].

North of this mountain is a spring issuing from rocks (i.e., the dragon pond). This is [the place where] the Buddha rinsed his mouth and chewed a twig of a *khadira* tree (Skt. *dantakāṣṭha*) [to clean the teeth and the tongue] after receiving a meal offered by a mountain deity. For this reason, [*khadira* trees] were planted [around the site] and now they have become a dense forest. The temple [built here later] is called Dantakāṣṭha (Yangzhi; i.e., "Toothbrush").

Again, going east more than six hundred *li* from the dragon pond, crossing the Snowcapped Mountains and the Black Ridge, we arrive at the boundary of North India. All [the lands] beyond here are already Indian states. The style of clothing and the deportment [of the people in these regions] are not the same as those of Bactria (Daxia). [This area] is called the border state of the Mleccha [people] (Mieliche [lei], known as Gouzhuozhong, "Disgraceful Evil Race," in the Tang dynasty). On arriving in this region, we are halfway [through our travels to Central India].

Furthermore, going east, we reach the state of Lampāka (Lanbo; present-day Lamghān), which is exactlythe northern boundary of India. Speaking of India, its formal name is Tianzhu, and it is also called Shendu or Xiandou. These are all corrupted forms of pronunciation.

[India is bordered] by the Himalayas in the north and has oceans on three sides. In the configuration of the land, the southern part is narrow just like a waxing moon. The rivers are flat and wide and flow with abundant water. The circumference of the land is nineteen thousand *li.* More than seventy states are under the rule of one sovereign.

Again, going a hundred-plus *li* east, crossing over great mountain ridges and large rivers, we arrive at the state of Nagarahāra (Naqieluohe; present-day Jelālābād area),[55] which belongs to North India. There is a city called Kusumapura (Huashi) and two *li* east of the city is a stone stupa, three hundred *chi* in height. [The stupa] faced with stone stands erect like a mountain and has extraordinary engraving. This is exactly the place where formerly [Śākyamuni Bodhisattva] met Dīpaṅkara Buddha and received a prediction of his future attainment of buddhahood, and where [Śākyamuni] spread out a deerskin robe and laid out his hair to cover over the mud [in Dīpaṅkara's path]. [The site] still exists here after having passed through a *kalpa.* King Aśoka built the stone stupa. On the days of purification flowers rain from the heavens.

Moreover, in the city is the old foundation of a large stupa in which formerly the Buddha's tooth was deposited. There is another stupa, three-plus *zhang* high, and it is said that [this stupa] came from the sky. Since it is not manmade it truly has numerous miracles.

More than ten *li* southwest from the city is a stupa at the site where the Buddha traversed the sky from Central India and alighted. Next, a stupa to the east is the place where [Śākyamuni Bodhisattva] met Dīpaṅkara Buddha and bought flowers [to offer to him].

Furthermore, more than twenty *li* east from the city is a small rocky mountain ridge on which there is a stupa, two hundred-plus *chi* in height. There is a large cave on the precipice of the east bank. This is the dragon king's dwelling. Formerly the Buddha edified the dragon and left the [Buddha's] image here. [The image] is as brilliant as his true appearance. Those who pray with the utmost sincerity can see it clearly for a short time.

Outside of the cave is a square stone which contains an imprint of the Buddha's foot. The wheel mark [in the footprint] emits light.

There is also a stupa in the northwest corner of the cave, at the place where the Buddha walked about. In addition, next to it there is a stupa which contains [the Buddha's] hair and nail [relics]. A rock in the west of the cave [has an image of the Buddha] and on [the rock] there is also the pattern of the *kaṣāya* [robe] washed [by the Buddha].

Again, more than thirty *li* east from the city [of Kusumapura] is the city 498b
of Haḍḍa (Xiluo), where there is a two-storied pavilion. On the upper story the Buddha's parietal bone [relic] is placed. The circumference [of the bone] is one *chi* and two *cun;* its color is yellowish-white, and the pores are clear. Anyone who wishes to know whether his mind is good or bad can make an imprint [of the bone] with a plaster of incense and then examine the plaster of incense; [a good or a bad pattern] appears in accordance with his mind. Moreover, there is the Buddha's skull [relic], in appearance like a lotus leaf. Its color is the same as that of his parietal bone. There is [also] the Buddha's eyeball [relic], nearly as large as a crabapple (*nai*), which is clean and shines brilliantly. It is also contained in a seven-treasured bottle. The three [relics] left behind by [the Buddha] mentioned above are all contained in a sealed treasure box. There is [also] the Buddha's *saṃghāṭī* made of fine cotton, yellow in color, which is placed in a treasure box. It is in a slightly degraded condition. There is [also] the Buddha's staff with metal rings at the top; the rings are made of tin and the staff from sandalwood. It has been placed in a jeweled container.

These five sacred sites [have miraculous virtue]. The king [of Kāpiśī] ordered five men who practiced pure conduct to take full charge of these articles and protect them. [They decided to] collect a gold coin from those who come to see [the Buddha's parietal bone] and to ask those who want to make an imprint [of the parietal bone] for five [gold coins]. The fee [for inspection or imprinting] is high, but more and more people come to view and worship them. A small stupa northwest of the [two-storied] pavilion has many wonders. Whenever someone touches it, the bells of the stupa greatly shake.

Again, traveling five hundred *li* southeast through mountains and valleys, we come to the state of Gāndhāra (Jiantuoluo), which is also part of North India. There is a place where the great treatise masters, Venerable Manoratha and Venerable Pārśva, compiled the *Abhidharma-mahāvibhāṣā.* There are also the site where [Śākyamuni] Bodhisattva gave up his eyes [to donate them] through his thousand existences,[56] the place where the Buddha edified Hārītī (Guizimu),[57] and the place where Śyāmaka (Shangmojia, formerly called Shanzi [in China]) Bodhisattva was shot by the king [of Kāśi].[58] In addition, there is Mount Daṇḍaka (Danduoluojiashan, formerly called Tanteshan [in China]), on the ridge of which are the sites where Sudāna lived in seclusion and where a brahman beat [Sudāna's] son and daughter, and the blood dyed the ground [red]. Even today the trees and plants [of this place] are all deep red in color. A stone chamber between rocks is the place where [Sudāna's] wife practiced meditation.[59] There is also the place where a hermit named One Horn (Skt. Ekaśṛṅga) was bewildered by a woman.[60]

Again, crossing over the mountains to the north from this city and traveling more than six hundred *li,* we arrive at the state of Udyāna (the basin of present-day Swāt River; Wuzhangna, formerly called Wuzhang [in China]). This is a well-governed state of North India. Five *li* east of the capital city is a large stupa, which has numerous good omens. This is the place that the Buddha, who was then a hermit who practiced forbearance, was dismembered by King Kali (Jieli, who is called Douzheng, ["Fight" in the Tang dynasty]).[61] Moreover, the Buddha's footprint on a square rock is the place where the Buddha [formerly stepped on this rock], emitted light that shone upon a temple, and expounded a story of his past existence (Skt. *jātaka*) for heavenly beings. Furthermore, there is the place where in the past [when the Buddha was a bodhisattva] he copied a sutra [with a pen made out of] his broken bone in order to hear the [true] Dharma [from a brahman].[62] There is also the place where formerly King Śibi cut his own flesh and [gave it to a hawk] on behalf of a dove.[63] Furthermore, there is the place where when the Buddha was a king [called] Maitrībala (Cili) in the past, he stabbed himself so that five demigods called *yakṣa*s could gain nourishment from his blood.[64] Moreover, in a great temple is a wood-carved image of Maitreya Bodhisattva (Meijuliye, formerly called Mile [in China]). [The image] is golden in color, bright and brilliant; it is a hundred-plus *chi* tall. [The figure] was made by Madhyāntika Arhat (Motiandijia Aluohan, formerly called Motiandi Luohan [in China]). The arhat guided an artisan through supernatural power and they ascended to Tuṣita Heaven. They returned [to the heaven] three times in order to observe [Maitreya's] characteristics and they subsequently completed this good work. The image greatly possesses wonderful characteristics; it is impossible to give full details of them.

Again, crossing over a river through one state, we reach the state of Takṣaśilā 498c
(Dechashiluo), which belongs to North India. Seventy *li* northwest from the capital city is a stupa between two mountains, standing a hundred-plus *chi* in height. The Buddha formerly made a prediction that when Maitreya comes into the world the four great treasure houses, of which this place is one, will [emerge from the earth].[65] Moreover, twelve *li* north of the city is a stupa commisioned by King Candraprabha. On the days of purification it always emits mystic light, divine flowers rain down, and heavenly music is heard. Recently a leprous woman worshiped and repented of her sins at the stupa. She removed some soot and dirt [from the stupa] and applied scent on it. Soon thereafter she was cured [of the disease] and her body became sweet-smelling and clean. This is the same place that in the past, when the Buddha was King Candraprabha (Zhandaluobocipo, formerly called Yueguang, "Moonlight," [in China]), he [cut off] his own head and donated it.[66] He endured [giving up his body like this] and donated it for a thousand existences altogether.

There is also the pond where the dragon king Elāpattra (Yiluobo) heard the [Buddha's teaching]. At the place where [King] Candraprabha's eyes were gouged out,[67] a lofty stupa erected by King Aśoka stands at a height of ten *zhang*. In addition, there are the places where Prince [Mahā]sattva gave up his body and fed it to some tigers[68] and where he stabbed his body with a piece of bamboo and allowed beasts to drink his blood. Even today all the earth, plants, and trees [in this area] are dark red in color. Furthermore, there is the place where the Buddha edified the demon *yakṣa*s not to eat flesh.

Again, ascending the mountain to the southeast, after passing two states, crossing over an iron bridge, and traveling more than a thousand *li,* we arrive at the state of Kaśmīra (Jiashimiluo, formerly called Jibin [in China]), which belongs to North India. There are four stupas in the state. Each contains one-plus-*sheng* relics. Four hundred years after the Buddha's *parinirvāṇa,* Venerable Pārśva, who renounced the world at the age of eighty and who attained the fruit of no more learning (i.e., arhatship), led five hundred arhats here.

They produced the *Upadeśa* (*Wupodishuo*), and annotated the *Sūtram-piṭaka* (*Sudelanzang,* formerly called *Youpotishe lun* [in China]). Next, they composed the *Vinayavibhāṣa* (*Pinaiye Piposha lun*) and after that, the *Abhidharma-mahāvibhāṣā* (*Apidamo lun*). Each of these three treatises contains a hundred thousand *gāthās*, and have six million six hundred thousand words altogether. The Tripiṭaka is fully annotated [in the three treatises].

There is also the Buddha's tooth, one and a half *cun* long, yellowish-white in color, which emits light on the days of purification. In addition, there is a standing statue of Avalokiteśvara. Those who wish to see [Avalokiteśvara] must fast and then they can see him [within the statue].

Again, going east, after passing three states we come to the state of Cīnabhukti (Zhinapudi), which belongs to North India. Going more than five hundred *li* southeast from the capital city we arrive at Tamasāvana (Anlin) Temple, more than twenty *li* in circumference. There are several hundreds of thousands of sites for stupas in which the Buddha's relics are placed, and stone chambers as well. A thousand buddhas of the auspicious *kalpa* expounded the Dharma in this place. Three centuries after Śākyamuni's *parinirvāṇa,* Kātyāna (Jiaduoyanna, formerly called Jiazhanyan [in China]), composed the *Da zhi lun* (*Great Wisdom Discourse*) here.[69] A stupa in the temple stands more than twenty *zhang* high. There is also the site where the four [past] buddhas (i.e., Krakucchanda, Kanakamuni, Kāśyapa, and Śākyamuni) spent their daily lives.

Again, going east after passing four states, we come to the state of Mathurā (Motuluo guo, formerly called the state of Motouluo guo [in China]), which is part of Central India. In the capital city there are three stupas as well as numerous sites of the four [past] buddhas and various stupas for [the Buddha's disciples and bodhisattvas], such as Śāriputra (Shelizi), Maudgalyāyana (Moteqieluozi, formerly called Mulian [in China]), Pūrṇamaitrāyaṇīputra (Mancizi, formerly called Fulouna [in China]), Upāli (Youpoli, formerly
499a called Youpoli [in China]),[70] Ānanda (Anan), Rāhula (Luohuluo), and Mañjuśrī (Manzhushili). In the three purification months every year and on the six purification days every month, all the monks and nuns assemble and offer worship to all the stupas. Those who study the Abhidharma offer worship to the memorial stupa for Śāriputra. Those who learn meditation offer worship to the stupa for Maudgalyāyana. Those who hold fast to the recitation of sutras offer worship to the stupa for Pūrṇamaitrāyaṇīputra. Those who learn

the Vinaya offer worship to the stupa for Upāli. The nuns' group offers worship to the stupa for Ānanda. Those who have not yet received the complete set of precepts offer worship to the stupa for Rāhula. Those who learn Mahayana [Buddhism] offer worship to the stupas for various bodhisattvas.

(In searching for these various stupas it is not always possible to find the remains. By responding to standing figures, [the people] set up offerings and devote their hearts [to stupas] such as those for Rāhula and Mañjuśrī. Judging from the descriptions in sutras, these bodhisattvas have not yet entered *parinirvāṇa,* so they can know it.)

Six *li* east of the city is a temple on a cliff, built by Venerable Upagupta (Wupojuduo). Inside [the temple] is a stupa for the Buddha's fingernail relic. North of the temple is a stone chamber. Twenty-plus *li* southeast of the stone chamber is a large dried-up pond, and beside the pond is a stupa. The Buddha once roamed around here, and this is the place where a monkey had some honey and offered it to the Buddha. [The Buddha] diluted [the honey] with water so all the people could have a drink of it. The monkey was happy but he later died after falling into a pit. He was then reborn in the realm of human beings. In a grove north of the pond is a place where the four [past] buddhas roamed. There are more vestiges.

Again, going northeast more than four hundred *li,* after passing a state we reach the state of Śrughna (Sululena), which belongs to Central India. The eastern border [of this state] is formed by the Ganges River (Qingqiehe, formerly called Henghe [in Chinese]). The north is contiguous with the Himalayas. Southeast of the city is the Yamunā River (Yanmouna), which issues from the mountains in the northwest of the state and runs through the state territory. The eastern border of the capital city is next to the Yamunā River.

There is a stupa outside of the eastern gate of a great temple west of the river. The Buddha once expounded the Dharma and delivered people [from the transmigration of birth and death] here. On one side is a stupa for the Buddha's hair and fingernail relics.

Going more than eight hundred *li* east from the Yamunā River, we come to the origin of the Ganges River.[71] The width [of the river here] is three or four *li* [and it runs to] the southeast; at the place where it enters the sea its width is more than ten *li*. The color of the water is blue and its taste is sweet. Fine sand courses, following the water. [The river] is commonly called the

Water of Great Virtue (Fushui; Skt. Mahābhadra). Those who bathe [in the Ganges River] have their sins removed, or if someone takes his own life and submerges [in this river], wishing to be reborn in heaven and receive happiness, he will be able to have a mysterious response.

Again, going southeast from this point, after passing six states we arrive at the state of Kapitha (Jiebita; i.e., Sāṃkāśya), which belongs to Central India. There are ten sites of *deva* shrines (Skt. *devakula*). [Heretics reside alongside Buddhists and] they serve Maheśvara in the same way [as Buddhists do].[72] They all made the image of the deity [Maheśvara], which in appearance is like a phallus, very long and gigantic. The common people do not take this to be unwholesome; they say that all sentient beings are born from the *liṅga* (Maheśvara's icon in the shape of a male sexual organ).

Twenty-plus *li* east of the capital city is a great temple, and within a large fenced area beside [the temple] are three sets of treasured stairs built by Śākra-devendra for the Buddha. The middle set was entirely gold-plated, the left was made of crystal, and the right of silver. They lie north and south and go down to the ground on the east side. This is the place where the Buddha descended after he ascended from Jeta Grove (Shiduolin, formerly called Zhituolin [in China]) to heaven and went to the Wholesome Dharma Hall (i.e., Śākra-devendra's palace; Shanfatang) where he expounded the Dharma
499b for his mother for three months. A hundred years ago the [original] stairs still existed but they now have all vanished. Later kings [of various states restored the stairs by] copying them. Their height is more than seventy *chi*. On the top a monastery was built. Beside [the restored stairs] is a stone pillar, smooth and glossy, which projects an image within itself according to whether one has committed an evil act or performed a meritorious deed. It was built by King Aśoka. To the side of the stairs is a stupa, the site where the four [past] buddhas spent their daily lives. Moreover there is a place where the Buddha bathed; a stupa was built at that site. There is a monastery where the Buddha entered meditation, and on its side is a rock that the Buddha walked around [to take a break]. The base of the rock is fifty paces long and it is seven *chi* in height.[73] All the spots on which [the Buddha] stepped have the pattern of a lotus flower. Furthermore, small stupas on both sides of [the rock] were built by the king of Brahma Heaven. In front of [these stupas] is the place where Utpalavarṇā Bhikṣuṇī transformed herself into a wheel-turning noble

king in order to get to see the Buddha before others. The Buddha told the *bhikṣuṇī,* "You are not the first [to see me]. Subhūti (Subudi, formerly called Xuputi [in China]), meditated in a stone chamber. Since he knows all phenomenal things are empty, he is the first one who saw my *dharmakāya.*"

Again, going two hundred *li* north from here, we arrive at the state of Kānyakubja (Jieruojushe), which belongs to Central India, and which is [known in the Tang dynasty as the state of] Qunücheng ("City of Women Who Are Bent"). The western part of the capital city is close to the Ganges River. [The city] is more than twenty *li* long and four or five *li* wide. [This state] is the most powerful one and governs five Indian metropolises.

Formerly the king was called Śīlāditya (Shiluoyiduo, called Jieri, "Day of Abstinence," in the Tang dynasty). He was from the merchant-farmer caste (*feishe*; Skt. *vaiśya*). When he first intended to ascend the throne [after his elder brother, the king, was killed], there was an Avalokiteśvara image on the bank of the Ganges River. He asked it for advice. [Avalokiteśvara] told him, "You were originally a *bhikṣu* who practiced in this grove (*lanruo biqiu;* Skt. *āraṇya-bhikṣu*). King Śaśāṅka of Karṇasuvarṇa persecuted the Buddhist Dharma, and you, king, must restore it. If you continue to have the mind of kindness toward people you will become a king of five territories. Be carfeul! Do not ascend the lion's sat.[74] Do not use the title "Great King" for yourself, either." Then, together with a boy king (*tongzi wang*),[75] King [Śīlāditya] subjugated and destroyed the non-Buddhists, King Śaśāṅka, and his followers.

Moreover, [Śīlāditya] laid down strict orders. Those who ate meat would have their tongues cut out, and those who destroyed life would have their arms cut off. [The king,] along with his widowed sister[-in-law], managed state affairs. He built more than a thousand stupas along the Ganges River, each [of which] is more than a hundred *chi* tall.

For twenty years, once every five years he held an [offering] assembly to save all sentient beings, even though the state coffers were depleted by this. He kept weapons but he did not expect the weapons to be useful [for the assembly]. On the first day of the assembly, monks from various states gathered together. For twenty-one days the four kinds necessities (i.e., food and drink, clothing, bedding, and medicine) were offered to them, and the monks were asked to discuss among themselves. If there was [a monk present] who virtuously upheld the [Buddhist] precepts and practices, or whose virtue was excellent, he ascended the lion's seat. The king received the precepts from him. The king showed respect toward those who were pure yet had no learning. Those who displayed vile behavior were expelled from the state territory.

[A stupa] northwest of the city was built by King Aśoka. In the past, the Buddha expounded the Dharma for seven days in this place. Around it are a stupa for [the Buddha's] hair and nail [relics] and the site where the four [past] buddhas spent their daily lives. Moreover, south [of this stupa] there is a temple adjacent to the Ganges River that has the Buddha's tooth, which is one and a half *cun* long. The luster and the color [of the tooth] change [in the morning and evening]. It is contained in a treasure box. People come from remote as well as neighboring areas to look at it, up to a hundred or a thousand [visitors] a day. Those charged to protect the relic are bothered [by the visitors] and collect heavy inspection taxes of cash or precious items from them. Nevertheless, those who happily worship [the Buddha's tooth] do not refuse to pay large amounts of money. On the days of purification [the Buddha's tooth] is taken out [from the box] and placed on a raised seat. [Peo-
499c ple] scatter flowers [over it] but even though [the flowers] pile up, the tooth is never covered over.

Again, more than a hundred *li* southeast of the city is a stupa at the place where the Buddha once expounded the Dharma for seven days. There are relics inside and sometimes [the relics] emit light. Beside [the stupa] is the site where the Buddha spent his daily life. There is another stupa near the Ganges River four *li* north of the temple, at the place where the Buddha once expounded the Dharma for seven days and five hundred hungry ghosts attained enlightenment and were reborn in heaven. Next to it is a stupa [containing the Buddha's] hair and nail [relics], and also another site where the four [past] buddhas spent their daily lives.

[Traveling on,] we come to the state of Ayodhyā (Ashutuo), which belongs to Central India. There is a stupa in a large temple near the bank of the Ganges River five *li* north of the capital city, at the site where the Buddha expounded the Dharma for the sake of heavenly and human beings for three months. [This is also another] place where the four [past] buddhas spent their daily lives. Next, five *li* west [of the temple] is a stupa for the Buddha's hair and nail [relics]. In a great grove of *āmra* trees five *li* southwest of the city is an old temple. [From] this place Asaṅga Bodhisattva ascended to a heavenly palace at night, where he received from Maitreya the *Yogācārabhūmi* (*Yuqie shidi lun*), the *Mahāyānasūtrālaṃkāra* (*Dasheng zhuangyan jinglun*), the *Madhyāntavibhāga* (*Zhongbianfenbie lun*), and other texts, and then descended to discourse on them for sentient beings during the day.

A hundred-plus paces northwest from the grove is a stupa for the Buddha's hair and nail [relics]. Near the Ganges River southeast of the city is a stupa at the place where the Buddha once expounded the Dharma for three months. There is a blue stone stupa for the [Buddha's] hair and nail [relics] and another site where the four [past] buddhas spent their daily lives.

Again, going southeast, after passing through two states we come to the state of Prayāga (Boluoyeqie), which belongs to Central India. The southwest border of the capital city is formed by the Yamunā River. [At a place where the river] curves there is a stupa. This is the where the Buddha once subjugated non-Buddhists. There is a stupa with the [Buddha's] hair and nail [relics] and the place where he roamed [for leisure]. There is also the place where [Ārya]deva Bodhisattva composed the *Guang Bai lun.*[76] In the city there is a *deva* shrine. The branches and foliage of a large tree in front of the [shrine] hall have grown thick, and there are cannibalistic spirits [in the tree]. So human remains can be seen piled up around [the tree]. Anyone who enters the shrine will lose their life without fail. [Recently someone] was thrown down from the tree; he had been tempted by the spirits.

[An area] east of the city where two rivers (i.e., the Ganges and Yamunā) meet is more than ten *li* around. The land is level and lushly vegetated, with fine sand completely spread out. In ancient and modern times, when kings and nobles offer donations all the people come [here]. [This place] is called the Field of Great Almsgiving (Dashichang). Great King Śīlāditya also followed this observance.

At the mouth of the confluence [of the two rivers] east of the field, every day several people commit suicide by [going into the churning waters and] drowning. The common people call it the "place to be reborn in heaven." Those who come to to do this fast for seven days and then plunge into the river midstream. [People] come here from remote as well as neighboring areas. Even mountain apes and beasts of the fields such as deer wander about the water's edge, fast, and die by drowning, too. Once when King Śīlāditya was giving alms, a couple of rhesus monkeys, [a male and a female,] were nearby. The female was killed by a dog. The male carried the dead body [of the female] and threw it into the river, then it committed suicide after fasting for many days.

Again, going more than five hundred *li* from a large forest southwest of
500a this place, we reach the state of Kauśāṃbī (Jiaoshangmi), which belongs to Central India. There is a great monastery in the old palace of the capital city. [The monastery building] is sixty *chi* high. A buddha statue of carved sandalwood, above which is a stone canopy, was made by King Udayana (Wutuoyana, formerly called King Youtuoyan, and called Chuai in the Tang dynasty). Mysterious [events] and light occasionally arise there. Various kings have tried to move [the statue] relying on force, but in the end no one could transfer it.

In the past, the Buddha ascended to heaven and expounded the Dharma for his mother. King [Udayana] asked Maudgalyāyana to use his supernatural power to ascend to heaven with an artist so that he could to try to make an image of the [Buddha's] form. When the Buddha descended from heaven, the statue rose to its feet and received him. The Buddha said to [the statue], acknowledging [its service], "Please serve only Buddhism."

A hundred-plus paces east of the monastery is the site where the four [past] buddhas spent their daily lives. The Buddha's bathroom and well remain, and even today [the well] still has enough water to draw.

In the southeast corner of the city there are the house of the elder Ghoṣila (Jushiluo), a Buddhist monastery, a stupa for the [Buddha's] hair and nail [relics], and the place where the four [past] buddhas spent their daily lives.

A stone chamber nine *li* west of the city is the site where the Buddha subjugated a poisonous dragon. Next to it is a large stupa, more than twenty *zhang* high. This is the place where the Buddha roamed around [in leisure] as well as a stupa for the [Buddha's] hair and nail [relics]. People who are ill go to pray there, and many of them are healed. [The Buddha prophesied] that the Dharma left by Śākyamuni will be destroyed in this state. When people, regardless of their high and low social positions, enter the territory [of this state], they spontaneously feel sentimental (i.e., nostalgic and softhearted).

Traveling seven hundred *li* northeast of the [dragon] cave, crossing over the Ganges River to the north bank, we come to the city of Kaśapura (Kāśapura or Kājapura; Jiashebuluo). This is the place where Dharmapāla Bodhisattva subdued non-Buddhists. The Buddha once expounded the Dharma for six months here, and there is the place where he roamed around [in leisure], as well as a stupa for the [Buddha's] hair and nail [relics].

Again, going a hundred eighty *li* north from this place, we arrive at the state of Viśāka (Bingsuojia), which belongs to Central India. South of the capital city is a temple and a stupa that rises to a height of over twenty *zhang*. The Buddha once expounded the Dharma for six years in this place. Next to it is a strange tree, seventy *chi* in height. [The tree] does not change over time. It grew vigorously from a twig the Buddha had tossed away after cleaning his teeth with it. Various people of wrong views and non-Buddhists vie with each other trying to cut [the tree] down, but it soon grows back as before. Those who try to cut down [the tree] receive misfortune. Beside [the tree] is a place where the four [past] buddhas spent their daily lives and a stupa for the [Buddha's] hair and nail [relics]. The corners of the foundation [of the stupa] are connected. A grove is reflected in a pond.

Again, going five hundred *li* northeast from here, we come to the state of Śrāvastī (Shiluofaxidi, formerly called the state of Shewei [in China]), which belongs to Central India. The capital city has been devastated. There is a small stupa on the eastern foundation of the old palace. This was [the capital city of the state governed by] King Prasenajit (Boluoxinashiduo, formerly called Posini, called Shengjun in the Tang dynasty). There is a place where a *bhikṣuṇī* built a monastery. Next, a stupa on the eastern side [of another stupa, formerly Prajāpati's monastery,] is the site of the old house of Sudatta (Sudaduo, called Shanshi in the Tang dynasty). Next to it is a large stupa. This is the place where Aṅgulimāla (Yangjulimoluo, called Zhiman in the Tang dydnasty) abandoned his evil mind [and took refuge in the Buddha].

About six *li* south of the city is the Jeta Grove, the Garden of Anāthapiṇḍada, offered by Crown Prince [Jeta, where Sudatta] built a temple. Today it is in ruins but there are still [two] stone pillars, more than seventy *chi* in height, which were built by King Aśoka. Only a brick chamber remains; everything else has vanished, and inside there is a golden image [of the Buddha] expounding the Dharma for his mother. Northeast [of the Garden of Anāthapiṇḍada] is a stupa at the place where the Buddha washed [the body of] an ill monk.

To the northwest is a stupa at the place where Maudgalyāyana tried to lift
500b up Śāriputra's sash. Not far from [that stupa] is a well, from which water was drawn and used for the Buddha. Furthermore, there is a path that Śāriputra along with the Buddha roamed [in leisure] as well as a place where they expounded the Dharma. There are also stupas to show wholesomeness where auspicious signs, heavenly music, and rare fragrance often descended [from heaven]. Some non-Buddhists once killed a woman in order to attempt to slander the Buddha. A stupa was built to mark the place. A hundred-plus paces east of the temple is a large, deep pit. This is the place where Devadatta, who intended to poison the Buddha, fell into [hell] while still alive. To the south is another large pit, where Kokālika (Quqieli) Bhikṣu, who tried to injure the Buddha, fell into [hell] while still alive. In addition, eight hundred paces to the south is another large, deep pit, the place where Ciñcā, a brahman woman, slandered the Buddha and fell into [hell] while still alive. These three large pits are all very deep, [seemingly] bottomless. Even when there is a large amount of rainfall and much [water] pours into them, there is no standing [water] visible within them afterward.

Seventy paces east from the temple is a monastery called Covered-by-Shadow (Yingfu), sixty *chi* in height. Inside there is a seated figure [of the Buddha] facing east. This is where [the Buddha] debated with non-Buddhists. Next, to the east is a *deva* shrine, as large as the monastery. In the early part of the day the shadow [of the shrine] covers the western area, but it never casts shade on the monastery, while by evening the shadow has moved east and consequently [the monastery] casts shades on the *deva* shrine. Moreover, four *li* east of [the shrine] is a large dried-up pond, which is the place where King Virūḍhaka (or Vidūdabha; Pilushijia, formerly called Liuli [in China]) fell into hell. Someone later erected [a stupa] there on which [the incident] was recorded. There is also the first temple built by Śāriputra at the place where he contested with non-Buddhists. A stupa was erected there and [this incident] was recorded on it, too.

Four *li* northwest of the temple is Andhavana ("Grove Where One Obtains His Eyes"), in which there is a stupa at the place where the Buddha roamed around [in leisure]. At the edge of this area is where King Prasenajit gouged out the eyes of five hundred bandits. [The bandits] heard of the Buddha's power of mercy and immediately recovered [their eyes]. They then abandoned the canes [they had used after losing their eyes], and these subsequently grew [into trees and become the Andhavana Grove].

Sixty *li* northwest of the city is an old city, the place where Kāśyapa Buddha was born during the time [in the present cosmic period] when the human life span was twenty thousand years. To the north of it is [a stupa for] the relics of this buddha's body (Skt. *śarīra*). King Aśoka built the stupa; this is recorded on its side.

Again, going five hundred *li* to the southeast, we arrive at the state of Kapilavastu (Jiebiluofasudu guo, formerly called Jiapiluo guo [in China]), which belongs to Central India. There is no longer anyone residing in the old capital city. In a monastery built on the foundation [of the former main palace hall] a statue of King [Śuddhodana] is set up. Beside [the monastery] was the main house of Lady Mahāmāyā (Mohe Moye, called Dashu, "Great Art," in the Tang dynasty). In a monastery built on the foundation [of this house] there is a statue of the lady. In a nearby monastery there is an image of [Śākyamuni] Bodhisattva when he descended to be conceived [by Lady Mahāmāyā]. [Each Buddhist school] holds a different view of [the date when he was conceived]. The Sthaviravāda school advocates that it is the fifteenth day of the fifth month [of the calendar] of the Tang dynasty. Various schools [other than the Theravāda school] say that it is the eighth of the fifth month in this [Tang calendar]. Probably this is simply due to the differing information [they obtained].

A stupa south of the city is the place where the Crown Prince (i.e., Siddhārtha) wrestled [with other boys] and threw an elephant over the city [wall], and where the elephant landed on the ground made a large hole. Near that place is a monastery in which a statue of the Crown Prince stands and the place where he studied his lessons. A nearby monastery was the main house of his wife. Statues of [his wife] Yaśodhārā (Yeshutuoluo) and [his son] Rāhula (Luohuluo) are found [in the monastery].

An alternative version holds that one early evening Crown Prince [Siddhārtha] went through the north gate of the city and departed. Moreover, in a monastery in the southeast corner of the city [there is an image of] the Crown Prince going beyond the sky riding a white horse. This is the place where [the Crown 500c
Prince] left the city. [Outside of] each of the four city gates is a monastery in which there are images of the old, the sick, the dead, and a *śramaṇa*. In a

nyagrodha grove four *li* south of the city is a stupa at the place where the Buddha attained enlightenment and expounded the Dharma to heavenly and human beings.

There is a stupa in the old city fifty *li* south of the city. This was the place where Krakucchanda (Jialuojiacuntuo) Buddha was born when the human life span was sixty thousand years [in the present cosmic period]. The stupa southeast of the [capital] city is precisely where this buddha passed away. King Aśoka built a stone pillar, three *zhang* in height, in front of it.

Moreover, there is a stupa in an old city more than thirty *li* northeast [of this city]. Kanakamuni (Jianuojiamouni) Buddha was born in this place when the human life span was forty thousand years [in the present cosmic period]. A stupa northeast of this city is placed precisely where this buddha passed away. King Aśoka built a stone pillar, two-plus *zhang* in height, for [this buddha] and this is recorded in an engraved inscription. More than forty *li* northeast of the city there is a stupa at the site of a tree under which Crown Prince [Siddhārtha] sat in meditation. There are several hundred to several thousand stupas northwest of the large city for the Śākya people who were killed [by King Virūḍhaka]. There are stupas for the four Śākya men who resisted King [Virūḍhaka's] soldiers. King Virūḍhaka was driven out of the city [of the Śākya clan] but [the four] men were not accepted [by the Śākya people]. They were punished and exiled from the state territory. [Their blood-lines,] however, have continued until now.[77]

A stupa among *nyagrodha* trees south of the city is the site where the Buddha returned to see his father, the king, for the first time [after he had attained enlightenment]. A stupa outside of the south city gate is where Crown Prince [Siddhārtha] had a contest with [the Śākya boys like] his brothers and shot [an iron drum].[78] More than thirty *li* southeast a spring gushed out when the ground was pierced by an arrow shot by the Crown Prince. It is commonly called Arrow Fountain (Śarakūpa). If people who are ill drink [this water] they will often be cured. Or if they take some of the mud and apply it to their forehead, all parts of their body that are in pain are healed. Moreover, ninety *li* northeast [of this place] is the Lumbinī Grove. There is a pond in which the Śākya people bathed. Flowers are reflected in the water.

Twenty-five paces north of the pond is an *aśoka* tree, which has already withered now. This is the place where [Śākyamuni] Buddha was born. A theory says that [his birthday] is the eighth day of the third month in the [Chinese calendar]. The Theravāda school asserts that it is the fifteenth day of the third month in the [Chinese calendar].

Next, to the east is a stupa at the site where two dragons bathed Crown Prince [Siddhārtha]. Immediately after his birth the [infant] Buddha walked seven paces in each of the four directions without support. Large lotus flowers emerged from the two places where he walked. After Crown Prince [Siddhārtha] was born from [his mother's] right side, Śakra-devendra received him in a cloth, and the four heavenly kings held him in their hands and placed him on a golden table.

Altogether four stupas were built [in memory of the four heavenly kings' service], and a stone pillar was erected to indicate it clearly. Next to [the four stupas] a small river runs to the southeast, commonly called Oil River. After Crown Prince [Siddārtha's] birth, heaven transformed an [ordinary] pond into a smooth and glossy pond so that [Lady Mahāmāyā] could cleanse her body to remove the filth [of childbirth]. [The pond] has now become a river, but the water's surface is still greasy, as if slicked with oil.

Again, traveling more than two hundred *li* east from this [river] through a wild forest, we reach the state of Rāmagrāma (Lanmo), which belongs to Central India. The capital city is in ruins. There is a stupa of the Buddha southeast of the city, which has settled lower than it was originally and now stands a hundred *chi* high. When it was built [it contained a] one-eighth share of the [Buddha's] relics. Mysterious light occasionally appears here. Nearby is a clean pond. A dragon that transformed into a snake emerged from [the pond] and circumambulated the stupa [in a clockwise direction]. Some wild elephants picked flowers to scatter [over the stupa]. King Aśoka intended to open [the stupa to distribute the relics] but the dragon [of this pond] protected [the relics] and would not allow him to do so.

Furthermore, a hundred-plus *li* east [of the temple of novices] is a large stupa at the site where Crown Prince [Siddhārtha] took off his valuable 501a
clothes when he arrived here, and where he sent [his driver] Chandaka along with the *maṇi*-stone from [his crown] back to his father, the king. Moreover, in the east there is a *jambu* tree [whose branches and leaves have already fallen off but the dried-up trunk still remains. There is a small stupa at the site where Crown Prince [Siddhārtha] exchanged his valuable clothes for a

tattered robe. A stupa near this place is where [Siddhārtha] took the tonsure. His age at the time is not certain; it is said that he was either nineteen or twenty-nine years old.

Moreover, traveling a hundred and ninety *li* southeast, we come to a stupa, three *zhang* in height, in a *nyagrodha* grove. In former times people collected the remains of the ashes and charcoal from the Buddha's funeral pyre and built a stupa here. If people who are ill pray here [for their recovery] they will be cured. There is also a stupa at the place where the four [past] buddhas spent their daily lives. It is more than a hundred *chi* in height and several hundreds of small stupas stand around it.

Again, going five hundred *li* northeast from here through a great grove along a rough and precipitous path, we come to the state of Kuśinagara (Jushinajieluo), which belongs to Central India. The city is dilapidated and only a small number of people live there. A stupa in the northeast corner of the city is an old residence of Cunda [who made offerings to the Buddha].[79] [Water of] the well [at this old residence] is still good. [The well] was dug in order to offer [water to the Buddha].

At a point four *li* northwest of the city we cross over the Ajitavatī River (Ashiduofadi, called Youjin, "Having Gold," in the Tang dynasty). Near the west bank [of the river] are groves of *śāla* trees. In the middle of two groves, several tens of paces from each other, are four [*śāla*] trees that are particularly tall. There was a great monastery made of bricks, with an image of the Buddha entering nirvana; he reposes with his head northward. [A stupa] nearby is more than two hundred *chi* tall. In front of it is a stone pillar that records the conditions of the Buddha's death. [Regarding the date of the Buddha's death,] some schools say it is the fifteenth day of the third month [of the calendar] of this land (i.e., the Tang dynasty). The Sarvāstivāda school advocates that is the eighth day of the ninth month of this [Tang calendar].

[Regarding the period since the time of the Buddha's death,] various schools hold different assertions. One school says that as of this year, the third year of the Longshuo era (663), it has been twelve hundred years. This [theory] relies on a record engraved on a stone pillar of the Bodhi (Puti) Temple. Another school says that it has been thirteen hundred years, another says that it has been fifteen hundred years, and yet another school says that nine hundred years have passed but it has been less than a thousand years [since the Buddha's passing].

Near the [brick] monastery are [two] stupas, one at the place where the Buddha fought a fire when he was the king of pheasants in the past, and the other where he saved living beings when he was a deer. Next, a stupa to the west is where Subhadra (Subatuoluo, called Shanxian, "Revelation of Wholesomeness," in the Tang dynasty), realized nirvana.[80] A stupa next to it is the site where Vajradhara fell down on the ground [in extreme grief over the Buddha's death].[81] Next, a nearby stupa is the site where the [Buddha's golden] coffin was detained for seven days. A stupa next to it is where his mother, [Lady Mahāmāyā,] descended and wept for [the death of] the Buddha after Aniruddha had ascended to [Tuṣita] Heaven and reported to her.

Crossing over the Nairañjanā (Nilianchanna) River north of the city, at three hundred paces there is a stupa. This is the place where the Buddha's body was cremated (*niediepanna,* called *fenshao,* "to burn," in the Tang dynasty). The ground is still yellowish-black and the soil there is mixed with ashes and charcoal. Those who pray wholeheartedly are able to obtain relics here. A stupa next to the place is the site where the Buddha revealed both of his feet [from the golden coffin] for Mahākāśyapa. There is a stupa and a stone pillar in front of it. The incident of the distribution of the relics to eight states is recorded with an engraved inscription [on this pillar].

Again, traveling five hundred *li* southwest from here through a great grove, we come to the state of Vārāṇasī (Poluoni, formerly called Boluona [in China]), which belongs to Central India. The west side of the capital city faces the Ganges River. The city is teeming with inhabitants. Northeast of 501b
the city is the Barṇa River. Ten-plus *li* northeast from the river is Deer Park (Skt. Mṛgadāva) Temple. A stupa on the southwest is more than a hundred *chi* tall. In front of it is a stone pillar, over seventy *chi* in height, transparent and clean. If people pray sincerely [here various] images appear in accordance with their good or evil [thoughts]. This is the place where the Buddha preached the Dharma for the first time after he attained buddhahood. There are three stupas nearby, at the site where the three [past] buddhas [Krakucchanda, Kanakamuni, and Kāśyapa] spent their daily lives. In the neighboring area are various stupas marking the places where five hundred *pratyekabuddha*s entered nirvana.

A nearby stupa stands where Maitreya Bodhisattva received a prediction about his future attainment of buddhahood. In addition, a stupa on the west is where Jyotipāla (Huming) Bodhisattva, who was [Śākyamuni] Buddha in the past, received a prediction of his attainment of buddhahood in the present age from Kāśyapa Buddha. Next, on the south is where the four [past] buddhas roamed around [in leisure]. [The site] is fifty paces long and seven *chi* high, constructed by piling up blue rocks. On this a statue of Śākyamuni [Buddha] walking is set up. The shape [of the statue] is particularly extraordinary: hair sticks up from the fleshy protuberance (Skt. *uṣṇīṣa*) on top of the head. His mysterious figure is completely visible and marvelously responsive to prayers. There are numerous sites in [Deer Park] Temple, several hundreds of monasteries and stupas, so it is difficult to give a complete account of [them all].

To the west of the temple is a clean pond, two hundred paces around. The Buddha formerly bathed here. Next, a small pond to the west is where the Buddha once washed utensils. Next, a small pond to the north is where the Buddha formerly washed his clothes. Dragons dwell in these three ponds and the water tastes sweet and pure. If someone touches [the water] in an arrogant [or aggressive] way, a beast called a *kumbhīra* immediately harms him. Near [the pond in which the Buddha washed his clothes] is a square stone with an imprint of the pattern of the Buddha's *kaṣāya* [robe]. If non-Buddhists or evil people tread on this spot rashly, the dragons of the ponds generate wind and rain and injure them.

There is another stupa next to this place. The Buddha was once the king of the six-tusked elephants. This is the site where he saw a hunter [who falsely] wore a Dharma robe [attempting to get close to the elephants to take their tusks], so [the Buddha] removed his own tusks and gave them to the hunter.[82] There is another stupa at the site where formerly, [in order to teach moderation,] the Buddha asked an elephant and a monkey about the size [of a *nyagrodha* tree they had seen].[83] Furthermore, another stupa in a great grove is the site where in the past, when the Buddha and Devadatta were kings of deer, the Buddha tried to sacrifice his life for a pregnant deer.[84] Deer Park was named for this [story].

Three *li* southwest of the temple is a stupa at the site where five [Śākya] people first received the Buddha. In addition, three *li* east from the great grove is another stupa [where] in the past, when the Buddha was a hare living together with other various animals, recognizing his body to be small he burned himself to offer it as food [to Śakra-devendra]. Because of this, Śakra-devendra was moved and descended to praise [the hare].[85] Consequently he caused an image of the hare to appear in the moon.

Again, traveling three hundred *li* following the Ganges River to the east, we arrive at the state of Yuddhapati (or Garjapatipura; Zhanzhu). The capital city, near the Ganges River, is teeming with inhabitants. There is a stupa in a temple northwest of the city in which a *sheng* of the Buddha's relics is deposited. Formerly the Buddha preached the Dharma here for seven days, and also it is the place where the four [past] buddhas walked about [in leisure]. North of the river is a stupa [at the site where] the Buddha subdued evil demons. [The stupa] has already partly collapsed to the ground. There is also the site where the Buddha expounded the Dharma for cannibalistic demons. Furthermore, crossing the river to the southeast and going more than a hundred *li*, we come to a stupa placed precisely [at the site where] the Buddha's relics were divided [into eight portions]. The bottle [of relics] and the remaining relics emit light on the days of purification.

Again, crossing the Ganges River to the northeast and going more than 501c
a hundred fifty *li*, we come to the state of Vaiśālī (Feisheli guo, formerly called Pisheli guo [in China]), which belongs to Central India. The capital city is in ruins; the circumference of its old foundation is seventy *li*. Only a small number of people still live here. The circumference of the imperial palace is five *li*. Six *li* northwest of the palace is a temple stupa at the place where [the Buddha] delivered the *Vimalakīrtinirdeśa.*

Furthermore, to the east is a stupa where Śāriputra testified to the fruit [of arhatship]. In addition, a large stupa to the east was built for one of the eight portions of the relics obtained by the king [of Vaiśālī]. The amount of relics [he obtained] was about one *hu,* from which King Aśoka took nine *sheng* and built other stupas in order to evenly [distribute the relics]. Later, a certain king further intended to open [the large stupa to take the remaining relics] when an earthquake occurred. [The king] thereupon stopped.

Next, to the south is a pond some monkeys dug out for the Buddha. To the west of the pond is where a group of monkeys climbed up into a tree with the Buddha's almsbowl and collected honey [for the Buddha]. To the south of the pond is where the monkeys offered the honey to the Buddha. Each [of these incidents] has been recorded on the stupas [in these sites].

About four *li* northeast from a temple is a stupa [built on] the foundation of Vimalakīrti's old residence, which still shows numerous wonders. A nearby house [appears to have been made by] piling up tiles, but it is traditionally said that it was made by piling up rocks. [The house] is precisely the place where [Vimalakīrti] preached the Dharma in the manifestation of an ill person. During the Xianqing era (656–661) of the Great Tang dynasty, the Imperial envoys Wei Changshi and Wang Xuance passed Vimalakīrti's residence heading toward India. They measured its foundation with their tablets. It was only ten times the length of a tablet. Because of this, it was designated as the ten-foot-square room (*fangzhangshi*). There are also the sites of Elder [Vimalakīrti's son] Ratnakāra's residence and Āmrapālī's residence, as well as where the Buddha's mother's sisters died. In all [these places stupas] have been put up with inscribed records.

A stupa four *li* north of a temple [located five or six *li* northwest of the capital city][86] is the site where heavenly and human beings gathered to send off the Buddha, who was leaving for Kuśinagara. Next, a stupa behind this place is where the Buddha took a final look back at the city of [Vaiśālī]. Next is the place where Āmrapālī donated her garden to the Buddha. A stupa beside this place is where the Buddha repeatedly foretold to Ānanda that he would soon enter nirvana. Moreover, a nearby stupa is where a thousand children met their parents.[87] These children are a thousand buddhas who appeared during the auspicious *kalpa*. A stupa built on the foundation of the lecture hall of an old multistoried building on the east sometimes emits light. This is the place where the Buddha expounded the *Pumenzhu* (*Dwelling of the Universal Gate*).[88]

A large stupa located fifteen *li* southeast of the city is where seven hundred wise people and sages reconvened [to compile the Buddhist teachings]. On each of the south and north banks of the Ganges River there is a stupa at the sites where Ānanda divided his body (i.e., relics) and gave them to two states.

Again, passing through a state traveling fifteen hundred *li* northwest, and passing through mountains and valleys, we come to the state of Nepāla (Nipoluo guo, a part of present-day Nepal), which belongs to North India. To the southeast, not far from the capital city, is Water-Fire Village. About one *li* east [from the village] is the Ajīva waterpool (Aqipomishui), the circumference of which is twenty paces. Even in times of drought or flood, [this pool] is calm and does not overflow but continually releases water. If a household fire is thrown into it the fire spreads all over the pond, and the smoke and flames rise several *chi* high. If water is poured over it the fire burns even more vigorously, and even if clods of earth are thrown onto it they completely burn up. Regardless of whatever is thrown [onto the flames], it all turns to ashes. If a cauldron is set up over the waterpool of fire to cook food, [it] is immediately cooked.

The *Xiande zhuan* (*Biographies of Virtuous People*) says:

> Formerly there was a gold chest in this water. Once, a certain king wanted someone to take it out for him. After the chest was raised out of the mud, people and elephants tried to pull it up but it did not move. One night a god said, "This contains a crown for Maitreya Buddha. Later when 502a
> Maitreya descends [to this world] to become [a buddha], it is intended that he will put on [this crown]. No one can obtain it." The fire is protection offered by a dragon.

A particularly outstanding temple stands on an isolated mountain located more than ten *li* south of the city. [The temple buildings] appear stacked one upon another; they look just like clouds. There are pine, bamboo, fish, and a dragon there and [animals] follow people obediently. If a person catches an animal and eats it, all the family members of the criminal are put to death. Recently the laws of [neighboring] states follow those of this state as to comings and goings. [The north of this state] borders the East State of Women (i.e., Suvarṇa) and the Tibetan regime. It is more than ten thousand *li* from the [lands controlled by either the] Tang dynasty or by India.

Again, going a hundred fifty *li* south and crossing the Ganges River, we arrive at the state of Magadha (Mojietuo), which belongs to Central India. A small number of people inhabit the city but there are very many people living in villages. The old city exists to the north of the mountain [of Rājagṛha and lies toward] the east. Two hundred forty *li* north is the Ganges River. A stone pillar in the northern part of the old imperial palace, several *zhang* tall, marks the place where formerly King Aśoka created the infernal regions. [Aśoka] is King Bimbisāra's great-grandson[89] and the husband of [King] Śīlāditya's daughter. The city governed by him was named Kusumapura (Huashi) (i.e., Pāṭaliputra). It was given this name because there were numerous flowers in the imperial palace.

There is a large stupa south of the stone pillar, one of [King Aśoka's] eighty-four thousand stupas. One *sheng* of the Buddha's relics are contained in it, and it sometimes shows bright good omens. It was comissioned by King Aśoka; Upagupta Arhat employed spiritual beings to construct it. In a monastery near [the large stupa] is a large boulder, at the place where the Buddha was about to enter nirvana. As he was traveling north toward Kuśinagara, he [stopped to] look back at Magadha in the south. He stepped on this rock and left an impression of both feet. [One footprint] is one *chi* and eight *cun* long, and six *cun* wide. [Both] footprints have wheel signs, and each one of the flower patterns on the ten toes is different from the others. Recently an evil king of Karṇasuvarṇa (i.e., Śaśāṅka) tried to destroy the Buddha's footprints. After they were chiseled off, however, [the flatness of the boulder] was restored and the [flower] patterns became as beautiful as before. [The boulder] was then thrown into the Ganges River but it soon returned to its original place. In the twenty-third year of the Zhenguan era (649) a [Chinese] envoy came here to copy the footprints.

Next to [the boulder] is a stupa at the site where the four [past] buddhas spent their daily lives. Southeast of the old city is a place where Nāgārjuna Bodhisattva subdued non-Buddhists. Next, in the north is a stupa for [a brahman who received instruction on] eloquence from [evil] spirits. Aśvaghoṣa dealt with him.

Furthermore, going southwest and crossing the Nairañjanā River, is Gayā city, in which a small number live, but there are more than a thousand households [of the brahman caste].[90] Going about six *li* southwest from the city, we come to Mount Gayā (Skt. Gayāśīrṣa, present-day Brahmayoni). The valley is deep, dark, and obscure. People call it the sacred mountain. From ancient times, sovereigns have officiated the rite of worshiping heaven and earth and report the succession to be accomplished. On the peak is a stone stupa, a hundred-plus *chi* in height, which occasionally emits strange light. The Buddha preached sutras such as the *Baoyun jing* (*Scripture on Treasured Clouds*) here.

Crossing the Nairañjanā River southeast of the mountain and going less than two *li*, we arrive at Mount Prāgbodhi (Boluojiputi), called Zhengjue ("Right Perfect Enlightenment") [in the Tang dynasty]. When the Buddha testified [to having attained right, perfect enlightenment], he first ascended

[this mountain], and due to this connection it was so named. The Buddha ascended the peak from the northeast ridge of the mountain and was about to enter the *vajra* meditation when the earth quaked and the mountain trembled. The [mountain] god, afraid, said to the Buddha, ["This mountain is not a good place to attain right, perfect enlightenment"]. So he went further to the southwest and arrived at a stone chamber on the midslope of the mountain, where he sat [in meditation]. The earth and the mountain quaked again. The Śuddhāvāsa [heavenly] god said to [the Buddha], "Fifteen *li* southwest of here, near the place where you practiced asceticism, there is a *vajra* seat 502b
under a *pippala* tree (i.e., the *bodhi* tree). This is the *bodhi* seat. All buddhas of the three periods of existence completely attained right, perfect enlightenment at that place." So the Buddha departed to go there, but he left his shadow [on the mountain] for the sake of the dragon of the stone chamber, [who had begged the Buddha to stay].[91] People of the world call it the "distinguished place."

The *bodhi* tree is surrounded by a fence made of brick, high and strong. It is wide from the east to west, with a circumference of about five hundred and forty paces. Rare trees and celebrated flowers planted in lines cast shade in rows. The main gate opens to the east and faces the Nairañjanā River. The south gate is contiguous with the great flower pond, and the west is blocked by strategic and impregnable topography. The north gate leads to a great temple. In the courtyard [of the temple] numerous sacred sites and various stupas are lined up. In the center of the fenced area around the [*bodhi*] tree is the *vajra* seat.

In ancient times, at the beginning of the auspicious *kalpa,* this *vajra* seat came into existence together with the earth, and is part of the trichiliocosm. Its bottom reaches to the gold layer and its top sits on the surface of the earth.[92] It is made of *vajra,* with a circumference of more than a hundred paces. The thousand buddhas [of the auspicious *kalpa*] were all seated here and entered the *vajra* meditation. Therefore, it is called [the *vajra* seat]. This is exactly the place in which they all attained enlightenment, so it is also called the "place of enlightenment" (Skt. *bodhimaṇḍa*). Even when the earth quakes, [this place] alone does not tremble. The date of the Buddha's attainment of enlightenment is controversial. Some [schools] say it is the eighth day of the third month [in the Chinese calendar], and others say it is the fifteenth day [of the third month in the Chinese calendar].

Outside of the north gate of the fence is Mahābodhi Temple, which consists of six compounds including a three-storied building. The fence [around the temple] is four *zhang* high, made of brick. The king of Siṃhala (present-day Ceylon) purchased this place and built this temple. There are only a thousand monks. [The temple] is maintained by the Mahayana-Sthaviravāda school (Dasheng shangzuo bu). There are relics of bones that look like human finger knuckles and relics [of bits of flesh] as large as pearls. The thirtieth day of the twelfth month in that land (i.e., India) is equivalent to the fifteenth day of the first month here [in China]. People call it the month of the great supernatural transformation (*da shenbianyue*).[93] On the evening [of the thirtieth day] [the relics] always emit light and bring about auspicious omens; rare flowers rain down from the sky and fill up the courtyard of trees. In the regular practice of that land, at this time a huge number of Buddhist monks and laypeople vie with one another in presenting offerings [to these sacred sites] for seven days and seven nights. They have generally two intentions: to see the light and auspicious omens, and to collect some leaves of the tree. [The *bodhi*] tree is bluish-green in color and it does not change color in winter or summer. Every year, on the [anniversary] day of [the Buddha's] entry into nirvana and in the late summer, the tree withers and drops [leaves] for a short time. Overnight [the tree] puts forth shoots and is restored to its former state.

After a time [the original tree] was cut down for King Aśoka's concubine. [Pieces of the tree] were collected [and placed] in an area several tens of paces west [from the original site of the tree], where [a brahman] burned them in order to worship heaven. Before the smoke and flames had dissipated, suddenly a couple of [*bodhi*] trees began to grow. Amid the raging flames the leaves grew densely and [the trees] were as luxuriant as [their previous condition]. Therefore [these trees] are called the ashen *bodhi* trees. On witnessing [this extraordinary event] King [Aśoka] gave rise to faith [in Buddhism]. He poured delicious milk on the remaining roots of the [*bodhi* tree]. By the next morning [the tree] had grown back, just as before. The king's concubine, angered by this, had someone cut down the tree again at night. King [Aśoka] again prayed for [the recovery of the tree] and poured milk on its base, and it soon grew back. [To protect it, the king had] rocks piled up around [the tree] to form a fence more than a *zhang* high.[94]

Recently, King Śaśāṅka of the state of Karṇasuvarṇa again had the tree cut down and made [his men] dig the ground deeply to a water vein [in order to uncover its roots], but they could not dig down far enough to reach the bottom of the roots. He then set fire to [the tree] and burned it. Furthermore, he had sugarcane juice sprinkled on to cause it to rot and then uprooted its base completely. Several months later, King Pūrṇavarman (Bucinafamo), 502c
who is called Manzhou here [in China], a great-great-grandson of the former King Aśoka, heard that the tree had been destroyed. He prostrated his body [in worship] and begged the [Buddhist] monks to circumambulate the large pit where the tree had been, into which milk from several thousands of cows was poured. On the night of the sixth day, a [*bodhi*] tree grew to a height of over a *zhang*. [Pūrṇavarman] was afraid that [the tree] might be cut down again in later ages, so a rock fence, two *zhang* and four *chi* high, was built around it. The tree is presently more than two *zhang* higher than the rock fence, and more than three *chi* in circumference.

To the east of the [*bodhi*] tree is a monastery made of blue bricks. Its height is more than a hundred sixty *chi* and one side of its foundation is more than twenty paces wide. Set into [the foundation] is a hook-shaped railing, one *zhang* in height, that surrounds [the temple building]. Each of the layered niches houses a gold image, and images of heavenly transcendents are engraved on each of the four the walls. At the top [of the monastery building] is a bronze *āmalaka* (called a treasure bottle (*baoping*) or jeweled platform (*baotai*) here [in China]). To the east next to [the monastery building] is a three-storied pavilion with particularly remarkable eaves. All [parts of the pavilion] are engraved with gold and silver ornaments. Outside of the triple gateways are niches; an Avalokiteśvara image is in the left [niche] and a Maitreya image is in the right [niche]. Both [of these figures] are made of cast silver and about a *zhang* tall. This monastery was built by King Aśoka. At first [the monastery] was small but it was later expanded and is now quite large.

According to the *Wang Xuance zhuan,* in the western states there are innumerable auspicious images. Moreover, the *Record of the Image of the Great Bodhi Tree* says:

> Formerly, the king of Siṃhala, called Brahma King Siri Meghavaṇṇa (Shimiqubamo, called Gongdeyun, "Clouds of Merit," in the Tang dynasty),

sent two *bhikṣu*s to visit this temple. The senior [*bhikṣu*'s] name was Mahāyaśas (Mohenan, called Daming, "Great Fame," here [in China]), and the junior [*bhikṣu*'s] name was Vyākaraṇa (Youpo, called Shouji, "To Predict the Future Attainment of Buddhahood," here [in China]). Those two *bhikṣu*s worshiped the *bodhi* tree and the *vajra* seat. After they finished worshiping, the temple would not accept them to reside there. The two *bhikṣu*s then returned to their own country. King [Siri Meghavaṇṇa] asked the *bhikṣu*s, "You went there to worship the sacred place and returned. How were the wonderful and auspicious omens?" The *bhikṣu*s replied, "There is no place in the great land of Jambudvīpa for us to stay." The king, hearing this, then sent an envoy carrying numerous pearls and valuables to present to Samudragupta (Sanmotuoluojueduo), the king of that country (i.e., India).

Because of this, since that time [many] *bhikṣu*s from Siṃhala [reside] here.

Furthermore, at the time when the venerable [buddha] image on the *vajra* seat was originally created, a foreign visitor told a crowd of people, "I have heard that a good skilled artisan has been invited to make an image. I am skillful and I can make this image."

The people said, "What is necessary [for you to make it]?" The man replied, "I only need incense, water, raw materials, and lamp oil." The materials to support [his work] were already available. He said to the monks of the temple, "I must close the door in order create [the image]. The time limit is up to the sixth month [from now]. Be careful! Do not open the door! Do not worry about food and drink for me, either!" The man then entered [the stupa] and did not come out again. Four days before the six-month deadline [for completion of the image], some people were commenting in a disharmonious way, "The inside of this stupa is cramped and he might slip out. How come he has not opened [the door] and appeared for so many months? I have doubts about his behavior." So they opened the stupa's door and they did not see the artisan, but the image had already been completed, except for
503a only a small incomplete part above the right breast. Later the sky god, surpised [at their behavior], admonished the people and said, "I am Maitreya Bodhisattva." The figure is seated on an east-west axis and is one *zhang*, one *chi*, and five *cun* in height. At its shoulders it measures six *chi* and two *cun* wide.

The knees are eight *chi* and eight *cun* apart from each other. The *vajra* seat is four *chi* and three *cun* in height, and one *zhang*, two *chi,* and five *cun* wide. The stupa, originally built by King Aśoka, had a hook-shaped stone railing.

In later ages there were two brahman brothers: the elder was Wangzhu ("Virtuous King") and the younger was Fanzhu ("Pure King").[95] The elder brother rebuilt the stupa to the height of a hundred *zhou.* The younger brother built the temple.[96]

That image was brought to completion by Maitreya himself. Since then, all Buddhist monks and laypeople attempt to copy its design but it is difficult to match its sacredness and extraordinariness. No one has yet been able to replicate it. Messengers from the king came to the [temple] seeking the services of various monks, and various messengers of this [land] (i.e., China) requested [the monks] with utmost sincerity and eagerness to circumambulate the image reciting a sutra as well as to repent of sins for a number of consecutive days. Concurrently [the Chinese messengers] explained the aim of their visit. They then obtained drawings that completely resemble [the image] and a textbook was produced for this image. Up to now there are ten fascicles that have been transmitted to this land (China). The skilled workmen for the [project] were Song Fazhi and others. They were extremely skillful in creating the sacred appearance [of the image] and copied the sacred countenance. [The replica image] arrived at the national capital [Chang'an], where Buddhist monks and laypeople vied with one another to [approach it and] touch it.

The record of Master [Xuan]zang's travels (*Da Tang xiyuji*) says:

> The illustration and the decoration above the right breast of the image was incomplete. That portion was filled in with numerous jewels. When one regards [the image's] appearance from a distance, he ends up being discontented. The image is in a seated position with crossed legs, the right leg crossed over [the left]. The left hand is held up and the right hand hangs down. The reason the image's [right] hand points down is because when the Buddha attained buddhahood he spoke to the king of devils (i.e., Māra) while pointing to the earth to bear testimony [of his attainment of buddhahood].
>
> When the [*bodhi*] tree was recently cut down by King Śaśāṅka, he ordered a minister to destroy the image, and then the king returned from the East. The minister, who originally had faith [in Buddhism, could not

destroy the image]. So he erected a brick barrier wall in front of the image [to hide it from view]. He felt ashamed that it was now dark [inside of the barrier], so he placed a lamp in there. An image of Maheśvara was drawn on the exterior [of the barrier wall]. [The minister] then reported having completed his mission [to destroy the image to the king]. When King Śaśāṅka heard [this], he became afraid. His whole body broke out in blisters, his skin was cracked all over, and he soon died. The minister swiftly returned [to the image] and removed the barrier wall. Even though many days had passed the lamp had not yet gone out.

Today [the image] is placed in a deep inner room. If at daybreak one holds up a mirror to reflect light onto [the image], its appearance can be seen. Viewers worship [the buddha image], pay respect to it, and [are so absorbed in devotion that they forget to depart from the place for a long time].

Moreover, according to the *Wang Xuance zhuan:*

This Chinese envoy, on receiving the imperial decree, went to Mahābodhi Temple in the state of Magadha and erected a stone tablet. On the eleventh day of the second month of the nineteenth year of the Zhenguan era (645), [the stone tablet] was raised to the west of a stupa under the *bodhi* tree.

The envoy manager and Clerk of the Transit Authorization Bureau, Wei Cai, wrote:

> Formerly, when the Han dynasty and the Wei kingdom ruled over the land, they waged war frequently. A hundred thousand troops were mobilized, and a thousand catties of gold were spent per day. They still esteemed the north and ruled there. They did not reach even as far as a village east of Mount Tianyan.[97] The great Tang dynasty encompasses the roads of the entire wide world and became the greatest of all rulers. They augment the refining influence of learning and art as universally as does heaven. Because of this, in all the states of India, Buddhist monks and laymen sincerely pledge allegiance to [the Tang dynasty].
> 503b His Majesty shows kindness toward their faithfulness and sincerity, and remembers them from a distance with a sacred thought. Therefore, he ordered an envoy [mission comprised of] twenty-two people, including Li Yibiao of the Grand Master for Closing Court, the Court of the Imperial Regalia, and the Senior Military Protector [as the senior

envoy], and Wang Xuance of the former District Magistrate of Huanshui of Rongzhou as the vice envoy, to conduct an imperial inspection tour to comfort the people of that state.

They then arrived at the *vajra* seat under the *bodhi* tree in the precincts of the Mahābodhi Temple. A thousand buddhas of the auspicious *kalpa* all attained buddhahood in the midst of it. They saw [the buddha statue with] reverently ornamented physical characteristics, which completely looked like the real features [of the Buddha]. The divine stupa and the pure pond were unexpectedly ingenious, unequaled by any others then in existence, something never before seen, and not described in detail in history books. His Majesty raised great glory from afar for the brilliant [*bodhi*] tree. Thereupon, he ordered his envoys to come here to pay their respects to it. This is the greatest affair of the age and an immortal, marvelous accomplishment.

What would one think if they just kept silent without chanting poems and did not include [this affair in] inscriptions on bronze and stone? Thereupon, they engraved [the following statement]:

The great Tang dynasty's comfort reaches afar. The one who squares with omens as the Son of Heaven lives long in prosperity. His edification covers the entire wide world. His power extends over the whole universe. [People in] India bow before him. Buddhist monks and laymen came to the ruler, and accordingly he issued brilliant envoys to worship and perform a mission at the place of attaining enlightenment, the *vajra* seat, where a thousand buddhas stayed for generations. The venerable appearance and physical characteristics [of the buddha image] were formulated by Maitreya. The divine stupa is splendid. The *bodhi* tree branches out with thick foliage. It never decays through *kalpa*s. Where else could the divine power go?

Furthermore, the record of Master [Xuan]zang's travels *(Da Tang xiyuji)* says:

The Buddha attained buddhahood on the eighth day of the third month in the Chinese calendar. The Sthaviravāda school says that it is the fifteenth day of the third month of this [Chinese] calendar. When [the Buddha] attained buddhahood he was thirty years old, or it is also said that he was thirty-five years old.

These differences are naturally distinct from one another in that land (i.e., India). Because of the different calendars used, there are discrepancies [in the dates]. Calculating by the Chinese calendar, [these dates] are originally different from one another. The three dynasties (i.e., Xia, Yin, and Zhou) settled [the calendar] correctly. Is it worth harboring doubt that [a period of time of the calendar] has been lengthened or shortened? Moreover, if you understand anything on the basis of one aspect, you will then go no further.

In a large monastery to the west of the [*bodhi*] tree is a standing brass figure facing east. [The figure] is decorated with rare and precious objects. In front of it is wonderfully patterned, extraordinary bright blue stone. In the past, on the day [the Tathāgata] attained buddhahood, the king of Brahma Heaven erected a hall adorned with the seven treasures, and Śakra-devendra fashioned a seat out of the seven treasures, which the Buddha occupied for seven days in contemplation. [The Buddha] emitted light that shone upon the [*bodhi*] tree. [Since that time] the treasures have turned into stone.

A stupa to the south of the [*bodhi*] tree is more than a hundred *chi* high. Formerly the Buddha bathed in a river (i.e., the Nairañjanā River) and contemplated while sitting upon a grass seat. Śakra-devendra transformed into a man [in order to collect] the grass called *kuśa* (called *jixiangcao,* "auspicious grass," here [in China]), and offer it for the Buddha's seat. King Aśoka built the stupa and recorded [the story].

Next, there is a stupa to the northeast at the place where when the Buddha testified to fruition a flock of small blue birds came and flew around the World-honored One, and also a group of deer presented a good omen. There are [two] stupas, on the right and left sides of a main street east of the [*bodhi*] tree. This is the place where the king of devils [Māra] tried to harass the Buddha but failed.

503c [A statue of] Kāśyapa Buddha is in a monastery northwest of the [*bodhi*] tree. It often emits light. It is commonly said, "If someone circumambulates [the image] with utmost sincerity seven times, he will naturally attain the wisdom of knowledge of one's former existences and those of others (Skt. *pūrvenivāsa-jñāna*)."

Moreover, northwest of the fence [surrounding the *bodhi* tree] is the *kuṅkuma* incense [stupa], one *zhang* and four *chi* in height. On the southeast corner of the fence [surrounding the *bodhi*] tree is a *nyagrodha* tree, and next to the tree is a stupa. In a monastery [near the stupa] a sitting [buddha] figure is enshrined. This is the place where formerly, when [the Buddha] testified to fruition, the great king of the Brahma Heaven asked him to turn the wheel of the Dharma (i.e., expound the Buddhist teachings). There is a stupa on each of the four corners inside the fence [surrounding the *bodhi* tree]. In the past, when [the Buddha] received the grass [for his seat] and went to the [*bodhi*] tree [to sit in meditation], he first went to the southwest [corner] and the earth quaked. Then he went to the northwest [corner], to the northeast [corner], and to the southeast [corner], and in each corner the earth quaked. He then went to the northwest, under the [*bodhi*] tree, and sat on the *vajra* seat facing east. Only then was the earth peaceful. Therefore, stupas were erected in commemoration of [this incident at each of the four corners].

To the southwest outside of the fence was the site of the residence of the two shepherd girls. Next to it is the place where they cooked milk-gruel [that was offered to Śākyamuni], and to the side is the place where he received the gruel. In all these places stupas were built to mark [and venerate] the sites.

Outside of the south gate of the [*bodhi*] tree is a large pond more than seven hundred paces in circumference. [Its water] is so clean and clear that fish and a dragon dwell within it. Next, a pond to the south was made by Śakra-devendra for the [the Buddha] to wash his robe. A large rock on the west side of the pond was brought from the Himalayas by Śakra-devendra for [the Buddha] to lay out his robe to dry in the sun. Next a stupa nearby marks the place where the Buddha donned an old robe. Next, a stupa in a grove to the south is where the Buddha received an old robe donated by a poor elderly woman.[98]

The pond of the dragon [king Mucilinda] is in a grove east of the [large] pond created [by Śakra-devendra]. [The dragon pond] is clean and the water is delicious. On the west bank is a small monastery in which a [buddha] image is enshrined. In the past, when the Buddha attained buddhahood he sat in meditation here for seven days. This is the place where the dragon king [Mucilinda] wrapped its body around the Buddha sevenfold times and transformed itself to have many heads in order to shade [and protect] the Buddha. In a monastery in the grove east of the pond of the dragon [king Mucilinda] is a buddha statue showing the emaciated body of Śākyamuni [when he was practicing austerities]. Next to this is the place where [the Buddha] roamed around in leisure. This place is seventy paces in length and on both its north and south sides is a *pippala* tree. [While doing ascetic practice Śākyamuni] leaned on the tree [for support] and stood up to walk around. This is the very place where [Śākyamuni] practiced asceticism for six years, taking only a single sesame [seed] and a grain of barley [for his daily food]. Today if people who are ill apply perfumed oil on this statue, many of them are cured. In addition, there is the place where the five *bhikṣus* [including Ājñāta-kauṇḍinya] dwelled.

Moreover, a stupa southeast [of the five *bhikṣus*' dwelling] is the place from where [Śākyamuni] Buddha went into the Nairañjanā River and bathed. Nearby is the place where the Buddha received and ate the milk-gruel. Next to this place are two stupas at the sites where [two] wealthy persons presented a wheat-honey cake [to the Buddha].[99] A stupa southeast of the [*bodhi*] tree marks where the four heavenly kings offered stone almsbowls to the Buddha.[100]

Next to this is a stupa at the place where after he had attained buddhahood the Buddha expounded the Dharma for his mother. Moreover there is the place where [the Buddha] liberated the [three] Kāśyapa brothers and their thousand disciples from [the transmigration of birth and death].[101] Outside of the north gate of the fence [surrounding] the [*bodhi*] tree is Mahābodhi Temple. As for courtyards and buildings, [the temple consists of] six compounds. The observation pavilion is three-storied. The fence surrounding [the temple] is five *zhang* in height. The Buddha's relics [contained in stupas] include [a bone relic] as large as a finger joint, lustrous, bright white, and transparent. A flesh relic is as large as a blue pearl, and its appearance is tinged with red. Every year, [on the days to complete] the Buddha's great supernatural transformation months (i.e., the first, the fifth, and ninth months when purification is observed), [the relics] are taken out and shown to the people. The date for this is the thirtieth day of the twelfth month in India,
504a which is equivalent to the fifteenth day of the first month in China.[102] At that time [the relics] emit light and flowers fall like rain. People greatly give rise to deep faith.

This temple regularly has a thousand monks [in residence], who study the teaching of the Mahayana-Sthaviravāda school. The monastic codes of conduct are clear and solemn. This temple was built at the request of the king of Siṃhala (present-day Sri Lanka) of the Southern Sea. Now four hundred years have passed [since then] and there are many people from Siṃhala at the temple.[103] Every year, when the *bhikṣus* are released from retreat, a large number of Buddhist monks and laypeople from the four directions gather together, [carrying] fragrant flowers and playing music, and tour throughout the grove to make offerings to [this sacred site] for seven days and nights.

All the monks of India enter summer retreat on the sixteenth day of the fifth month in the Chinese calendar, and the summer [retreat] ends on the fifteenth day of the eighth month in the Chinese [calendar]. These dates vary according to a calendar used in each locality; [the dates of the retreat] cannot be fixed. It is just as in some states north of the Himalayas there is a spring retreat or an autumn retreat. I think that in a place where there are high temperatures most of the year [this retreat period] was instituted to be three months [during the summer]. If a [calendar] month is advanced or delayed before or after [this period], then [the retreat dates] are not definite, and if it is based on the practice of the [Buddhist] Way, [the dates of the retreat] are not fixed. Therefore, the Vinaya regulates that traveling around for the three periods (i.e., the entire year) and entering a retreat somewhere else is an offense. [Monks] surely have a good relationship with [the Buddha during retreat], and concurrently they also provide salvation [for sentient beings].

Going east of the [*bodhi*] tree courtyard and crossing a river (i.e., the Nairañjanā River), there is a large grove in which a stupa stands. A pond on its north side is the place where in the past the Buddha attended his blind mother elephant when he was a fragrant baby elephant.[104] A stone pillar stands in front of the stupa. Formerly Kāśyapa Buddha sat in meditation here. Nearby is where the four [past] buddhas spent their daily lives. A small stone pillar in the grove is the place where Udrakarāmaputra (Yütoulan) made an evil vow.

Again, going east, crossing a yellow river, and going more than a hundred *li,* we come to Mount Kukkuṭapada (Ququchibotuo, formerly called Jizu, "Cock's Foot" [in China]). At the top there are three peaks that resemble the shape of a rooster's foot. On the summit is a large stupa that sends forth a mysterious light in the night, which illuminates the entire area. This is precisely the place where Mahākāśyapa entered meditation. In the past, the Buddha consigned to [Mahākāśyapa] a gold-brocaded *saṃghāṭī* robe and a *kaṣāya* made by the married sister of the Buddha's mother (i.e., Prajāpati) in order to pass them on to Maitreya. [The Buddha] ordered him to save the four kinds of [the Buddha's] disciples following the Dharma he had bequeathed. [Mahā]kāśyapa accepted the Buddha's instructions. Twenty years after the Buddha entered *parinirvāṇa,* [Mahākāśyapa] ascended the mountain carrying the robes in both hands in order to await Maitreya.

The mountain path is full of obstacles and rough. There are various groves and bamboos. Lions, tigers, and elephants come and go freely and approach close to you.

Dharma Master [Xuan]zang came to this place. He repeatedly thought to ascend [the mountain] but he had no means to undertake the journey. [Xuan]zang therefore related [his present condition] to the king and asked for guards and support. He received more than three hundred soldiers provided by the king, each equipped with a sharp weapon with which to cut a path through the bamboo. They advanced ten *li* a day.

At that time [the people of] that state heard that [Xuan]zang was going to the mountain. The number of men and women, adults and children, who wanted to worship him was fully a hundred thousand. They hurriedly followed after him one by one and together ascended [Mount] Jizu. They reached the recess of the mountain but a wall stood in their way and there was no path. Therefore, they [cut and] bound bamboo to make a ladder and climbed up one after the other. More than three thousand reached the summit of the mountain. As they looked out in the four directions they were very happy; their joy increased and they danced about. They saw the cracks in the rocks and scattered flowers as offerings.

Again, according to the *Wang Xuance zhuan:*

In the third month of the seventeenth year of the Zhenguan era (643) of
504b the Great Tang dynasty, a brilliant imperial decree was issued. [His Majesty] dispatched an envoy party including Li Yibiao, Grand Master for Closing Court, the Court of the Imperial Regalia, and Senior Military Protector,

[as the senior envoy,] and Wang Xuance, former District Magistrate of Huanshui of Rongzhou, as vice envoy. They were sent to escort brahman guests who [wished to] return to their home country. In the twelfth month of that year they arrived in the state of Magadha. Accordingly they made the rounds of inspection in the provinces and visited the Buddha's native place. They traveled to see the remains and traces. The sacred vestiges are deified. They felt omens when they were in [those] places.

On the twenty-seventh day of the first month of the nineteenth year [of the Zhenguan era] (645) they came to Rājagṛha. Thereupon they ascended Vulture Peak (Skt. Gṛdhrakūta). They looked around and gazed freely and extensively over the infinite views. A thousand-plus years have passed since the time the Buddha entered *parinirvāṇa.* The sacred sites and the remaining foundations solemnly and completely perdure. [The Buddha's] every action is entirely recorded on each stupa. They spontaneously thought of the magnanimity [of the Buddha and his] intellectual outlook. In such borderlands they suddenly could see personally the wondrous traces, and they could not restrain their emotions of grief and joy. Therefore, an inscription was made on the peak. By making [the inscription, this event] is passed on for all eternity. They wished to make His Majesty of the great Tang dynasty last as long and shine as brightly as the sun and moon and cause the Buddhist Dharma to be widely propagated and become as stable as that mountain.

The inscription says:

> In the great Tang dynasty all things spring up. [His Majesty] ascended the throne in accordance with auspicious omens. His glory extends throughout the world. His grace reaches to the four barbarian tribes on the borders of China. His edification is as lofty as that of the Three Augusts and the Five Thearchs. His virtue exceeds that of Xuanyuan (i.e., the Yellow Emperor) and Fuxi.
>
> [First,] he hangs a jade mirror high, lets his robe fall down, folds his hands, and allows matters to take their own course, [and then the land is ruled in an orderly way].
>
> [Second,] the way of enlightenment is spontaneous. One who is admired and respected by the scholastic community follows the world,

rests in his topmost position, and is venerated. The influence on customs, music, and all measures happened in the Middle Land (i.e., China), which is different from the border regions. Śākyamuni's teaching descended here, and his fortune is boundless.

[Third,] [the Buddha's] supernatural power is free from resistance. His transformation responding [to people's prayers] is vast and expansive. Sometimes he rises from the earth or descends from heaven. Ten billion suns and moons, the trichiliocosm, and the Dharma clouds all give support to him. The ingenious truth is altogether propagated by him.

[Fourth,] how luxuriant this mountain is! Extraordinary shapes increase, beautiful clouds scud above, and clear waves are seen below. This is the place where the wondrous spirits descend and gather, as well as the place wise and virtuous people pass by. Sacred sites remain on a lofty peak. We stand for a long time in the remains of the rocky edge.

[Fifth,] jagged and precipitous mountains in succession resemble a palace. We hear tinkling jeweled bells, smell extraordinary fragrance, and look at marvelous vestiges on the spendid mountain. We have engraved inscriptions on a virtuous stone tablet on the lofty ridge and propagate the pure and sincere edification of the great Tang dynasty, which is as permanent as heaven and earth.

Again, the record of Master [Xuan]zang's travels (*Da Tang xiyuji*) says:

Going sixty *li* east from this mountain, we arrive at the city of Kuśāgrapura (Jushejieluobuluo). There is a stupa outside of the north gate at the site where the Buddha stretched out his hand and five lions emerged [from the tip of his finger] to subdue Devadatta's intoxicated elephant.[105] Furthermore, a stupa to the northeast is the place where Śāriputra heard Aśvajit's exposition of the Dharma and testified to the sacred [fruition]. A stupa close to a large pit north of this stupa is the place where Śrīgupta tried to injure the Buddha by means of setting up a pit of fire.[106]

Again, going east, we come to Mount Gṛdhrakūṭa (Gulituoluojuzha, called Jiufeng, or Jiutai, formerly called Qishejue shan, "Vulture Peak," here [in China]). There is a large rock near [a monastery on the mountain], one *zhang* and four or five *chi* in height and more than thirty paces wide. This is the place where Devadatta threw [a rock] at the Buddha.[107] At the

foot of a cliff to the south is a stupa. The Buddha expounded the *Lotus Sutra* here. A large stone chamber in the mountain cliff south [of the 504c
monastery] is where the Buddha entered meditation in the past, when Ānanda was frightened by [the king of] devils [Māra] in a separate room. [The Buddha] pierced the rock [wall] with his hand and patted the crown of [Ānanda's] head [to comfort him]. Today the hole made [by the Buddha can still be seen]. A large rock northeast of the monastery is the site where the Buddha dried his robe in the sun, on which the patterns of the robe can be clearly discerned. On a rock next to it is an impression of the Buddha's [footprint].

West of the north gate of a mountain city is Mount Vipula.[108] [To the north of] a cliff on the southwest face [of the mountain] there used to be five hundred hot springs. Even today there are still several tens of [hot] springs. To the west is the *pippala* stone chamber in which the Buddha often resided in the past. A cavern in the back wall is the *asura* palace.

Going one *li* from the north gate of the mountain [city], we come to the monastery of Kalandaka Bamboo Grove [Garden]. A large stupa east [of the monastery] was [erected by] King Ajātaśatru (Asheduomotulu, called Weishengyuan in the Tang dynasty), namely King Asheshi. About six *li* southwest from the Bamboo [Grove] Garden is a large stone chamber in a big bamboo grove on the north side of the Southern Mountain (Skt. Dakṣiṇagiri, present-day Mount Baibhāra). This is the place where Mahākāśyapa compiled the Tripiṭaka together with a thousand arhats. Since [Mahākāśyapa] was a senior in the sangha (*shangzuo*), this [assembly] is called the *sthavira* (*shangzuo*) [assembly]. A stupa northwest of the [stone] chamber is where Ānanda came after he was reproached [by the other monks and did not attend the assembly], and where he testified to the fruit of arhatship.

Going about five *li* north of the mountain city, we come to the city of Rājagṛha (Heluoshejiliwen), called Xin Wangshecheng ("New Capital City") in the Tang dynasty. A stupa on the left side of the street outside the south gate is where Rāhula was ordained.

Again, going more than thirty *li* north, we arrive at Nālandā (Nalantuo) Temple, (called Shiwuyan si, "Donating without Loathing Temple," in the Tang dynasty). This is the greatest of the temples in Jambudvīpa; no temple or monastery is loftier. All five kings [contributed to] the construction [of this temple]; the supplies they provided doubled the prosperity [of the temple], and therefore, it was named after [their donations]. The temple has five compounds altogether, which share a great outer gate. The surrounding four-storied gates are more than eight *zhang* in height. [The wall is made] entirely of brick. Its lowest wall is six *chi* thick.[109] The outer wall, also of brick, is three-storied and about five *zhang* in height. [Water courses] run between all the compounds. Its ponds and moats are extremely deep.

There is plenty of fragrance from flowers, solemn and beautiful, and it is worthwhile to view them. Since the time [Nālandā Temple] was established, it has been protected, kept clean and majestic. Women are filthy and licentious and have not been allowed to live here in seclusion. There are normally more than four thousand resident monks. Visitors, both monks and laypeople, experts [on the teaching], heretics, and orthodox [followers] number more that ten thousand.They all are given clothes and food; no one suffers from a lack [of these supplies]. Therefore, [the temple] is also called Shiwuyan ("Donating without Loathing"). Inside of and near [the temple] numerous sacred vestiges appear over one another. It is impossible to record them all.

There are various *śāstra* masters whose knowledge is virtuous and profound. The king bestowed them manor estates, up to ten cities. Gradually the amount of the grants was lowered but it was not reduced to fewer than three cities. Today this temple has more than three hundred great virtuous monks who have received manors. Those who are above the level of being versed in sutras do not have charge of a service in the sangha. They set value on learning and love it; they ask questions about different teachings [of the Buddhist Dharma]. Therefore, as for all the monks throughout the land bordered by the four seas west from Agni, many study the philosophical principles [of Buddhism]. All masters who travel to and from the states where they are appointed to perform [Buddhist services] encounter no obstruction [in their travels]. Even through the kings protect their own states, they do not venture to interfere with [the monks' travel].

Again, going east and entering mountains, traveling more than two hundred *li,* we come to the state of Īraṇaparvata (Yilanna[bofaduo]). There one can see the vestige of the Buddha's seat, which makes a slight depression

of about one *cun* in a rock. [The rock] is five *chi* and two *cun* long and two *chi* and one *cun* wide. There is [also] the trace of a water bottle in a depression 505a
of about one *cun* in a rock. There are patterns of an octopetalous flower, which seem to be newly produced. There is also a trace where the Buddha stood, a little longer than one *chi* and eight *cun* and about six *cun* wide.

Again, going northwest after passing seven states, we arrive at the state of Karṇasuvarṇa (Jieluona[sufalana]), where both heterodoxy and orthodoxy are concurrently practiced. Additionally there are three temples where dairy products are not eaten. [These temples] are for monks of Devadatta's school.

Furthermore, going seven hundred *li* southwest, we come to the state of Oḍra (Uḍra, Oḍḍa, Oṭa, or Utkala; present-day Orissa in Bengal; called Wutu in China). The eastern border [of the state] is the sea [coast]. In the coastal area of the city of Caritra (Faxing) many merchants and travelers stay [after crossing the sea].

Next, in the ocean to the south is the [island] state of Siṃhala (Sengqieluo; present-day Sri Lanka), called Zhishizi [in China]. [The state of Siṃhala] is about twenty thousand-plus *li* away from [the city of Caritra]. Every night, looking south [from the city], a treasure gem (i.e., a *maṇi* gem) on the top of the stupa of the Buddha's tooth [relic] in that state can be seen emerging from the horizon, shining as brightly as rising flames.

Again, going southwest we pass through various states in which there are also wondrous traces. Going about five thousand *li,* we reach the state of Kosala (Jiaosaluo), which forms the border of South India. [Buddhism] is worshiped more deeply here. More than three hundred *li* southwest from the capital city is Mount Bhrāmara (Heifeng, "Black Bees"). Here in the past a great king built a temple for Nāgārjuna Bodhisattva (Longmeng, formerly called Longshu [in China]). The temple is arranged in five tiers from top to bottom, made by chiseling rocks. Water channeled [from the high peaks of the mountain] runs around the [temple buildings] and drains into [a pond]. There are numerous various extraordinary things that reach other regions along [the watercourse].[110] Today sextons guard [the temple] firmly, and there are few visitors [to the temple].

The appearance of a stone image enshrined in a niche is extremely grand. On the day the temple was completed, Nāgārjuna went to the mountain and applied medicine to [the image], and it changed to a purplish-gold color. There is no equivalent to this in the world.

Moreover, there is a scripture depository containing innumerable folded and bound [sutras].[111] Elders say, from generation to generation, "All [sutras] are from the first assembly of the compilation of the teachings and the complete set [of teachings] exists now. Even though the Buddhist Dharma outside of [this temple] frequently experiences extermination, there is no change in this temple in regard to the preservation of the Buddhist Dharma. Recently a monk came and undertook a summer retreat there. He was able to study and recite [sutras] but he was not allowed to take them out [of the temple]." These things are explained in detail. The path [to the temple] is quite deep and steep. It is difficult to visit and make inquiries there.

Again going south, we arrive at the state of Āndhra (Andaluo), which belongs to South India. More than twenty *li* southwest of the capital city is an isolated mountain, on the ridge of which there is a stone stupa. This is the very place where Chenna (Dignāga) Bodhisattva composed the *Yinming lun* (*Discourse on the Clarification of Causes*).

Again going a thousand *li* south, we reach the state of Dhānakaṭaka (Duonajiezhejia guo), which belongs to South India. There are [two] great temples on the hillsides east and west of the capital city. Formerly the king built them for the Buddha by excavating into the mountains and removing rocks. They were created to be extremely splendid and extensive. Wandering sages and virtuous people would take a rest here. Before a thousand years after the Buddha [entered nirvana], there were a thousand ordinary monks in these places. They all testified to arhatship on the day they were released from retreat and flew away beyond the sky. Today [the temples] are quiet and no one is there. [Near] those places is [the site for] the *śāstra* master Bhāviveka (Popifeiqie, called Mingbian in the Tang dynasty), namely the master [who wrote] the *Boruodeng lun shi* (commentary on Nāgārjuna's *Mūlamadhyamakakārikā*). Before [an image of]
505b Avalokiteśvara he took no food and drank only water for three years. He set his mind and entreated to await and see Maitreya. Avalokiteśvara then revealed his physical form to [Bhāviveka and said,] "Now, recite the *vajra-dhāraṇī* for three years at Vajrapāṇi's place in a cave in the great mountain

located south of the city." The deity [Vajrapāṇi] gave an instruction [to Bhāviveka], "There is an *asura* palace in this rock cave. If you entreat according to the Dharma, the rock wall will surely open for you. You should immediately enter and wait for Maitreya to appear. I will report to you just at the moment [Maitreya emerges]." Three more years passed. [Bhāviveka] then chanted a spell to some mustard seeds and struck the rock wall, and [the wall] broke open, revealing a cave. At that time a great number of people all saw and marveled at this. The *śāstra* master [Bhāviveka] stepped through the opening and then looked at the people and commanded them [to follow after him] repeatedly. Only six people entered after him. The rest of the people said that the cave was full of poisonous snakes. At that moment the rock door immediately closed and again formed a wall.

Again going more than six thousand *li* south, we come to the state of Malakuṭa (Moluojuzha), namely the southernmost coastal border of Jambudvīpa. Mount [Malaya] produces Borneo camphor (Skt. *karpūra*). There are also sandalwood trees as well as *karpūra* trees. [The trunk of a *karpūra* tree looks like] that of pine tree and the tree has no leaves, but it is fragrant and [white in color], just like ice or snow. This is precisely Borneo camphor.

In the ocean south of here is a palace of heavenly beings, which is the place where Avalokiteśvara Bodhisattva (Guanzizai pusa, "Bodhisattva Who Observes Freely," formerly called Guanshiyin pusa, "Bodhisattva Who Hear the Sounds of the World" [in China]), usually resides. Facing the ocean is a city. The state, formerly called the Land of Lions (i.e., Siṃhala), is about three thousand *li* across the ocean from here. Without a large group it is impossible to reach this place.

Going more than four thousand *li* northwest from here, witnessing various miracles in the states we pass through en route, [we come to the state of Mahāratha (Mohelata)]. In the southeast corner of the state [of Siṃhala is Mount Laṅkā]. Several thousands of *li* [south] is Nārikeladvīpa, [which means "Coconut Island"]. The people here are [small], only three *chi* tall. They [have beaks like those of] birds, and they eat only coconuts.[112]

Again, we arrive at the state of Mahāratha. The king of this [state] does anything he wishes at will; he has not submitted to [King] Śīlāditya. There are more than a hundred temples and five thousand monks.

A temple on a mountain on the eastern border of the state was built by an arhat (i.e., Acala). In a large monastery building, a hundred-plus *chi* in height, a stone image is enshrined. [The image] is more than eight *zhang* long. A stone canopy above [the image], comprised of seven layers altogether, floats in the air. Each [layer of the canopy] is separated from the other by three *chi*. None among those who worship and come before [the image] fails to exclaim at the extraordinary sight. One legend says, "It is held [in the air] by the power of the arhat's vow"; another says, "It is held by the power of medicine or incantation."

Again going northwest beyond two states, we come to the state of Mālava, which belongs to South India. More than twenty *li* northwest of the capital city is a great brahman village. There is a large depression nearby in which water will not remain even though it flows into [the hole]. This is the place where in the past a greatly self-conceited brahman slandered the Mahayana [teaching] and fell into hell alive.

Again going northwest, we reach the state of Aṭāli (Azhali), which belongs to South India. This state produces peppers and [a type of incense called] *kunduruka.* The leaves of the [*kunduruka*] tree look like those of the wild pear tree.

Furthermore, making a tour to the northwest and passing through more than ten states, we arrive at the state of Pārasya (Bolasi; present-day Persia), which is not under Indian sovereignty. This state produces great
505c quantities of gold, silver, brass, *sphaṭika* (quartz), and crystal. When people die their corpses are mostly left unattended. The almsbowl of the Buddha is kept in the palace here. The northwest [region of Pārasya] borders on the state of From (Fulin; i.e., the Eastern Roman Empire). This state produces white dogs. Originally the red-headed duck was born in a cave here.

According to the *Liang gongzhi tu* (*Illustrations of Tributes to the Liang Dynasty*):

On an island in the southwestern sea ten thousand *li* north of Pārasya, there is the Western State of Women (Xinü), which is not under Indian sovereignty. Every year [the state of] From sends men to mate with [the women of this state].

Sacred vestiges have been briefly explained just as mentioned above. They are completely enumerated in worldly historical records, and fully recorded in the large original version [of the record of Master [Xuan]zang's travels (i.e., the *Da Tang xiyuji*)].

Verses say:

Rare precious sound flows afar.
Then, looking back I think of the East.
Being delighted with the wind and admiring the Way,
I respectfully plan to cross over to the West.
The subtlety is complete at the tip of a brush.
Fortune is as subtle as a thin silk.
Phenomena are entrusted to temporarily take shapes.
Clouds and fog shine.
In the remains numerous images flow.
Truth deepens its meaning.
I give vent to my interest and open my mind.
Ordinary people are led to the sacred way.
A thousand buddhas assimilate.
To ten thousand virtuous people, dawn has come.
His Majesty makes a comment from his feeling:
"Buddhist monks and laypeople are equally treated."

[End of] Fascicle Twenty-nine of *A Forest of Pearls from the Dharma Garden*

Fascicle 30

Chapter Twenty-two

Preservation of the Buddhist Teaching

(This chapter consists of ten parts:) (1) Introduction, (2) Punishment, (3) Careful Consideration, (4) Speaking and Listening, (5) Bodhisattvas, (6) Arhats, (7) Monks and Nuns, (8) Wealthy People of Virtue, (9) Heavenly Kings, and (10) Spiritual Beings.

1. Introduction

The Dharma is not spontaneously propagated; its propagation depends on human beings. People are led toward wrong or right. The Dharma expels people's wrongdoings. If you wish to preserve the Three Treasures, you must be full of virtuous conduct; be first versed in the precepts, the doctrine, and the whole purpose [of Buddhism] and recite them from memory; spare no pains; and do not be fond of acquiring a widespread reputation. Buddhist clergy and laypeople have a basis for their happiness. Practitioners of this realm admire and honor the conduct of diligence. When monks and laypeople rely on each other the Dharma can exist eternally. Therefore, the *Sifen lü* (T. 1428; Skt. *Dharmagupta-vinaya*) says, "If a wrong system is not instituted, a right system is then exercised. In this way gradually the Dharma is caused to exist eternally."

If the Dharma derives from ordinary human feelings, words carry no fixed rules. On reflection this would be the same as vulgar [teachings]. How could 506a
they deliver sentient beings?

You should withdraw from selfishness and examine yourself as a human being. Therefore, the [*Sifen*] *lü* says, "If a wrong system is instituted, then a right system will be severed. In this way gradually the Dharma is caused to be quickly destroyed."

I frequently see that the emperor and many leaders from distinguished, high-ranking families ask monks or nuns to heal them of diseases. Some of [these monks or nuns] practice medicine, acupuncture, and moxibustion in order to seek and covet fame and wealth. Some of them gamble in games of dice (*shupu*), sing songs, and play without managing their behavior. Some of them are entrusted to arrange a marriage or act as a go-between for marriage. Some of them allot wine and meat openly to the people who come to their assembly. Some indulge in luxurious living necessities as well as items of amusement and go about on the back of a caparisoned horse. Some of them chat pleasantly while holding the wrist [of another]; they belong to the same class as worthless vulgarians. Some of them keep bad company and associate with ill-bred people.

[Such monastics] cause the roads to be full of debauched sounds that pollute the sensibilities of ordinary people. Noble and distinctive people know this simultaneously and it passes through to heaven and is heard there. Thereafter, just like blindly following the roar of thunder [heaven] completely removes wrongs and falsehoods and purifies the people. Unless monks and nuns are upright and honest, they cannot rely on the sacred teaching. This is because laypeople do not recognize the virtuous. Due to these causes a few monks slander immeasurable good monks.

Certain [monks or nuns] diligently seek learning and have extensive knowledge in the Tripiṭaka. Certain [monks or nuns] talk about [the Buddhist teaching] and lead and benefit sentient beings through all four seasons without fail. Certain [monks or nuns] exclusively abide in meditation and concentration and continually sit [in meditation] without lying down. Certain [monks or nuns] read and recite sutras and discourses, always diligent without negligence. Certain [monks or nuns] worship [the Three Treasures] and repent [their sins] six times a day; they practice the [Buddhist] Way day and night. Those who enter [monastic life] wear a robe made of rags and beg for alms. They are frugal and lead a simple life. They let things take their own course. Certain [monks] dwell in mountains and forests practicing *dhūta* and asceticism. Certain [monks or nuns] devote themselves to engaging in meritorious and beneficial conduct and make offerings to the Three Treasures. Certain [monks or nuns] organize a purification [ceremony] or a lecture meeting and educate secular people in order to cause them to enter the [Buddhist] Way. Certain [monks or nuns] engage in producing [buddha] images or in building a Buddhist monastery.

In this way I have briefly listed the categories that can be exhaustively recorded. Distinguished monks like these always rely on the place where the Buddha is worshiped and the Buddhist Way is practiced. They wholeheartedly practice merit and wisdom. They do not forget [their practice] even for a very short time; they have no time to become defiled by worldly matters. Because [these distinguished monks are not in the public eye,] princes and noble people do not know [of them. Instead,] they form close friendships with humble people (i.e., corrupt monks or nuns) who are habitually defiled for a long time. Because of this, these people are not right. Even when [these corrupt monks or nuns] see that a sage monk does something for the sake of ordinary people they only give rise to anger and haughtiness. Have they ever paid respect to [such a monk]? Think about this matter quietly! Wouldn't [this attitude] be false?

2. Punishment

After the Great Sage (i.e., the Buddha) hid himself in the west, the true teaching flowed to the East. [The transmission of] the Buddhist Dharma was entrusted to us. Kings ordered [the people] to protect and hold it. The king's law has gradually changed and declined as time passes. The charter observed or violated has gradually become almost exhausted. If those who hear a sermon are insulted all the worse contrary [to their expectation], Buddhist clergy and laypeople will become wild and evil; they will [give rein to] passion and oppose [the precepts] for a long time. If we intend to bring them to justice, correct evil, and follow wholesomeness, we should rely on the government's power to control and purify people. On the contrary, the sangha is powerless and the [monastics'] pure minds are defiled. Their minds have become debauched and it is truly difficult to control them. [This situation] causes the great teaching to cease and the transmitted [degraded] teaching to be substituted for [the great teaching].

Therefore, the [*Dafangdeng*] *daji jing* (T. 397) says: 506b

> If in the future all kings and those of the four castes are able to give up their lives to protect the Dharma to preferably protect a single *bhikṣu* who

practices in accordance with the Dharma, and to not protect immeasurable various evil *bhikṣu*s, kings such as this will be reborn in the pure land after giving up their own life. If [they] follow evil [*bhikṣu*s] they will not be able to be reborn in a human body for immeasurable generations.

If the king and others do not control [evil *bhikṣu*s], then they will cut off [the seed of] the Three Treasures and take by force the vision of sentient beings. Even if they cultivate almsgiving (Skt. *dāna*), precepts, and wisdom for immeasurable generations, [their meritorious acts] will be destroyed and lost.

Furthermore, when a *bhikṣu* who has committed a sin should be punished, give him hard labor for one or two months, forbid him to talk or sit with others, exile him to between one and four other countries where there are places to practice the Buddhist Dharma. If evil *bhikṣu*s are managed in these ways, all good *bhikṣu*s can comfortably receive the Dharma. Therefore this allows the Buddhist Dharma to last eternally without destruction.

Moreover, the *Sapoduo lun* (T. 1440) says,[113] "One receives a *duṣkṛta* [offense] because he has gone against the king's institution."[114]

Furthermore, the *Shengman* [*shizi hou yisheng dafangbian fangguang*] *jing* (T. 353; Skt. *Śrīmālādevī-siṃhanāda-sūtra*) says:

O World-honored One! I will denounce those who should be denounced and I will embrace those who should be embraced. Why? Because by denouncing [evil] and embracing [good] we enable the true Dharma to last eternally. Then heavenly and human beings will fill [the world and beings of] the evil realms will decrease. We will be able to follow the wheel of the Dharma turned by you, the Tathāgata.

Again, the *Nirvana Sutra* (T. 374, T. 375) says:

[The Buddha said,] "Good people! Listen attentively! Listen attentively! I must speak for your sake about acts for longevity attained by me, the Tathāgata. Bodhisattvas attain long life because of the cause and condition of these acts.

If you wish to attain long life, you must have thoughts of compassion for all sentient beings, just in the same manner as you think of a child. Give rise to great compassion, great mercy, great joy, and great almsgiving.

Accept the precept of not killing. Teach and cultivate the good Dharma. You must also establish all sentient beings in the five precepts and the ten wholesome acts. Further you must enter all the evil realms, such as hell and the realms of hungry ghosts, animals, and *asura*s, and deliver suffering sentient beings from these [realms]. Liberate those who have not yet been liberated from [the transmigration of birth and death]. Ferry to [the yonder shore] those who have not been ferried. Cause those who have not yet attained nirvana to attain it. Soothe all those who have various fears. Because of the cause and condition of acts like these, bodhisattvas attain longevity and freedom in various wisdoms, and they will be reborn in heaven after their life comes to an end."

Kāśyapa Bodhisattva addressed the Buddha, "O World-honored One! In the Buddhist Dharma there are those who violate the precepts, those who commit the five deadly sins, or those who slander the true Dharma. Why should we consider these people in the same way we think of a child [with compassion]?"

The Buddha answered Kāśyapa, "Good people! Suppose there is one man in the whole corps of officials who violated the king's law, and the king has him executed in accordance with his crime without overlooking it. I, the Tathāgata, the World-honored One, do not act in this way. To those who slander the Dharma I will give [the seven deeds]: *quqian jiemo* (Pāli *pabbājaniya-kamma*), *heze jiemo* (Pāli *tajjaniya-kamma*), *shezhi jiemo* (Skt. *utkṣepaṇīya-karma*), *juzui jiemo* (Pāli *paṭisāraṇiya-kamma*), *bukejian jiemo, miebin jiemo* (Pāli *nāsana-kamma*), or *weisheejian jiemo* (Pāli *pāpikāya diṭṭhiyā appaṭinissagge uppamahepaneya-kamma*).[115]

Good people! I, theTathāgata, the World-honored One, make acts of subjugation like these to those who slander the Dharma. It is because I 506c
want to show all the people who do evil acts that there is retribution for their evils. After I enter nirvana, there is a *bhikṣu* who observes the precepts. He completely possesses a dignified manner and protects and maintains the true Dharma. If [this *bhikṣu*] sees a person who destroys the Dharma, [he] can expel the person, berate, and remedy the person by punishment. You should know this person will attain immeasurable, innumerable merits. Consequently, if a good *bhikṣu* sees a person who destroys the Dharma, but leaves that person alone without berating him, expelling him, accusing

him of his offense, and punishing him, then you must know that this person is an enemy of the Buddhist Dharma. If [the offender] can be expelled, berated, accused of his offense, and punished, this is my disciple and a true *śrāvaka*."

Again [the Buddha] said, "I, the Tathāgata, now entrust the transmission of the supreme true Dharma to all kings, ranking officials, prime ministers, *bhikṣu*s, *bhikṣuṇī*s, *upāsaka*s, and *upāsikā*s. All these kings and the four kinds of my disciples must exhort and encourage all scholars to attain the powerful precepts, meditation, and wisdom. If there are those who do not learn these three classes of the teachings, who are negligent, who violate the precepts, or who slander the true Dharma, then kings, ranking officials, and the four kinds of my disciples must strenuously punish them."

Moreover, [the *Nirvana*] *Sutra* says:

If there is a *bhikṣu* who has always abundant endowments for himself,[116] he can further protect and maintain the Buddhist precepts that he has received. He can expound the Dharma as powerfully as a lion roars and extensively preach the wondrous Dharma, that is to say, [scriptures] from sutras (i.e., the Buddha's exposition of the Dharma in prose) up to *adbhuta-dharma* (i.e., accounts of miracles performed by the Buddha or other deities). He extensively explains the nine kinds of scriptures mentioned above for others. He benefits and comforts all sentient beings. Therefore, he chants such words as "In the *Nirvana Sutra* it is instituted that all *bhikṣu*s should not keep slaves, cattle, sheep, and unlawful things. If there is a *bhikṣu* who keeps impure things like these, you must punish him." The Tathāgata earlier said in a scripture for various different schools, "If there is a *bhikṣu* who keeps unlawful things like these, the king of such-and-such state should punish him in accordance with the law, and urge him to return to secular life."

Suppose that when a *bhikṣu* can expound the Dharma in this way, just as powerfully as a lion roars, some [monks] who violate the precepts hear these [*bhikṣu*'s] words, become enraged, and kill this Dharma master. The Dharma preacher, even if his life comes to an end, is called one who observes the precepts and who benefits himself and others due to [his conduct]. On account of this condition, I let kings, the whole body of officials, prime ministers, all *upāsaka*s, and others protect the Dharma preachers. This is extensively clarified in this sutra.

When Juede ("Realization of Virtue") Bhikṣu protected the true Dharma,[117] he controlled all the *bhikṣu*s [saying,] "You cannot violate the precepts and keep unlawful things." A group of *bhikṣu*s heard his words and came to kill him.

At that time there was a king called Youde ("Virtuous").[118] Regardless of risking his life [the king] protected and supported Juede Bhikṣu. He fought against [the evil *bhikṣu*s] and rescued the Dharma master. From that time on [the king] was able to continually meet a buddha. Consequently both of them attained buddhahood."

The Buddha said, pointing to himself, "The king of that time is myself, and the Dharma preacher *bhikṣu* is Kāśyapa Buddha."

[The Buddha said,] "All people are able to accomplish this diamond body (Skt. *vajrakāya*) as a result of protecting the Dharma."

Furthermore, [the Buddha] said, "In the evil world with defilements 507a
after my nirvana the land will be desolate and disordered. [The people] will take things from each other by force and everyone will be starving. At that time, out of hunger many people will renounce the world [without] having awakened the aspiration for enlightenment. Such people are designated as the bald-headed. When these bald-headed people see a pure *bhikṣu* who observes the precepts, fully possesses a dignified manner, and protects and maintains the true Dharma, they try to expel him and drive him out of [the sangha], kill, or injure him."

Kāśyapa Bodhisattva addressed the Buddha, "O World-honored One! How can those who observe the precepts and protect the Dharma travel around in the villages and cities to educate [the people]?"

[The Buddha said,] "Good people! For this reason I now approve that [*bhikṣu*s] who observe the precepts may rely on laymen who have swords and canes with them and take them as companions. If all those such as kings, ranking officials, the wealthy, elderly people, and *upāsaka*s have swords and canes in order to protect the Dharma, I say that these people are designated as ones who observe the precepts. Even if they have weapons they must not destroy life. If they can act in this way, then they can be designated as primary in observing the precepts."

[The Buddha] again said, "In my teaching I also say that if there is one who commits one of the four grave offenses (Skt. *catvāraḥ pārājayika-sthāniyā*) or the very minor *duṣkṛta* offense,[119] you must severely punish him. If sentient beings do not protect and maintain the Buddhist precepts, how can they see the buddha-nature? Even though all sentient beings possess the buddha-nature, they must follow the observance of the precepts, and later they will see it. Because of seeing the buddha-nature they are able to attain highest, perfect enlightenment."

[The Buddha] further said in verse:

If *bhikṣu*s study and achieve
Precepts, meditation, and wisdom,
They should know
They will soon be close to great nirvana.

Again the *Yuedeng [sanmei] jing* (T. 639; Skt. *Samādhirāja-candrapradīpa-sūtra*) says in verse:

Even though you extensively read numerous sutras
And rely on erudites, if you violate the precepts,
Even the erudites cannot deliver you.
The violation of the precepts results in suffering in hell.

Moreover, in the [*Dafangguang*] *shilun jing* (T. 410; Skt. *Daśacakrakṣiti-garbha*) the Buddha says in verse:

A true good person of the *kṣatriya* [caste]
Gives an offering to the true Dharma,
And enables the three vehicles to flourish,
He will attain the sea of merits.
He fully possesses the seven treasures and others
That are replete throughout Jambudvīpa.
He offers them to all buddhas.
That merit is still limited.
Consequently, in the four continents around Mount Sumeru
If he builds monks' quarters to offer,
Even though he attains great merit,
It is not as good as protecting the true Dharma.

If for the sake of all buddhas
He builds many stupas and temples,
Even though he attains great merit,
It is not as good as protecting the true Dharma. 507b
For instance, it is just as when five suns come out
And can exhaust the ocean,
He who protects my Dharma
Exhausts the trammels of defilement.
For instance, it is just as a disaster caused by strong winds arises
And completely smashes all mountains;
He who protects my Dharma
Also destroys all defilements.
For instance, it is just as the disaster of a flood breaks out,
And [the water] flows around and destroys the earth;
He who protects my Dharma
Also extinguishes all defilements.

3. Careful Consideration

If you wish to become a great physician to propagate the Tripiṭaka, you must first accommodate yourself to the faculty of others. Treat your own troubles by yourself and then help others manage theirs. The Dharma can last eternally. You must not speak of the distinguished teaching in vain for your fame and wealth. Not cultivating even a single practice is consequently the same as being haughty.

Therefore, the *Da*[*sheng*] *zhuangyan jinglun* (T. 1604; Skt. *Mahāyāna-sūtrālaṃkāra*) says:

> There are two kinds of haughtiness. One is the haughtiness [that arises] when a person obtains a house, material goods, wealth, and other such things, and the other is that which arises when he is praised by other people.

Of these two kinds of haughtiness, the former is often seen in laymen who become haughty when they attain wealth and high position. They open the gate of self-indulgence and create the cause to fall into hell. The latter is often seen in those who have renounced the world. They avariciously study for fame and wealth, striving for humility. They expect others to praise them and that gives rise to haughtiness. They are muddled in their frame of mind and get lost in the thought of a sage. The blind do not see the [Buddhist] Way and wander about in the three evil realms.

Therefore, the *Nirvana Sutra* says:

> The Buddha said to Kāśyapa, "Seven hundred years after my nirvana Māra-pāpīyān (i.e., the devil king Pāpīyān) will gradually ruin my true Dharma. For instance, just as a hunter may put on a Dharma robe, the devil king Pāpīyān is also like this. He transforms himself into the figure of a *bhikṣu*, a *bhikṣuṇī,* an *upāsaka,* or an *upāsikā.* He also transforms himself into one who has attained the stage of *srota-āpatti-phala* up to the stage of arhatship, as well as the physical form of a buddha. The devil king makes this impure body into a pure body and ruins my true Dharma."

Again, the [*Nirvana*] *Sutra* says:

> If there is a *bhikṣu* who preaches the Dharma for others in order to benefit and nourish himself, all of this [*bhikṣu*'s] followers and dependents also imitate their teacher and avariciously seek to benefit and nourish themselves. That person then personally causes people to become evil in this way.

[The *Nirvana Sutra*] further says:

> Suppose there is a *bhikṣu* who observes the Buddhist precepts, yet in order to benefit and nourish himself he acts together and exchanges visits with those who violate the precepts, or he is intimate with and close to them and shares their pursuits. This [*bhikṣu*] is called [a monk who] has violated the precepts and is also called an impure monk.

[The *Nirvana Sutra*] again says:

> Furthermore, there is one who is continually submerged in delusion and yet is not an *icchantika.* What is this? If a person practices almsgiving, precepts, and good acts [while still sinking in delusion], this is called continually sinking in delusion.

Therefore, the [*Nirvana*] *Sutra* says:

> Good people! There are four good things by which one obtains evil effects. What are the four? The first is to read and recite sutras in order to surpass

others; the second is to receive and observe the pure precepts in order to benefit and nourish oneself; the third is to practice almsgiving because of others' dependents; and the fourth is to concentrate one's thought to attain 507c
the abode of neither thought nor non-thought (Skt. *naiva-saṃjñā-nāsaṃjñāyatana;* nirvana for non-Buddhists). By these four good things one obtains evil effects."

Again, [the *Nirvana Sutra*] says:

It is because this *icchantika* exterminates all wholesome roots and does not [possess] the ability [to become a buddha]. Even if this person hears and receives the *Great Nirvana Sutra* like this for a hundred, a thousand, or ten thousand years, in the end he cannot awaken the aspiration for enlightenment. Why? It is because he has no wholesome nature.

Moreover, the [*Nirvana*] *Sutra* says:

Good people! Incalculable years after my nirvana all sages of the four paths [to nirvana] will enter nirvana too. During [the period of] the semblance Dharma after [the period of] the true Dharma, there will be *bhikṣu*s who appear to observe the precepts and who read and recite a few sutras but they will be covetously addicted to food and drink and nourish their bodies. They will wear coarse and ugly clothes. They will be haggard in appearance and have no dignity or virtue. They will raise cattle and sheep and carry firewood and straw on their shoulders. Their beards, fingernails, and hair will all grow abundantly. Even though they wear a *kaṣāya,* they will still look like hunters. They will walk slowly with mincing steps, just as a cat stalks a mouse. They will always repeat this, "I have attained arhatship." They will often suffer from various diseases and sleep amid dung and filth. They will outwardly present themselves as virtuous yet harbor greed and jealousy inside. They are just like brahmans who receive the ascetic practice of silence. They are in fact not *śramaṇa*s, even if they look like a *śramaṇa.* Having outrageous wrong views, they will slander the true Dharma. People like these break the precepts, right practices, and dignified deportment established by the Tathāgata. While speaking of the fruition of liberation and the teaching to leave behind impurity, they will destroy the very profound esoteric teaching. Each of them, personally in accordance with his thought, will speak against sutras and precepts and claim, "The Tathāgata entirely allows us to eat meat and to drink wine." They will personally produce a discourse like this and say that it was spoken by the Buddha. They will dispute among themselves. Each one will declare himself to be a *śramaṇa* and Śākyamuni's son.

Good people! At that time, furthermore, there will be various *śramaṇa*s who amass raw grain, accept fish and meat, make food with their own hands, and possess a bottle of oil, a treasured canopy, and leather shoes. Being intimately close to kings, ranking officials, and wealthy elderly people, they will practice divination by physiognomy or astrology, and will diligently practice medical science. They will keep slaves; [collect] gold, silver, and miscellaneous treasures; study various mechanical arts; engage themselves in clay works with artists, book production, educational affairs, planting, and the art of casting a spell on people. They will combine various medicines, sing songs, and play music. With incense and flowers they will adorn their bodies. They will be skillful in gambling in games of dice (*shupu*), encirclement chess (*weiqi;* Jp. *go*), and other games. For a *bhikṣu* who can leave behind all evil affairs like these, I say, "This person is truly my disciple."

If, on the contrary, [*bhikṣu*s] learn these things,[120] are intimate with and close to kings, princes, ranking officials, and various women; laugh loudly or stay in silence; arouse many suspicions toward all teachings; chatter and speak recklessly about merits or demerits, good or bad appearance, wholesomeness or unwholesomeness, or wonderful clothes and various impure things like these; sing their own praises to their donors; roam about going into and out of impure places, such as wine stores, brothels,
508a and gambling places, then I immediately do not allow the people like these to stay among the *bhikṣu*s. They must leave the monk's order, return to secular life, and be employed by other people. For instance, they are just like millet splits; they should be completely extinguished without any remainder. You must know that this is established in the sutras and precepts and entirely spoken by the Tathāgata. If there are those who follow what a devil says, they are the devil's dependents. If there are those who follow what the Buddha teaches, then they are bodhisattvas.

Consequently the [*Fozang*] *jing* (T. 653) says:

A *bhikṣu* who violates the precepts must cut his flesh in order to compensate to his donors for myriad *kalpa*s. If he is reborn as an animal, he will always bear a heavy burden. Why? It is just as when a hair is split apart to become a hundred billion portions, the *bhikṣu* who violates the precepts still cannot reconcile [his sin with the donors'] offering even as much as a portion of [a single hair], not to speak of [the four necessities:] clothes, food and drink, bedding, and medicines [that donors have offered to him].

Again, [the *Fozang jing*] says:

[He who violates the precepts] is happy to see women and is not close to men. Consequently he loathes those who observe the precepts and becomes intimately attached to [those who] violate the precepts. [Those who violate the precepts] always praise almsgiving while they do not praise observance of the precepts, forbearance, diligence, meditation, and wisdom. They do not appreciate the tranquil state of complete extinction (i.e., nirvana), leaving [impurities] far behind, or dwelling alone in a quiet place. They are always fond of ridiculously talking about faults of those who observe the precepts, [but] they do not praise those who practice *dhūta,* or when they refer to that [practice] (i.e., *dhūta*) they unrestrainedly verbally abuse it.

The [*Nirvana*] *Sutra* again says:

Good people! The Tathāgata's true Dharma is about to be extinguished. At that time there will be many *bhikṣu*s who act evil. They do not know the Tathāgata's depository of subtle esoteric teachings. They are very lazy and negligent. They are unable to read, recite, enhance, or discriminate the Tathāgata's true Dharma. For instance, it is just like an idiotic thief who gives up the true treasure and [instead] carries off grass and wheat husks on his shoulders.[121] Since they do not understand the Tathāgata's depository of subtle esoteric teachings, they are negligent and lack diligence even in this sutra. How sad! This is a great danger! You should be afraid of the future world. How miserable sentient beings will be! They will not diligently listen to and receive this Mahayana sutra, the *Great Nirvana Sutra.* Only all bodhisattva *mahāsattva*s will be able to take the true meaning in this sutra beyond its written language. Following [this sutra] without offense they will preach it for sentient beings.

Next, good people! It is just like a herdswoman who sells milk waters it down by twenty percent in order to make an excessive profit. She sells it to another pasture woman, who further dilutes it with water by another twenty percent and then resells it to a woman who lives near a city. That woman then dilutes it by adding twenty percent more water and again resells it to a woman in the city. After obtaining the [diluted milk], that woman again dilutes it by another twenty percent and takes it to the market to sell.

On that occasion a man [is planning a banquet] for his son who is getting married. He needs good milk to provide for his guests and visitors. He goes to the market in order to buy [milk]. The [woman] who is selling the milk asks him for a high price. The man replies, "Your milk contains much water. It does not deserve the price, but I now wish to offer hospitality to my guests and visitors, so I must take it." He buys [the milk] and returns to his house. He boils it to make porridge but it has no milk flavor at all. Even though it has no flavor, it is still a thousand times better than a bitter
508b taste. Why? Because the taste of milk is the best among all tastes.

Good people! After my nirvana, for eighty-odd years the true Dharma will not be extinguished. At that time this sutra must be widely circulated in Jambudvīpa. At that point there will be numerous evil *bhikṣu*s who plagiarize this sutra, or divide it to make many parts. They will be able to ruin the form, the fragrance, and the relish of the true Dharma. Even though evil people read and recite sutras like this, they will exterminate the Tathāgata's profound, esoteric, important meanings and install [in the sutra] meaningless words decorated with worldly adorned language. They will take the fore and attach it to the rear, the rear to the fore, the fore or the rear to the middle, or the middle to the fore or the rear. You must know that all evil *bhikṣu*s like these are a devil's companions. They will accept livestock and all impure things and say, "The Tathāgata has completely allowed us to raise them." They are just like the pasture woman who adds so much water to [the pure] milk. All evil *bhikṣu*s are also like this. They will disorder this sutra with worldly words and cause many sentient beings to be unable to recite [the sutra] correctly, to copy it correctly, to take it correctly, to hold it in reverence, to gasp in admiration of it, to make an offering to it, and to show respect to it. Because these evil *bhikṣus* aim to only benefit and nourish themselves, they cannot extensively propagate and circulate this sutra. What they can distribute and circulate is minuscule and not worthy of mention. It is just as that poor pasture woman's [milk] is watered down and resold from hand to hand, and [in the end] it has no true flavor. Even if [the *Nirvana Sutra* is diluted in this way and] has lost its original flavor, it still surpasses other sutras; [the *Nirvana Sutra*] serves a thousand times more than [other sutras], just as the taste of that [watered-down] milk still surpasses by a thousandfold all bitter tastes. Why? Because this Mahayana sutra, the *Great Nirvana Sutra,* is the most honored among the sutras for *śrāvakas*, just as cow's milk is supreme in flavor. For this reason it is called the *Great Nirvana* [*Sutra*].

4. Speaking and Listening

Just as the *Nirvana Sutra* says:

> Next, good people! If my disciples receive, hold, read, recite, copy, and speak this *Nirvana Sutra,* do not preach it at the wrong time, do not preach it in wrong countries, do not preach it without being asked to do so, do not preach it rashly, do not preach it here and there, do not preach it to praise yourself, do not preach it to disparage others, do not preach it to extinguish the Buddhist Dharma, and do not preach it to cause worldly law to flourish.
>
> Good people! If my disciples who receive and hold this sutra preach it [in unacceptable circumstances mentioned above] from "at the wrong time" up to "to cause worldly law to flourish," then the people will despise and slander them. Accordingly they will say, "If the Buddha's treasure the *Great Nirvana Sutra* has such awesome power, why does [the Buddha] allow [the disciples] to preach it [in unacceptable circumstances mentioned above] from "at the wrong time" up to "to cause worldly law to flourish"? If those who hold the sutra make such a statement, we must know that this sutra is powerless. If [the sutra] is powerless, even if we were to receive and hold it we must consider that there would be no benefit." Due to slighting and slandering the *Nirvana Sutra,* they will cause incalculable sentient beings to fall into hell. [If anyone preaches the sutra under these

wrong conditions,][122] then that [person] is an evil friend to sentient beings
508c and not my disciple but a devil's dependent.

If you preach the sutra only to benefit and nourish yourself, to attain the five desires or fame, then your service is no different than trading and will quickly extinguish the true Dharma.

Furthermore, the *Nirvana Sutra* says:

> How is it that sandalwood is traded for a common tree? It is just as one of my disciples makes a speech and preaches the Dharma to laypeople for the sake of receiving an offering; the laypeople are self-indulgent and not interested in listening to him; the laypeople sit on a high place while the *bhikṣu* stays in a lower place; [the laypeople] offer various kinds of dishes, food, and drink yet they are still not willing to listen to him. This is designated as sandalwood being traded for a common tree.
>
> How is it that gold is traded for brass? Brass is compared to form, sound, smell, taste, and touch. Gold is compared to the precepts. If all my disciples violate the precepts they have received because of the cause and condition of form, this is designated as gold being traded for brass.
>
> How is it that silver is traded for tin? Silver is compared to the ten wholesome acts and tin is compared to the ten evil acts. If all my disciples reject the ten wholesome acts and commit the ten evil acts, this is designated as silver being traded for tin.
>
> How is it that silk is traded for coarse woolen cloth? Coarse woolen cloth is compared to being unrepentant and unashamed [of one's sins], and silk is compared to being repentant and ashamed [of one's sins]. If all my disciples reject being repentant and ashamed [of their sins] and become unrepentant and unashamed [of their sins], this is designated as silk being traded for coarse woolen cloth.
>
> How is it that nectar is traded for poison? Poison is compared to various kinds of offerings and nectar is compared to all sorts of purity. If all my disciples, before all the laypeople in order to benefit and nourish themselves or praise themselves, say, "I have attained purity," this is designated as nectar being traded for poison.

Furthermore, the *Lotus Sutra* says:

Bodhisattva *mahāsattvas*! Do not be on intimate terms with kings, princes, ranking officials, and directors of officials. Do not be on intimate terms with non-Buddhists such as brahmans and the followers of Nirgrantha [Jñātaputra] (i.e., a founder of Jainism), as well as those who produce worldly literary works and who praise non-Buddhist books or all codes of evil conduct such as hunting and fishing. Do not be on intimate terms with people who seek a *śrāvaka*. Moreover, taking the characteristic that the female body allows you to give rise to thoughts of [sexual] desire, you should not preach the Dharma for women. Do not wish to see them, either. If you enter another's house, do not talk with young girls, virgins, or widows.

Again, do not be close to the five kinds of males who have sexual abnormalities and consider them to be good friends. Do not go into another's house alone. If you have a reason to enter alone, just think of the Buddha wholeheartedly. If you preach the Dharma for women, do not smile, exposing your teeth, and do not reveal your inmost thoughts. Consequently, still do not be intimate and friendly with [women] for the sake of the Dharma, not to mention of other matters. Do not wish to raise young disciples, novices, and young boys. Do not hope to have the same teacher as theirs, either. Always be fond of meditation. Cultivate your mind in a quiet forest.

Furthermore, the *Fozang jing* says:

As for impure preachers of the Dharma, there are five kinds [of faults]. First is to claim that one personally completely knows the Buddhist Dharma. The second fault is to have differences from all other sutras when explaining a Buddhist sutra. Third is to harbor doubts about all teachings and not to believe in them. Fourth is to refute the teachings of other sutras 509a
only with what one personally knows. Fifth is to preach the Dharma for others only in order to benefit and nourish oneself. As for preachers like these, I say they will fall into hell and not reach nirvana.

[The *Fozang jing*] also says:

I sought this Dharma treasure working assiduously in defiance of hardships for a long time, but these evil people abandon it and never preach it.

Merely by the different meanings of words in the sutra, they mutually discuss right or wrong and do not follow the true Dharma. They are arrogant and conceited in regard to the sacred Dharma. They preach [the Dharma] as they please in order to seek to benefit and nourish themselves. When a *bhikṣu* preaches the Dharma, mixing it with non-Buddhist connotations, any good *bhikṣu*s [in attendance] must leave their seats. If they do not do so, they are not good *bhikṣu*s. They are not called followers of Buddhism, either. ["It is very difficult to preach the Dharma."][123] As for those who speak like this, I say that they are called and considered to be disciples of the non-Buddhist Nirgrantha. They are not the Buddha's disciples. [The way of Nirgrantha] is designated to [lead to] hell and [the realms of] animals and hungry ghosts. Why? Because one sits on the raised seat [to preach] before he has testified the Dharma, this is a case where one teaches others without having personal knowledge. By law he will fall into hell.

Moreover, in the future *bhikṣu*s will be fond of reading non-Buddhist scriptures. When they preach the Dharma they will revise the diction [of sutras] to make the people happy. At that time devils will help confuse the people and hinder the wholesome Dharma. If there are those who covetously attach to sounds and words and who skillfully elaborate on the diction [of the sutras], or those who are fond of reading non-Buddhist scriptures, then all the devils will misguide these people and cause their minds to be [un]peaceful.

Furthermore, it is just like a group of blind people who give up things they have obtained and want to go to a great assembly of almsgiving, yet they fall into a deep ditch [on the way]. My disciples are also just like this. They abandon coarse clothing and food and pursue the great assembly of almsgiving seeking good offerings. Because of [gaining] worldly profits, they lose great wisdom and fall into the deep ditch, [namely] Avīci Hell.

Again, [the *Fozang jing*] says:

Impure preachers of the Dharma commit an offense extremely often. They also become evil friends for sentient beings and slander the buddhas of the past, present, and future as well. [If they are placed among sentient beings in Jambudvīpa,] it is as if these people completely take by force sentient beings' lives in the trichiliocosm. The sin of an impure preacher of the Dharma is more than this. Why? Because such a person ruins all buddhas' highest, perfect enlightenment and helps devils in their works. He also causes sentient beings to receive various afflictions for a hundred or a thousand generations. He is only able to create defilement but is unable to liberate [sentient beings]. You must know that such a person becomes an evil friend to all sentient beings. He engages in wild talk and slanders all buddhas among the mass of people. Due to this cause and condition he falls into the great hell. He teaches matters of wrong views to many sentient beings. Therefore he is called one who has evil wrong views.

Furthermore, [the *Fozang jing*] says:

Śāriputra! At that time a *bhikṣu* who violates the precepts consequently speaks on the Buddhist Dharma with various laypeople in order to obtain a cup of wine. What do you think about this? He is very greedy and vehemently idiotic. He is greatly delighted with reading sutras. Covetous of the advantage of non-Buddhist scriptures, he commits impurities.

Śāriputra! If there is a *bhikṣu* who is aged and virtuous, who is a dragon
[deity] among *bhikṣu*s, and who has profound wisdom, such a person is 509b
able to believe in the laws of nothingness (*wu suoyou;* Skt. *nāstitva*) and emptiness of self (*zixiang kong;* Skt. *svalakṣaṇa-śūnyatā*) and the law of non-self (*wuwo wuren;* Skt. *nirmamo nirahaṃkāro*). Why? Because this person is not delighted with noisy chit-chat, sleeping, and being officious. He does not manage and engage in worldly affairs for laypeople. He does not go on errands carrying documents. He does not practice medicine. He does not read medical prescriptions. He does not engage in peddling. He is not pleased to discuss matters in worldly speech. He is delighted by and only wishes to speak of supramundane matters.

Śāriputra! I now clearly and comprehensibly tell you: Good *bhikṣu*s who seek to benefit themselves just at that [evil] time should not go about among the masses; they should not even have a night's lodging [with them]. Only arhats who have already cut off defilement and those related to a buddha or bodhisattva in the past among sick *bhikṣu*s are excluded.

Why? Śāriputra! Because the people of that time are full of the poisons of avarice, anger, and ignorance. They are inactive, fearful, and incessantly pressed. Good people who seek to benefit [themselves] should always go to a quiet, open place among mountains or forests; consequently they end their lives just as a wild animal dies.

Again, [the *Fozang jing*] says:

My true Dharma does not stay long in the world. Why? Because sentient beings' merit and wholesome faculties have already been exhausted. The defiled world is just around the corner.

Moreover, the *Daji yuezang jing* (i.e., *Dafangdeng daji jing,* T. 397) says:

If there is a sentient being who wishes to seek highest, perfect enlightenment only by relying on reading or reciting [sutras], this person is often happy to become attached to common customs. Because of his attachment to common customs he is unable to control defilement of his mind. How could such a person control other people's defilement?

Good people! Those who are happy to become attached to reading or reciting [sutras] in order to seek enlightenment then have jealousy and seek fame and wealth. They haughtily presume on their [abilities] and disrespectfully slander others. They still cannot attain wholesome faculties in the realm of desire; much less can they attain all wholesome faculties in the realms of form and nonform.

Furthermore, the *Moheyan dabaoyan jing* says:[124]

For instance, it is just as a pharmacist roams around carrying medicines and yet he cannot treat his own disease. The erudite one who has the disease of defilement is also like this. Even though he has learned much, if he does not control defilement he cannot benefit himself; he merely has nothing to use. For instance, it is just like a dead person wearing a gold necklace. A learned [*bhikṣu*] who violates the precepts yet wears the Dharma robe and accepts others' offerings is also like this.

Furthermore, the [*Da*]*fangguang shilun jing* (T. 410; Skt. *Daśacakra-kṣitigarbha*) says:

If there is a sentient being who gives rise to vulgar and ignorant, abusive speech and considers himself to be intelligent, he consequently does not leave behind wrong views. He seeks others' profit for himself and gives rise to jealousy. He is avariciously attached to fame, praises himself, and slights others. He cannot protect his bodily, verbal, and mental [acts]. He always thinks of evil.

Such a person often makes this statement, praising himself, "I am a person of the Mahayana." He also teaches others to read and recite [sutras]. He simply praises himself and slanders others. Because of this, even 509c
though he praises the Mahayana, he cannot control himself. Following the Mahayana path he wishes to teach others to practice the Mahayana. He consequently says, "It is difficult to obtain a human rebirth."

He also loses the vehicles of *śrāvaka*s and *pratyekabuddha*s and he will probably fall into the evil realms. He does not wish to be on intimate terms with various intelligent people. Nevertheless he says, "I expound the Dharma as powerfully as a lion roars. I am a good follower of the Mahayana." He can be compared to a donkey that has a lion's pelt draped upon it and considers itself to be a lion. Someone seeing [the animal] from a distance may think that it is a lion and there is no way to discriminate before the donkey brays, but after it cries out everyone far and near know it is not a real lion and those who see it spit at it, saying, "This worn-out, cantankerous donkey is not a lion."

Consequently he who defames and violates the Buddhist precepts and who commits evil conduct does not become a vessel of the Dharma (i.e., a person capable of receiving the Dharma) anywhere at all. If he says of himself, "I am [a follower of] the Mahayana who can destroy the battle array of defilement for all sentient beings. I also abide in the eightfold holy path and enter the city of nonfear for the sake of sentient beings," there is no correct point [in what he says].

Again, the *Fozang jing* says:

There were five *bhikṣu*s in the past world. The first was called Pushi, the second was called Ku'an, the third was called Saheduo, the fourth was called Jiangqu,[125] and the last was called Upananda. These five *bhikṣu*s were teachers of the sangha. Pushi knew the true meaning of emptiness and the law of nonacquisition (Skt. *aprāptitva*) taught by the Buddha. All the other four *bhikṣu*s fell into a wrong path and often spoke of *astyātmā* (existence of a self). The *bhikṣu* Pushi was slighted by the four groups

> [of the Buddha's disciples (i.e., monks, nuns, laymen, and laywomen)] and had no influential power. Many people loathed and looked down on him. The four evil *bhikṣus* often taught people by the path of wrong views. In the Buddhist Dharma they were not respectful to each other and they opposed each other. Therefore, they destroyed the Buddhist Dharma.
>
> Moreover, [the *Fozang jing*] says:
>
> All these evil men destroyed the Buddha's true Dharma. They also gave many people great afflictions. [Consequently,] after these evil men died they fell into Avīci Hell, where they must lie on their backs for nine thousand trillion years, on their stomachs for nine thousand trillion years, on each of their left and right sides for the same period of time, and where they are burned and scorched with heated irons. After leaving here on their deaths, they are [successively] reborn in Tapana Hell, Pratāpa Hell, Saṃjīva Hell, and Kālasūtra Hell. [In each of these hells] they receive various sufferings for the number of years mentioned above. After dying in Kālasūtra Hell they are again reborn in Avīci Hell.
>
> [The *Fozang jing*] further says:
>
> [Including] those who were close to these people, good virtuous friends, and various donors, there are altogether six hundred four trillion people who are reborn and die along with these four teachers; they are also burned and boiled in the great hells.

Moreover, [the *Fozang jing*] says, "They transmigrate in this way; they receive suffering for a *kalpa* and are burned for a great *kalpa.* Therefore they are continually in the hells."

Again, [the *Fozang jing*] says:

> After these four evil people as well as the six hundred four trillion people are burned for a great *kalpa,* from Avīci Hell they transmigrate to another
510a place yet still exist in a great hell. Why? Śāriputra! If one has committed a sufficiently grave offense, the retribution is not small. In another place he will receive great suffering for incalculable years and then be reborn in the world. These four sinners and the six hundred four trillion people

as well as other people whose sins have not been exhausted, even after dying there, are reborn here in a great hell.

Again, [the *Fozang jing*] says:

After a long time, even if they escape from suffering of hells and are able to be reborn in the human realm, they are congenitally blind for five hundred generations. Later they can meet Yiqieming Buddha.[126]

Furthermore [the *Fozang jing*] says:

They renounce the world in [Yiqieming] Buddha's Dharma, and industriously practice diligence for ten trillion years, just as if brushing away sparks from their hair, but they do not attain the third rank of bodhisattvas (*shunren*), not to mention attainment of the fruition of the Buddhist Way (i.e., nirvana).

Again, the *Nirvana Sutra* says, "Sunakṣata Bhikṣu recited and obtained the twelve kinds of scriptures."

The [*Da*] *zhidu lun* says:

Devadatta renounced the world and studied the [Buddhist] Way. He recited and attained a collection of sixty thousand teachings." I will explain this. These two persons both neither studied expedient means, the true buddha-nature in the [Buddhist] Way, and methods of practice such as contemplation on the four bases of mindfulness (Skt. *catvāri smṛty-pasthānāni*), nor did they observe the five *skandha*s, impermanence, suffering, emptiness, non-self, and their own possessions. They avariciously became attached to their own views, other people's views, and the views of sentient beings. They caused high treason and slandered the Tathāgata. For these reasons, while alive these two persons fell into Avīci Hell, where they received endless suffering. It is difficult to completely explain customary examples like this.

5. Bodhisattvas

Just as the *Jiashe jing* says:[127]

At that time the Buddha said to Mahākāśyapa, "I, the Tathāgata, will soon be in nirvana." Kāśyapa addressed the Buddha, "O World-honored One! I pray that you, World-honored One, will stay in the world for another *kalpa* or so to protect the true Dharma."

The Buddha said to Kāśyapa, "Even if a thousand buddhas appear in the world and educate ignorant people by manifesting various supernatural powers and expounding the Dharma, those ignorant people cannot cause their evil desires to stop. Kāśyapa! In the future, five hundred years after the latter days, there will be various sentient beings who possess wholesome roots and whose minds are pure. They will be able to protect my Dharma to requite the Buddha's kindness."

Kāśyapa addressed the Buddha, "O World-honored One! I have cultivated only a little and my wisdom is slight and inferior. I am not adequately capable of shouldering such an important task. There are other bodhisattvas who are adequately capable of bearing an important task like this. For instance, suppose there is a man who is extremely old, a hundred and twenty years old. He has a serious disease and cannot get up and remain upright. Then a man who is very wealthy brings jewels and valuables to the ill man's place, and says to him, 'I have some business and must go to another place. I entrust my valuables to you. Please protect them for me and wait for my return. Then you must return them to me.' The old ill man
510b has no children; he leads a solitary life. His condition worsens and he dies shortly after the [wealthy] man departed. All the property entrusted to [the old man] are entirely scattered and lost. When the [wealthy] man comes back and seeks [his property], it is nowhere to be found.

"O World-honored One! *Śrāvaka*s are also like this. Their wisdom is scant and shallow and their cultivation is very slight. Moreover, they have no companions and are not able to reside in the world for a long time. If the true Dharma is entrusted to them, it will soon be scattered and extinguished."

The Buddha praised Kāśyapa, "I already clearly know this, but the reason I entrust it to you is to enable those ignorant people to hear of this and then give rise to repentance."

At that time Kāśyapa addressed the Buddha, "O World-honored One! I now further speak of a second allegory. Let us say there is a person of great physical power and vigor who has no distresses. His life span is immeasurable; he is a billion years old. He was reborn in a good family and possesses money and jewels. He is good at observing the pure precepts. Having great compassion, he holds happiness in his mind. He benefits many people and causes them to attain comfort. At one time a person comes to his place bringing treasures. [That person] says, 'I have some business and must go to another place. I entrust my treasure to you and you must properly protect it. I may be back in ten or twenty years. Please await my return and then you must return my treasure to me.' The man receives the treasure, stores it, and protects it. The person [who entrusted the treasure to him] returns and immediately [the treasure] is given back to him.

"O World-honored One! Bodhisattva *mahāsattva*s are also like this. If the Dharma treasure is entrusted to all bodhisattvas, nothing will be lost and destroyed at the end of incalculable *kalpa*s. It benefits immeasurable boundless sentient beings without cutting off the Three Treasures. O World-honored One! I am not capable of holding such an [important] matter. Only bodhisattvas are adequately capable of receiving it. O World-honored One! Maitreya Bodhisattva Mahāsattva is here in the assembly with us. If you, the Tathāgata, entrust [the Dharma] to him, even five hundred years after [the latter day period in] the future, when the Dharma is about to be extinguished, all the teachings you, the Tathāgata, have collected [for incalculable *kalpa*s] will be protected, widely expounded, and extensively spoken. Why? Because Maitreya Bodhisattva will testify to the attainment of highest, perfect enlightenment in the future world. Just as the crown prince of a king, [after ascending the throne,] must attend to royal affairs and govern the world in accordance with the law, Maitreya Bodhisattva is also like this. He regulates the rank of the Dharma King and protects the true Dharma."

At that time the Buddha praised Kāśyapa, "It is just as what you have spoken!" He then extended his right hand and touched Maitreya on the crown of his head, and said, "Maitreya! I entrust you with [the Dharma]. When the true Dharma is extinguished five hundred years after the latter days in the future, you must protect the Three Treasures and not allow them to become extinct." At that time, when the Tathāgata touched Maitreya on the crown of his head, there were six kinds of quakes in the trichiliocosm and light filled the entire trichiliocosm.

At that time all the heavenly beings from Pṛthivī Heaven and the four highest heavens of the six heavens in the realm of desire up to Akaniṣṭha

Heaven joined their hands in prayer, addressing Maitreya Bodhisattva
510c Mahāsattva, "The Tathāgata entrusts the Dharma to you, Saint. We pray that you, Saint, will receive this true Dharma in order to benefit all heavenly beings."

At that time Maitreya Bodhisattva stood up from his seat, bared his right shoulder, knelt on his right knee, respectfully joined his hands in prayer, and addressed the Buddha, "O World-honored One! I still receive suffering for myriad *kalpa*s in order to benefit all sentient beings. Furthermore, you, the Tathāgata, entrust me with the true Dharma, which I must accept. O World-honored One! I now receive it[128] and in the future world I will expound the Dharma of highest, perfect enlightenment that you, the Tathāgata, have collected for incalculable *kalpa*s." When Maitreya said these words, there were six kinds of quakes in the trichiliocosm.

Moreover, the [*Dafangdeng*] *daji jing* says:

At that time the World-honored One said to Maitreya who held the premier place (Skt. *pūrvaṃgama*) as well as all bodhisattva *mahāsattva*s of the auspicious *kalpa*, "All good people! In ancient times when I practiced the way of the bodhisattva, I once made this offering to all the past buddha tathāgatas. Because of this wholesome root they helped me create the cause of highest, perfect enlightenment. I now feel pity for all sentient beings. Therefore I will divide this reward into three parts; I will keep one for myself; the second will be given to *śrāvaka*s who firmly comply with meditation and contemplation on liberation after my nirvana in order to cause them to have no deficiencies, and the last part will be given to *śrāvaka*s who violate the precepts but who read and recite sutras and to those who shave their heads and who put on a *kaṣāya* [robe during the periods of] the true Dharma and the semblance Dharma in order to cause them to have no deficiencies.

"Maitreya! I now further consign to you all *śrāvaka*s, *bhikṣu*s, *bhikṣuṇī*s, *upāsaka*s, and *upāsikā*s who harmonize the three kinds of acts [of body, speech, and mind]. Do not cause them to come to an end being deficient and solitary! I also consign to you those who wear a *kaṣāya* and who have damaged the Buddhist precepts [in the periods of] the true Dharma and the semblance Dharma. Do not cause them to come to an end being deficient in all necessities of life. Do not cause *caṇḍāla* kings to annoy and kill each other and suffer bodily and mentally, either. I now further consign to you the various donors. I now have people both capable and incapable of receiving the Dharma who renounce the world for my sake and who make offerings to me. You also must protect, hold, raise up, and educate those people.

"O Maitreya! If people read, recite, receive, and hold fast to this Buddhist teaching in the present and future worlds, they will attain ten kinds of pure merits. What are the ten? Since from the beginning they are pure, they defy [evil acts] from the destruction of life up to wrong views (Skt. *mithyādṛṣṭi*). These are the ten kinds of merits. In a billion rebirths from this life forward they always attain these ten kinds of pure merits. If someone hears this Buddhist teaching with the utmost mind, that person will abide in ultimate reality and attain the eight kinds of pure merits. What are the eight? The first is long life; the second is correctness; the third is wealth and high position; the fourth is fame; the fifth is to be continually protected by all deities; the sixth is having no deficiency in necessities; the seventh is exhausting all karmic hindrances (Skt. *karma-* 511a
āvaraṇa); and the eighth is that when his life is about to come to an end, the buddhas in the ten directions and all members of sangha will emit great light to shine upon his eyes and cause him to see that he will be reborn in the good realms. In a billion rebirths he will continually attain these eight kinds of merits.

"I now further briefly explain this. This person will attain thirteen kinds of pure merits. What are the thirteen? First, after the transmigration of birth and death comes to an end he will no longer give rise to absurd ideas and evil views. Second, he will not be reborn in the land of the five defilements where there is no buddha.[129] Third, he will always be able to see a buddha. Fourth, he will hear the true Dharma at all times. Fifth, he will always be able to make offerings to the sangha. Sixth, he will meet a virtuous friend or teacher who will lead him to the Buddhist Way. Seventh, he will always comply with the six *pāramitās*. Eighth, he will not fall into the Hinayana. Ninth, he will always bring sentient beings to [spiritual] maturity through great compassion, great mercy, and the great power of expedient means. Tenth, he will continually make the superb vow. Eleventh, he will not leave behind the Dharma mentioned above at any time [from the beginning] up to enlightenment. Twelfth, he will be able to swiftly complete the six *pāramitās*. Finally, he will achieve buddhahood in highest, perfect enlightenment."

If there are those who receive, hold, transcribe, explain for others, and cultivate in accordance with this teaching of the *Yuezang* section [of the *Dafangdeng daji jing*] the merits they will obtain are just as explained previously.

Again, the [*Dafangdeng*] *daji jing* says:

At that time a boy called Wushengyi ("Supreme Intention") addressed the Buddha,[130] "O World-honored One! All the people of other buddha lands always speak these words: 'The *sahā* world ("land of endurance," i.e., this world) is disorderly and filthy.' I, however, now see it as pure at all times."

The Buddha said, "It is so. It is so. It is just as what you say. Furthermore, all bodhisattvas of this world make various kinds of images of heavenly and human beings and animals, roam about in Jambudvīpa, and edify various kinds of sentient beings like these. If sentient beings are controlled by heavenly and human beings, it is not considered to be difficult. If sentient beings are controlled by animals, it is, however, considered to be difficult."

"In the Eastern Sea outside Jambudvīpa there is a lapis lazuli mountain called Lake (*hu*)[131] which contains various treasures. In that mountain there is a cave called Diverse Colors (Zhongzhongse). This is a place where a bodhisattva formerly resided. Now a poisonous snake that dwells within [the cave] cultivates the compassion of a *śrāvaka*. There is another cave called Immortality (Wusi), also the former residence of a bodhisattva. There a horse cultivates the compassion of a *śrāvaka*. Again, another cave called Good Abiding Place (Shanzhuchu) is also a place where a bodhisattva formerly resided. There a sheep cultivates the compassion of a *śrāvaka*. The tree goddess on that mountain is called Supreme (Wusheng),[132] and there is a *rākṣasī* called Wholesome Conduct (Shanxing; Skt. Śīrṣupacālā?). They each are surrounded by five hundred dependents.These two females always make offerings together to these three animals.

"In the Southern Sea outside Jambudvīpa is a crystal mountain, in which there is a cave called Best Quality (Shangse). This is also a place where a bodhisattva formerly resided. There a rhesus monkey cultivates the compassion of a *śrāvaka*. There is another cave called Vow (Shiyuan), also a former residence of a bodhisattva. There a rooster cultivates the compassion of a *śrāvaka*. Again in another cave, called Dharma Seat (Fachuang), also a bodhisattva's former residence, a dog cultivates the compassion of a *śrāvaka*. In [the mountain] are the fire goddess and a *rākṣasī* called Seeing-by-Eyes (Yanjian), each of whom is surrounded by five hundred dependents. These two females always make offerings to the three animals including the rooster. 511b

"In the Western Sea outside Jambudvīpa is a silver mountain called Moon of Enlightenment (Putiyue), where there is a cave called Diamond (Jingang; Skt. Vajra), also a bodhisattva's former residence. There a boar cultivates the compassion of a *śrāvaka*. In another cave called Fragrant Merit (Xianggongde), a bodhisattva's former residence, a mouse cultivates the compassion of a *śrāvaka*. Again, in another cave called Lofty Merit (Gaogongde), also the former residence of a bodhisattva, a cow cultivates the compassion of a *śrāvaka*. On the mountain are the wind goddess called Stirring Wind (Dongfeng) and a *rākṣasī* called Heavenly Protection (Tianhu), each of whom is surrounded by five hundred dependents. These two females always make offerings to these three animals.

"In the Northern Sea outside Jambudvīpa is a golden mountain called Characteristics of Merit (Gongdexiang), in which there is a cave called Bright Star (Mingxing), also a bodhisattva's former residence. There a lion (called a tiger in this region) cultivates the compassion of a *śrāvaka*. In another cave called Pure Path (Jingdao), a bodhisattva's former residence, a rabbit cultivates the compassion of a *śrāvaka*. Again, in another cave called Joy (Xile), also the former residence of a bodhisattva, a dragon cultivates the compassion of a *śrāvaka*. In the mountain are the water goddess called Water Deity (Shuitian) and a *rākṣasī* called Cultivation of Shame (Xiucankui), each of whom is surrounded by five hundred dependents.These two females always make offerings to these three animals.

"These twelve animals go around in Jambudvīpa day and night at all times. They are respected by human and heavenly beings and accomplish

merits. They have already made a profound important vow at all buddhas' places. While one animal travels about to edify [sentient beings] for a day and night, the remaining eleven animals peacefully abide and cultivate compassion. Each in turn makes a round and then it starts over again. On the first day of the seventh month the mouse first goes around to edify all mice by virtue of the *śrāvaka* vehicle, causing them to abandon evil acts and urging them to cultivate wholesome things. In this way [the mouse] goes in order and on the twelfth day he returns and goes again.[133] In this way twelve months consequently come to an end. The cycle goes through to the twelfth year in this way as well. The twelve animals continually
511c control all sentient beings. Therefore there are many merits in this land. Even animals can edify [sentient beings] and speak on the path of highest enlightenment. For this reason all bodhisattvas of other lands should respect the world of this buddha."

I will explain [more] about these twelve animals. All these are the [expedient means] of bodhisattvas to edify [sentient beings] and lead them with compassion. Therefore, they take various forms such as that of a human being or of an animal. They preserve the world and cause it to not become extinct. Therefore, the human path first came into existence and is applicable to caves where these bodhisattvas resided, which now belong to these animals. [The animals] protect, maintain, and benefit [the world]. Therefore in China, the animals of the zodiac signs are used according this [sutra], not other sutras.

6. Arhats

According to the *Fufazang* [*yinyuan*] *zhuan* (T. 2058):

The Buddha entrusted the true Dharma to Mahākāśyapa and ordered him to protect and maintain it and to cause the king of Paranirmitavaśavartin Heaven, dragons, spirits, and kings and their servants who have wrong views to not possess it, slight it, or ruin it. After [Mahākāśyapa] received the entrustment, he held a meeting for compiling the Tripiṭaka and circulated it among human and heavenly beings. Kāśyapa further entrusted the [true] Dharma successively to Ānanda. In this way [the true Dharma] was passed down through many hands, altogether twenty-five people, until it came to Siṃha (Shizi). These are all sages of the six supernatural powers in Jambudvīpa. Mahākāśyapa is currently in a cave of the western peak of Vulture Peak (i.e., Gṛdhrakūtaparvata) where he sits in the meditation of complete extinction.

When Maitreya Buddha descends in five billion six hundred and seventy million years, he will transmit the *saṃghāṭī* [robe] entrusted to him by Śākyamuni Buddha. He will extensively reveal supernatural powers. Later he will enter nirvana.

Furthermore, in the state of Juqu, two thousand *li* south of the state of Kustana, three arhats who have nothing more to learn are in meditation in the mountains. For countless years they sit upright as if they are alive. On the fifteenth day foreign monks enter the mountains and shave [the arhats'] beards and hair. Moreover, according to various sutras and vinayas, the Buddha ordered the great arhat Piṇḍolabhāradvāja to not enter nirvana and to propagate the Buddhist Dharma in the three realms of existence, to bless and benefit sentient beings, and to cause them to escape the transmigration of birth and death.

The *Ru Dasheng lun* (T. 1634) further says:[134]

> The sixteen arhats who have nothing more to learn, such as Piṇḍolabhāradvāja and Rāhula, as well as nine billion and nine hundred million arhats all received *śalākā* (chips used for calculation) before the Buddha and abided in the Dharma without advance or retreat.

Furthermore, according to what a new translation of the *Da Aluohan Nantimiduoluo suoshuo fazhuji* (T. 2030; Skt. *Nandimitrāvadāna*) says:

> In eight hundred years, after the Bhagavān (i.e., the Buddha) entered *parinirvāṇa,* in the capital of King Mahāsena of Siṃhala there was an arhat called Nandimitra (called Qingyou, "Blessing Friend," in the Tang dynasty). He had already completed the conditions to edify people and was about to enter *parinirvāṇa.* He assembled all *bhikṣu*s and *bhikṣuṇī*s.
>
> [Nandimitra said,] "Those who have doubts should promptly ask me." [The assembly] was much obliged for his announcement and wept for a long time. They then asked, "We have not known until what time the superior, true Dharma given by the World-honored One Śākyamuni lasts." Then, Venerable [Nandimitra] said to them, "You! Listen to me attentively!

The Tathāgata has previously spoken the *Fazhu jing* (T. 390; Skt. *Mahāparinirvāṇa-sūtra*). I must now further briefly explain it for you. When the Buddha Bhagavān entered *parinirvāṇa,* he entrusted the highest
512a Dharma to sixteen great arhats and all their dependents. He ordered them to protect and maintain it, to cause it to not vanish, to be prudent in conduct, and to be a true field of merit for all donors; this causes the donors to attain great rewards."

After all the people heard these words, they understood a little but they were still anxious and sad. They repeatedly asked, "We do not know of the sixteen great arhats mentioned by you. What are their names?"

Qingyou (Nandimitra) replied, "The first venerable is called Piṇḍolabhāradvāja.[135] Together with his dependents, a thousand arhats, he mostly resides in Aparagodānīyadvīpa (i.e., Godānīyadvīpa, west of Mount Sumeru). The second venerable is called Kanakavatsa. Together with his dependents, five hundred arhats, he mostly resides in Kāśmīra in the north. The third venerable is called Kanakabharadvāja. Together with his dependents, six hundred arhats, he mostly resides in Pūrvavidehadvīpa in the east.

"The fourth venerable is called Śobhita (or Suvinda). Together with his dependents, seven hundred arhats, he mostly resides in Uttarakurudvīpa. The fifth venerable is called Nakula. Together with his dependents, eight hundred arhats, he mostly resides in Jambudvīpa. The sixth venerable is called Bhadra. Together with his dependents, nine hundred arhats, he mostly resides in the continent of Danmoluo. The seventh venerable is called Kālika. Together with his dependents, a thousand arhats, he mostly resides in the continent of Sengqietu. The eighth venerable is called Vajraputra. Together with his dependents, eleven hundred arhats, he mostly resides in the continent of Bolana. The ninth venerable is called Jīvaka. Together with his dependents, nine hundred arhats, he mostly resides on Mount Gandhamādana. The tenth venerable is called Panthaka. Together with his dependents, thirteen hundred arhats, he mostly resides in Trāyastriṃśa Heaven. The eleventh venerable is called Rāhula. Together with his dependents, eleven hundred arhats, he mostly resides in the continent of Biliyangqu. The twelfth venerable is called Nāgasena. Together with his dependents, twelve hundred arhats, he mostly resides on Mount Bandubo. The thirteenth venerable is called Aṅgaja. Together with his dependents, thirteen hundred arhats, he mostly resides on Mount Guangxie. The fourteenth venerable is called Vanavāsin. Together with his dependents, fourteen hundred arhats, he mostly resides on Mount Kezhu. The fifteenth venerable is called Ajita. Together with his dependents, fifteen hundred arhats, he mostly resides on Vulture Peak (i.e., Gṛdhrakūtaparvata). The sixteenth venerable is called Cūḍapanthaka. Together with his dependents, sixteen hundred arhats, he mostly resides on Mount Īṣadhara. 512b

"All these sixteen great arhats completely possess immeasurable merits such as the three transcendental knowledges, the six supernatural powers, and the eight stages of meditation for liberation (Skt. *aṣṭā-vimokṣa*). They have abandoned the defilements of the three realms of existence, recite and hold the Tripiṭaka, and have extensive knowledge of non-Buddhist books. They have received the Buddha's decree. Therefore, they extended their own life spans so that they can always follow, protect, and hold the World-honored One's true Dharma which must abide in this world, and they are a true field of merit for all donors; this causes the donors to attain great rewards.

"If all kings, prime ministers, ranking officials, elderly wealthy people, laypeople, and men and women in this world eagerly awaken aspiration for the pure mind, they will arrange either a great assembly for almsgiving for the sake of monks who come from the four directions, a *pañca-vārṣika* assembly,[136] a great assembly to celebrate the completion of a new monastery, a new buddha image, a new copy of a Buddhist scripture, or new banners, or a great meritorious assembly for a monk who was invited arrives at the place where he will reside. Otherwise, they visit such places as a walking place in a monastery to make a donation of fabric to the sangha and very good various mats for sitting and sleeping, clothes, medicine, and food and drink (i.e., the four necessities).

"At that time these sixteen great arhats and all their dependents, according to the place from which they have accepted an invitation, disperse and direct their courses. They manifest themselves in various forms, hiding their [original] sacred features. Appearing to be the same as ordinary people at all times, they secretly receive offerings and cause all donors to attain wonderful rewards. In this way the sixteen great arhats fully benefit sentient beings by protecting and maintaining the true Dharma.

"[The sixteen great arhats] come to this Jambudvīpa when human life span is extremely short.[137] When [the people] become ten years old, the disaster of war breaks out and they kill one another. At that time the Buddhist Dharma is about to temporarily vanish. After the war the people's life span gradually increases to about a hundred years. The people of this continent hate the previous war that caused heartless injury and put them in misery. They recover happiness and cultivate wholesomeness, and when these sixteen great arhats and all their dependents come to the human realm again they praise and clearly speak the highest true Dharma, liberate immeasurable sentient beings, and cause them to renounce the world. [The arhats] make abundant beneficial things for all sentient beings. In this way, consequently the life span of the people of this continent increases to sixty thousand years and then the highest true Dharma becomes prevalent and flourishes in this world endlessly. Later when the human life span becomes seventy thousand years, the highest true Dharma eternally vanishes.

"On that occasion the sixteen great arhats and all their dependents come and gather together in this continent. With supernatural powers they create a stupa of seven treasures, solemn, beautiful, lofty, and spacious, in which all the relics of Śākyamuni Tathāgata, Arhat, Samyak-saṃbuddha ("Fully Enlightened One") are collected. At that time the sixteen great arhats and all their dependents circumambulate the stupa. They bring various fragrant flowers to use as an offering. They respectfully sing the praises of [the stupa]. After circumambulating it a hundred thousand times, looking up respectfully and worshiping, they soar into the sky together. Facing toward the stupa they say, 'We salute the World-honored One,
512c Śākya[muni] Tathāgata, Arhat, Samyak-saṃbuddha! We previously received his orders to protect and maintain the true Dharma as well as to create various abundant benefits together with heavenly and human beings. The Dharma store has already vanished. Our relation to it has already been completed. Now we are leaving for nirvana.' After saying these words, they all enter nirvana without residue (Skt. *nirupadhiśeṣaṃ nirvanam*) at the same time. By the power of the vows previously made in meditation, a fire arises and burns up their bodies. Just like a blazing lamp it extinguishes their skeletons with nothing remaining. Then the stupa sinks into the earth and goes down to the edge of the diamond layer (i.e.,

the bottom of the lowest layer of the earth), where it stops and remains. At that time, the highest true Dharma of the World-honored One Śākyamuni is extinguished eternally and never reveals itself in this trichiliocosm.

"Right after this, in this buddha land seven thousand million billion *pratyekabuddhas* appear at the same time. When the human life span becomes eighty thousand years, the sacred group of *pratyekabuddhas* again all enter nirvana. Next, afterward Maitreya Tathāgata, Arhat, Samyaksaṃbuddha appears in the world. At that moment Jambudvīpa is expansive, solemn, and pure."

The details are just as is explained in the sutra.

7. Monks and Nuns

Just as the *Pinimu jing* (T. 1463; Skt. *Vinayamātṛkā*) says:

> If monks and nuns, those who renounce the world, have causes and conditions for five issues, they can cause the true Dharma to not quickly vanish. First, they completely possess the phrases of sutras learned by recitation, are able to investigate exhaustively the sequences and all significances, and further teach their followers and disciples in order to cause them [to understand] the same as what they know. Such a person can cause the Buddhist Dharma to last long in this world. Second, they extensively learn the Tripiṭaka, completely possess the meanings of the passages, and are further able to teach the four categories of Buddhists (monks, nuns, laymen, and laywomen) in accordance with what they understand. Even though they die, they cause the true Dharma to continue without being disrupted in later ages. Such a person can cause the true Dharma to not be cast down. Third, if in the sangha there is a senior monk of great virtue who is valued by the four categories of Buddhists, who is able to diligently cultivate the three kinds of acts, and who gives up managing secular affairs, then his followers and disciples will continue [his practice] one after another. If everything goes like this, such a person also causes the true Dharma to last long. Fourth, if there is a *bhikṣu* whose nature is gentle, whose speech contains no contradictions, who hears of wholesomeness and follows it, and who hears of evils and keeps far away, or if there is [a *bhikṣu*] who is outstandingly talented, intelligent, and virtuous, if [such

a person] gives instruction, [other people] wll receive his words with respect and practice it. This person also can cause the Buddhist Dharma to last long. Finally, if *bhikṣus* are mutually compliant, they will neither help one another in factions to benefit their own situations nor dispute right or wrong. [Such *bhikṣus* will also cause the Buddhist Dharma to last long]. These five issues can cause the true Dharma to spread without disruption. This is called the upper seat in preaching the Dharma.

8. Wealthy People of Virtue

Just as the *Youposai jie jing* (T. 1488) says:

At that time there was a son of a wealthy person of virtue in the assembly called Sujāta. He addressed the Buddha, "O World-honored One! The six non-Buddhist masters always speak their teachings and instruct sentient
513a beings. They say, 'If you can respectfully worship the six directions in the morning, you will be able to increase your wealth and lengthen your life span. Why? The eastern land belongs to Śakra-devendra, who protects and helps those who make an offering to him. The southern land belongs to King Yama, who protects and helps those who make an offering to him. The western land belongs to the god Varuṇa, who protects and helps those who make an offering to him. The northern land belongs to the god Kubera, who protects and helps those who make an offering to him. The lower land belongs to the god of fire, Agni, who protects and helps those who make an offering to him. The upper land belongs to the god of wind, Vāyu, who protects and helps those who make an offering to him.' Is there something much like these six directions in the Buddhist Dharma?"

The Buddha replied, "Good man! In my Buddhist Dharma there are also six directions, what are called the six *pāramitās*. The east is precisely [the *pāramitā* of] giving alms (Skt. *dāna*). Why? Because what appears at the beginning is the origin that emits the light of wisdom. The east belongs to the minds of sentient beings. If there is a sentient being who can make an offering to the [*pāramitā* of] giving alms, his life span and wealth will increase. The south is precisely [the *pāramitā* of] the precepts (Skt. *śīla*). Why? The term *śīla* is designated as an honor. If someone makes an offering to this, he will also be able to increase his life span and wealth. The west is precisely [the *pāramitā* of] forbearance (Skt. *kṣānti*).

Why? The west is designated as the rear, because all evil things are left behind. Those who make an offering to it will be able to increase their life span and wealth. The north is precisely [the *pāramitā* of] diligence (Skt. *vīrya*).[138] Why? The name of the north is Victory Over All Evil Things. Those who make an offering to it will also be able to increase their life span and wealth. The lower direction is precisely [the *pāramitā* of] meditation (Skt. *dhyāna*). Why? Because the three evil realms can be correctly observed through it. Those who make an offering to it will also be able to increase their life span and wealth. The upper direction is precisely [the *pāramitā* of] transcendental wisdom (Skt. *prajñā*). Why? The upper direction is supreme. Because it is supreme, those who make an offering to it will be able to increase their life span and wealth.

"Good man! These six directions belong to the minds of sentient beings. They are not just like what the six non-Buddhist masters speak of."

[Sujāta asked,] "Who can make offerings to these six directions?"

[The Buddha replied,] "Good man! Only bodhisattvas can make offerings to them."

9. Heavenly Kings

Just as the *Shelifu wen jing* (T. 1465) says:

> Śāriputra addressed the Buddha, "Why did you, the Tathāgata, say to Śakra-devendra as well as the four heavenly kings, 'I will soon enter nirvana. Each of you, protect and maintain my Dharma at your own locality. After I leave the world, the four great *bhikṣus* Mahākāśyapa, Piṇḍolabhāradvāja, Kuṇḍapadhaṇiyaka, and Rāhula will remain without entering nirvana and circulate my Dharma'?"
>
> The Buddha replied, "At the time when the semblance teaching [is practiced] the root of faith will be weak and fragile. Even though people [can] awaken to faith, they cannot firmly keep it and they cannot be moved by all the Buddha's disciples. Even if someone exclusively tries to achieve [the Way] for many years, it will not be as good as the wholesomeness of one thought made during the time the Buddha resided in the world. Therefore, Maitreya will descend to be reborn [in this world] and allow you to enter nirvana." 513b

The *Za ahan jing* (T. 99) further says:

> At that time the World-honored One said to Śakra-devendra and the four heavenly kings, "I, the Tathāgata, will soon enter into nirvana without residue (Skt. *nirupadhiśeṣaṃ nirvanam*) and *parinirvāṇa.* Each of you, protect and maintain my Dharma at your own locality. When the Dharma is extinguished a thousand years after my nirvana, a wrong law will appear in the world. The ten wholesome acts will be completely annihilated and a great number of various troubles will fill Jambudvīpa. The Tathāgata's skull [relic], the Buddha's teeth [relics], and the Buddha's almsbowl will be placed in the east."

(After this, [the sutra] tells of heavenly kings, Śakra-devendra, the four kings, and the six desires. They are fully described in the sutra. It is impossible to explain it in detail here.)

Moreover, the *Sheng tianwang* [*banruo boluomi*] *jing* (T. 231) says:

> Again, sentient beings saw that this bodhisattva had only just attained enlightenment, or that the Bodhisattva had attained enlightenment in the remotest past. Again, [sentient beings] saw that in one world the four heavenly kings presented an almsbowl [to the Bodhisattva], or that the four heavenly kings presented an almsbowl to him in worlds in the ten directions as numerous as grains of sand in the Ganges River. Śāriputra! At that time the Bodhisattva liberated sentient beings. Therefore, he received many almsbowls.
>
> He held [all the bowls] one over the other in his hand and combined them into one. All the heavenly kings did not see this. Every one of them thought, "The World-honored One uses only my almsbowl."

Furthermore, according to what the [*Fo*]*boji* (*Records of the Buddha's Bowl*) says:[139]

> When Śākya[muni] Tathāgata resided in the world he used the blue stone almsbowl, which had a capacity of more than three *dou.* After the Buddha's nirvana, in accordance with the law of conditions that bowl went to bless sentient beings. At last the edification left by [the Buddha] arose in the Chinese territory. This record came from North India. There were a couple of sheets of paper that arrived at Shijian Monastery in the third month of

the Jiazi year. Saṃghayaśas, a young meditation master, made it publicly known in the Chinese land.

10. Spiritual Beings

Just as the [*Dafangdeng*] *daji jing* says:

At that time the various heavenly beings, all the various dragons, and even all *koṭa-pūtana*s (extremely malodorous spirits) attained increasing powerful and superior faith in the Three Treasures. They made this [vow], "From now on we will all protect and maintain the true Dharma."

If all kings see that there are those who renounce the world and receive and hold the Buddhist precepts for the Buddha's sake in this way, those who shave their beards and hair for the Buddha and yet who do not receive the Buddhist precepts, those who have received [the precepts] and yet violate them, or those who do not accumulate any [good], and if it is the case where in accordance with the condition of the event [those kings] punish and flog such people with a whip, we will no longer protect, maintain, raise, and educate such kings and we will abandon them and leave their countries. Once we abandon and leave them, their lands will have various flattery, frauds, fights, epidemics, famines, and wars. Accompanying those, the wind and rain [will come at] the wrong time, and drought and intense heat will arise. The rice plant seedlings will be damaged. We will cause all the World- 513c
honored One's *śrāvaka* disciples in their countries to depart and go to other countries. We will cause their countries to become empty and have no field of merit. If there are the World-honored One's *śrāvaka* disciples or even those who wear just a fragment of a *kaṣāya* [robe], if there is the case where an official flogs them with a whip and the *kṣatriya* king does not protect them from [that official], we will leave that country as well.

Again, the [*Dafangdeng*] *daji jing* says:

At that time the World-honored One entrusted China to Viśvakarman and his five thousand dependents, the head of the *yakṣa*s Kapila and his five thousand dependents, up to the Great Heavenly Woman Shuangtongmu and her [five thousand dependents].[140] Each of seventeen great generals leads their five thousand dependents.

[The Buddha said,] "You! Genial men (Skt. *bhadramuka*)! Protect and maintain the Chinese land together! Cause all that land's tactile defilements, fights, enmity, anger, competitions, disputes, battles between two camps, famines, epidemics, wind and rain at the wrong time, freezing cold, and intense heat to completely stop! Block unwholesomeness and all evils! Cause sentient beings' anger, rudeness, hardships, tactile defilements, and tasteless things to completely come to an end! This is because you enable my Dharma eye to last long, and because you hand down the seed of the Three Treasures without ceasing to exist."

Verses say:

Ah! Great Sage!
He realizes all things completely and clearly.
Every wrong is examined.
Just like an echo he rewards our voices.
If he does not aid us by extending blessing,
Who would awaken and return to sincerity?
Truly the [Buddhist] Way should be revered.
It truly guides deluded sentient beings.
Even the evil waves of a hundred rivers are
Swallowed altogether as one taste.
There are accepting and refusing things.
There is, however, no waxing and waning of good and bad.
The eightfold wrong path vigorously spreads.
With the four lines (i.e., *gāthās*) [the evil] struggles for fame.
If we know wrong and examine right,
The Dharma will abide peacefully.

[End of] Fascicle Thirty of *A Forest of Pearls from the Dharma Garden*

Fascicle 31

515a

Chapter Twenty-three

Seclusion

(This chapter consists of two parts:) (1) Introduction and (2) Quoted Testimonies.

1. Introduction

I have heard that when sages and virtuous people adapt themselves to the times, their traces (i.e., ways to educate people) have no set pattern. All countries where they reside are benefited. Earthly people adhere to their fortune. The wisest people are undisturbed by good or evil. If one waits for the time with a right mind, he will be equal to heaven.

Formerly, during the reign of Emperor Wu (265–290) of the Jin dynasty, there was Jīvaka from India. At the beginning of the reign of Emperor Wu (420–422) of the Song dynasty, there was Beidu in Pengcheng. They both revealed auspicious signs and brightly awakened the common people. In the Qi (479–502) and Liang (502–557) dynasties there was the *śramaṇa* Baozhi, who appeared for the first time in the beginning of the Yongming era (483–493). He seemed dark and insane; his body was as black as dirt, but he had stored up [knowledge of events] in the past and knew [what would happen] in future. Frequently in the midst of miracles he sat up straight and expressed his words. It was rare for him to make a mistake. The common people followed him, yet his whereabouts were as elusive as clouds. While his manifested form was covered in dust and dirt, his spirit roamed in a profound and tranquil state. Even water could not make him wet, and fire could not scorch him. Snakes and tigers could not attack and harm him. Even if he was repeatedly restricted to Jiuguan [where the Lord of Heaven resides], his body had no hindrance after all. When he spoke about the Buddhist doctrine he did so more skillfully than *śrāvaka*s. When he talked about his secret logic, he was like a hermit or someone of noble character.

Since it is possible for something good to be in the world, wholesomeness arises in response, and since evil is also possible, unwholesomeness comes out in response. It can be said that [Jīvaka, Beidu, and Baozhi] are as like suspended from the sun or moon or sheltered under metal or stone. Boundless merit is seen here!

2. Quoted Testimonies

Just as the *Sheng jing* (T. 154) says:

> The Buddha said to the *bhikṣu*s, "Once in the past, incalculable *kalpa*s ago, there were a sister and her younger brother. The sister had a son, and the son, along with his uncle, served the court as weavers. They saw rare treasures and good things in the treasury and discussed and said, 'We weave assiduously, in spite of hardships, and now know about many goods in the treasury. We had better take some and use them to relieve our poverty.' They watched [and waited] for the people to become still, then bored a tunnel through the ground and stole government property of incalculable quantity.
>
> "The next day the superintendent of the treasury realized that some of the goods had decreased in number and reported it to the king. The king proclaimed, 'Do not announce it publicly and cause outsiders to know about this. The thieves, an uncle and his nephew, think that I, the king, am unaware of it.' The king said, 'They will certainly return some day.
> 515b Just guard closely and wait for them to come. When you catch them, detain them. Do not let them escape!' The superintendent of the treasury received the edict and increased the guards.
>
> "After a long time the [two] men returned to steal again. The nephew instructed his uncle, 'Uncle! You are now old. You have a weak constitution and little strength. If you are caught by a guard you will not be able to escape by yourself. My strength is great and vigorous. I will rescue you, uncle.' The uncle entered into the hole and was arrested by a guard, who called all the other guards. The nephew grabbed [his uncle], but he could not overpower [the guard]. Afraid that they would discover [the uncle's identity], the next day [the nephew] cut off his uncle's head, came out of the tunnel, and returned home carrying [the severed head].

"At daybreak the next day the superintendent of the treasury thoroughly reported [the events to the king]. The king again proclaimed, 'Take out the corpse on a carriage and place it at a crossroads. If anyone weeps over it and tries to retrieve the corpse, it will the head of the thieves.' [The corpse] was abandoned at a crossroads and watched for days.

"People and horses filled the area and they ran swiftly, blocking the roads. The thief (i.e., the nephew) loaded firewood onto two vehicles with a great noise and then piled it on the corpse. A guard reported this to the king. The king proclaimed, 'Watch secretly! If someone comes to burn it, arrest, bind him, and bring him to me!' Thereupon the nephew instructed some boys to carry torches and dance around. The large crowd of people was noisy. A torch was thrown onto the firewood and it burned fiercely. The guards could not determine [who had lit the pyre]. They fully reported this to the king. The king again proclaimed, 'If [the body] has been cremated, then increase [the guards]. Watch [the remains] closely! Whoever comes to take the remains is the head [of the thieves].'

"The nephew was again aware of [the trap]. Simultaneously [with the incident mentioned above] he brewed wine without permission, making [the wine of] particularly superior quality. He then secretly took the wine to sell to the guards. The guards were hungry and thirsty every night. When they saw the wine, they crowded together and drank it. They drank too much, became drunk, and passed out. [The nephew] then put the remains into wine bottles and left. The guards were not aware of it.

"The next day the guards again reported to the king. Again the king proclaimed, 'Although we kept close watch both front and rear, we were not able to get the decapitated head after all. This rebel is cunning. We must set another plan.'

"The king then picked out his daughter, adorned with treasures. The girl calmly stood in a chamber. On the bank of a river many people guarded her, watching for anything wrong or reckless. Certainly someone would try to come to the girl desiring carnal pleasure. She would welcome him, catch him, cry out, and cause the people to detain him.

"On a night some other day the nephew came stealthily looking for [the girl]. He pushed a stump into the river and let it float away with the stream's current. He then cried out, shouted, and ran away. The hidden guards, surprised, went to the place, thinking there was an unusual person there, but they saw only the stump of a tree. This [occurrence] frequently went on in exactly this way all through the night every day. The guards [became used to it, disregarded it,] and fell asleep. The nephew then rode on the stump and arrived at the girl's chamber.

"The girl grasped his garments. The nephew said to her, 'Rather than holding onto my clothes you should hold my arms.' The nephew was very cunning by nature. He had come prepared with the [severed] arms from a corpse which he now handed to the girl. She let go of his clothes, grasped the arms, shouted loudly, and waited for the guards to wake up. The nephew was able to escape.

"The next day [the guards] reported to the king in detail. Again, the king proclaimed, 'This person used expedient means. He has creative talentand no equal [in the world]. We have tried to arrest him for a long time but we have not been able to do so. What should we do now?'

"The girl became pregnant and gave birth to a boy in ten months. The boy was very well-featured. [The king] had a wet nurse take [the baby boy]
515c and travel all over the country. [He said,] 'If there is anyone who sees the baby and makes cooing sound at him, capture him and bring him to me!'

"[The wet nurse] carried the baby all day long but no one fondled it or made cooing sound. The nephew had become a seller of cookies and lived under a furnace. The baby cried with hunger, so holding the baby the wet nurse went to that place and bought some cookies to feed to the baby. When the nephew saw the baby he made a [gentle] cooing sound at it. [The wet nurse] fully reported this to the king. The king again proclaimed, 'Why did you not capture and bring him to me?' The wet nurse replied, 'The baby cried with hunger. A seller of cookies gave him some cookies and made a [gentle] cooing sound for [the baby]. I did not know that he is the thief. Why do you wish to imprison him?'[141]

"The king again told the wet nurse to hold the baby and go out. [He said to her,] 'If you see anyone come close to the baby, capture him and lead him here!'

"The nephew now sold good wine. He called the wet nurse and spies and offered some wine to them. They became drunk and fell asleep. Then [the nephew] stole the baby away. When they sobered up and awoke, the baby was gone. They reported to the king in detail. The king again proclaimed, 'You are stubborn and stupid! You greedily relished alcohol and did not capture the thief, and furthermore you have now lost the baby.'

"The nephew had now obtained the baby. Taking [the baby] he went to another country. Seeing the king [of that country], he advanced and expressed thanks to him, and responded to his questions. Referring to sutras, he explained the meaning. The king was very happy and offered [the nephew] an official salary and rank, appointing him as a ranking official. [The king] said to him, 'In my country there is no one who matches you in wisdom and expedient means. I wish to give a girl in marriage to you, or my daughter must become your mate. Tell me exactly what you want!' [The nephew] replied, 'I dare not do so. If you, king, see and have pity for the realities of my life, I would like to ask for a princess from my home country.' The king said, 'Good! I will comply with your ambition.' The king who personally considered [the nephew] to be his son sent a messenger to ask for a princess [from the man's home country]. The king [of the nephew's original country] promptly agreed, and he sent a messenger [to report,] 'I would like you to come to receive my princess. Please dispatch that crown prince.'[142]

"Five hundred well-disciplined warriors on horseback were [mustered]. Because the nephew was a [hunted] thief, he felt afraid. [He thought,] 'If I go to that country the king will certainly realize it is me and I will undoubtedly be arrested.' So he addressed the king [who favored him], 'O king! If I am to be sent to that country, you must make sure that the people's clothing and the horses' saddles and bridles are all the same. I can then go to receive my wife.' The king affirmed his request and ordered to arrange two hundred fifty mounted warriors on horseback in the front and another two hundred fifty mounted warriors on horseback in the back. The nephew was in the middle of [the entourage]. He mounted a horse and did not get off.

"The girl's father, [the king,] personally came out and observed the [company] again and again. The king rode among the warriors on horseback, personally captured the nephew, and came out. [He said to the nephew,] 'You did these evils. You used expedient means of [dividing the group] in the front and the back. It was impossible to arrest you!' [The nephew] bowed his head to the ground and replied, 'Indeed, you are right.' The king said, 'Your sagacity is matchless in the world. According to what you wish, I will match you with my daughter. [You two] can become a married couple.'"

The Buddha said to all *bhikṣu*s, "If you wish to know, the nephew of that time was myself; the king of the foreign country was Śāriputra; the uncle was Devadatta of today; the girl's father king was Śuddhodana; the mother was Lady Māyā; the wife was Gopikā; and the son was Rāhula." When the Buddha said this, everyone rejoiced.

516a Moreover, the [*Da*] *zhidu lun* says:

Bodhisattvas ponder and meditate on the characteristics of emptiness and impermanence. Therefore, even if they have the exquisite five desires, they do not give rise to any defilement. For instance, it is just as the ranking official of a king conceals his sin in the mind, and other people do not know it. The king says, "Go get a [healthy] sheep without fat and bring it to me! If you do not obtain it I will punish you." The ranking official uses his wits: he ties up a big sheep and feeds it well with grass and grain. But three times a day he allows a wolf to threaten and frighten it, so even though the sheep is well-nourished and big, it has no fat. [The ranking official] then takes the sheep and gives it to the king. The king sends a man to butcher [the sheep], which is big but does not have fat. The king asks, "What did you do to obtain such [a sheep]?" The answer is what was described above. Bodhisattvas are also like this. They see the wolves of impermanence, suffering, and emptiness and the fat of all defilements is extinguished while the flesh of all merits grows big.

Again, the *Xianyu jing* (T. 202) says:

At that time in Magadha there was a wealthy man of virtue, to whose wife a boy was born. The baby had complete features and was very lovable and respectable. On the day of his birth a golden elephant spontaneously appeared in the [family's] storehouse. [The baby's] parents were happy. Because of this good omen, a pseudonym was established [for the baby]; he was called Nāgapāla.

As the boy gradually grew older, the elephant also grew. When the boy was able to walk, the elephant walked, too. [The elephant] was never separated from [the boy] whenever [the boy] went out, returned, advanced, or stopped. If [the boy] thought he did not need [the elephant], then [the elephant] stayed in [the storehouse]. Instead of urine and feces when the elephant relieved itself, there was only good-quality gold. For this reason the storehouse was filled with treasures. When Nāgapāla grew up, he always traveled to the east or to the west riding [the elephant], and the animal went slowly or swiftly according to [Nāgapāla's] wish. The elephant was in accordance with his feelings.

King Ajātaśatru heard [about the elephant] and asked [Nāgapāla] to show it. Nāgapāla and his father rode the elephant and arrived at the [palace] gate. The king allowed them to enter [the palace] riding the elephant. They dismounted from the elephant and paid their respects to the king. The king was greatly delighted. He ordered them to be seated, offered meals to them, and had a brief discussion with them. Shortly they said good-bye to the king and were about to leave. The king said to Nāgapāla, "I will keep the elephant here. Do not depart with it!" Nāgapāla sadly accepted [the king's] instruction with respect, left [the elephant], and walked out of the palace empty-handed. Not long after, the elephant submerged into the earth and it rose up again outside the [palace] gate. Nāgapāla took it back and then rode on it.

Nāgapāla worried about being killed by the king [for having taken the elephant]. So he joined the Buddha, renounced the world, and attained the path of arhatship. He always pondered on one thing (Skt. *cetanā*) together with other *bhikṣu*s in a forest. The golden elephant was before his eyes all the time.

The people of Śrāvastī heard that there was a golden elephant and vied with one another to go see it. [Their gathering] was [extremely] noisy and unpeaceful. [The *bhikṣu*s] were disturbed and stopped practicing the [Buddhist] Way. At that time all the *bhikṣu*s expressed their thoughts to the Buddha. The Buddha said to Nāgapāla, "Because of this [elephant, the sangha] has become disrupted. Send it away, order it to leave!" [The elephant,] however, was unwilling to leave [Nāgapāla]. The Buddha again said [to Nāgapāla], "You must say to [the elephnant], 'I have already exhausted the fate allotted in my current life. I no longer need you.' If you repeat it three times in this way, the elephant will be extinguished." At that time Nāgapāla received [the Buddha's] instruction with respect and spoke to [the elephant]. At that moment the golden elephant entered into the earth.

The Buddha said to the *bhikṣu*s, "Why does [Nāgapāla] obtain this reward? In the past, at the time of Kāśyapa Buddha, the human life span
516b was twenty thousand years. After that buddha's nirvana, stupas were erected. Inside one of the stupas there was an image of the Bodhisattva who rode [an elephant] when he originally descended from Tuṣita Heaven to enter the womb [of Lady Māyā].[143] At that time a small piece of the elephant's body came off. A person found the broken part and repaired it. Accordingly he made a vow, 'Please, in the future, may I have noble status and no financial deficiency!' That person died and was reborn in heaven. He completed his life in heaven and descended to be reborn in the world. He remained noble constantly. He had a golden elephant that followed, attended, and guarded him. The person who repaired [the image of] the elephant at that time was Nāgapāla of today. Since he repaired the elephant [image], he spontaneously receives this merit. According to his respectful mind he believes in the Three Revered Ones. Therefore, he has now encountered me and attained the [Buddhist] Way."

The *Za baozang jing* further says:

In former times King Milinda (Greek Menandros) was bright and erudite, skilled in everything. He claimed that in knowledge there was no match for him. A group of his vassals had no answer to this.

On one occasion all the vassals addressed the king, "There is a *bhikṣu* called Nāgasena who is matchlessly bright. He now resides in the mountains." The king wished to test him and sent a messenger to offer a bottle of *koumiss,*[144] filled to the brim. The king did this with the implication, "My wisdom is perfect. Who might be able to add more to it?" Nāgasena received the *koumiss* and immediately understood the [king's] intention. From his disciples he collected five hundred needles and thrust them into the *koumiss,* yet the *koumiss* still did not spill over the brim. Subsequently he sent it back to the king. On receiving it the king understood [Nāgasena's] intention. He quickly sent a messenger to invite Nāgasena, who came and was led into the palace. The king gave him coarse food. After having three or five spoonfuls of the food [Nāgasena] said that he was already sated. Later exquisite delicious food was given, and at that time he again ate. The king asked him, "Previously you said you were already sated. Why do you now eat again just as you did before?" Nāgasena replied, "Previously, I was full of coarse food but not yet sated with exquisite food."

Then [Nāgasena,] facing the king, said, "You should now gather all the people in your hall and cause it to be filled." [The king] subsequently summoned people to gather in [the hall] until there was no more room left. The king arrived later and wished to enter the hall. Since all the people were afraid of him, they all completely prostrated from fear. The interior [of the hall] then became spacious and could hold many more people. At that time, Nāgasena said to the king, "Coarse food is just like these people and exquisite [delicious food] is just like you, the king. When the people see the king, who does not withdraw from his way?"

The king again asked, "Who attains the [Buddhist] Way, those who have renounced the world or those who remain householders?" Nāgasena answered, "Both attain the [Buddhist] Way." Again the king asked, "If both [householders and renunciants] can attain the [Buddhist] Way, why is it necessary to renounce the world?" Nāgasena replied, "For instance, it is just like traveling more than three thousand *li* from here. If you dispatch a healthy youth on a horse with provisions and a weapon in his hand, he can reach there promptly, can he not?" The king answered, "Yes, he can." [Nāgasena said,] "If you dispatch an old man on a [frail,] lean horse, moreover having no provisions, do you think he can reach there?" The king answered, "Even if he had provisions, I am afraid that he would still not reach there, not to mention having no provisions." Nāgasena responded 516c
to [the king], "Those who have renounced the world and attain the [Buddhist] Way can be compared to the healthy youth. Those who remain householders and attain the [Buddhist] Way are just like the old man."

The king further asked, "As for the sun above us, its essence is singular. Why is it extremely hot in summer and tremendously cold in winter? In summer the daytime is long, but in winter it is short." Nāgasena replied, "On Mount Sumeru there are upper and lower paths. In the summer the sun goes on the upper path. It is a long road and the sun moves slowly, shining on the golden mountains. Therefore the daytime is long and has scorching heat. In winter the sun goes on the lower path. It is a short road and [the sun] moves swiftly, shining on the great sea. [Therefore, the daytime] is short and it is tremendously cold."

Verses say:

Seclusion is a skillful change.
Making wholesomeness spreads in the unseen world.
How great is the one of benevolence and intelligence!
The policemen from the palace undergo a transition.
The sheep grows big without becoming fat.
Nāgapāla is accompanied by a heavenly being.
Merit complies with what we receive.
In the unseen fate we unite with [the Buddha's] faculty.
Tranquility is deep silence.
Movement is brightness of the spirit.
Everlastingly we are managed from a distance,[145]
Through the long ties full of earnest activity.
No image is [found] when we return to the origin.[146]
The light is hidden and the shadow is gone.
His hiding and revealing are unpredictable.
Truth or falsity is difficult to know.

Miracle Stories

(Thirteen stories are briefly cited.)

[Liu Sahe, a *Śramaṇa* of the Western Jin Dynasty]

During the Western Jin dynasty there was a shrine called the Shrine for Master Liu Sahe to the west of Anren Temple in a town of [current] Ci province. Formerly, in the final years of the Western Jin dynasty (265–316), this area was originally called Wencheng prefecture, [named for] a place where Lord Wen of Jin found a shelter. On the tableland to the southeast not far from [Ci] province lived a man called Sahe, whose family name was Liu. The shrine dedicated to him was magnificent and gorgeous.

Sahe was no different from ordinary people [before he renounced the world]; he often thought of destruction of life and did not revere the [Buddhist] Dharma at all. Sahe died from an illness but he rose from the dead. He said, "I saw Avalokiteśvara in the netherworld, who said to me, 'Your sin is heavy. You must receive suffering [in hell]. I, however, think that your sin was caused by your ignorance. I will let you go for the time being and bring you back to life. The stupas of King Aśoka are located in Luoyang, Qicheng, Danyang, and Guiji. You may go and worship there. Then you will be absolved of your former sin.'" Sahe reformed his previous conduct after he revived.

[According to] local custom the Buddha was not worshiped [in that place]. 517a
[Liu Sahe] heard that [the Buddha was worshiped] in a town [in Ci province] so he went there and asked questions in detail. He began to edify the people with expedient means and spread the benevolent way (i.e., Buddhism). The people of the Ji tribe [of that area] were especially upright and honest. They believed in what [Sahe] taught. Every year on the eighth day of the fourth month a large number of people gathered on the tableland. Everyone brought wine and pastries as well as offerings of vegetarian food. From dawn till noon they drank as much as they could and had fun while offering the vegetarian food. At noon they stopped [drinking and amusing themselves], and in the afternoon they glorified the Buddha together and sang praises for the Three Treasures. Then they stayed until dawn of the next day.

[Liu] Sahe subsequently renounced the world. His Dharma name is Huida. The common people looked up at him and respected him as if recollecting the Buddha. Moreover, Sahe performed miracles and the people's faith in him grew stronger. During the day he expounded for the people in a high stupa, and at night he entered a cocoon to conceal himself. He came out of the cocoon in the early morning. At first he did not fix his abode. Therefore the people called him Sage Suhe; the word *suhe* means "cocoon" in the Ji tribal language. He was called so because he spent the night in a cocoon. Due to this, today according to that local custom every village has a Buddhist temple with a standing figure of [Liu Sahe]. [His statue] is called the Buddha of the Tribal People's Teacher.

The statue presently worshiped in the shrine of Anren Temple is extremely dignified [in appearance]. Many local people offer prayers and vows to the statue. In the first month every year the statue is put on a palanquin and is carried on a tour from village to village. What village will be visited is determined by the will of the statue; it cannot be controlled by human effort. If the statue intends to go to a certain village, only two people can lift and carry it. If the mark on the statue's forehead is clear and its facial expression is peaceful and happy, few people in that village will die or decline in health for an entire year. [On the contrary,] if the statue does not want to go to another village it cannot be moved even by ten people. If the mark of its forehead shrivels and it has a sad and gloomy appearance, that village will certainly experience calamity in the coming year. Therefore even today people often consider [the reaction and appearance of the statue] to tell their fortune.

The people also think that [Huida] is Avalokiteśvara, who temporarily transformed in order to edify them and who called himself Huida for that reason. A sutra [supposedly composed by Huida] is circulated among the common people. It was written entirely in a tribal language. If people read it, they spontaneously understand it. Therefore, in the lands of the eight provinces along the Yellow River, Ci, Xi, Lan, Shi, Dan, Yan, Sui, and Yin,[147] there is no one who does not respectfully believe in the teaching. All the people perform the religious functions just as [Huida] explained. Even today, on each of these tablelands, an earthen stupa stands. A pole made out of cypress wood is affixed to the top [of the stupa] and a cocoon is connected to the pole. This is modeled after Huida's style of living.

After propagating Buddhism in his home village, [Liu] Sahe traveled east to Danyang, where he worshiped many stupas. After that, he went west to [Mount] Yuyu in Fanhe county in Liang province, where he worshiped a [buddha] image that had appeared from the mountain. He continued traveling and passed away in the desert to the west of Jiuquan city in Su province. His remains are scant and look like sunflower seeds. There is a hole in the center of each bone, and they can be strung together [like beads]. So in local custom a person who has a disaster simply goes to the desert and looks for [one of the bones] and if he is able to find it his misfortune will end, but if he is not his fortune is lost. Someone once looked for [a bone] but could not find it. So he took a bone [from the left hand] of the Avalokiteśvara image. When night came, the bone [that he had taken] disappeared. When he looked for it the next morning, it had returned onto the hand of the [Avalokiteśvara] image. Due to this incident, the local people's esteem for the bones increased.

[Beidu, a *Śramaṇa* of the Western Jin Dynasty]

The original domicile of the *śramaṇa* Beidu of the Western Jin dynasty is unknown. He came from Jizhou and was around seventy years old,but he did not reveal his family name. He did not ardently pursue [Buddhist] practice. and the people of that time did not yet value him. He once lodged at someone's house where there was a golden image. Beidu got up at daybreak and left with [the golden image]. The master of the house chased him, whipping his horse [to go faster], but even though Beidu went slowly, [the master] who rushed his horse could not catch up with him. [Beidu] came to the Mengjin River and crossed over it in a small cup. Accordingly, he was called Beidu ("Crossing Over in a Cup"). 517b

Later the people often saw him in Pengcheng. He was always [seen] on a road. No one knew where he lived. Shouldering a bamboo container, he went or stayed in accordance with his feeling. One early morning when [soft] snow congealed he pounded ice and washed and bathed himself. The color of his skin was luminous and he did not appear to be cold and miserable.

During the Yixi era (405–418) he temporarily stayed in Guangling. Liu Fan of Peiguo, Regional Inspector [of Yanzhou], had previously heard [Beidu's] name. The Buddhist practitioner (i.e., Liu Fan) wished [to see him]. [Beidu] came still carrying the bamboo container on the shoulder. [Liu Fan] bade his people to lift up [the container], and though they tried repeatedly they were not successful. Fan personally got up to examine it. There was only a tattered Buddhist surplice [in the container]. When Beidu left there, he carried the bamboo container in his hand as if it were as light as swan's down.

[Beidu] passed away during the Yongchu era (420–422).[148] Kumārajīva heard that Beidu was in Pengcheng. He lamented, "I used to play with this youngster. It has been several hundreds of years since we parted from each other." At that time [the people] awoke to the fact that Kumārajīva was also a holy man.

[Zhu Fotudeng, a *Śramaṇa* of the Western Jin Dynasty]

Toward the end of the Western Jin dynasty was Zhu Fotudeng, a man from the Western Region (i.e., Central Asia). In appearance he seemed to be about a hundred years old. There was an opening on the left side of his torso, about four or five *cun* around. He filled it in with silk fabric. On the day of purification he went to the waterside and pulled his intestines and stomach out through the hole. After washing them, he put them back through the opening. At night he removed the silk fabric. Light [poured out of the opening] illuminating his room, and he read books. Even if he never understood thoroughly a multitude of books, when he debated and explained with various scholars he had no hindrance. So everyone held him in high esteem.

During the Yongjia era (307–313) he traveled to Luo[yang], at the time Shi Le stationed troops in Hebei and menaced people by killing. Many monks and laymen were murdered. Fotudeng went to [Shi Le's] camp gate and foretold whether he would have good or back luck [in his battles]. Every time [Shi] Le saw [Fotudeng] he bowed to him. Fotudeng edified [Shi Le] and caused him to believe in the Buddhist [Dharma]. [Shi Le] lessened the cruelties and reduced punishments. Because of this, in the central district (i.e., present-day Hebei province) eighty or ninety percent of the people escaped from [being killed].

[Shi] Le and Liu Yao had a conflict and split from each other. Thereby [Shi Le] consulted with Fotudeng, who said, "You will capture him alive. What are you worried about?" Applying sesame oil on the palm of his hand, [Fotudeng] had [Shi Le] look at it. [In the oil Shi Le] saw that [Liu] Yao was arrested and his elbows were bound with a red rope. Later, as a matter of fact [Shi Le] captured [Liu Yao] in just the same way as what he had seen in the palm of [Zhu Fotudeng's] hand.

On the eighth day of the fourth month of the fourth year of the Jianping era (333) [Shi] Le went to a monastery and sprinkled hydrangea tea on the image of the infant Buddha [to celebrate the Buddha's birthday]. There was a breeze and a bell rang. Fotudeng looked at [the bell] and said to the those gathered, "Do you understand the sound of this bell? The bell says that there will be imperial mourning in the country by the end of this year."

In the seventh month [Shi] Le died. Shi Hu [subsequently] ascended to the throne and served Master [Fotudeng] even more devotedly than [Shi] Le had done. [Fotudeng] made a tour to edify the people riding in the imperial carriage, and used [the carriage] even when he entered and came out of [the palace]. He had extremely numerous aspects of auspicious signs and [his responsiveness to people's] receptiveness have been left out and not explained.

517c In the last year of [Shi] Hu's [reign] Fotudeng said to his disciples, "A misfortune is happening. The time has not matured yet. I will pass away."

In the *wushen* year (348) the Crown Prince murdered his mother and brother. In a fury [Shi] Hu killed the Crown Prince as well as his wives and children. Next year [Shi] Hu died. Thereupon there was Ran Min's rebellion.

[Zhu Fotudeng] was buried to the west of [the capital] Ye. Someone said that on the day Fotudeng died a merchant saw him in some quicksand. When [Shi] Hu opened [Fotudeng's] coffin he only found a robe and a bowl.

When Fotudeng was in the Central Plains he met with unfortunate disorders, yet he was able to pass through smoothly and edify with benevolence. His virtue was of the highest. If he was not a Great Sage (i.e., a buddha), how could he relieve such distess? He built monasteries in more than nine hundred and eighty places altogether. [The number of] all the monks and laypeople who were delivered by [Fotudeng] was half of the population in the world!

[Shi Daojin, a *Śramaṇa* of the Western Jin Dynasty]

In Ye during the Western Jin dynasty there was Fotudeng's disciple Daojin. He was versed in both Buddhist and non-Buddhist studies and was esteemed by Shi Hu. His talk once came to the issue of recluses. [Shi] Hu said to Daojin, "Yang Ke is one of my subjects. I have summoned him for more than ten years but he has never respected my orders. Therefore I went to inspect him and found him laying [on the bed] haughtily. Although I lack virtue, I reign over all nations. Wherever I go riding in the carriage, even heaven seethes and the earth is in an uproar. Even though I cannot cause lifeless things to kneel down, why is an ordinary man so arrogant toward me? Formerly my father went to Qi, where he killed the Chinese gentlemen first. Could my father's men of virtue and learning have been wrong?" Daojin responded to him, "In ancient times Shun considered Pu Yi, [who declined Shun's offer of the throne,] to be excellent; Yu came to Bocheng [Zigao, a marquis who left the government service when Shun abdicated the throne for Yu, to ask the reason for his resignation]; [Marquis Wen of] the state of Wei paid respects to [Duan] Ganmu over the horizontal front bar on his carriage; the Han dynasty praised Zhou Dang, [who cut off communication with the outside world at the time Wang Mang usurped the throne]; Guan Ning did not respond to [the offer from] the Cao [royal] family [of Wei of the Three Kingdoms]; and Huangfu [Fanghui] did not yield to the Jin dynasty. The Two Sages and the Four Men of Virtue all strengthened their principles. They only wished to harshly [criticize] avaricious competition and enhance pure customs. I hope you, Your Majesty, follow the virtue of Shun and Yu and do not imitate your father in torturing. Your deportment is certainly recorded. How could you cause the history of [your state,] the Later Zhao, to include no biography of recluses in the consequence?" [Shi] Hu was happy with these words. He then sent [Yang] Ke back to the place where he had resided and selected ten households to supply to [Yang Ke].

Daojin returned and fully explained [matters] to Fotudeng. Fotudeng gazed at him and said with a smile, "Your words are good, but [Yang] Ke's life is still at risk."

Later in Qinzhou there was a war. [Yang] Ke's disciples put Ke on the back of a cow and they fled to the west. The military chased and captured them, and at that time they killed them.

[Shi] Hu once took a nap and dreamed that a flock of sheep came from the northeast carrying fishes on their backs. He woke up and visited Fotudeng. Fotudeng said, "This is inauspicious! Will the Xianbei tribe control the Central Plains?" As a matter of fact, the Murong family [of the Xianbei tribe] later occupied that region.

[Shi Tanshi, a *Śramaṇa* of the Song Dynasty]

In Chang'an during the periods of the Song dynasty and the unjustified Wei dynasty there was Shi Tanshi, a man of Guanzhong (in present-day Shaanxi province). After renouncing the world he had many extraordinary traces. At the end of the Taiyuan era (396) of Emperor Xiaowu of the [Eastern] Jin dynasty, he went to Liaodong bringing several tens of volumes of sutras and vinayas, and he propagated the [Buddhist] edification, clearly taught the three vehicles, and established the law of precepts in order to refuge in the Three Treasures. Probably this is the time when Koguryo first heard of the
518a [Buddhist] Way. In the beginning of the Yixi era (405) [Shi Tanshi] returned to Guanzhong and illuminated the Three Guardians.

Tanshi's feet were whiter than his face. Even if he waded in a muddy pool with bare feet, he was never covered with mud. All the people in the world called him the *upādhyāya* White Feet.

At that time Wang Hu, a man of Chang'an, suddenly saw his paternal uncle who had died several years ago, who returned to Hu in his [original] form. Leading Hu, [the uncle] traveled throughout the hells and showed [Hu] the various forms of retribution. When Hu returned home, the uncle said to [Wang] Hu, "You already know about the law of cause and effect. You must serve in White Feet's monastery." Hu visited sanghas throughout the land [looking for the one called White Feet] and saw only Tanshi's feet were whiter than his face. Accordingly he served [Tanshi].

At the end of the [Eastern] Jin dynasty Helian Bobo of the Xiongnu from the northern region expressed an exclamation for [Tanshi]. At the same time he released *śramaṇa*s; none were killed. Tanshi thereafter slipped away into the hills and valleys, where he cultivated *dhūta* practices. Later, Tuoba Tao gained Chang'an again and monopolized power in the Guanzhong and Luoyang areas.

On that occasion Cui Hao from Boling, who had learned a heresy when he was young, was suspicious and jealous of Śākyamuni's teaching. He already held the unjustified rank of Bulwark and was relied upon and trusted by [Tuoba] Tao. Moreover, together with Celestial Master Kou, he said to [Tuoba] Tao that Buddhist education did not serve any purpose and was harmful to the people's well-being. They persuaded [Tuoba Tao] to persecute [Buddhism]. Tao was totally deluded by their words. In the seventh year of the Taiping era according to the unjustified dating (415), they consequently destroyed the Buddhist Dharma. Military soldiers were separately dispatched to burn and plunder monastery buildings. All the monks and nuns within the land governed by [Tuoba Tao] were ordered to abandon the [Buddhist] Way. If any of them fled or hid themselves, in every case [Tao's] men were dispatched to pursue them and arrest them. If they were caught they were decapitated without fail. No *śramaṇa*s could be found in [Tao's] territory anymore. Tanshi confined himself in a deep, dark place that the soldiers could not reach.

At the end of the Taiping era (430) Tanshi knew that the time to edify [Tuoba] Tao was approaching. On New Year's Day of the Chinese lunar calendar, during the court ceremony, [Tanshi] suddenly arrived at the palace gate carrying a staff with metal rings attached to the top. An official's report to [Tuoba Tao] said, "There is a Buddhist monk whose feet are whiter than his face. He has entered through the gate." Tao, according to military law, ordered [his men] to behead [the monk] repeatedly but [the monk] was not injured. [The monk] suddenly spoke to Tao and Tao, furious at him, personally slashed him with his sword, yet [the monk's] body was unharmed. Only at the place where the sword touched his body there was a mark just like a line on textiles. At that time in the north garden there were tigers that had been raised in a cage. Tao ordered his people to feed Tanshi to them. All the tigers hid themselves and dared not approach [Tanshi] at all. When [Tao] tried to bring Celestial Master [Kou] near [the cage] the tigers roared.

Tao, for the first time, knew the nobility and loftiness of the Buddhist edification, which the teaching of the Yellow Emperor and Laozi cannot match. Accordingly [Tao] invited Tanshi to the palace, worshiped him by bowing his head to [Tanshi's] feet, and repented of his lapse from faith [in the Buddhist Dharma]. Tanshi expounded the Dharma for [Tao] and clearly spoke of the law of cause and effect. Tao became aware of great shame and fear and thereafter fell ill in an epidemic. Subsequently both Cui [Hao] and [Celestial Master] Kou came down with malignant diseases. Since the fault derived from them, Tao thereupon punished and killed [all the members of] these two families; their entire clans were completely annihilated. [Tao] made a declaration throughout the country and restored the right teaching. Soon [after this] Tao died. His grandson Jun succeeded to the throne and then greatly propagated the Buddhist Dharma, which has flourished up to the present day. It is unknown where Tanshi later died.

[Shi Falang, a *Śramaṇa* of the Song Dynasty]

In Gaochang (in present-day Turfan) during the Song dynasty was Shi Falang, a man of Goachang. He performed [cultivation] intensively and diligently in his childhood and often received various omens and auspicious
518b signs. He concealed his ability and cultivated virtue. No one was able to determine on what he relied [for his cultivation].

Falang's teacher, Shi Fajin, was also a *śramaṇa* of noble conduct. Once when Fajin closed the door to sit alone, he unexpectedly saw Falang before him. He asked [Falang], "Where did you come from?" [Falang] replied, "I came in through the door lock." He continued, "I came together with a monk who has come from a distance. It is already about noon. I hope you will provide a meal for us." Fajin immediately arranged a meal for them. [Fajin] heard only the sounds of spoons and bowls and did not see the men, somewhat to his surprise.

Formerly, Huiyuan of Mount Lu sent a *kaṣāya* [robe] to Fajin on one occasion. Fajin considered it to be a donation [to the sangha]. Falang said, "The sangha has already gone. You must accept it on some other day." Later [Falang] saw that the one who did the cooking went to Fajin and took the robe, and Fajin gave it to him. [Falang] inquired of those who always handled the cooking [about taking the robe from Fajin]. They all said they had not taken it. He just then knew that the [*kaṣāya*] had been taken by the incarnate form of a former sage.

When the Wei savages destroyed the Buddhist Dharma, Falang went to Kucha in the west. The king of Kucha formed an agreement with the great meditation master of his country [and said], "If one who has attained the [Buddhist] Way comes here, he must preach for me. I will surely make an offering to him." When Falang arrived, [the great meditation master] reported it to the king. The king treated [Falang] with the courtesy worthy of a sage.

[Falang] later died in Kucha. On the day he was cremated, a spring gushed out from his both shoulders and shot straight up into the sky. The people sighed in wonderment at the uncommon occurrence, collected his bones, and erected a stupa. Later the people of the Western Region came to this land and fully conveyed this matter.

[Shi Shaoshi, a *Śramaṇa* of the Song Dynasty]

At Tongyun Monastery on Mount Min in the Song dynasty was a *śramaṇa* called Shaoshi. Originally his family name was Shao and his first name was Shi. He was a man from Shikang. He appeared to be mentally deranged, but he deeply respected the Buddhist Dharma.

In the early Song dynasty (420–479),[149] he renounced the world and entered the [Buddhist] Way. He called himself Lord Shi. Day and night he went in and out, or going and returning. If he went to someone's house and slept on the ground, a death would occur in that house. If he came to a person and begged for a mat, there would certainly be the death of an infant [in that person's house]. All the people of the time took these as omens.

On the eighth day of the fourth month there was the Buddhist ceremony in Chengdu. Shi transfomed into the form of a lion and prowled among the crowd. On that day [the people of] Pi county also saw Shi transform into a lion.[150] In other words, the people realized that [Shi] manifested himself in two different places at the same time. Regional Inspectors Xiao Huikai and Liu Mengming and others all deferred to and served him.

At a later time, one morning suddenly [Shi] put on a cloth cap and visited [Liu] Mengming. Awhile after this Mengming died. Prior to this Mengming's adjutant, Shen Zhongyu, had changed the rules on flogging with a whip and exercised strict control on daily rules. Shi said to Zhongyu, "Grievous crying of the world arises from here! If you do away with the rule of flogging with a whip, you will be able to become Regional Inspector." Zhongyu trusted in his words and removed [the rule]. When Mengming died, as a matter of fact Zhongyu exercised authority over provincial affairs.

On the first day of the ninth month of the first year of the Yuanhui era (473) in the Song dynasty [Shi] died at Tongyun Monastery on Mount Min.[151] At the moment of his death he spoke to a monk called Fajin, "You should take my corpse outside and quickly put my shoes on my feet." [Fajin] complied with [his request] and his corpse was taken out and placed in the monastery. A couple of days later, [the corpse] could not be found anywhere.
518c Suddenly a person came from Pi county, saw Fajin, and said, "Yesterday I saw Lord Shi in the city. He had a shoe only on one foot. He said ramblingly, 'I have nothing proper. I have lost one of my shoes.'" Fajin was surprised by this so he checked with a novice, who answered, "Recently when the corpse was put out, I was frightened and could not get one shoe onto his right foot aptly, and then I lost it." [Shi's] conduct was odd and could not be fathomed. It is unknown where he ended up after that.

[Shi Huian, a *Śramaṇa* of the Song Dynasty]

At Pipa Monastery in Jiangling during the Song dynasty was Shi Huian, whose original domicile is unknown. He renounced the world at the age of eighteen and stayed in Pipa Monastery. His style and features were common, and he was slighted somewhat by others. When he was a novice, in the presence of numerous monks he was made to purify his body with water. Huian held up an empty bottle from which water fell down ceaselessly. At that time everyone considered him to be extraordinary.

After he received the full set of [two hundred and fifty] precepts, he gradually manifested mysterious trances. One time, in the evening of the last day of the month, together with his fellow student Huiji [Huian] ascended the hall to join a semimonthly assembly (Skt. *upavasatha*). Before the door of the hall opened, Huian interlaced his fingers with [Huiji's] and together they passed into the hall through a crevice in the wall. He did the same when they went out. Huiji was very frightened and dared not speak. Later [Huian] went to the area under a stupa along with Huiji and then he said to Huiji, "I must go far away. I will now part from you." Soon [Huiji] saw heavenly musicians and fragrant flowers spread out throughout the air, and he was merely afraid and could not speak at all. Huian again said, "Be careful! Do not speak recklessly of the vestiges I have shown in sequence. If you speak of this you will surely be punished. The only [exception] is a layman in the southwest. He is a bodhisattva who has newly awakened the aspiration [for enlightenment]. You can speak to him [of these things] in detail for my sake." Thereupon [Huian] departed.

[Huian] then traveled on the Xiang River [in a ship] in a company of merchants. Midway he had diarrhea, which was extremely serious. He said to the shipowner, "My life must come to an end. Just take me off [the ship] and leave me on the shore. I do not need a wooden container (i.e., coffin). After my breath is exhausted, I will give [my body] to the insects and birds." In accordance with his [last] wish the merchants took him out and laid him on the shore. At night they saw flames come out of his body. The merchants felt that this was strange and dreadful. They went to see and [found that Huian's] breath was already exhausted. The merchants then traveled on to Xiangdong [county], where they saw Huian who had already arrived there before them. Suddenly [he disappeared and] his whereabouts were once again unknown.

Huiji later came to Zhiqi Monastery. He visited Liu Qiu, a recluse of Nanyang, and talked about the events [he had witnessed with Huian] in detail. Qiu promptly stood up and bowed to [Huian] from a distance. [Qiu] said to Huiji, "This is one who attained enlightenment and entered the light-of-fire *samādhi* (Skt. *ekajvālībhūto dhyāyati*)."

[Gao Yang, Emperor of the Northern Qi Dynasty]

The emperor of the [Northern] Qi dynasty, whose posthumous name is Yang, was the second son of Gao Huan, Counselor-in-Chief of the Northern Wei dynasty. Cheng, his brother born from [Gao Huan's] legal wife, was hot-tempered and was killed by his servant. Yang succeeded to his position and became Counselor-in-Chief in his place. The Wei dynasty's power was

coming to an end. Yang built an altar in the southern suburb. Using divination by means of stalks of milfoil, [Yang] saw signs of great violence, excellent luck, and the Chinese character *han* (the Chinese people). Therefore, he erected a gold statue. Once it was drawn [the statue] was accomplished. Wei
519a Shou composed a letter of abdication, which the emperor of the [Eastern] Wei dynasty signed. Accordingly, [Yang] took over the throne abdicated [by the emperor] and started the great Qi dynasty.

Generally in what [Yang] performed it is not determined whether he was ignorant or intelligent. He left political affairs to Chief Administrator Yang Zunyan. The emperor built many Buddhist monasteries. Monks and nuns overflowed throughout the provinces. In winter and summer he made offerings and donations and practiced the [Buddhist] Way ceaselessly. One time the meditation master Sengchou admonished the emperor, "My donor, you are ruled over by *rākṣasa*s. See by yourself on the surface of the water." The emperor followed his admonition and [looking at his reflection in the water] he saw a crowd of *rākṣasa*s just behind him. Consequently, he did not eat meat, banned hunting using hawks, and ceased government-managed fishing and butchering. Strong-smelling foods and spices were completely disposed of and could not be brought into a market.

The emperor often sat in meditation and did not come out all day long. He worshiped the Buddha and circumambulated [the image of the Buddha] as swiftly as wind blows. He received the precepts from Great Superintendent Fashang at Zhaoxuan Monastery. His face covered the earth, and he allowed his superiors to step on his hair when he received the precepts.

Prior to this the emperor was in Jinyang. He had his man mount a camel and ordered, "Go to a monastery and take a container of sutras!" The messenger asked where the monastery was. The emperor said, "Just go out of the city, leave everything to the camel!"

As soon as [the messenger] went out, he arrived at a mountain just as if he was dreaming. Midway up the side of the mountain was a Buddhist monastery. A crowd of novices said from the distance, "Gao Yang's camel is coming!" They then guided [the messenger] and introduced him to an elderly monk. [The messenger] paid respects to [the monk]. [The monk] asked, "What do you think about Gao Yang as emperor?" [The messenger] said, "He is capable and virtuous [for the throne]." [The monk] asked, "Why are you here?" [The messenger] said, "To take a container of sutras." The monk said, "Yang stayed in a monastery and yet he was negligent in reading sutras. Have him go to the eastern part of the north ward where we will give them to him!"

The messenger returned and reported this to [the emperor]. The emperor first went to the Buddhist monastery of Mujing in Gukou (in present-day Shaanxi province). There was a fool who had given himself to the monastery. He did not understand language, but he abruptly said to the emperor, "I will be leaving. Come afterward!" That night the fool died. The emperor subsequently passed away in Jinyang.

[Shi Senghui, a *Śramaṇa* of the Qi Dynasty]

In Jingzhou (in present-day Hubei province) during the Qi dynasty was Shi Senghui. His secular family name was Liu but his original domicile is unknown. He resided in Jingzhou for several decades. When Liu Qiu (438–495) of Nanyang (in present-day Henan province) built Zhiqi Temple,[152] he invited [Senghui] to reside there.[153]

When the people of that time saw [Senghui], he was already fifty or sixty years old, but he did not appear to have grown older in the long run. His behavior tended to be thoughtless, and he had no dignity in his demeanor. When he went to the house of an ill person, if he was displeased the ill person assuredly died; if he was joyful, then the ill person certainly recovered his health. At that time all the people considered this (i.e., his mood) to omen [the fate of an ill person]. Generally, regarding even those with whom he had no acquaintance, he completely knew their relatives and could relate who were alive and who were dead.

Senghui once came to the Yangzi River area and asked the officer of a ferry to take him across the river. The officer, however, said coercively, "Since the boat is small, you cannot cross this time." In an instant Senghui could already be seen on the shore of the other side of the river. All the people [on both shores] marveled at the miracle.

Zhen Tian of Zhongshan (in present-day Guangdong province) and Che Tan of Nanping (in present-day Fujian province) invited Senghui on the same day. Senghui went to both places. Later, both families investigated and then learned that [Senghui] had manifested himself in two different bodies.

During the time of the Yongming era (483–493) of the Qi dynasty, Crown Prince Wenhui (458–493) was traveling to the capital [from his post in Xizhou] and dropped in for a visit with Baozhi. Baozhi, patting the prince's back, said, "A red dragon!" and said nothing else.

Later, Senghui returned to Jingzhou. He came across Liu Jingrui, Administrator of Zhenxi. [Senghui] abruptly began to weep bitterly and clung to [Jingrui]. Several days later Jingrui, as [Senghui] had feared, was killed by the Regional Chief. Later, when [Senghui] went to Chengnan in Xiangzhou,
519b he suddenly said, "Stone tablets are buried in the earth here." People cautiously dug in the area and found two stone tablets, just as [Senghui] had said.

It is unknown where he later died. Some people say that he died at Changsha Temple in Jiangling (in present-day Hubei province) during the Yongyuan era (499–501).

[Shi Baozhi, a *Śramaṇa* of the Liang Dynasty]

In the capital city of the Liang dynasty there was Shi Baozhi, whose original family name was Zhu. He was a man from Jincheng (in present-day Shaanxi province). He renounced the world when he was young and stayed at Daolin Temple in the capital city. He studied [Buddhism] under the *śramaṇa* Sengjian as his *upādhyāya* and learned meditation practices.

At the beginning of the Taishi era (465–471) of the Song dynasty [Baozhi] suddenly adopted an unusual lifestyle: he had no fixed adobe and no regular times for drinking and eating, he let his hair grow to several *cun* [without care], he always walked around on streets and lanes barefooted, and he carried a monk's walking stick, on top of which were suspended a pair of scissors and a mirror and sometimes one or two rolls of silk fabric.

During the Jianyuan era of the Qi dynasty (479–482) his strange behavior eventually became remarkable. He would not eat for several days and yet he did not look as if he were starving. What he talked about with other people seemed difficult to understand in the beginning but later [all his words] proved true. Sometimes he composed poems, which were just like prophecies. The common people of the capital city all served him.

Emperor Wu of the Qi dynasty (r. 482–493) thought that Baozhi misled people, and confined him in Jiankang prison. The next morning the people saw [Baozhi] going into a marketplace. When they went back to the prison to investigate [they found] Baozhi still confined there. Baozhi said to a warden, "A couple of carriages' worth of food for me will be delivered outside the gate. There will be cooked rice filled in a golden bowl. You can go and accept it for me." Later, Wenhui, Crown Prince of the Qi dynasty, and Ziliang (460?–494), the king of Jingling, both sent gifts of food to Baozhi. [The delivery situation] was just as what he had described. The Director of Jiankang Lü Wenxian reported this event to Emperor Wu. The emperor immediately invited [Baozhi] [to the palace] to reside in an inner hall. Once after a palace banquet was dismissed, Baozhi left [the palace], following the other people. Not long afterward a person called Baozhi together with seven monks was residing on Mount Jingyang. The emperor was angry and sent his men to investigate why [Baozhi] had departed. The doorkeeper explained, "Baozhi went out a long time ago and has not returned. [When he went out] he must have painted his body with black ink [as a disguise]."

Archbishop Faxian once intended to send a garment to Baozhi and dispatched messengers to the two temples, Longguang and Jibin, in search of him. Monks in both temples said, "He stayed here last night but left this morning." [The messengers] further went to a place where [Baozhi] often visited, the house of Guang Houbo, to look for him. [Hou]bo said, "Baozhi was here yesterday and circumambulated a buddha image chanting a sutra. He went to bed at dawn and he has not yet woken up." The messengers returned and reported this to Faxian. It was then known that [Baozhi] had manifested himself in [three different] bodies and stayed in three different places.

Baozhi frequently walked with one shoulder bared even in the dead of winter. The *śramaṇa* Baoliang (444–509) wished to send a monk's robe to [Baozhi]. Even though Baoliang had not spoken of it to [Baozhi], Baozhi suddenly came, pulled out the robe, and left. Moreover, he went to ask a person for chopped fresh fish. The person provided it for [Baozhi] completely, and Baozhi ate to the full then left. After [Baozhi] had departed, the person saw in the basin the fish [that he had chopped for Baozhi] alive and swimming as it had been before.

Later, Baozhi let Emperor Wu use his supernatural power to see Emperor Gao (i.e., the emperor's father) in his grave. [Emperor Gao] was continuously tormented by the suffering of being pierced with an awl. From that time on, Emperor Wu never again used an awl.

When Hu Xie, Chamberlain for the Palace Garrison of the Qi dynasty, fell ill, Baozhi was asked [to cure him]. Baozhi sent a note, reading, "Hu will bend down tomorrow," and rather unexpectedly he did not visit the next day. On that day Xie passed away, and his body was carried back to his home.
519c Baozhi said, "My statement, 'Hu will bend down tomorrow,' meant 'tomorrow a corpse will come out [to return home].'"[154]

Yin Qizhi, Defender-in-Chief of the Qi dynasty, was attending Chen Xianda [who was appointed] to the garrison at Jiangzhou, so he came to Baozhi to say goodbye. Baozhi drew a tree on some paper. On the tree he added a crow and said, "In an emergency you should climb up on this." Later, Xianda rebelled and kept Qizhi in the garrison at Jiangzhou. When [Xianda] was defeated, Qizhi deserted and went to Mount Lu. Men on horseback were chasing [Qizhi] and coming close when he found a tree in a forest, and there was a crow on the top of the tree, just as Baozhi had drawn. [Qizhi] took the hint and climbed up the tree. The crow unexpectedly did not fly away. The pursuers saw the crow, thought no one was there, and the soldiers turned back. Thus [Qizhi] escaped from the difficulty.

Sang Yan, Commandant of Garrison Cavalry of the Qi dynasty, intended to rebel and went to visit Baozhi. When Baozhi saw [Sang Yan] from afar, he ran out and shouted, "He will surround the imperial palace, intending to rebel. He will be beheaded and disemboweled." Ten days later the incident happened. Yan had staged a revolt and headed toward Zhufang (in present-day Jiangsu province), but he was apprehended by some people, beheaded, and disemboweled, just as [Baozhi had described].

[Hui,] the Zhonglie king in Poyang during the Liang dynasty, once courteously asked Baozhi to come visit. As soon as they met, Baozhi abruptly ordered [Hui] to quickly look for a bramble (*jing*). After [Baozhi] obtained it, he placed it on a gate. No one could understand the reason for this. Shortly after, the king was transferred to Jingzhou to serve as Regional Chief. There are numerous examples of [Baozhi's] foresight like this.

Baozhi often came and went between Xinghuang Temple and Jingming Temple. After the reigning emperor (i.e., Emperor Wu of the Liang dynasty) ascended the throne, [these two temples] were greatly esteemed. During the previous Qi dynasty many temples had forbidden Baozhi to enter. When the reigning Emperor [Wu] succeeded to the throne, he issued an imperial decree stating, "Lord Baozhi's daily life is detained in the world of dust and dirt, but his spirit wanders about in the profound and tranquil state. Water cannot wet him and fire cannot scorch him. Not even a snake or tiger can attack and frighten him. Regarding his understanding of the Buddhist doctrines, he is above a *śrāvaka*. As for reclusion, he is the same as an immortal who lives incognito or a person of noble character. How could worldly people vainly detain and control him out of ordinary feelings? Why has the meanness and indiscretion [of the Qi dynasty's policy regarding him] come to this? From now on [Baozhi] is to be allowed to go in and out [of these temples] as he likes. He cannot be forbidden to do so." Thereafter, Baozhi frequently went in and out of the royal residence [according to his wishes].

There was a drought in the winter of the fifth year of the Tianjian era (506) and a sacrificial worship rite had been wholeheartedly performed, but it still did not bring rain. Baozhi suddenly submitted a report to the authorities, saying, "I am ill and unable to recover. The government officials beg me to regulate [the drought]. If I do not accept [this task], officials of all ranks and descriptions will be flogged with whips or canes. I wish that the *Śrīmālādevī-siṃhanāda-sūtra* will be presented in a lecture at Huaguang Sanctuary in order to pray for rain." The emperor immediately ordered the *śramaṇa* Fayun (467–529) to conduct a lecture on the *Śrīmālādevī-siṃhanāda-sūtra.* The night after the lecture was completed it snowed heavily. Baozhi said again, "The basin needs [to be filled with] water. Lay a knife over it." Suddenly it rained heavily, and all the high and low lands benefited from this.

The emperor once asked Baozhi, "I have not yet been able to remove defilements. How can I harness them?" [Baozhi] replied [with only one word], "Twelve." Intelligent people thought that he meant that the twelve causations are the medicine for curing defilements. Again [the emperor] asked about the meaning of "twelve." [Baozhi] answered, "It is written in a water clock that ticks away the time." Intelligent people thought that this meant that it is written in the twelve hours [of each day and night]. Furthermore [the emperor] asked, "When will I be able to peacefully learn and practice [the Buddhist Way]?" [Baozhi] replied, "Peace and happiness become cessation." Intelligent people understood that "cessation" means 520a
coming to rest; when the emperor reaches the world of peace and happiness, he will simply rest in [the Buddhist Way].

Later Fayun lectured on the *Lotus Sutra* at Hualin Hall. When he came to the phrase, "Even if an evil wind blows [against the boat],"[155] Baozhi suddenly asked whether or not there was wind. [Fayun] replied, "In reality in the worldly sense, there is; but in ultimate reality there is not." Baozhi exchanged questions and answers [with Fayun] three or four times, and then he said, smiling, "If the real thing is not real existence, this is beyond comprehension and difficult to understand." The intention of his expressions was obscure. All examples of his expressions are like this.

A man called Chen Zhenglu along with his entire family very sincerely served Baozhi. Once Baozhi manifested his real form for them, and his bright countenance was just like that of a bodhisattva image. Baozhi was well known for revealing wonders for more than forty years. Those, both men and women, who respectfully served him were countless.

In the winter of the thirteenth year of the Tianjian era (514) [Baozhi] said to someone in the rear hall of the imperial palace, "A bodhisattva is leaving." Less than ten days later he passed away without having become ill. His body was fragrant and pliable, and his appearance was peaceful and happy. Just at the moment of his death he lit a candle and gave it to Wu Qing, Houseman of the Rear Cabin. Qing immediately reported this to the emperor, who lamented, "The Great Master will no longer stay [in this world]. Regarding the candle, he meant to entrust me with future affairs." Accordingly, [Baozhi's body] was courteously carried to the grave and buried in the Dulong mound on Mount Zhong. Kaishan Monastery was subsequently built around his grave. An imperial decree was issued for Lu Chui (470–526) to make an epigraph in the graveyard and for Wang Yun to engrave an inscription on a tablet of the temple gate. [Baozhi's] image was transmitted and exists in various places.

In the beginning when Baozhi began to reveal his deeds, he was around fifty or sixty years old, but he did not appear to age right to the end. So his age could not be definitively determined. A man called Xu Jiedao, who resided [north of Jiuritai] in the capital city, personally said, "I am the younger brother of Baozhi's wife's father and four years younger than Baozhi." Counting Baozhi's age at death [from Jiedao's statement], [Baozhi] would have been ninety-seven years old.

(This story is found in the *Gaoseng zhuan* compiled in the Liang dynasty [*Liang Gaoseng zhuan*].)

[Xu Guang, a Layman of Wu Kingdom]

Xu Guang lived in the Wu [kingdom of the Three Kingdoms] (222–280). He often practiced sorcery. In the city he planted melons, dates, mandarin oranges, and a chestnut tree, [which grew instantly]. He promptly harvested [the fruit] and ate it. The trade of the fruit vendors in the shops diminished [in the proportion to what Xu Guang expended]. Generally it is said that he produced effects of floods and droughts.

He frequently passed by the gate of Great General Sun Lin. Lifting his lower garments he passed by quickly, spitting left and right. Someone asked him why he did this and he replied, "Bloodshed covers the road. It smells of blood. I cannot stand it!" [Sun] Lin heard this and killed [Xu Guang] by beheading him, but there was no blood. When Lin dethroned a youthful ruler and placed Emperor Jing [on the throne], he led his people to pay respects to Jiangling (i.e., the mausoleum of the founder of Wu kingdom in present-day Jiangsu province). There was a great violent wind and something like a granary fell down from the sky onto Lin's carriage, which collapsed and broke. [Lin] turned his head and saw Xu Guang [sitting] in a pine tree, clapping his hands, waving his fingers, and chuckling sneeringly at him. Lin asked his aides but no one else saw [Xu Guang]. Lin loathed this. Emperor Jing abruptly put him to death. All four [of Sun Lin's] brothers were massacred in one day.

(This is found in the *Yuanhunzhi* [*Records of Resentful Spirits of Those Who Died Unreasonably*]).

[The *Soushen ji* (*Records of Inquiries of the Spirits*), Miscellaneous Legends, and Records Such as Those of the Earth Transcendents]

Regarding Laozi during the time of the Zhou dynasty, his family name is Li, 520b
first name Dan, and pseudonym Boyang. He was a man from the Quren community of Lai village in Ku county, Chu state.[156]

His mother was moved at the sight of a shooting star and became pregnant. Even though he received the energy (*qi*) from heaven (i.e., he was a Son of Heaven), he was born to the Li family, and therefore he took Li as his family name. Some say that Laozi was born before the Creation. Another opinion is that he is a heavenly spirit or a sort of sprite. Or, according to another account, his mother conceived and carried him for seventy years before he was born; at his birth he cut his mother's left armpit to come out, and since he was born with gray hair, he was called Laozi (i.e., "Old Boy").

Another version says that his mother had no husband and the name Laozi is her family name. Or Laozi's mother happened to arrive under a plum (*li*) tree and then gave birth to Laozi. Right after his birth, Laozi said, pointing the tree, "I will take this as my family name." Some say that Laozi intended to go west out across the frontier pass[157] and that Yin Xi, Director of the pass, knew that [Laozi] was extraordinary. [Xi] tried to become his disciple and asked [Laozi] the art of the [Daoist] Way. Laozi was surprised at this and lolled out his tongue; consequently, he was called Lao (i.e., "old") Dan (i.e., "to loll"). These are all wrong.

According to the *Jiubian* (*Nine Changes*) and the *Xiansheng Shierhua jing* (*Scripture of Sir Laozi's Twelve Transformations*), Laozi assuredly used the name Dan before he traveled through the pass. Laozi frequently changed his first name and pseudonym. It is simply not the case that he used only Dan. According to the *Jiugong* (*Nine Palaces*), the *Sanwu jing* (*Scripture of Three-Five*), and the *Yuanchen jing* (*Scripture of the First Day of the Year*), the reason for this is that there are unlucky times in one's life, and when such a bad time comes, if a person adapts to the changes of the energy [of Nature] by changing his first name and pseudonym, then he can prolong his life span and avoid misfortunes. Nowadays those who attain the Way in the world do so in the same way. Laozi lived in the Zhou dynasty for more than two hundred years, during which time he certainly repeatedly met with misfortune. Therefore, he had numerous first names and pseudonyms.

Pengzu during the time of the Yin dynasty has the posthumous name Keng. He is the great-great-grandson of Emperor Zhuanxu. At the end of the Yin dynasty he was already seven hundred and sixty-seven years old, yet he was not infirm with age. He was fond of peace and quiet from his early days, had little interest in worldly affairs, did not seek fame, and did not adorn himself with a chariot and [fine] clothes. He only considered it his duty to preserve his health and regulate himself. The king heard about him and made him Grand Master in honor of his long life, but [Pengzu] led a quiet life, and often on the pretext of illness he did not participate in state affairs.

[Pengzu] was skilled in the art of nourishing energy and guiding the breath, and took [medicines such as] cinnamon water, powdered mica, and powdered deer horn. He always looked young. He held his breath and practiced abdominal respiration. From dawn to noon he sat upright. He rubbed his eyes, scoured his body, moistened his lips, swallowed saliva, practiced breath control several tens of times, and then began his daily actions. Sometimes when he felt tired or uneasy in his body, he performed the practice of guiding the breath into the body and holding it (i.e., breathing deeply) in order to cure the affected part. [Consequently,] [he cultivated] sensitivity throughout the body; he caused [sensitivity] to work in the head, the bodily orifices, the five viscera, the four limbs, and even the hair. He performed this practice from the nose and mouth to the tips of the ten fingers until he felt that breath entirely filled his body. The king personally visited and asked him for instructions but he would not tell anything. [The king] sent presents of curios as valuable as several tens of thousands of catties of gold altogether. Pengzu received all of them and then gave them to the poor; he kept nothing at all. 520c

Furthermore, there was [a female transcendent called] Cainü who also attained the Way when she was young and who knew the method to nourish life. She was two hundred and seven years old, but she looked like she was only fifteen or sixteen years old. The king respectfully served her; he built a splendid building decorated with gold and gems for her in the side quarters of the palace. Moreover, he requested Cainü to ride in a light carriage as an imperial emissary and go to Pengzu to ask him about the Way. Cainü fully received [from Pengzu] all important methods and instructed the king in them. The king tried them and they had effect. He then intended to kill [Pengzu in order to monopolize the methods]. Pengzu knew of this and he left [China] and disappeared. More than seventy years later, there was report that someone saw [Pengzu] in the west in the desert.[158]

The king was not always able to practice Pengzu's Way, but he still attained a long life of a hundred and three years. He was full of energy, and in appearance he looked like he was around fifty years old. He later indulged in lewdness with a woman from the Yun area (in present-day Hubei province). [Consequently] he lost the Way and died. The common saying, "Pengzu's Way was not taught to the people," came about because the king prohibited his teaching.

In the time of the Yin dynasty when Pengzu left [China], he was seven hundred years old; his life span did not come to an end.

(The two stories above are found in the *Shenxian zhuan* [*Biographies of Divine Transcendents*].)

During the Han dynasty, there was a hole of unlnown depth in the suburb of Luoyang. A woman who wished to kill her husband said to him, "I have not yet seen that hole." The husband personally took her to see it, and the wife pushed him into it. After [falling] for awhile he reached the bottom of the hole. Afterward the woman threw food [into the hole] as if making offerings to him.

At the very moment [this happened her husband] was passed out due to the shock of the fall, but he soon recovered consciousness. He found the food, and having eaten it his spirits lifted a little. He walked at a leisurely pace looking for a way out and found a cave. He crept into it and advanced several tens of *li,* bumping against rock and twisting his body [to get through the passage]. [Eventually] the cave opened up, and he saw a dim light. He was then able to walk normally. He traveled more than a hundred *li.* He felt that the ground underfoot was covered by something like dust, and he smelled nonglutinous rice.[159] He ate something [that seemed to be dust], which was fragrant and good. Immediately he wrapped some of it [to carry] for provisions. He went on further, nourishing himself with it. It was difficult to know how many *li* he walked in the dark. Soon [the cave] became bright and more spacious.

When he ran out of provisions, he entered a large city whose city walls were in good repair and well maintained, and the palace buildings were splendid; all the high pavilions and mansions were decorated with beaten gold. Even though there were no sun and moon, it was brighter than the world of the three sources of light (i.e., sun, moon, and stars). All the inhabitants [of this place] were three *zhang* tall, wore robes made out of feathers, and played wonderful music unheard in the common world. He told them [what had happened to him] and asked for aid. An extremely tall man said to him, "Go further!" He went on, [as he had been told,] and passed through nine places like this altogether.

In the last place he was suffering from starvation. The extremely tall man pointed to a sheep under a cypress tree in a courtyard; the circumference of the cypress tree was nearly a hundred arm-widths. [The extremely tall man] ordered him to kneel down and pluck one of the sheep's whiskers with his hands. [When he did so] first he got a pearl. The extremely tall man took [the pearl], as well as what he got next, [after plucking another whisker,] and he was directed to eat what he got when he plucked one last whisker. Immediately his hunger was relieved. He asked [the extremely tall man] the names of the nine places [he had passed through] and earnestly entreated him to let him stay there. [The extremely tall man] answered, "Due to your fate, you cannot stay here. Go back to [Luoyang] and ask Zhang Hua, and you will know everything about this place." Thereupon, he followed the cave passages and emerged at Jiaozhou (in present-day Guangxi province).

[From there] he returned to Luoyang and visited [Zhang] Hua to show what he had obtained. Zhang Hua said, "This dust-like substance is the saliva 521a
from a dragon that has collected on the bottom of the Yellow River. The mud is from the foot of Mount Kunlun. The earthly immortal of the nine places is called the high steward of the nine lodges (*jiuguan dafu*). The sheep is called *chilong* (i.e., "idiotic dragon"). If one eats the pearl obtained from the first whisker, one's life span will be equal to that of the universe; what is obtained from the next one prolongs the life span; and the last one merely satisfies hunger." Seven or eight years passed while the man was traveling this way.

In the fifth year of the Yongping era of the Han dynasty (62) Liu Chen and Ruan Zhao of Yan county (in present-day Zhejiang province) went to Mount Tiantai together, but they became lost and could not find their way back. They wandered around for thirteen days. Their provisions ran out and they were about to die from starvation when they saw a mountain in the far distance. On the mountain was a peach tree full of fruit, but there was no path to reach it. They climbed, grabbing onto vines, and somehow they were able to reach the top. After they each ate several pieces of fruit, their hunger abated and they became full of vigor.

They descended the mountain. With a cup they collected water to wash their hands and to rinse their mouths when they saw the leaves of a turnip flowing out of a hillside. [The leaves] looked very fresh. In addition, a cup floated to them, filled with sesame rice. They went into the water together and pushed upstream.

They traveled two or three *li,* crossing over a mountain, and came to a great gorge. On the stream bank were two girls whose features were excellent and outstanding. Seeing both [Chen and Zhao] holding the cup [of sesame rice, the two girls] said, smiling, "Mr. Liu and Mr. Ruan, you caught the cup we lost in the stream some time ago." [Though the girls] were unknown to Chen and Zhao, they greeted the men by their family names as if [Chen and Zhao] were old acquaintances. Then both the girls asked [Chen and Zhao], "Why did you take so long to get here?" [The girls] then led the way to their house.

The house had copper roof tiles, and inside there were large beds next to each of the south and east walls enclosed with red silk curtains. There were bells on the corners of the curtains, and [the fabric of the curtains] was interwoven with gold and silver [threads]. Ten maidservants sat at the side of each bed. The girls ordered them, "Mr. Liu and Mr. Ruan crossed over the rugged mountain. Even though they had jade fruits a little while ago, they must be still hungry. You should quickly make a meal for them." [Chen and Zhao] ate sesame rice, dried and seasoned goat meat, and beef, all of which were very delicious. After the meal wine was served and a group of ladies came. Each of the ladies carried three or five peaches and said, smiling, "We are here to congratulate you on the arrival of your husbands." At the height of the wining and dining music played. When night fell, [Chen and Zhao] were told to go to their respective beds and the girls followed them. [The girls'] voices were clear and pleasant and dispelled the people's gloom.

Consequently [the two men] stayed there for half of a year. The weather [in that place] was everlasting spring, and the plants [grew luxuriantly] just as in spring. Various kinds of birds sang. In due course, [Chen and Zhao] longed for [their homes] and became sad. They anxiously asked [the girls] to let them go home. The girls said, "You are affected by sinful karma. What should we do?" Consequently [the girls] invited thirty or forty ladies, those who had come previously [to congratulate Chen and Zhao], for a [farewell] party with music. Then [the girls] together saw Liu and Ruan off, showing the way back to their homes.

After they came out [from the mountain] and returned home, [they found that] their relatives and old friends were dead, the circumstances of the village and houses had changed, and there was no one they knew living there. They searched for their relatives and found the descendents of the seventh generation after them. [The descendents told them,] "We heard [from our parents] that our ancestors went into the mountains, got lost, and could not come back."

In the eighth year of the Taiyuan era of the Jin dynasty (383) [Liu Chen and Ruan Zhao] suddenly left home and went missing.

During the time of the Han dynasty, Huang Yuan of Mount Tai (in present-day Shandong province) opened the gate [of his house] at daybreak and saw a [strange] black dog lying on its belly outside of the gate, watching over his house as if it was Huang's family dog. Yuan put [the dog] on a leash and went to a neighboring village to hunt. He spotted a deer toward nightfall and 521b just then unleashed the dog.

The dog seemed to run very slowly, yet when Yuan followed after the dog to the best of his ability he could not catch up. After going for several *li* he reached a cave. He entered it and advanced more than a hundred paces when he suddenly came to a level thoroughfare. There were lines of locus and willow trees and a house surrounded by a wall.

Yuan passed through the gate, following the dog. There was an array of several tens of rooms with barred windows in which there were girls. Their features were attractive, and their garments were resplendent. Some of them played the Chinese musical instruments *qin* and *se*; some played a game of Chinese chess. When he came to the northern mansion he saw a residence of three divisions. Two waiting women watched over the house; they seemed to look for [a stranger], and when they saw Yuan they looked at each other and said, smiling, "This is Miaoyin's husband, brought by the black dog." One of the waiting women remained behind while the other entered the mansion. Soon four maidservants came out and delivered a message, "Lady Taizhen addresses Mr. Huang, 'I have a daughter who has reached the age of marriage. According to fate she must become your wife.'"

It was already dusk. [The maidservants] led Yuan inside, where there was a hall facing the south with a pond in front. In the pond was a platform, and on each of the four corners there was a hole one *chi* in diameter. Light emitted from these holes and illuminated the curtained seats.

Miaoyin was beautiful and wonderful in appearance. Her ladies in waiting and maidservants were also attractive. Once the wedding ceremony was over, they consummated their marriage. [Their intimacy] was just as if they were close companions of long standing.

Several days later, Yuan wished to go home temporarily in order to report [the marriage to his family]. Miaoyin said, "The realm of human beings is different from that of divine beings. Originally [our marriage] will not be long-lasting." The next day [Miaoyin] untied her jade pendant to exchange as a keepsake of their separation. She came to the stairs [to see him off], weeping copiously. They would not have the chance to meet again. [Miaoyin's] love and respect [for Yuan] increased even more. [She said,] "If you are able to continue loving me, you should perform purification on the first day of the third month." Her four maidservants accompanied him to outside of the gate. Within a half day he arrived back at his house in a state of rapture.

Each time the date [Miaoyin had mentioned] (i.e., the first day of the third month) came, [Yuan] saw that a curtained carriage for women appeared in the air and seemed to be flying.

(The three stories above are found in the *Youming lu* [*Records of the Other World and This World*].)

The *Shuyi ji* (*Records to Give Accounts of Extraordinary Things*) says:

> On Mount Lu there is a three-stone bridge. The length is several tens of *zhang* and the width is less than a *chi*. If you look down from it, [you see that] it is deep, expansive, and bottomless. During the Xiankang era [of the Eastern Jin dynasty (335–342)], Yu Liang, Regional Inspector of Jiangzhou, welcomed Wu Meng. Leading his disciples, Meng ascended the mountain, traveling to see the sights. Accordingly they passed this bridge. They saw an old man sitting under a cassia tree; he held a jade cup filled with nectar and gave it to Meng. Meng passed it round to his disciples. Again they proceeded and arrived at a place with a lofty tower, spacious buildings, a palace made of jade, and a golden building. Fine jade stones shone brightly, and the brightness and colors were dazzling. Vast amounts of jewels, valuables, and jade articles were beyond recognition. All [of the people in Meng's party] saw several people, who said to Meng, "If we had known each other in the past we would have arranged the juice of jade (i.e., the elixir of life) throughout the day."

Again, the *Shuyi ji* says:

> Single-horned is a man from Yijunjiang who could be several hundreds of years old. The common people forgot his name and a horn sprang up from the crown of his head, so he was called Single-horned. He [disappeared] suddenly and was gone for years, or he would not speak for several tens of days. When he had something to say, his purpose and intention

were profound. No one could judge him. At his residence he educated himself with virtue. He was also strikingly knowledgeable in teaching and guiding. One day he left home and eventually entered a river in front of his house, where he transformed into a carp. The horn was still behind its head. He frequently returned for a brief time and his appearance was 521c
just as usual. He had a feast with his descendants and several days later he left again.

The original domicile of Soldier Changsheng in a village in Gucheng [prefecture] (in present-day Shandong province) is unknown. He died and came back to life several times. People of the time considered that this was not right. Later there was a heavy flood, which caused damage in various places. Thereupon the soldier stood on Mount Quemen and shouted, "Here is Servant Changsheng!" He further said, "It will rain once again, but it will surely stop in five days." When the rain stopped, [the people] went up the mountain and looked for [Changsheng] to deify him, but they only found a soldier's robe, stick, and leather belt. Several tens of years later he became the gatekeeper of a city in Huayin [prefecture] (in present-day Shaanxi province).

Qin Gao is a man from Zhao (present-day Shanxi province). By means of playing a Chinese zither (*qin*) he became a houseman of King Kang [of Song state]. He performed the art of Xuan[zi] and Peng[zu] and floated between Jizhou (present-day Hebei, Shanxi, northern Henan provinces, and western Manchuria) and Dang prefecture (part of Henan, Shandong, Jiangsu, and Anhui provinces). More than two hundred years later, he once went into the Dang River to try to catch a child dragon. He promised his disciples, saying, "On the chosen day, you must all purify yourselves and stay at a shrine set up near the river." As a matter of fact [Qin Gao] emerged riding a red carp, entered the shrine, and sat down there. Ten thousand people in Dang prefecture came to see [the event]. [Qin Gao] stayed there for a month and then went back into the river.

Guan Xian is a man of Song state (present-day Henan province). He was a fisherman by occupation and lived near the Sui River for more than a hundred years. Whenever he caught fish he released, sold, or ate them himself. He always wore a cap and a belt, and he was fond of planting lychee and ate the flowers and fruits.

Lord Jing of the state of Song asked him about his Way [for longevity] but he would not reveal it, so [Lord Jing] immediately killed him. Several tens of years later [Guan Xian] [was seen] sitting on the city gate of Song playing a Chinese zither. He left after several tens of days. The people of the state of Song worshiped him with respect in each household.

(These three stories are found in the *Soushen yiji* [*Separate Records of Inquiries of the Spirits*].)

Chapter Twenty-four

Supernatural Beings

(This chapter consists of two parts:) (1) Introduction and (2) Quoted Testimonies.

1. Introduction

Regarding supernatural beings, Gan Bao's [*Soushen*] *ji* (*Records of Inquiries of the Spirits*) says:

> [Supernatural beings] are likely those who are haunted by vital energy. When the internal vital energy is disordered the [haunted] substance changes into outward form. The body and spirit, the substance and the vital energy, function with the influence between inside and outside. If you know the foundation of the five primary elements (i.e., metal, wood, water, fire, and earth) and are versed in the five faculties (i.e., facial expression, language, vision, hearing, and thought), although [all things] disappear or appear, ascend or descend, and change or move in complicated ways, all these signs, whether good or ill, can be discerned and discussed.

This is the common people's familiar view and it has not reached the Great Sage's law of cause and effect. If we examine the changes of these signs to be collections of sentient beings' good or bad acts done in previous existences, accordingly we sense that the maturation of karma in the present existence just reveals itself. Cause and condition converge upon each other and the law of nature is inevitable. Therefore, there are these signs. This is not worthy of feeling surprised by.

2. Quoted Testimonies

Just as the *Fo benxingji jing* (T. 190) says:

At that time the Buddha said to all the *bhikṣus*, "I remember that in ancient times there was a king of horses, called Keśi. His countenance was well formed. His body was as perfectly clean as white agate, snow, silver, a
522a complete full moon, or white lotus (Skt. *kumuda*) flowers.[160] His head was of a deep purple color. He ran as swiftly as the wind. His voice sounded like a wonderful drum.

"During his reign there were five hundred merchants in Jambudvīpa, and all the merchants wished to go onto the great sea. They purchased equipment and provisions and traveled to [the shore of] the great sea. Then they prayed to the god of the sea, prepared all the ships, and hired five crew members. They [were traveling in order to] seek for valuables. At that time all the people going by sea abruptly happened to meet a violent wind, which blew the ships to Rākṣasīdvīpa, the country of numerous *rākṣasī*s. When the ships were about to arrive at that country, a gale blew and struck the ships, completely destroying them. All the merchants at that time swam through the current and floated away, and they were about to reach the shore of that country.

"At that time the *rākṣasī*s heard that there were ships wrecked in the great sea, and they [thought that they should] immediately go to meet and save [the victims]. [They planned] to take hold of the five hundred merchants at a time and together with them they would indulge in the pleasures of the five desires and be very happy. After giving birth to boys and girls [fathered by] the merchants they would confine the merchants in an iron city and subsequently the merchants would settle there.

"The [*rākṣasī*s] transformed from their original forms, making themselves well-featured. They were more attractive than human women but not as good as heavenly women. They bathed themselves using heavenly fragrant water, dabbed balm on their bodies, adorned themselves with various garments and necklaces of precious stones, put on heavenly caps of beautiful flowers, and hung treasured bells.

"Quickly running to where the merchants were they said to them, 'All you sages! Do not fear! Do not have any worry! Give us your hands! Give us your arms! Give us your wrists!' At that moment, the merchants ultimately feared death and wished to protect their lives. Accordingly they thought that [the *rākṣasīs*] were real [human] women and reached out their hands and arms [to the *rākṣasīs*].

"When the *rākṣasīs* had saved all the merchants [from the great sea], they said with mercy and sympathy, "From where have you come such a long way? You should become our husbands. Have pity on us and become our masters for our sakes! We have no one who loves and thinks of us. Please be the object in which we can take refuge, and remove and destroy our worries and afflictions! You must become the heads of our families for our sakes. We will follow and serve you and not cause you to have any deficit or loss."

"At that time all the merchants felt anguish. They wept and wailed aloud, breathing heavily [in distress]. They comforted and advised each other, and gained peace of mind by turns.

"They went to the city of the *rākṣasīs*, [Rākṣasīnagara]. Before arriving, midway in the journey, they saw a place where the land was spacious and completely flat and straight. In the forest there were luxuriant flowers, fruits, branches, and leaves. Various kinds of birds flew around and gathered. There were incalculable kinds [of birds] such as [parrots, mynahs, and *kokila*s]. Moreover, there were ponds and swamps filled with flowers and birds. Seeing this, the people were delighted and their worries and afflictions were wiped out.

"The city of *rākṣasīs* was surrounded by four pure walls, which looked like jade and snow or an iceberg. This city was sitting on the ground, yet if observed from at a distance, it appeared to be a group of white clouds rising up from the earth. The city was adorned, just as is fully explained in the sutra (i.e., the *Fo benxingji jing*).

"At that time all the *rākṣasīs* proceeded to the city, leading all the merchants. They had [the merchants] remove their old clothes to bathe in hot 522b
water of various fragrances, then seated them on various kinds of beautiful seats and amused them by means of the five desires. The [*rākṣasīs*] made all the sounds of the five notes of traditional music before [the merchants]. [The merchants] greatly enjoyed themselves for a long time. Afterward, the *rākṣasīs* said to all the merchants, 'Good! Sages! You cannot go out to the south of this city to visit a certain place.'

"[The chief] merchant (Skt. *sārthavāha*), whose intelligence was profound and exquisite, who was bright and astute, promptly felt suspicious and thought, 'Why will they not allow us to travel to the south? I will watch for a chance. When all the women are asleep, I will seek out the place they forbid us to go in order to see the good or bad things that are there.' At that time, having thought of this, the chief merchant then waited and watched for when all the *rākṣasī*s fell asleep. He then got up calmly, not making any sound, and holding a sword he went out of the house.

"He made inquiries, pursuing his intent. He advanced slowly and [eventually] arrived at a small area where he saw a narrow path and a fearful place without any grass or trees. It was very horrible. Then he heard someone crying out in great agony. It sounded like the cries of pain in Raurava Hell. On hearing this his hair stood on end and he stopped, remaining silent. After a while the gasping abated. He returned to the path and went on slowly. He saw an iron city (Skt. *ayomaya-nagara*), high and huge. This was the place from where the agonizing cries had come. He approached the city and went around [its perimeter walls] but did not find a gate. When he came to the north side, there was a tree called a silk tree (Skt. *śirīṣa*) growing near the city. The tree was lofty and rose over the city wall. The chief merchant saw this, promptly climbed the tree, and looked down at the interior of the city. He saw numerous dead people, more than a hundred, in the city. There were dead people whose [bodies] had already been half-eaten, those who had not yet died and whose bodies were dismembered, those who sat on the ground, suffering from hunger and thirst, or those who were [completely] emaciated, whose bodies were only skin and bones. Their eyes were sunken deep in their heads and they looked like heavenly bodies in the bottom of a well. They were deluded and agonized and laid on the ground. Their hair was disheveled and their bodies were covered with dust. Though they were very emaciated, they cut others' flesh and devoured one another. For this cause and condition, they cried out in great agony. It was just like the place of King Yama. [The chief merchant] saw all sentient beings suffering greatly [in this way]. On seeing this, the great chief merchant was also [frightened]. He grapsed the silk tree with his hands and shook it. When a branch moved, all the other branches and leaves of the tree rubbed against each other and made a sound.

"At that time, all the suffering people heard the sound and looking up above the city wall, they saw the chief merchant in the silk tree. On seeing him, they mournfully shouted, 'What are you? Are you a deity, a dragon, a *yakṣa,* Śakra-devendra, or King Mahābrahman? We are in great hardship. 522c
Did you come here to save us from suffering out of pity for us?' On that occasion, joining their palms, the people worshiped him from a distance by touching their heads to the ground. With mournful loud cries, looking up at him they spoke in this way, 'Good! Virtuous One! Are you going to save us from suffering and allow us to reach a place we love?' Hearing these words from those suffering people, the chief merchant was then depressed and unhappy. Sad and troubled in mind and body, he replied to them, 'All of you should know that I am neither a deity, nor a dragon, nor even King Mahābrahman. We were, however, born in Jambudvīpa, from where we reached here. Seeking wealth we traveled out on the great sea. As we were about to reach land we encountered a sudden gale and our ships were broken apart [and destroyed]. We met various ladies who approached and saved us from hardship. Since then we have been enjoying pleasure together with all the ladies and receive happiness in this way. How can I now relieve you from suffering?'

"At that moment the chief merchant again asked them, 'All you people! Why are you here and having trouble like this?' The suffering people immediately replied, 'Good! Good man! We were also like that. We traveled with five hundred people, too. Our ships were destroyed and we reached a shore where we also met *rākṣasīs*. Together with them we enjoyed the [pleasures of] the five desires. The[*rākṣasīs* then] led us and imprisoned us in this iron city. Since the time we came into this city, two hundred and fifty people have been already eaten by them. Now only two hundred and fifty people remain. We also mated with them and had boys and girls. The *rākṣasīs*' language is delicate and their voices are pleasant and attractive. They, however, greedily eat flesh. Therefore, even the children we had together have all been eaten. All of you! Be cautious! Do not receive pleasure and give pleasure together with them! Why? Because they are very fearful and they have no compassion.'

"At this point the chief merchant again asked them, 'You people! Are there any expedient means to be able to escape from this hardship?' They

promptly responded, 'There is one expedient means.' The chief merchant again asked, 'Good! What is that expedient means? Please explain it for me!' They replied, 'On the fifteenth day it will be a full moon, the great day of pleasure of the fourth-month festival. When the moon meets with the Pleiades and becomes full (Skt. *kārtikapūrṇamā*), there will be a king of horses called Keśi (called Duomao, "Hairy," in the Sui dynasty.) His countenance is well-formed, and those who see him enjoy [his appearance]. He is as white as a *ke* shell.[161] His hair is of a dark purple color. He goes as swiftly as the wind. His voice sounds like a wonderful drum. In any place where he stops there is [spontaneously produced] nonglutinous rice (Skt. *śāli*),[162] which has no husk and bran originally and [the rice kernels] are very large, bright white, and completely fragrant and delicious. This is what that horse eats. After having the rice he will come to the seashore and reveal half of his body. Speaking in a human voice he will say, 'Who wishes to be saved from the great sea of painful hardship?' He will repeat this three times. 'I must now enable the people to smoothly cross over to the yonder
523a shore.' If you meet a horse like this, you will be able to escape from hardship. There is no other way [to be rescued] except for this. If you want to escape from all hardship, do not speak of this to others!'

"Again the chief merchant asked, 'Have you ever seen the horse king? If you have seen him, why did you not feel an affinity with him? Why did he not let you cross over [to the yonder shore]? From whom did you first hear of this matter?' They replied, 'We heard the voice like this from the sky, and there was one who believed it. Seeking the voice from the sky, he visited the horse king's place in Uttarakuru. Even though he went to that place he did not receive the horse king's words and returned. We were all attached to the *rākṣasī*s. Therefore we are like this now, suffering from this difficulty.'

"The chief merchant again said to them,[163] 'Leave here and come with us to visit that horse king's place together.' They responded, 'We want to climb the city wall but it rises up higher [when we try to do so]. We dig a hole in the ground in order to escape, but then the hole closes up. We have no hope of extricating ourselves from this place. We will certainly be eaten by the *rākṣasī*s. How can we see our parents and dependents again? You people! Be careful! Do not be self-indulgent! Leave here as you like! Quickly go to your parents and your own dependents! Return to your home villages! We only wish for you to be harmonious in your intentions. We were originally born in a certain town of a certain city of such-and-such place. Ah! If you go to that place, please visit our parents and all our good friends for our sakes!' After saying this, they further told him,[164] 'Do not resolve later to go out on that great sea. Why? There are various fearful things in the great sea. Just stay in your place and live in accordance with proper ways! Remain with your parents, wives, children, and dependents! Do not separate from them again! Practice generosity well, do many meritorious acts, and strictly observe purification and the precepts. These are primary.'

"At this point, after hearing their words, the chief merchant felt great fear. He immediately descended from the tree. At this moment, all the people exclaimed, screaming and crying for a short time, 'Alas! This is extremely painful. How can we see the subtle land (i.e., their home land) in Jambudvīpa again? If we had known of this distressing place from the first, we would rather have remained there and eaten cattle's dung to survive. We would not have come here seeking wealth.'

"At that time, the chief merchant, following the former path, returned to the place he had left [his party]. He saw that his fellow merchants and all the *rākṣasī*s were still asleep as before. At that moment the chief merchant went back to sleep.

"At daybreak he thought, 'How can I make all the merchants understand this matter? If I abruptly speak of this, it will leak out immediately. If the *rākṣasī*s hear of it, I am afraid that they will take us to the place of hardship. My words about this matter must be concealed. So, on the day of the festival in the fourth month when the horse king [Keśi] is coming, I will tell them. Why? From former days a verse says: 523b

Generally in a place of knowledgeable people,
If one carelessly speaks his mind,
That matter must leak out.
Everyone who hears it transmits it.
On this account he is blamed.
In that case he receives great suffering.
Therefore a wise man does not
Carelessly spread his words.

"At that time, the chief merchant concealed the matter and remained silent. When the happy festival day of the fourth month came, then for the first time he told all the merchants about the matter. [He said,] 'All of you! Be cautious now! Do not be self-indulgent! Neither feel a persistent attachment to passions, be covetous of women, nor be greedy for food or other wealth! I am overwhelmed with pity for you, so I now secretly tell you this.' All the merchants heard now what the chief merchant said. It was just as when in a mountain forest a lion suddenly roars loudly, all the lesser beasts near that mountain hear its roar and feel great fear. All the people said to each other, 'We have not yet escaped from hateful events of the great sea.'

"A day passed and at nightfall the merchants saw all the *rākṣasīs* sleeping deeply and peacefully. [The merchants] secretly and stealthly got up from their beds and went together to the designated place. They arrived there and then addressed the chief merchant, 'Good! Chief merchant! We wish you tell us what you saw.' At that time the chief merchant explained the events he had witnessed. The people were sad and melancholy after hearing it. They addressed the chief merchant, 'Oh, chief merchant! We must quickly go to the horse king's place. We wish to stay in a proper place so that we will be able to reach our original birthplace of Jambudvīpa.' Thereupon, all the merchants went to the horse king's place.

"At that time the horse king [Keśi] came to the seashore. Revealing half his body he chanted three times in a human voice, 'Who wishes to cross over the sea of [painful] hardship to the yonder shore? I will smoothly carry [that person] on my back to cross over, and allow him to reach the other shore.' After hearing the horse king said this, all the merchants were so overjoyed that their hair stood on end. Joining their palms, they all worshiped the horse king by touching their heads to the ground. They said, 'Good! Horse king! We wish to cross over and we want to reach the yonder shore. We pray to you to save us and take us from this shore to the yonder shore.'

"At that time the horse king said to all the merchants, 'You must know that those *rākṣasīs* will soon be here. Some of them will lead boys and the other will lead girls. They will pitifully and mournfully weep and show their misery. You cannot give rise to a mind of a persistent attachment to passions at that moment. If you do so, even if you are riding on my

back, you will definitely fall down and be eaten by those *rākṣasī*s. If you 523c
think like this, 'She is neither my betrothed nor mine. They are not my children,' even if you grasp only a single piece of my hair with your hand and hang on to it, at that point I will smoothly take you to the yonder shore promptly.' After saying this, [the horse king Keśi told all the merchants,] 'Now you should ride on my back or grasp a part of my body, feet, or legs.' Thereupon, all the merchants followed his words and grabbed onto him. The horse king then carried those merchants on his back, speaking in a compassionate voice. He flew in the sky and traveled as swiftly as a wind.

"At that time all the *rākṣasī*s heard the horse king's compassionate voice. They also heard the sound of the horse's galloping, like that of a violent wind. They suddenly awoke and looked for the merchants, but they had all disappeared. They searched for them here and there, and then they saw in the distance the merchants riding on the horse king, having fled during the [*rākṣasī*s'] unguarded moment. After seeing this, [the *rākṣasī*s] quickly led the children and ran to the seashore. They shouted in pitiful voices and mournfully wept and wailed; they were in great distress.

"Each of them said, 'You! All the sages! Now you are leaving us. Where are you going? You cause us to have no husbands. You are our husbands. You previously fell into the great fear of a disaster at sea, from which we saved you. We only wish you to remain together with us as our husbands. Now you abandon us and cast us away. Where are you going? You have no sense of moral obligation. Why do you give us up? If we have made a violation we now supplicate you for a chance to repent of it. From now on we will never make evil acts. Those who do not need us in that way should now take these children and leave together with them.' Even though the *rākṣasī*s made such pitiful groundless statements at that time, the horse king Keśi still carried the five hundred merchants away, smoothly crossing over the great sea to the yonder shore, and they arrived in Jambudvīpa.

"*Bhikṣu*s! What do you think? What an extraordinary figure the horse king Keśi of that time was! He was precisely me, myself. What a remarkable man the chief merchant among the five hundred merchants was! He was precisely Śāriputra. What great people the five hundred merchants were! They were all precisely the wanderer Sañjaya[-vairaṭī]'s five hundred disciples. At that time, when all those five hundred merchants came to the place of hardship, I delivered them from the hardship and caused them to reach the yonder shore. Then they returned to Sañjaya in the place of wrong views. Śāriputra led them to my place after educating them. In the wild land of wrong views I edified them and caused them to attain liberation from the sea of birth and death. For this reason, you must give rise to a mind of reverence and respect in the Buddha's place."

Furthermore, the *Jiu zapiyu jing* (T. 206) says:

In ancient times five Buddhists were traveling together. When they encountered a snowstorm, they went to a shrine to [seek shelter and] sojourn. In the [shrine] building there were images of spirits, which were respectfully
524a worshiped by the people. Four of the travelers said, "This evening it is very cold. We should take these wooden images and burn them to use in cooking." The other traveler said, "These [images] are worshiped by the people. You cannot damage them." So they left [the images] as they stood without burning them.

In this room evil spirits always ate human beings. They said to one another, "We will eat just the one man as only he is afraid of us. The other four are evil and we should not attack them." The one who dared not destroy [the images] heard the spirits' speaking in the night. He got up and shouted to his companions, 'I am leaving." The other four then said, 'Why don't we destroy the images and burn them to use in cooking?' Then they took [the images] and burned them. The cannibalistic spirits were frightened and promptly ran away.

A person's learning of the [Buddhist] Way is also like this. He continually needs a strong will. He should not be timid and enable evil spirits to harm human beings.

Therefore, the *Vimalakīrtinirdeśa* (T. 475) says, "For instance, it is just as when a person is frightened, nonhuman beings take advantage of it."

The *Pusa chutai jing* (i.e., *Pusa cong Doushutian jiangshen mutai shuo guangpu jing;* T. 384) further says:

At that tme the World-honored One told Zhi[qing]jing ("Purity of Intelligence") Bodhisattva, "A bodhisattva who will take up a [buddha's] place in the next existence (Skt. *eka-jāti-pratibaddha*) was born into a humble family by way of skillful expedient means. He wished to be able to manifest himself and to remove the defilement of ignorance (Skt. *avidyā-saṃyojana*). He stayed in his mother's womb for ten months. On the day he was born he manifested himself without hands and feet. His parents saw him and thought he was an evil spirit. They deserted him in a wild plain and let no one see him. Several days after that, the mother became pregnant again. When full ten months had passed, she gave birth to a boy. The boy had regular features that were extremely wonderful and very rare in the world. He was born in the daytime and died the night [of the same day]. His parents wept aloud, hitting their chests and facing toward heaven. [They said,] 'God of mountains! God of trees! Why do you not sympathize with us? Previously we had a child but he [was born] with no hands and feet. So we deserted him in the wild plain. Now we had a child whose regular features were matchless and whose appearance was just like that of gods in heaven, but now again [we lost our son]; he was born in the daytime and died that night. Our hearts are broken! How can we deal with this?'

"Again, several months passed and the mother became pregnant again. After ten full months she gave birth to another boy, who had three heads, eight feet, four eyes, and eight arms. Those who saw him had goosebumps [in fear]. His parents and whole family were willing to part with him and intended to get rid of him. The bodhisattva's incarnation made them unable to get rid of him. The parents asked him, 'Are you a heavenly being, a dragon, or a spiritual being?' At that time the newborn promptly said to his parents in verse:

> I am neither a heavenly being, a *yakṣa,*
> An *asura,* nor a *garuḍa.*
> To remove ignorance for my mother's sake,
> I was reincarnated in my parents' house.
> Their previous child [born] without hands and feet was
> Also myself.
> The one who was born in the morning and died in the evening was
> A supreme revered one of the eighth stage [of the bodhisattva's path].
> I have now received the form
> Of three heads, eight hands, and eight feet.
> Why do you give me up and get rid of me?

Your path goes to the gate of hell.
You destroy the foundation of wholesomeness by burning.
You seek extinguishment and also want hardships.
524b I now recover my body
And reveal my original form of regular features.
Observing the precepts and not losing my vow,
I entrust my life to my parents' family.
I abandon my life from beginning to end.
[My lives] are as numerous as particles of fine dust.
Sentient beings' diseases are numerous.
I prescribe the medicine of nectar.
I urge and cause them to enter the [Buddhist] Way and examine themselves.
I do not cause them to enter wrong paths.
All heavenly beings receive happiness.
Nectar is the medicine to get rid of diseases,
And a medicine that does not go against the sacred teaching.
It is the medicine for liberation and nirvana.

Verses say:

[Merchants] sought treasures, lost ships, and failed to cross the sea.
They floated around thinking of human beings who would rescue them.
Many illusory seductive women just then came in haste.
The goblins deceived human feelings.
Under a false pretext they approached and saved [the men] from a disaster at sea.
Deceptively using affectionate voices.
If [the men] were not carried on the horse king [Keśi]'s back,
They would be in danger and difficulty contrary to peace.

Miracle Stories

(Twenty-six stories are briefly cited.)

[The Mystery of Blood that Happened to Liu Chong from Dongyang]
Liu Chong from Dongyang (in present-day Zhejiang province), whose pseudonym is Daohong, lived in Hushu (in present-day Jiangsu province).

Every night several *sheng* of blood flowed to the gate and into the yard. It was unknown from where [the blood] flowed. This incident happened for three or four [nights in a row].

Later, Chong became Assault Resisting General and was dispatched on an expedition to the north. Before he left he cooked some rice, but all [the rice] 524c
changed into worms. Other members of his family steamed or stir-fried [rice], but it all turned into worms as well. The hotter the fire became, the more vigorous the worms were. Chong consequently went on an expedition to the north. His army was defeated at Tanqiu, and [Liu Chong] was killed by Xu Long.

[The Mystery of Dragons in the Time of Lord Zhao of Lu State]

In Lord Zhao's nineteenth year of the state of Lu (524 B.C.E.), dragons fought each other in the deep waters of the Wei River outside the gate of Shi in Zheng state.

The *Jing Fang Yizhuan* (*Annotation of Changes*) says, "When people's minds are uneasy, it gives rise to the mishap that dragons fight in their town."

[The Mystery of Dragons in the Reign of Emperor Hui of the Han Dynasty]

In the morning of the first day, the Guiyou day, of the first month of the second year of Emperor Hui of the Han dynasty (193 B.C.E.), two dragons appeared in the well of Zuowenling in Tingdong village, Lanling county (in present-day Shandong province).

The *Jing Fang Yizhuan* says, "When a man of virtue is murdered, it gives rise to the mishap that dragons appear in a well. When a punishment is too cruel, it gives rise to the mishap that a black dragon comes out of a well."

[The Mystery of Snakes in the Reign of Emperor Wu of the Han Dynasty]

In the tenth month of the fourth year of the Taishi era during the reign of Emperor Wu of the Han dynasty (93 B.C.E.), a snake appeared in Zhao;[165] it came into the city from outside the city wall. The snake fought with a snake of the city near the shrine of Emperor Xiaowen, and the city's snake was killed. In the fall, two years later, the incident of Crown Prince Wei was caused by Jiang Chong, a man from Zhao.[166]

[The Mystery of a Serpent in the Reign of Emperor Huan of the Han Dynasty]

When Emperor Huan of the Han dynasty ascended the throne (147), a large serpent appeared in Deyang Hall of the Imperial Palace. Chunyu Yi,

Market Director of Luoyang, said, "That the snake has scales is an omen of warfare."

[The Mystery of Fishes that Happened during the Taikang Era of the Jin Dynasty]

During the Taikang era (280–289) of the Jin dynasty, two carp appeared on the roof of an arsenal. An arsenal is a storehouse of weapons, and [a fish's] hard scales are a kind of weapon (i.e., armor), too. Moreover, fish are of extreme *yin* and a roof is of grand *yang*. The emergence of a fish on a roof symbolizes that the extreme *yin* offends the grand *yang* by means of the disaster of warfare.

Later, at the beginning of Emperor Hui's reign period (290–306), Yang Jun, father of the empress dowager, was killed [by Empress Jia] when arrows flew around above a palace gate. [The empress dowager] was dethroned to the staus of a commoner. She died in a room deep in the recesses of a palace. At the end of the Yuankang era (299) Empress Jia controlled a dictatorship, and she slandered the Crown Prince and killed him. Soon thereafter she was dethroned [and killed], too. In the past ten years misfortune fell upon the emperor's mother and wife. Since that time on, disorder was brought upon the world.

The *Jing Fang Yizhuan* (*Annotation of Changes*) says, "Fish strangely coming out of water and jumping onto a road indicates entering into a war."

[The Mystery of Rats in the Reign of Emperor Cheng of the Han Dynasty]

In the ninth month of the fourth year of the Jianshi era (29 B.C.E.), during the reign of Emperor Cheng of the Han dynasty, south of the city of Chang'an there were some rats that took the yellow dead leaves of cypress trees in their mouths, went up into trees such as cypress and elm, and built nests in the trees in the graveyard of the local residents. Among these trees, paulownia and cypress were in the majority. In the nests there were no baby rats, but instead several *sheng* of dried-up dung. At that time a courtier commentator said, "I am afraid that a fire will break out."

Rats, [however], are small thieving animals; they go out during the night and hide in the daytime. Yet just now they had came out of a den and climbed up a tree [to make nests]. This is an omen that a humble person is going to occupy a high-ranking position. Tongbo county (in present-day Henan province) is the place where Empress Wei Si's garden was located.[167]

After that, Empress Zhao ascended the most august position from a humble station, just as Empress Wei [Si] had done, but she did not have a son after all and was killed. This symbolizes that in the following year (28 B.C.E.) a hawk burned its nest and killed its babies.

The *Jing Fang Yizhuan* (*Annotation of Changes*) says, "If a vassal embezzles 525a
public funds and deceives his sovereign, it causes the weird case where rats make nests [in trees]."

[The Mystery of a Dog in the Reign of Emperor Jing of the Han Dynasty]

In the third year of the reign of Emperor Jing of the Han dynasty (154 B.C.E.), a dog mated with a domestic pig in Handan (in present-day Hebei province). At that time, the king of the state of Zhao rose in revolt in league with six states. He contacted the Xiongnu from outside [of the Han territory] and took them as reinforcements.

According to the book *Wuxingzhi* (*Annals of the Five Primary Elements*), the king of the state of Zhao was muddled and confused and caused a peculiar affair in which a pig mated with an animal of another species. The Xiongnu are like a race of dogs and pigs.

[The Mystery of Evil Spirits in the Reign of Emperor Zhang of the Han Dynasty]

Shou Guanghou, who lived during the reign of Emperor Zhang of the Han dynasty (76–88), was able to denounce various evil spirits and cause them to bind and reveal themselves.

Among the people of the county in which he lived, there was a woman who had an illness caused by an evil spirit. When Guanghou performed an exorcism, a large snake, several *zhang* long, died outside of the gate of [her house].

There was a tree in which a dryad lived. People who rested [under the tree] died, and any birds that flew over it fell to the ground. When [Guang]hou exorcised it, even though it was the middle of summer the tree withered and a large snake, seven or eight *zhang* long, died and hung from a branch.

Emperor Zhang heard about this and summoned [Guanghou] to question him. [Guanghou] said, "There are such things." The emperor said, "In this palace building there are evil spirits. After midnight, several people wearing red clothes with disheveled hair always walk in a line, holding a lamp. Can you exorcise them?" Guanghou replied, "Yes, I can do it. They are merely minor evil spirits."

The emperor had his three attendants disguise themselves as the evil spirits. When [Shou] Guanghou performed the exorcism, the three fell down to the ground and ceased to breathe. The emperor, terrified, said, "These were not mischievous spirits. I was just testing [your power]!" He immediately had [Guanghou] unbind them by a spell.

[The Mystery of a Buzzard that Happened to Jia Yi]

When Jia Yi was Grand Mentor for the king of Changsha, on the *gengzi* day of the fourth month a buzzard flew into his house and perched on the corner of his seat. The buzzard stayed there for a while and then flew away. Yi looked in a book to divine it, and it said, "If a wild bird flies into a room, the master will soon be leaving the house." Yi was afraid of this, so he composed the *Funiao fu* (*Poem of a Buzzard*), in which he expressed [the wish] to see life and death as equal, fortune and misfortune to be the same, and to make determinations by means of leaving his fate to heaven.[168]

[The Mystery of a Public Inn in the City of Anyang]

In the south of the city of Anyang (in present-day Henan province), there was a public inn, but it was impossible to lodge there. Those who stayed there were killed. A scholar who was passing by, however, intended to stay overnight there. An inhabitant of the village said, "You cannot stay in this [inn]. From the beginning up to today, of those who have taken lodging for the night no one has survived." The scholar replied, "This is nothing difficult. I can settle the matter by myself." Consequently he stayed in the inn.

The scholar then sat up straight, reading a book aloud. He stopped after a while. After midnight someone wearing black single-layer clothing came and called the manager of the inn from outside the door. When the manager of the inn responded to her, she asked, "Is there anyone in the inn?" The manager answered, "Until a few minutes ago a scholar was reading a book here. He just stopped, but he does not seem to have gone to sleep." The person clicked her tongue and departed. Soon another person wearing a red cloth headdress came and called the manager of the inn. When the manager responded to him, he asked, just as the previous person had done, "Is there anyone in the inn?" The manager answered in the same way as before. The
525b man clicked his tongue and left as well. The scholar then thought that no one else was there and arose. He [disguised himself] and went to where [the two

persons] had previously called out, and called the manager of the inn. The manager replied again. [The scholar] asked if anyone was staying in the inn. The manager replied in the same way as he had done previously. [The scholar] then asked, "Who is the one in black clothing who came awhile ago?" [The manager] answered, "It is a sow from next door on the north side." [The scholar] asked again, "Who is the one wearing a red cloth headdress who just came?" [The manager] answered, "It is an old rooster from next door on the west side." [The scholar] asked, "Who are you?" [The manager] answered, "I am an old scorpion." So, the scholar secretly recited from a book and did not dare sleep until the morning light.

After dawn the villager came to see [the scholar] and said with surprise, "How is it you're still alive?" The scholar said, "Go and get a sword for me, and I will slay the mischievous spirits with you." So they dug the place where the manager had spoken the night before, and as expected they found an old scorpion as large as the musical instrument *pipa.* Its tail with its venomous stinger was several *chi* long. They found an old rooster next door on the west side and a sow next door on the north side. They killed all three. The deadly nature of the inn was consequently suppressed. There was no longer any disastrous violence there.

[The Mystery of a Serpent in Minzhong Prefecture in the Eastern Yue Region]

In Minzhong prefecture (in present-day Fujian province) in the Eastern Yue region there is Mount Yongling which is several tens of *li* high. In the cave north of its base there was a huge serpent, seven or eight *zhang* long, with a girth of one *zhang.* The people of the local community were always in fear of it. Since [the serpent] took a heavy loss of lives, the Commandant of Dongye county and the Senior Subalterns of the cities within the county offered sacrifices of a cow and a sheep [to the serpent],[169] but there was no good result. Appearing in a person's dream or divined by a sorcerer [the serpent] demanded a twelve- or thirteen-year-old girl to eat. The Commandant, the District Magistrate, and the District Chief were all very concerned about this, but the [the serpent's] ferocity never ceased. Together they asked for girls born of slaves as well as from criminal families and raised them. On the day of the sacrificial offering, the first day of the eighth month, they sent one of the girls to the entrance of the serpent's cave. The serpent came out at night and gulped the girl down. This situation was repeated every year and nine girls were sacrificed up to that time.

At that time (i.e., in the tenth year of this awful incident) [the officials] recruited and searched for a girl beforehand but they could not find one [for the sacrifice]. The family of Li Dan of Jiangle county had six daughters but no son. The youngest daughter, called Ji, wished to respond to the call but her parents would not allow her. Ji said, "You, my parents, are not blessed in your progeny; you only have six daughters and no son. Although you have children, it is as if you have no children. I have no opportuity to perform a feat and rescue my parents just as Ti Ying did.[170] I am incapable to offer provisions to you. On the contrary, I idly spend food and clothing [given by you]. I would rather die than to live bringing no benefit for you. If you sell my body [to be used as a sacrifice], you can obtain some money and in this way I can offer provisions to you. Wouldn't that be good?" Her parents loved [Ji] and pitied her, and they would not allow her to go. So Ji secretly left home; [her parents] could not stop her.

[Ji] went and asked the high-ranking officials for a good sword and a dog that would [attack and] bite a snake. On the first day of the eighth month she went to a shrine [near the snake's cave] and sat there, concealing a sword in her bosom, with a dog. She had previously prepared cakes from several *dan* of rice, smeared them with honey and roasted wheat powder, and placed them at the entrance of the cave.

The serpent came out that night. Its head was as large as a granary, and its eyes were just like mirrors, two *chi* in diameter. [The serpent] sniffed fragrant rice cakes and ate them first. Thereupon, Ji loosed the dog on it and the dog bit it. Ji cut [the serpent] from behind and wounded it. Since [the serpent] could not stand severe pain, it rushed out of the cave and reached
525c the courtyard [of the shrine], where it died. Ji went into the cave and found the skulls of the nine girls. She took them all out and shouted with anger, "You were weak and cowardly. Therefore, you were eaten by the serpent. You are very pitiable." Thereafter, the girl Ji walked slowly home.

The king of Yue heard about this. He married Ji and made her the queen. Her father was appointed governor of Jiangle county and her mother and sisters were all granted rewards. From that time on in Dongye county there was no more evil demon. A folk song [in praise of Ji] remains even today.

[The Mystery of a Mouse that Happened to Wang Zhounan from Zhongshan]

During the Zhenshi period (240–253) [of the Wei kingdom], Wang Zhounan from Zhongshan (in present-day Hebei province) was the Magistrate of Xiangyi county (in present-day Henan province). A mouse came out of a hole and climbed into his office. The mouse said, "Zhounan, you will die on a certain day of a certain month." Zhounan walked hurriedly [to the mouse] and did not respond to it. The mouse then returned into the hole.

Later, on the day [mentioned by the mouse] it came out again. This time it wore a headdress and black clothes and said, "Zhounan, you will die at high noon." Again, Zhounan did not respond to it and the mouse went back into the hole, but it soon came out once again and then went back into the hole once more. Going back and forth [between the hole and the office] the mouse repeatedly spoke, just as it had done before. Just at high noon the mouse again said, "Zhounan, if you do not respond to me, what more can I say?" When the mouse finished speaking, it fell down and died. Thereupon, the [mouse's] headdress and clothes disappeared. Zhounan hurried over to look at it and it was completely just like an ordinary mouse.

[The Mystery of a Tree that Happened to Zhang Yi in Guiyang]

Zhang Yi, the Governor of Guiyang prefecture (in present-day Hunan province) and a man from the Jiangxia area (in present-day Hubei province), whose pseudonym is Shenggao, resided in Yanling (in present-day Henan province). In a field there was a big tree measuring ten arm-lengths and it covered six *mu* of land; the branches and leaves of the tree cast shade on the ground underneath and grain and plants would not grow there. [Shenggao] sent his workers to cut down the tree. When the workers chopped the tree several times, there was a rush of blood-red sap [from the gashes in the tree]. The workers were astounded and returned to tell Shenggao about it. Shenggao cried out in anger, "Since the tree is old, the sap is red. How is this strange?" Accordingly, he went to cut the tree himself and [saw] a great deal of blood-red sap flowed out. Shenggao tried again to cut the branches. There was a hollow in [the tree] from which an old gray-haired man, four or five *chi* tall, jumped out and came toward Shenggao. Shenggao drew his sword and he killed all four or five old men [who had jumped out of the hollow in the tree one after another]. All the people by his side fell prone on the ground in horror. [Only] Shenggao, a man of marvelous mind, remained calm as before. All the people slowly examined [the old men]. They were creatures who were part human being and part beast.

Is this what [Confucius] described, "Evil spirits of senseless beings are demons called *kui* or *wangliang*"?[171]

In the year Shenggao cut the tree, he was summoned by the Minister of Works and appointed as the Censor and the District Magistrate of Yanzhou.

[The Mystery of a Public Inn that Happened to Song Daxian in Nanyang]

[This is a story of] a man of Nanyang called Song Daxian. In the west suburbs [of Nanyang] there was a public inn but no one could lodge in it, [because] anyone who stayed at the inn would be harmed. Daxian considered himself to be not at risk since he kept to the right path. He stayed on the second floor of the inn, where he played a Chinese zither (*qin*). He had neither a weapon nor a stick.

In the middle of night an apparition came up the stairs and spoke to Daxian. [The apparition] glared hatefully at him and gnashed his teeth; he had a forbidding countenance. Daxian, however, kept playing the Chinese zither. Thereupon, the apparition left.

[The apparition] returned, bringing the severed head of a dead person from a marketplace and said to Daoxian, "You should rather cook and eat
526a it." Accordingly he threw the head in front of Daxian. Daxian said, "Very good! I was going to sleep without a pillow tonight. I now have this [as a pillow]." [The apparition] left.

[The apparition] again came back after awhile and said, "Would you like to wrestle with me?" Daxian replied, "All right!" Before he had finished replying, [the apparition] drew close to him and Daxian then grasped its waist in advance. The apparition anxiously cried out, "Murder!" Daxian then killed it.

The next morning, [Daxian] examined [the apparition], which was an old fox. Thereafter, no evil incident happened in the inn; there were no longer any harmful or fearful things there.

[The Mystery of Evil Spirits in an Inn of Luling County during the Wu Kingdom]

During the period of the Wu kingdom (222–280), evil spirits frequently appeared in a two-story inn in a city in Luling county. Those who lodged there were inevitably killed. Later no envoys or officials dared to stay at the inn.

At that time, there was a brave and strong man from Danyang (in present-day Jiangsu province) whose family name was Tang and whose first name was Ying. When he arrived at Luling as an envoy he went to the inn to take lodgings. A [local] official informed him that he should not stay in the [inn], but Ying did not listen to his admonition and sent all his followers outside to stay alone there. He had only a large sword.

[Ying] lay down [to sleep]. At midnight,[172] someone knocked on a small side door, and far away from [the door] Ying asked whom it was. The person answered, "The Regional Retainer Clerk is here to greet you." Ying replied, "Show him in." After exchanging greetings [the Regional Retainer Clerk] left. After a short while there was again a knock on the door just as before and the person said, "The Commandery Governor is here to greet you." Ying again let [the Commandery Governor] in. Even after [the Commandery Governor,] who wore black clothes, had left, Ying thought he was a human being without doubt. Soon thereafter, [however,] again someone knocked on the door and said, "The Regional Retainer Clerk and the Commandery Governor are here to visit you." Ying then felt suspicious and thought, "This time of night is not appropriate for [official] visits. Moreover, the Commandery Governor and the Regional Retainer Clerk should not travel together." He realized that they were evil spirits.

Holding his sword, [Ying] invited in [the Commandery Governor and the Regional Retainer Clerk]. He saw that they were both dressed up. They together stepped forward and seated themselves. The one referred to as the Commandery Governor spoke to Ying.

Before [the Commandery Governor] had finished speaking, the Regional Retainer Clerk jumped up and went behind Ying. Ying turned around and struck him with his sword. [The one referred to as] the Commandery Governor left his seat and ran away. Ying hurriedly chased him and caught up with him at the wall at the rear of the inn. Ying slashed at him and inflicted several wounds. Ying then went back [to his room] to sleep.

At daybreak Ying led the people to search the place. They found traces of blood, and following them they caught all [the evil spirits]. The one referred to as the Commandery Governor was the evil spirit of an old fox, and the one referred to as the Regional Retainer Clerk was the evil spirit of a large old wild cat. After that, there were no more strange incidents and never again any evil spirits.

[The Mystery of an Old Man in Eastern County During the Jian'an Era]

During the Jian'an era [of Emperor Xian of the Han dynasty (196–219)], there were strange incidents in a household in Eastern County. For no reason, an earthenware vessel spontaneously made loud noises, just as if someone had struck it. Plates and a table suddenly disappeared before one's eyes. Every time a hen laid an egg it disappeared. This situation lasted for several years. [The family] was bitterly disgusted with it.

[The family members] then made a lot of good dishes, covered them, and placed them in a room. They hid behind a door and watched [what would happen]. Just as they had thought, [the strange incident] happened again: [the earthenware] made [the same] noises as before. Immediately they closed the door and tried to find [the cause of the noises] in the room, but nothing could be seen. So they began randomly striking the floor with a stick. After a while, they struck something in a corner of the room and someone groaned.
526b Intending to kill it, they opened the door and found an old man, about one hundred years old. They could not communicate to him in language at all. In appearance he looked like a beast.

Subsequently they investigated [the old man]. Then they found [the old man's] family living several *li* away, and they said that more than ten years had passed since the old man had disappeared. They were grieving and were happy that he had been found.

More than a year later, [the old man] disappeared again. It was known that in the Chenliu area (in present-day Henan province) an apparition just like this one appeared. People of that time considered that it was the same old man.

[The Mystery of an Old Fox Disguised as a Father during the Jin Dynasty]

During the Jin dynasty period, in Wuxing (in present-day Zhejiang province) there was a man who had two sons. When [the boys] were working in the fields, their father came and scolded and beat them. They went home to tell their mother. The mother asked their father [why he had acted in such a bad way]. The father was very surprised [to hear of it], but then realized that it had been done by an evil spirit. He ordered [his sons] to kill it [when it returned].

The evil spirit then became inactive and did not return to them. The father was worried his sons might be troubled by the evil spirit, so he personally went to see how they were. The sons thought that he was the evil spirit, so they killed and buried [their own father]. The evil spirit then went to their home [ahead of them], disguising itself as their father, and said to the family members, "My two sons have already killed the evil spirit." When the sons returned home in the evening they rejoiced over it along [with the family members]. Consequently, no one was aware of [what had heppened] for years.

Later, a [Dharma] master stopped by [to visit] the family and told the two sons, "Your father has a serious malicious vapor." The sons reported this to the father, who became very angry. The sons went out to the door and told the [Dharma] master, "Please leave here quickly." The [Dharma] master, however, raised his voice and came into [the house]. The father then revealed himself to be a large old fox and crept under the bed, but it was finally caught. [The two sons then realized that] they had killed their real father. They reinterred their father's body and went into mourning. One of the sons committed suicide, and the other died in anger and resentment.

(The eighteen stories above are found in the *Soushen ji* [*Records of Inquiries of the Spirits*].)

[The Mystery of Crows Building Nests in a Palace Building in Nanjing during the Jin Dynasty]

The *Nanjing siji* (*Records of Monasteries of Nanjing*) of the Jin dynasty says:

> Bodi Monastery is located in Qingling city in Xinlin, Moling county (in present-day Jiangsu province). Emperor Jianwen raised it in the second year of the Xian'an era (372) of the Jin dynasty, and it was originally called Xinlin Monastery.
>
> At that time Daorong, a nun of Wujiang Monastery in Liyang prefecture (in present-day Anhui province), practiced asceticism and was able to communicate with spiritual beings. She could foretell fortune or misfortune. She was known as a sage nun in the world.
>
> At the beginning of the Xian'an era (371) some crows built nests in a palace building. The emperor often had a fortune-teller interpret this. [The fortune-teller] said, "There is a female master in the southwest. She should be able to dispel this strange incident."
>
> [The emperor] immediately dispatched a messenger to Wujiang and invited the sage nun. He asked her if this incident was auspicious or

inauspicious. The nun said, "If you cultivate virtue, you will be able to exorcise disasters. If you observe purification in your mind and body, you will be able to avoid and defend from [misfortunes], too." The emperor then set up a seven-day purification rite; he worshiped [the Buddha] and repented of his sins devotedly and diligently. Before the Dharma assembly came to an end, the flock of crows suddenly left, carrying away their nests. [The palace building] was quickly emptied [of the crows' nests]. The emperor's respect for and faith in [the Buddha] deepened and increased. Accordingly, for the sake of the sage nun, [Emperor Jianwen] erected this monastery.

[The Mystery of a Wild Cat Disguised as a Man's Wife during the Jin Dynasty]

In the time of Lord Haixi (i.e., Sima Yi, the dethroned emperor; r. 365–371) there was a man whose mother had died, but since his family was poor he had no money to bury her. So he moved the coffin with her corpse deep into the mountains. At the side [of her grave] he made wooden shoes day and night without taking a rest.

Toward the evening a woman holding a child in her arms came and stayed overnight [at his place]. When night came, the filial son had not yet finished making wooden shoes, and the woman repeatedly asked him to go to sleep.
526c Then she went to sleep near the fire. In reality [the filial son saw] a wild cat clutching a dark-colored chicken, so he beat them to death and threw them into a pit in the back yard.

The next day a man came and asked him about [the woman] in detail, "Where is the one who came here yesterday and who stayed here last night?" The filial son replied, "There was only a wild cat. I promptly killed it." The man said, "You have killed my wife under a false accusation. How can you say that she was a wild cat? Where is it now?" Therefore together they went to the pit and saw that the wild cat had become a woman. The man then bound the filial son and turned him over to government officials, who [ruled that] he must atone for his crime with death. [The filial son], however, said to the director, "This is in fact an evil spirit. Just bring a hunting dog and you will know whether or not it is an evil spirit."

[The man] came again to urge them to put to death the filial son. The director then asked him about the task of a hunting [dog]. "Can we unleash a [hunting] dog?" [The man] replied, "I am afraid of dogs by nature. Do not unleash it!" [The director] released the dog, and [the man] then transformed to an old wild cat. Therefore it was shot and killed. The woman had already changed back to a wild cat.

[The Mystery of a Wild Cat Disguised as a Woman that Gave Birth to Babies during the Jin Dynasty]

During the Taiyuan era (376–396) of the Jin dynasty, Chun Yujin, who was young and fair-skinned, resided in front of a stupa of Waguan Temple [in Jinling in present-day Jiangsu province]. He sent a guest south of Shitou city [two *li* west of Jinling], where he met a girl who had a beautiful face and figure. [Yu]jin was glad to meet her. While speaking, they felt they were getting along with one another. He took her to the northern corner of the city, where they both had a thoroughly good time. Afterward they separated from each other, but they set a time for their next meeting. Moreover, [Yujin] said that he wanted to marry her. The girl said, "If I were to take a husband like you, I would not regret it even if I died. I have many brothers, and both my parents are well. You must ask my parents [for permission to marry me]."

Thereupon, [Yu]jin had the girl's maidservant ask her parents' intention. Without objections, her parents approved their marriage. Accordingly, the girl ordered her maidservant to take a hundred catties of silver and a hundred rolls of silk fabric to [Yu]jin as dowry for their marriage.

Some time later, they had two children. [Yujin's wife told him,] "You will become the Directorate of the Palace Library." The next day, just as she had said, horse-mounted messengers came to summon [Yujin] and led him [to the capital] on vehicles and horses and with drum and fife bands before and after [the procession].

Shortly after, as a hunter passed by and greeted [Yu]jin, several tens of dogs owned by [the hunter] attacked [Yujin's] wife and children and mauled them to death. [The woman and children] all turned into wild cats, and at the same time the silk fabric, gold, and silver became grass and human skeletons.

[The Mystery of a Girl Possessed by an Evil Spirit in the Time of Zhang Chun of the Jin Dynasty]

During the Yongchu era of the Jin dynasty (420), Zhang Chun became Governor of Wuchang. At that time a man had married off his daughter, but before [the girl] boarded the carriage, she suddenly lost consciousness. She then went out and attacked the people, taking advantage of the circumstances, and said, "I am not happy to marry and do housework." A vulgar sorcerer said, "This is an evil spirit." [The sorcerer] took the girl to the riverside.

(The three stories above are found in the *Youming lu* [*Records of the Other World and This World*].)[173]

[The Mystery of Evil Spirits in the House of Liang Daoxiu during the Song Dynasty]

During the time of the Song dynasty (420–479), Liang Qing, a man from Anding (present-day Jingchuan in Gansu province), whose pseudonym was Daoxiu, lived in Huan Xuzhou's former residence near the Right Directorate for Imperial Manufactories of Yangzhou.

In the second month of the fourteenth year of the Yuanjia era (437), a strange luminous object often appeared, and the sound of a bamboo fence tearing apart could be heard. [Qing] ordered a maidservant called Song Luo to go and see [what happened]. She found a man who said, "My family name is Hua and my first name is Furong. I am a messenger of the Most August Liujia, and I came down from Taiweizi Palace. I stopped by here, my former residence." Thereupon, he stayed [in Qing's house] and would not leave.

Moreover [Hua Furong had] the head of a bird and a human body. Whenever someone looked at [Furong], he struck that person. [Furong] threw excrement and filth at Qing. [Furong] was intimidated by shooting a bow and disappeared at [the sound of] the bowstring. At the same time he dyed the arrow with a deep red-colored fluid.

527a Furthermore, [Furong] manifested himself as something resembling an ape, which hung down from trees. [Qing] ordered his man to stab [Furong]. Pierced in the buttocks, [Furong] fell down to the ground and immediately disappeared. A day later [Furong] returned, walking with a limp on the roof. He approached a maidservant and begged for food. [The maidservant] made rice balls and gave them to him. He ate two *sheng* [of rice] at once.

Several days later, numerous evil spirits came in groups. Their ugliness was unspeakable. Dust and stones flew about on the curtain around Song Luo's bed and did not stop until morning for many days in succession.

A maidservant called Caiju met an evil spirit on a street. [This evil spirit] wore clothes and a headdress, rode a horse, and was guarded by several tens of subordinates. He said to Caiju, "I am a transcendent from heaven. Do not call me an evil spirit." [Caiju] asked him, "Why do you always throw filth?" He answered, "Excrement and filth are a symbol of wealth. Throwing them is a sign of relocating soon."

Soon, as had been expected, Qing became a military general as well as Governor of Beilu prefecture. Since [Liang] Qing had been harassed by the vice and maliciousness [of evil spirits] for a long time, he summomned a foreign monk called Poluodie to chant a spell. All the evil spirits were afraid. Some went over a wall or ran into a hole in a wall. All cried out in voices like a bird's chirping. Thereafter, they stopped [coming out].

Shortly after Qing had settled down in the prefecture of his appointment, Song Luo again saw at midnight that several tens of thousands of people [were carrying] weapons in a dignified manner. One of them, who wore a headdress, gave her a letter in which about seventy Chinese characters were written on coarse paper. The handwriting was beautiful; it was modeled after the style of the former [calligraphers Wang] Xi[zhi] and [Wang] Xian[zhi]. Furthermore, the spirit sang a song, "I ascend the Peacock Tower. I hear the sound of the phoenix drum coming from the distance. I descend to the vicinity of Mount Zou from where the states of Liang and Lu are seen."

This evil spirit had an uncle called Cao. When [Cao] died, he wept and offered condolences in the same way as the people of this world. He [wished] to hand down an instruction, so he asked Song Luo for a box of paper [and wrote a message], the title of which read, "The late Kong Xiuzhi's blank letter with awe in order to offer condolences on his uncle's death." The description was full of sadness [about the deceased], and the writing was well arranged in order.

Moreover, he said [to Qing], "Recently, when I went to the west, I saw a *śramaṇa* who called himself Damocha. He asked me for news of you and entrusted to me five balls of incense to give to you." Qing had once taken an official trip to Dunhuang and remembered that he had seen the monk [there].

After a maidservant gave birth to a baby in Qing's house, the evil spirits stopped [appearing] there.

In Langye (in present-day Shandong province) Wang Chengzhi's wife, who was from the Xie family of Chen prefecture, gave birth to a son. His childhood name was Nuzi ("Slave"). Years later, Wang sent for his wife and maidservants and made [his wife from] the Xie family a concubine in order to benefit himself. In the eighth year of the Yuanjia era (431) [the concubine] died of an illness. The great tomb of the Wang family was in Guiji [in Zhejiang province]. [The concubine] was temporalily buried on the east ridge of a mountain in Jiankang.

After [Wang Chengzhi] returned from the burial and performed the rites to pacify the spirit of the diseased (*yü*), he entered the memorial hall with the spirit. He [was seated,] leaning on an armrest, when suddenly he was thrown into the air and fell to the ground. Then an angry voice said, "Why did you not sing a funeral song? Would you cause me to go all the way [to the other world] quietly?" Chengzhi said, "This is not a formal funeral. Therefore, I simply did not prepare complete rites."

(The two stories above are found in the *Yiyuan* [*Park of Wonders*].)

In the Zhou dynasty, Zhongni (i.e., Confucius) said to Ji Huanzi, "I have heard that evil spirits of senseless beings are called *kui* or *wangliang*."[174]

(Wei Zhao's annotation says: "Lifeless things mean mountains. *Kui yizu* is a hill man so called by the Yue people, or it is called *duzu* ("one foot"). *Wangliang* is a mountain spirit. It is fond of imitating a human voice and confuses human beings.")

527b This story is found in the *Guoyu* (*Talks of States*).

The *Shiji* (*Records of the Grand Historian*) says, "The First Emperor of the Qin dynasty said, 'The mountain spirits merely foresee things a year ahead.'"[175]

[The Mystery of Men Who Ate Shrimp and Crab in the Western Mountains]

Deep in the mountains in the western direction, there are men who are more than one *chi* tall. They bare their bodies and catch shrimp and crab. It is not their nature to be afraid of people. When they see a person staying in the mountain, they are happy and broil shrimp and crab depending on that person's fire. They watch until the person is out and then they steal their salt in order to eat the crab. They are called *shanxiao.* They have voices that sound like spontaneous crying. People always use bamboo chopsticks to set off firecrackers in a fire. ([In the two Chinese characters for the word "firecracker"] the first character is pronounced *pu* and the second is pronounced *bi.*) Accordingly all *shanxiao* are afraid of [firecrackers]. If you offend them, they will cause you to have a chill or fever. (Even though they have the form of humans, they are simply a kind of evil spirit. They are found everywhere in the mountains.)

(The story above is found in the *Shenyi jing* [*Scripture on Miracles*].)

[The Mystery of Wood Caught in a Crab Weir Made by the Wang Family during the Song Dynasty]

At the beginning of the Yuanjia era (424) of the Song dynasty, a man from Fuyang (in present-day Zhejiang province), whose family name was Wang, set up a crab weir in the backwaters of a river.

In the morning when he went to inspect it, he found a piece of wood, about two *chi* long, had caught in the weir and broken it, [so] all the crabs had escaped [from the weir]. [Wang] then repaired the weir and took out the piece of wood and put it onto the bank. The next morning he went back to inspect the weir again and found that the piece of wood had been caught in the weir and broken it, just as before. So Wang again repaired the weir and took out the piece of wood. The following morning he saw that the same thing had happened. Wang suspected that the piece of wood was mysterious so he put it into a crab cage, tied it to a pole, and left for home carrying it on his shoulder. [He said,] "When I get home, I will cut up [this piece of wood] with an axe and then burn it."

Three *li* before he reached his house, he heard [something] suddenly move [in the crab cage]. He turned his head and saw that the piece of wood [which he had put in the cage] previously had transformed into a monster, with a human face and the body of a monkey, with one arm and one leg. [The monster] said to Wang, "In my nature I am fond of crabs. It was I who entered the water, broke your crab weir, and went into it to eat the crabs these days. I feel ashamed of what I did. I hope you will understand and forgive me. Please open the cage and let me out. I am a mountain deity. I will surely help you and cause you to catch lots of crabs in your weir." Wang, [however,] said, "You are the one who committed the savage act. [You committed] numerous offenses from the first to the last. Naturally you must die." By all possible means the monster entreated [Wang] to release him, [but] Wang looked the other way and did not respond to him. The monster said, "What is your full name? I want to know it." He asked the question repeatedly. Wang still did not answer. When they approached the house, the monster said, "Since you will not release me and you will not tell me your full name, either, what more can I do? I must simply die." When Wang reached his house, he made a fire and burned [the monster].

After that, there was no longer anything strange at all. The local people said [the monster] was called a *shanxiao* (mountain dryad, nymph, or sprite). If it knows someone's full name it can harm that person. The reason [the monster] repeatedly asked Wang [his full name] is that it intended to kill him and save itself.

(The story above is found in the *Shuyi ji* [*Records to Give Accounts of Extraordinary Things*].)

[The Mystery of Zhang Liang, a Traitor during the Tang Dynasty, and a Thunderclap]

Zhang Liang, a traitor of the Tang dynasty, was formerly Commander-in-Chief of Youzhou. While he was worshiping at Zhiquan Monastery, he saw a large [buddha] statue whose major and minor physical characteristics were perfect. Thereupon, he made an exceptionally [generous] offering [to the statue].

[One time] Liang was struck by a thunderbolt. A pillar of the hall exploded, and a piece of the wood [pillar] hit Liang on one of his temples, but he was not gravely injured. So he went to the monastery to worship the statue, and
527c one of the statue's temples was seen to have a broken part.

This is found in the *Mingbao ji* [*Records of Rewards and Retributions from the Unseen World*].

Furthermore, during the Zhenguan era (627–649), this same statue suddenly had a mark around its neck. The large [mark] looked like a thread. At that time all people who saw it considered it to be an inauspicious omen. Soon afterward, just as they thought, Liang was executed as punishment. The mark [around the statue's neck] actually remains today.

(This is found in the *Mingbao shiyiji* [*Gleanings of Anecdotes of Rewards and Retributions from the Unseen World*].)

[End of] Fascicle Thirty-one of *A Forest of Pearls from the Dharma Garden*

Fascicle 32

Chapter Twenty-five

Transformation

(This chapter consists of three parts:) (1) Introduction, (2), Proficiency in the Law of Supernatural Transformation, and (3) Abhorrence of Desire.

1. Introduction

The Sage's activities indiscriminately pervade without hindrance. He exerts influence in numerous areas. You cannot seek anything through making a single way. You cannot deduce anything with only a principle. Therefore, he responds to coarseness with coarseness and to precision with precision. Coarseness or precision is in accordance with the faculty of each sentient being. Reason is certainly so.

Consequently, as for emitting great light and manifesting various supernatural transformations, this is merely his response to the leader of all the great bodhisattvas of the ten directions, the one to whom he hands down the honored position. If he places himself in the secular world and makes contact with vulgar beings, this is in order to stop evil and restore righteousness. Furthermore, one must follow the law of conditions. With proficiency in transformation he assesses people's feelings. One cannot clearly understand indirect symbols through marvelous truth, but he transforms himself and shows the form and substance of wonders, and through this he blocks the ignorant views toward wonders.

For instance, the Sage also joins herds of deer or horses to liberate them. At the time when he is among deer or horses, is he the same as deer or horses? If he was no different from deer or horses that comply with ordinary people of the world, it is clear that he would not rely on supernatural transformation.

528a

2. Proficiency in the Law of Supernatural Transformation

Just as the *Garland Sutra* (T. 278) says:

> Sons and daughters of the Buddha! It is just as the transformed body of a tathāgata preaches incomparable clouds of the Dharma like this. All worlds, such as the realm of ultimate reality (Skt. *dharmadhātu*) and the realm of space, are weighted and measured throughout by the use of a single hair tip. On each tip of hair in one moment [a tathāgata] transforms into a body equal to a single atom of the indescribable, indescribable buddha land. He consequently completes it until the end of the future. Each transformed buddha has a head equal to a single atom of the indescribable, indescribable buddha land. In each of these heads is a tongue equal to a single atom of the indescribable, indescribable buddha land. Each tongue produces a voice equal to a single atom of the indescribable, indescribable buddha land. With each voice [a tathāgata] preaches a sutra equal to a single atom of the indescribable, indescribable buddha land. In each sutra he delivers a teaching equal to a single atom of the indescribable, indescribable buddha land. In each teaching he explains sentences equal to a single atom of the indescribable, indescribable buddha land. Again, in a *kalpa* equal to a single atom of the indescribable, indescribable buddha land, he speaks different sentences. His voice fills the entire universe (*dharmadhātu*).
>
> Among all sentient beings there is no one who does not hear it. Until the very end of the future he continually preaches the Dharma. The voice of a tathāgata does not vary, has no breaking off, and never comes to an end. This is the Dharma abided by the vigorous Nārāyaṇa-streamer (Naluoyanchuang) Buddha for all buddhas' sakes.

Again, the *Garland Sutra* says:

> All buddhas entirely have eight kinds of subtle voices. Each voice entirely has five hundred subdivisions of exquisite voice. It is incalculable. A hundred thousand kinds of voices are considered to be solemn. The music of immeasurable and boundless exquisite voices is completely pure. The significance of all buddhas' true Dharma can be widely expounded. [All buddhas] completely leave behind fear, peacefully abide in fearlessness,

and expound the Dharma, just like a great lion's roar. They completely cause all sentient beings of the entire universe to hear their voices and attain realization according to the various good acts they originally practiced. This is the glorious manifestation of all buddhas' supreme, highest verbal acts.

Furthermore, the *Chuchu jing* (T. 730) says:

At that time the Buddha smiled. Five-colored light came out from his mouth. There are five kinds of causes for this. The first is that [the Buddha] intended to cause the people to wonder about it and to benefit from doing so. The second is that he was concerned that people would say that the Buddha unconsciously smiled. The third is that he manifested the light from his mouth for sentient beings. The fourth is that he smiled at all those who are insincere. The last is that he smiled at the arhats who are attached to emptiness yet who have not attained the way of bodhisattvas. After the light returns into him from the crown of his head he surely shows his great intelligence to the people.

Moreover, the *Foshuo xinming jing* (T. 569) says: 528b

At that time the World-honored One smiled at a brahman. Five-colored light came out from his mouth and shone upon beings of the five realms in the ten directions. He intended [the light] to reach the people's minds, and he was delightful to cause hungry ghosts to be able to eat to the full, the pain in the hells to cease, and animals' minds to open and their sins to be removed. Seeking the light, they came to the Buddha's place.

In the ways in which all buddhas smile there is always auspiciousness. When [a buddha] gives a prediction to a bodhisattva about his future attainment of buddhahood, the light, after shining all over the ten directions, enters the crown of his head. When he gives the prediction to a *pratyekabuddha,* the light enters the middle of his forehead. When he gives the prediction to a *śrāvaka,* the light enters an aperture near his shoulder blade. When he speaks about the issue of rebirth in heaven, the light enters his navel. When he speaks about descending to the human realm, the light enters his knees. When he speaks about going to the three types of suffering (Skt. *tri-duḥkhatā*), the light enters the arches of his feet.

All buddhas hope [the people] do not smile out of desire, do not smile in anger, do not giggle, do not smile unrestrainedly, do not smile out of cupidity, do not smile to attain honors, or do not smile to gain wealth. Now the Buddha universally and equally feels compassion for sentient beings and makes a great benevolent smile, without these seven types of smiles.

The [*Da*] *zhidu lun* further says:

Just like when the Buddha turned the Dharma wheel for the first time, bodhisattvas immediately came from other lands. They intended to measure the Buddha's body, but even though they went above beyond immeasurable buddha lands in space and arrived at the World Above [Lotus] Flowers (Huashang shijie), they saw the same Buddha's body as before. Accordingly they said in verse:

Space has no limit.
So too the Buddha's merit.
When we intended to measure the Buddha's body,
We toiled in vain and could not accomplish it.
Although we went above and beyond
Immeasurable buddha lands in space,
We saw the same Lion of the Śākyas (Śākyasiṃha)
As before, with no difference.
The Buddha's body is just like a golden mountain.
It produces the great light.
All marks of his physical excellence are spontaneously dignified.
They are just like flowers spreading out in spring.

Again, the *Chuchu jing* says:

When the Buddha resided in the world, all the heavenly beings, spiritual beings, dragons, and human beings went to the Buddha's place, where they heard the teachings [sitting] in several hundreds of thousands of rows. They all saw the Buddha's face before and behind him. What is the reason for this? It is because during the time of the Buddha's previous existence, when he spoke there was neither front nor rear. Therefore, everyone was able to see the Buddha's face; they all lay down in the direction in which the Buddha faced, because they revered the Buddha.

3. Abhorrence of Desire

Just as the *Da zhuangyan famen jing* (T. 818; Skt. *Mañjuśrīvikrīdita-sūtra*) says:

> At that time there was a courtesan in Rājagṛha called [Superior] Golden-colored Light Virtue ([Sheng] Jinse Guangming De).[176] Due to the cause and condition of good conduct in her previous existence, she had a graceful figure and completely possessed the thirty-two marks of physical excellence (Skt. *dvātriṃśatī-lakṣaṇa-rūpa*). Her body was of authentic golden color and radiated light. Her deportment was attractive and elegant. She was rare in the world. She was bright and intelligent and eloquent without hindrance. Her language was clear, subtle, profound, and pliable. She always spoke with a 528c smile. Wherever she went, golden light shone entirely upon that place. Her clothing was all golden-colored, too. All the people who saw her constantly had her on their minds, became attached to her, and never dismissed her from their thoughts. Wherever she traveled, everyone followed her.
>
> There was a wealthy man's son called Superior Awesome Virtue (Shangweide). Since he wished to take pleasure [with the courtesan], he gave her many valuables, and they made an agreement with each other. [She] boarded a carriage [adorned with various treasures] and he adorned himself, and then together they went to a garden.
>
> At that time, as a result of her previous existence a benefit was secretly bestowed on the woman called [Superior] Golden-colored [Light Virtue]; she was edified by Mañjuśrī, who caused her to enter the [Buddhist] Way. This is because [Mañjuśrī] freely manifests miracles through supernatural power.
>
> [Superior Golden-colored] was asleep with her head on Superior Awesome Virtue's lap. Through supernatural power [Mañjuśrī] manifested himself at the place where she was sleeping and caused her to have the marks of death. [Her body] was swollen, rotten, and stinking. It was hardly possible to come close to her. Her belly broke open in an instant, her liver and bowels split, and her five viscera were exposed. It was smelly, filthy,

and detestable. The impure things, such as urine and feces, [from her body] flowed over a road. All her sense organs and joints [polluted all over the place] and were eaten by flies and maggots. It is impossible to describe it.

At that time the wealthy man's son saw the corpse and felt great fear. His hair stood on end [in horror] and he thought, "I have now nothing with which to save myself. I look throughout the four directions, but there is no place in which I may take refuge." His fears increased more and more, and he cried out loudly in fear. Because of two kinds of causes the wealthy man's son gave rise to great fear: first, he was afraid because he had never seen such a fearful thing as this before; second, he was afraid because the people knew that he had come with her, and now she had suddenly died here, so they might think that he had intentionally killed her. King Ajātaśatru would not examine all the reasons for this and would sentence him to death with an unjust view.

At that time the wealthy man's son was alone in the grove; he did not see even a single other person. [He thought,] "Among all ordinary people and sages, who can rescue me?' Even though the past good conduct of the wealthy man's son was ripe for [a reward], because he had not heard the Dharma spoken by Mañjuśrī along with the woman Golden-colored, Mañjuśrī, through supernatural powers, promptly caused all trees in the grove to intone a verse.

The wealthy man's son felt great joy after hearing [the verse]. He considered himself to be very fortunate. He abandoned the corpse, came out of the grove, immediately went to the Buddha's place, and fully explained his fearful story.

At that time the Buddha said to the wealthy man's son, "You! Do not be anxious and fearful! I will give you fearlessness in all things. If you take refuge in the Buddha, you will be fearless in everything." The wealthy man's son addressed the Buddha,[177] "From what do all fears arise?" The Buddha replied, "You feel fear due to causes and conditions from greed, anger, and ignorance. You must know that in all fears there is neither the subject, nor function, nor persistence. Where is the sensation of desire you earlier had now?" The wealthy man's son said, "Due to [the causes and conditions of] lewdness and evil speculation we see among these [phenomena], ordinary people give rise to covetous attachments. In the sacred

Dharma there is nothing like these things." Thereafter, the Buddha through various kinds of expedient means expounded the Dharma.

At that time the wealthy man's son attained the clear cognition in accordance with the Dharma (*shunfa ren*). At that time the woman [Superior] Golden-colored [Light Virtue], knowing that the wealthy man's son had received edification, adorned five hundred horse-drawn carriages, and 529a
accompanied in front and behind she came to the Buddha's place. She withdrew and stayed to one side.

At that time Mañjuśrī asked the wealthy man's son, "Do you recognize this young lady?" The wealthy man's son replied, "I now truly recognize her." Mañjuśrī said, "How do you know her?" At this moment the wealthy man's son immediately faced Mañjuśrī and said in verse:

I see that her features are just like bubbles on water.
All my perceptions are completely like foam.
I contemplate that her thought is the same as heat haze.
In this way I recognize her.
I see that her acts are [impermanent,] like plantains.
I know that her views are just like illusion.
The woman's name is expediently established.
In this way I recognize her.
Her body has no sensation, just like a tree,
And also like grass, or tiles, or pebbles,
But her mind cannot be seen.
In this way I recognize her.
All ordinary people appear to be charmed.
They are perverted and give rise to evil speculation.
This is not in what intelligent people are steeped.
In this way I recognize her.
Just like the corpse in that grove,
Stinking, rotten, horrid, and impure.
The nature of a body is like this.
In this way I recognize her.
The past is originally not extinguished.
The future will not come into existence, either.
The present does not remain even for a brief time.

In this way I recognize her.
Mañjuśrī must listen to me attentively.
It is hardly possible to requite his kindness.
I had originally much avariciousness.
As I saw impurity, I was liberated.
Her body did not die in fact.
He showed her death in order to edify me.
He manifested it out of compassion for sentient beings.
Who can see this without awakening the aspiration for enlightenment?
Greed, anger, and ignorance like this,
As well as all defilements,
The Dharma of the true nature of these things is
Good and very subtle.

At that time the Buddha said to Ānanda, "In the past I already edified these people, the woman [Superior] Golden-colored [Light Virtue] and the man Superior Awesome Virtue, and caused them to awaken the aspiration for enlightenment. Now they have further heard the Dharma and attained the clear cognition in accordance with the Dharma. In the future, ninety, a hundred, or a thousand *kalpa*s later, this woman, Golden-colored, will be able to become a buddha called Light of Treasures (Baoguang) Tathāgata. [Superior] Awesome Virtue, the wealthy man's son, will attain the status of a bodhisattva at Light of Treasures Buddha's place and he will be called Light of Virtue (Deguang). He will be able to become a buddha after the nirvana of Light of Treasures [Tathāgata] and will be called Flames of Treasures (Baoyan) Tathāgata."

529b Furthermore, the *Guanfo sanmei*[*hai*] *jing* (T. 643; Skt. *Buddhadhyāna-samādhisāgara-sūtra*) says:

The Buddha said to Ānanda, "Formerly when I was in summer retreat, there was a courtesan in Vārāṇasī. She stayed in a high building and was called Wonderful Intention (Miaoyi). In ancient times she had had a relationship with the Buddha.

"At that time, the World-honored One created three youths through supernatural power. [The boys] were all fifteen years old, well-featured, and superior to all people in the world. On seeing them, the courtesan felt happy in body and mind. She addressed [the boys], 'Young sirs! This house I live in now is like that of Śrī-mahādevī. It is comfortable due to the power of wealth and adorned with numerous treasures. May I now present myself and my servants to you? I will completely sprinkle water and sweep [to cleanse my house]. If you can think of, accept, and follow my wishes, I will offer all of this to you; I will begrudge nothing.' After she said these words, the transformed boys sat on mats. Soon afterward the woman drew intimately close to [one of them] and addressed him, 'Sir! I hope you will fulfill my intention.' The transformed boy did not defy her [intention] and complied with what she wanted. She had already approached him.

"The night of the first day she was not yet tired. On the second day her affectionate feeling gradually came to an end. On the third day she said, 'Sir! We should get up and eat and drink.' The transformed boy immediately got up, but he pestered her incessantly.

"The woman felt wearisome and penitent. She said, 'Sir! Does an extraordinary person [act] like this?' The transformed boy told her, 'In my former worldly ways I generally had an affair with a woman for twelve days and only then took a rest.'

"The woman heard this and felt just like a person choking on food. Since she could not spew nor swallow it, her body was as painful as if it had been pounded with a pestle. On the fourth day she felt as if she had been run over by a vehicle. On the fifth day she felt as if an iron pellet had entered her body. On the sixth day all her joints ached as if an arrow had pierced in her heart. She thought and said, 'I have heard people speak about King Śuddhodana's son in the city of Kapilavastu. His body is purplish gold-colored and possesses the thirty-two marks of physical excellence. He commiserates with the ignorant and relieves suffering people. He usually resides in that city and continually performs meritorious liberation. Radiating golden light, he relieves all people. Why does he not come to rescue me today? From now on until the last moment of my life I will no longer covet carnal pleasure at all. I would rather be kept in a den with a tiger and a wolf than have this misery without sensual desire.'

"The transformed boy said in anger, 'You are a worn-out filthy woman! You want to discontinue our affair. Now I would like to unite with you.

It would be better to have an early death. If my parents and members of the same clan come and look for me, where can I hide? I would rather commit suicide by hanging myself. I will not be able to tolerate the humiliation.' The woman said, 'You are a bad person! I do not need you. If you wish to die, do as you like.' At that moment the transformed boy took a sword and stabbed himself in the neck. Blood flowed in torrents, staining the woman's body. [The transformed boy] weakened and fell to the ground. The woman could not stand it.

"On the second day [after this tragedy the boy's body] was congested with blood and turned blue. On the third day it became swollen and puffy. On the fourth day it broke out in sores. On the fifth day it began to rot. On the sixth day the flesh fell off. On the seventh day there were only the stinking bones. A substance like glue or lacquer stuck fast to the woman's
529c body. All the urine and feces discharged from his body, various evil insects, the blood that had burst out of him, and pus completely covered her body. The woman was extremely offensive and detestable, but she could not escape from [the situation].

"The woman made a vow: 'All heavenly gods and hermits! If King Śuddhodana's son can save me from this suffering, I will offer this house and all my jewels and valuables.' When she had this thought, the Buddha, accompanied by Ānanda and Nanda, with Śakra-devendra before him and the Brahma King at the rear, emitted a halo from his head that shone upon heaven and earth. All the people saw the Tathāgata going to visit the woman in her high building.

"When the woman saw the Buddha, she felt ashamed. There was no place to hide the boy's bones. She took some white cotton cloth and wrapped up the stinking corpse, but the offensive smell was the same as before; it was impossible to hide [the corpse] away.

"The woman saw the World-honored One and bowed to him. Out of shame she covered the bones with her body, but the stinking bones suddenly appeared on the woman's back. The woman was extremely ashamed and said with tears in her eyes, 'The Tathāgata's merit and benevolence are boundless. If you can cause me to leave behind this suffering, I will pray to become your disciple. My intention will never retrogress until my last moment.'

"Through the Buddha's supernatural powers the stinking bones disappeared. The woman was greatly delighted. She bowed to the Buddha and addressed him, 'O World-honored One! I now offer to you, the Buddha, all what I have valued.' The Buddha fluently offered prayers for her sake in a purevoice. Hearing the prayers the woman was greatly delighted and promptly attained the path of *srota-āpatti-phala.* Her five hundred maidservants, on hearing the Buddha's voice, all awakened aspiration for the highest *bodhi.* Incalculable practitioners who cultivated pure acts saw the Buddha's manifestation of the miracle through supernatural power, and attained the clear cognition regarding the unproduced nature of all existences (Skt. *anutpattika-dharma-kṣānti*). Among all heavenly beings led by Śakra-devendra, there were those who awakened aspiration for *bodhi* and those who attained *anāgāmi-phala.*"

Moreover, the [*Zhuanji*] *Baiyuan jing* (T. 200; Skt. *Avadāna-śataka*) says:

When the Buddha was residing in the world, in Śrāvastī a wealthy man's wife gave birth to a boy. The boy was extremely ugly; he looked like an evil spirit. All those who saw him deserted him. He eventually grew up, but his parents loathed him. They ordered [someone] to abandon him far away. Even the animals that saw his ugliness harbored fear, not to speak of human beings. Moreover, one time he went to a grove where he earned a living by collecting fruit. Every flying bird and running beast was frightened of him.[178] He was completely isolated from the world and lived alone.

The World-honored One felt benevolence [toward this man]. Leading the *bhikṣus*, he went to the grove, intending to liberate him. When [the ugly man] saw the Buddha, he ran away from him but through supernatural power the Buddha prevented him from leaving. At that time all the *bhikṣus* sat cross-legged under the trees and concentrated their minds on one point. The World-honored One transformed himself into a bad-looking person holding a bowl filled with food, and slowly approached the ugly man. [Seeing that the bad-looking person's] appearance was similar to his own, [the ugly man] felt happy. [He thought,] "This person is now truly my companion." Soon [the bad-looking person] came to him and talked with him, and they ate from the same bowl. When they had finished eating,

the transformed man suddenly became regular-featured, [no longer bad-looking]. The ugly man asked, "How did you now suddenly become regular-featured?' The transformed person replied, "I ate this food and saw with a wholesome mind the *bhikṣus* sitting in mediation under those trees.
530a This caused me to become regular-featured." After hearing this, the ugly man subsequently did [what the transformed person had done], and soon he also attained regular features. He felt happy. He immediately faced the transformed person and deeply gave rise to faith in and understanding of him. Thereupon, the transformed person returned to his original form [as the Buddha]. The [formerly] ugly man saw the thirty-two major and eighty minor marks of physical excellence of the Buddha. Light shone upon all, as bright as a hundred or a thousand suns. The man stepped forward and worshiped [the Buddha] by bowing his head to the Buddha's feet, then he withdrew and sat to one side. The Buddha expounded the Dharma for him in various ways. The man attained *srota-āpatti-phala* and immediately requested to renounce the world before the Buddha. The Buddha said to him, "Welcome, *bhikṣu*!" His beard and hair spontaneously fell off and a Dharma robe was put on him. Thereupon, he became a *śramaṇa.* With devotion and vigor he practiced and received training, and attained the fruit of arhatship.

At that time all the *bhikṣus*, seeing this incident, asked the Buddha to explain for them the original causes and conditions of [the ugly man's] former existence. The Buddha said to the *bhikṣus*, "Formerly, a buddha who appeared in past incalculable worlds was called Puṣya. He sat cross-legged under a tree. Maitreya and I were both bodhisattvas [at that time]. We went to [Puṣya] Buddha's place and made various offerings. Accordingly I raised my foot and spoke in verse to praise [Puṣya] Buddha for seven days:

> In heaven and earth there is nothing better than the Buddha.
> Nor is there in the worlds in the ten directions.
> Even if we can completely see all the places in the world,
> There is no one who can come up with one like the Buddha.

"At that time the Bodhisattva finished speaking this verse.

"Then, in that mountain there was a spiritual being who transformed into an ugly form and came to scare me. Through supernatural power I caused the place where he walked to become a steep precipice, and he was unable to pass through it. At that time that [spiritual being], a mountain deity, had this thought, 'Because I frightened him with an evil intention, he made the place where I am now steep and difficult and disabled me from passing through it. I must now go to him and repent of my previous sin.' After having this thought [the mountain deity] subsequently came to me, repented, made a vow, and left."

The Buddha said to the *bhikṣus*, "If you want to know [who was that mountain deity, it is the ugly man who has now attained arhatship.] Because he frightened me, he had an ugly appearance for five hundred generations, and those who saw him were horrified and ran away. Because he repented [of his sin], he has now met me, renounced the world, and attained the [Buddhist] Way." Hearing this, the *bhikṣus* rejoiced and upheld and practiced the teaching.

Verses say:

The Great Sage manifests a transformation.
Complying with circumstances, he enlightens the people.
He bears beauty and reveals gracefulness.
Opening the mind and awakening correspond to each other.
He subdues evil ways,
Manifests a transformation through supernatural power,
And hides and reveals himself to benefit the people,
Who follow his lofty traces.
Sentient beings stop slandering.
They receive realization vigorously.
He secretly contrives at will.
Those who see him give rise to respect.
We, however, seldom meet this sage,
A matchless spiritual dragon.
Sentient beings have merits
In meeting this auspicious sign. 530b

Miracle Stories

(Twenty-five stories are briefly cited.)

[Preface to Divine Changes and Numerous Kinds of Transformations]

The way to save with benevolence shakes the divinations of the old system. The origin of the method to propagate edification is hard to surmise. Here is the Great Sage outside of China, not a person of common capability in this region. If you seek the very source of things, it is impossible to trace it back to the origin. If you investigate something exhaustively, it is impossible to accomplish it. Even though ordinary people and sages are distinguished from each other, there is commonality in transformation. Truly it is because in intelligence there is shallowness and depth, in hindrance there is coarseness and refinement, in faculty there is greatness and smallness, and in edification there is expansiveness and narrowness. It can probably be said that to reach the origins of birth and death is a transformation. If you rely on the Buddhist teaching and clearly believe in causality and that causes and conditions take advantage of each other, then you will achieve transformation. If you rely on non-Buddhist or secular teachings, you will not attain the right path. Just believe that all things come into existence through conditions and do not rely on the belief that they are brought about by causes.

Therefore, Gan Bao's record (i.e., *Soushen ji*) says:

> In heaven there are five kinds of energies that transform and form all things. When the wood [energy] is pure, it is benevolence. When the fire [energy] is pure, it is propriety. When the metal [energy] is pure, it is righteousness. When the water [energy] is pure, it is intelligence. When the earth [energy] is pure, it is gratitude. When the five kinds of energies are all pure, a sage's virtue becomes complete. When the wood [energy] is impure, it is weakness. When the fire [energy] is impure, it is lewdness. When the metal [energy] is impure, it is wildness. When the water [energy] is impure, it is avarice. When the earth [energy] is impure, it is obstinacy. When the five kinds of energies are all impure, it results in vulgar people. In the Middle Land (i.e., China) many sages appear as a result of the intersection of harmonious energies, while in inaccessible remote areas there are many monsters, produced by peculiar energies.

Once you receive energy [from heaven], you certainly have a form. Once you have a form, a disposition certainly arises. Therefore, those who eat 530c grain are intelligent and civilized. Those who eat plants are mighty yet unintelligent. Those who eat mulberry [leaves] produce raw silk and become moths. Those who eat meat are brave and violent. Those who eat earth have no mind and do not breathe. Those who eat vapors have spiritual intelligence and longevity. Those who eat nothing are immortal and become deities.

There is no male among those who are thick-waisted, and there is no female among those who are slim-waisted.[179] There is no male who neglects having sexual intercourse [with a female]. There is no female who neglects raising [a child]. Insects that undergo three transformations [in a life-cycle] first become pregnant and later mate. Beasts that mate indsicriminately (i.e., that can mate with either sex) spontaneously have both sexes within. Ivy is parasitic and twines around the trunks of tall trees. The moss called *nüluo* lives on the mushroom called *fuling* (i.e., *Poria cocos*). Trees take root in the ground. Duckweed spreads its roots in water. Birds fly through the sky. Beasts run on the ground. Insects hibernate, confining themselves in the earth. Fish live hiding in deep pools.

Originally those that spring up in the sky come close to the upper part, those that spring up on the earth come close to the lower part, and those that spring up with the change of times come close to the sides. Every being follows [the nature of] its species. A thousand-year-old pheasant enters the sea and becomes a large clam. A hundred-year-old chickadee enters a large river and becomes a clam. A thousand-year-old large turtle can speak with human beings. A thousand-year-old fox stands up [on its hind legs] and becomes a [human] beauty. Even if a thousand-year-old snake is cut apart, its body becomes joined again. A hundred-year-old mouse can divine. [Each of these is] the culmination of fate.

On the vernal equinox day a hawk is transformed into a pigeon. On the autumnal equinox day a pigeon is transformed into a hawk. These are changes in time. Therefore, decayed grass becomes fireflies, rotten reeds become crickets, rice plants become rice weevils, and wheat becomes butterflies. Wings grow, eyes are formed, and mind and wisdom come into existence. This is the change from ignorance to intelligence; it is the change of energy. When a crane changes into a roe deer, a snake changes into a freshwater turtle, or a cricket changes into a shrimp, [these creatures] do not lose their original blood and energy (i.e., constitution), but their forms and generic characters change. Examples like these are too numerous to enumerate.

To move in response to a change is said to follow the common way. If one takes a wrong step, he may cause an absurd disaster. Therefore, that the lower half of one's body engenders the upper part is the inversion of energy. That a human being gives birth to an animal, or an animal gives birth to a human being, is a disorder of energy. That a man is transformed into a woman or a woman is transformed into a man is the transformation of energy.

Niu Ai of the state of Lu fell ill, and in seven days he transformed into a tiger. His form changed, and his nails and fangs completely came out. As his elder brother entered [the room], he attacked and ate his brother. This is because at the time he was a human being he did not know he was going to become a tiger, and at the time he was a tiger he did not know he had once been a human being.

During the Taikang era (280–289) of the Jin dynasty, Ruan Shiqin of Chenliu (in present-day Henan province) was bitten by a pit viper. He was unable to stand the pain and smelled the wound several times, and then two pit vipers grew in his nose.

During the Yuankang era (291–299) [of the Jin dynasty], Ji Yuanzai of Liyang (in present-day Anhui province) was entertained with a dish on a big turtle as a guest, and then he had an induration [in the stomach]. A doctor treated it with medicine, and several *sheng* of baby turtles were purged [from his bowel]. Each was as large as a coin and possessed a head, feet, and shell. Even the pattern of the shell was complete. However, they died due to being harmed by the medicine.

A wife is not the energy of Nature's nourishing. The nose is not a place to conceive a child. The place for the passage [of food] (i.e., the alimentary
531a canal) is not a means for reproduction. Observing such cases from this point, regarding the birth and death of all things and their changes, unless you understand thoroughly the will of the gods, even if you seek them, how could you know from where they come? That decayed grass changes into fireflies is, however, due to decomposition. That wheat changes into butterflies is due to moisture. In this case, the changes of all things have

reasons. When a farmer wants to stop the wheat from changing, he soaks it in lye. When a sage manages the changes of all things, he accomplishes [the changes] by means of the Way. Are those sorts [of changes] not [just as what I have mentioned above]?

Even someone who realizes phenomena is now assuredly not capable of investigating exhaustively the culmination of change. This is because sentient beings' original consciousness (Skt. *vijñāna*) is formed through having been influenced by miscellaneous acts. The seed of a cause has already ripened, and a condition is externally formed availing itself of [the seed of its cause]. In accordance with the law of conditions, sentient beings and insentient things arise and change. If first there is no seed [of a cause], even if there is an encounter with a condition, the condition is coarse and its power is weak. Moreover, a thing cannot change alone. Therefore causes avail themselves of conditions. The seed [of a cause] does not grow alone, and a condition must avail itself of a cause. Therefore conditions do not manage [changes] alone. When a cause and a condition harmoniously unite, their power and function are equal to each other. All kinds of things come into existence through this process. Only one is not capable to achieve [changes]. I earnestly desire that this will be clarified in the future. I hope that people will examine other divinations with suspicion.

[The Transformation Ability of Zuo Ci in the Zhou Dynasty]

Zuo Ci, whose pseudonym was Yuanfang, from Lujiang (in present-day Anhui province) had a supernatural power. He was once present at a gathering of Lord Cao. Lord [Cao] said, "For today's party I regret we cannot have the fresh meat of sea bass from Songjiang (in present-day Jiangsu province)." [Yuan]fang responded, "I can get it." He asked for a copper container, which he filled with water. He lowered a baited line from a bamboo pole into the container and started fishing. Immediately he caught a sea bass. Lord [Cao] clapped his hands in joy, and all the participants were surprised. Lord [Cao] said, "One fish is not enough for all the people. If you can get two, it would be good." [Yuan]fang thereupon began to fish with bait. In an instant he landed [another sea bass]. Both [fish] were more than three *chi* long, lively and beautiful. Lord [Cao] immediately prepared a fresh sea bass dish in front of everyone and offered it to all the people.

Lord [Cao] said, "Now we already have sea bass. I simply regret we do not have fresh ginger from Shu (i.e., Sichuan province)." [Yuan]fang replied, "I can get it." Lord [Cao] was afraid that [Yuanfang] might buy [the ginger] in the neighborhood so he said, "I formerly sent a messenger to Shu to buy brocade. You should order your man to contact my messenger and have him buy two more rolls of brocade." [Yuanfang's] man left and soon came back with fresh ginger. Moreover, [Yuanfang's] man said, "Lord, I met your messenger at the brocade store. I passed on your order to him to buy two more rolls."

More than a year later, Lord [Cao's] messenger returned with two more rolls of brocade [as he had been requested]. When [Lord Cao] asked the messenger [why he had bought two more rolls, the messenger] replied, "Formerly, on such-and-such day of such-and-such month, I met a person at the store who told me to buy two more rolls of brocade on your orders."

After that, Lord [Cao] went on an outing to the suburbs, accompanied by just more than a hundred officials. [Yuan]fang entertained them with a jar of wine and a piece of dried meat, himself going around and serving wine to each official. [Although he had only one jar of wine,] all the officials could have enough to get drunk. Lord [Cao] investigated this after returning [and found that] all of the wines and dried meats from a wine seller had disappeared [in the night] on the day before.

Lord [Cao] thought ill of [Yuanfang] and secretly intended to kill him. When Yuanfang came to Lord [Cao's] place, [Lord Cao] was planning to detain him. [Yuan]fang, however, entered into the wall and quickly disappeared. [Lord Cao] then offered a reward for anyone who could apprehend
531b him. Someone saw him at a marketplace and tried to arrest him, but all the people in the marketplace [suddenly] became the same in appearance as [Yuan]fang.

Later, someone else saw [Yuan]fang on the mountaintop in Yangcheng (in present-day Henan province). A passerby chased him. [Yuan]fang hid among a flock of sheep. The passerby knew that [Yuan]fang was with the sheep and said to him, "Lord Cao is not plotting to kill you. He originally tried to judge your [magical] skills. Since they have been examined, he merely wants to see you." An old ram suddenly appeared from among the sheep, bent its knees, stood up like a human being, and said, "That cannot be!" Then the people said, "This ram is [Yuanfang]!" They competed with one another in approaching [the ram] intending to catch it, but then the flock of sheep, several hundreds, all turned into rams that all bent their knees and stood up like human beings all at the same time. [The rams all] said, "That cannot be!" Thereupon, no one knew which [ram] to catch.

The *Laozi* says, "What I consider to be great calamity is that I have a body. If I had not the body, what great calamity would I have?"[180] It is said that people like Laozi are able to have no body. Is [Yuanfang] far behind?

[The Transformation Ability of the Deity's Daughter on Mount Sheduo]

The daughter of the deity of Mount Sheduo died and was reincarnated as a strange grass with luxuriant leaves, yellow flowers, and fruit that resembles that of a love vine (i.e., dodder). So if you take this strange grass as medicine, you will be always loved by people.

In the thirty-third year of King Xuan of the Zhou dynasty (794 B.C.E.), King You was born. In that year a horse was transformed into a fox.

In the second year of King Xian of the state of Jin (654 B.C.E.), King Hui (r. 676–652 B.C.E.) of the Zhou dynasty resided in Zheng (in present-day Henan province). The people of Zheng entered his palace and most of them cast off their skins and were transformed into the tortoise-like creature called *yu,* which spat out [sand] onto the people.

When Chang Hong was killed, a man of Shu (present-day Sichuan province) hid [Hong's] blood [in a container]. Three years later it had turned into jasper.

During the reign of Emperor Ling of the Han dynasty (r. 168–189), the mother of the Huang family of Jiangxia (in present-day Hubei province) took a bath in a tub and did not rise [from the bath] for a long time. She was transformed into a large turtle. A maid was startled and ran to tell about it. When the people of the family came, the turtle dived into the deep waters [of a river]. After that, [the turtle] appeared sometimes. An ornamental hairpin and a silver hairpin [the mother] had [been wearing when] she took a bath were still on the [turtle's] head. From that time the Huang family did not dare eat turtle meat through successive generations.

On the last day of the sixth month of the first year of the Baoding era of Wu (266), the eighty-year-old mother of Xuan Qian of Danyang (in present-day

Jiangsu province) also turned into a large turtle while she was bathing in a pool. The situation was just like that of the Huang family. [Xuan] Qian's four brothers closed the door to prevent [their mother from going out]. They dug a large hole [in an earthen-floored part of] the hall and filled it with water. The turtle entered it and swam around in the water. For a couple of days, [the turtle] often craned its neck to look around, looking for a chance [to escape]. When the door was slightly open, [the turtle quickly escaped by] rolling out, jumped into deep water [of a river] by itself, and never returned.

[The Transformations of Gun of the Xia Dynasty and the King of Zhao, Ruyi]

Gun of the Xia dynasty was the father of Emperor [Yu]. The king of Zhao, Ruyi, was a son of [Gao]zu of the Han dynasty. Nevertheless, Gun became the animal called *huangxiong* ("yellow bear"),[181] and [Ru]yi became a blue dog.[182]

[The Transformation of a Woman during the Reign of King Xiang of Wei State]

In the third year of King Xiang of Wei state, a woman transformed into a man and fathered a child with his wife.

531c Therefore the *Jing Fang Yizhuan* says:

> A woman is transformed into a man. This is to say *yin* is vigorous [and foreshadows that] a person of humble origins may become a ruler. A man is transformed into a woman. This means that *yin* surpasses *yang* and is an omen of calamity and the ruin [of the state].

[The Transformation of a Man during the Jianping Era of the Han Dynasty]

During the Jianping era of the Han dynasty (6–3 B.C.E.), in Yuzhang prefecture (in present-day Jiangxi province) there was a man who transformed into a woman. She then married a man, became his wife, and gave birth to a child.

Chen Feng in Chang'an said, "That *yang* turns into *yin* means a loss in the near future. That she gave birth to a child who carries on the family line means that only one more generation will be carried on, but [the bloodline] will then be cut off." Therefore, this was the cause of the demise of Emperor Ai and Emperor Ping [one after another] and then Wang Mang seized [the throne].

[The Transformation of a Man during the Jian'an Era of the Han Dynasty]

In the seventh year of the Jian'an era of the Han dynasty (202), in Yuejun (in present-day Sichuan province) a man was transformed into a woman.

Zhou Qun said, "In the reign of Emperor Ai there was an extraordinary [event like] this. It means that an event that changes the [imperial] line will occur." In the twenty-fifth year [of the Jian'an era] (220) Emperor Xian [usurped the throne and then] was installed as Lord of Shanyang.

[The Transformation of a Woman during the Yuankang Era of the Jin Dynasty]

During the Yuankang era of the Jin dynasty (291–299) in Anfeng prefecture there was a girl called Zhou Shining. From the age of eight, she gradually transformed into a man. When she attained the age of seventeen or eighteen, her disposition also became [that of a man]. Her physical body did not completely change from a female [to male]; it was not completely the body of a man. She took a wife but they had no children.

[The Transformation of a Hermaphrodite during the Reign of Emperor Hui and Emperor Huai of the Jin Dynasty]

During the reign of Emperor Hui (r. 290–306) and Emperor Huai (r. 306–311) of the Jin dynasty, in the capital city Luo[yang] there was a hermaphrodite who was content with both [sexes]. [This person,] however, was extremely fond of lewdness.

The disturbances of war in the world causes the disorder of the male and female energies (i.e., *yang* and *yin*), and a malformation is thus created.

Furthermore, in the years of the Zhongxing era, there was a woman whose female organ was on her belly. She lived in Yangzhou and also possessed a lewd nature.

The *Jing Fang Yizhuan* says:

> How strange! When a woman gives birth to a child, if the female organ is on the neck, [it means] the world is greatly disordered. If it is on the belly, [it means] the world will fall into trouble. If it is on the back, [it means] there will be no successor in the country.

[The Transformation of a Man in the Reign of Emperor Jing of the Han Dynasty]

In the ninth month of the first year of the reign of Emperor Jing of the Han dynasty (156 B.C.E.), a man more than seventy years of age lived in Xiami county in Jiaodong prefecture (in present-day Shandong province). He grew horns on which hair grew.

The *Jing Fang Yizhuan* says, "When an ignorant prime minister monopolizes political affairs, there is the strange event that a man grows horns." The *Wuxingzhi* says, "It is improper if a man grows horns. It is as improper as the event that feudal lords raise an army [against the central government] and advance on the capital city." After this event, the Revolt of Seven States broke out.[183]

[The Transformation of a Rooster in the Reign of Emperor Xuan of the Han Dynasty]

In the first year of the Huanglong era of Emperor Xuan of the Han dynasty (49 B.C.E.), in the stable called Luling in Weiyang Palace, a hen transformed into a rooster. Its feathers changed, too, but it could neither crow nor grow, and it had no spurs.

In the Chuyuan era (48–44 B.C.E.) of Emperor Yuan, at the house of a scribe of the Office of the Counselor-in-Chief, a hen turned into a rooster that had a cockscomb and spurs. It crowed and grew to maturity.

In the years of the Yongguang era (43–39 B.C.E.) someone presented a horned rooster [to Emperor Yuan]. In the *Wuxingzhi* [these events] are considered to be omens of Wang [Mang's usurpation].

[The Transformation of Mud Crabs and Crabs in the Taikang Era of the Jin Dynasty]

In the fourth year of the Taikang era (283) of the Jin dynasty, in Guiji prefecture (in present-day Zhejiang province) all mud crabs and crabs transformed
532a into rats. They spread all over the fields, eating the paddies voraciously, and this caused a disaster.

At first [after being transformed the rats] had fur and flesh, but they did not have bones. Regarding their behavior, they could not cross the footpaths between the rice fields. Several days later, all [the rats] turned into female [rats].

In the sixth year [of the Taikang era] (285), a two-legged tiger was caught in Nanyang (in present-day Henan province). A tiger is of the *yin* essence but dwells in *yang*. It is an animal of metal (in the five primary elements of metal, wood, water, fire, and earth). *Nanyang* (i.e., south *yang*) is the name of fire. [That is to say,] the metal essence enters into fire and loses its form. [This was] a strange [omen] of the disorder of the imperial house.

[The Transformation of a Catfish that Happened to Confucius When He Sang a Song While Playing a Stringed Musical Instrument in an Inn in Chen State]

Confucius had met with a hardship in Chen state.[184] He sang a song while playing a stringed musical instrument in an inn. During the night a man who was more than nine *chi* tall appeared. He wore black clothing and a high crown. His shout was loud enough to move things around him. Zigong approached and asked him, "Who are you?" Abruptly [the man] lifted up [Zigong] with his hands and held him under his arm. Zilu brought [the man] out and fought with him in the yard but for some time [Zilu still] could not win. Confucius, observing [the fight], saw that the man's fighting chariots sometimes spaced apart as if he was opening his hands. Confucius said [to Zilu], "Why don't you try to pull on his fighting chariot and shake it?" Zilu did as [Confucius had said] and easily threw [the man] to the ground. [It was seen that] he was really a giant catfish, more than nine *chi* long.

Confucius exclaimed, "Why did this fish come here? I have heard that when [all] creatures get old a multitude of spirits possess them. [I am wondering if] this [monster] appeared because my fortunes have declined. Could it be because I have met with hardship, my provisions have run out, and my attendant fell ill? When the six kinds of domestic animals as well as turtles, snakes, fish, snapping turtles, grass, and trees get old, spirits all dwell in them, and they can become monsters. So people call them *wuyou*. The term *wuyou* refers to the fact that each of the five primary elements possesses such a thing. The word *you* means "old." Accordingly, when creatures get old, they become monsters (*guai*). If they are killed they just come to an end. What are we worried about? Perhaps heaven has not deserted the intellectuals and supports my life with this [fish]. If this is not the case, why have we come to this situation?" [Confucius] sang while playing the stringed musical instrument unceasingly.

Zilu cooked [the catfish], which was good, and it nourished the ill [attendant]. He consequently departed with [everyone] the next day.

(The thirteen stories above are found in the *Soushen ji* [*Records of Inquiries of the Spirits*].)

[The Transformation of Yi Ba, an Official of Yuzhang Prefecture during the Jin Dynasty]

During the Jin dynasty there was a minor official called Yi Ba in Yuzhang prefecture (in present-day Jiangxi province). In the Yixi era (405–418) he was off duty and returned home. Then he disobeyed, deserted, and did not return to [his post]. The prefecture [office] sent men to pursue him, and when they found [Yi Ba] he spoke to them as usual and offered a meal to them. When a messenger hurried him to get ready [for a journey], Ba accordingly said, "You! See my face!" Thereupon, [the messenger] looked at him. [Ba] opened his eyes wide; he had yellow spots on his body. Raising one leg he went out of the gate. His house had been built leaning against a hill. When [Ba] came to the foot of the hill, he transformed into a large tiger with three legs. The leg he had raised had become its tail.

(This story is found in the *Yiyuan* [*Park of Wonders*].)

[The Transformation of a Girl Whose Family Name was Peng and Whose First Name was E, of Yiyang County during the Jin Dynasty.]

At the time of the Yongjia revolt (311) during the Jin dynasty there were no regular rulers in the prefectures and counties; it was a jungle. In Yiyang county there was a girl whose family name was Peng and whose first name was E. [She lived with] more than ten family members, including her parents and brothers. Her family was attacked by thieves from Changsha. At that time E, carrying a container on her back, had gone to draw water from a mountain stream. When she heard that the thieves had come, she ran back
532b home and saw that the walls had already been broken. She was overwhelmed by grief, and yet she fought the thieves. The thieves tied up E and packed her off to a place by a mountain stream, planning to kill her.

Next to the mountain stream was a big mountain with a rock wall several tens of *zhang* tall. Looking up, E called out, "Heaven, is there a god, or not? What offense have I committed to face [such suffering] as this?" Accordingly, she ran straight forward toward the mountain. The mountain split apart, and a level path like a grindstone several *zhang* wide appeared. Chasing E, the group of thieves also ran into the mountain; then [the rock walls of] the mountain closed together again, and it was completely restored to its previous state. All the thieves were crushed to death; only their heads stuck out from the side of the mountain. E then hid herself and did not come out again.

The water container [Peng] E had abandoned changed into a stone shaped like a hen. The local people accordingly called the mountain Mount Stone Hen and the stream E's Deep Water.

(This story is found in the *Youming lu* [*Records of the Other World and This World*].)

[The Transformation of Wu Daozong's Mother of Taimo County During the Jin Dynasty]

In the fourth year of the Yixi era (408) of the Jin dynasty, there was Wu Daozong in Taimo county in Dongyang prefecture (in present-day Zhejiang province). He had lost his father when he was young and lived with only his mother. He did not have a wife and children. Once when he had been hired and was not at home, his neighbor heard the sound of crashing stones coming from his house. [The neighbor] looked [into his house] but did not see [Daozong's] mother in the house, only a black spotted tiger. [The people of] the village were shocked. They were afraid that a tiger had gone into [Daozong's] house and attacked his mother. So they beat a drum to gather more people, and they all went to rescue her. They surrounded [Daozong's] house and rushed into it, but they did not see the tiger. Instead they found [Daozong's] mother, who spoke to them in the usual manner. They could not understand the meaning [of the event]. When her son came back his mother said to him, "A sin I committed in my previous existence now follows me. So I have had an incident of transformation [like this]." Later, the mother disappeared one day. Within the county troubles caused by a tiger frequently happened. Everyone said that it was because of the black-spotted female tiger. The common people were harassed by [the tiger]; it came among the people and attacked them, killing several people. Later, a man shot at the tiger as well as a white falcon, and at the same time a halberd pierced its stomach. The man, however, could not catch [the tiger]. Several days later the tiger returned to the house and lay down on the bed. It could not recover its human figure and died where it lay in the bed. The son (i.e., Daozong) wept bitterly and buried [the tiger] just as if he was burying his mother. From morning till the night he cried and attended [the grave].

(This story is found in *Qi Xie's Records* [*Qi Xie ji*].)[185]

[The Transformation of a Cow in Fuyang County during the Jin Dynasty]

During the Jin dynasty, among the villagers in Fuyang county there was a boy whose family had a pasturing cow. The cow abruptly licked the boy, and where [the cow had licked it] the skin all turned to white. The boy suddenly died. His family buried the boy and killed the cow in order to offer its meat to the guests of honor [at the funeral]. Those who ate the meat from the cow, more than twenty men and women altogether, were all transformed into tigers.

(This story is found in Gu Wei's *Guangzhou jilu* [*Records of Guangzhou*].)

[The Transformation of the Daughter of Emperor Yan]

Emperor Yan's [daughter] Nüwa went swimming in the Eastern Sea and drowned.[186] She was reincarnated as a bird called *jingwei,* whose appearance resembles that of a crow. She always carried bits of wood and stone from the Western Mountains in her mouth and tried to fill (*yin*) the Eastern Sea by dropping them there.

(The Chinese *yin* is the Chinese character *se,* "to block" or "to fill." It is prononced the same way as the Chinese word *yin,* "cause.")

Kuafu ran a race with the sun. He got thirsty and went to the Yellow River to drink, but the river water was insufficient to quench his thirst. He went to the north to drink water from a big swamp, but he died on the road before reaching there. His staff was tossed away, and it turned into a grove of teak trees.

(These two stories are found in the *Shanhai jing* [*Book of Mountains and Seas*].)[187]

[Transformations Found in Various Expositions and Miscellaneous Records]

532c The *Bowu zhi* says:

> Pine resin that falls into the earth changes to tuckahoe a thousand years later. Tuckahoe becomes amber (*hupo*) a thousand years later. Amber is also called *jiangzhu* ("pearl from a large river"). Today on Mount Tai there are tuckahoes but no amber. In Yongchang in Yizhou (in present-day Sichuan province) amber is produced but tuckahoe is not.

Furthermore, it is said that [amber] is made by burning a beehive. It has not yet been ascertained which of these theories is correct.

The *Shen Nong bencao jing* (*Shen Nong's Book of Plants and Medicines*) says:

> Take the shell off an egg. If the yolk and the white of the egg are mixed, cook it well. When the [cooked egg] is still soft, cut it as you like and marinate it in bitter wine. After several nights it will become firm. The hard stuff inside of the white powder is forgery (i.e., inedible).

(Everything commonly used in this world is served when it is made.)

The *Han Shi waizhuan* (*Han's Annotation on the Book of Odes*) says, "Confucius said, 'Aged leek becomes a stork. Aged cattail becomes a reed.'"

The *Soushen ji* says:

> A digger wasp called *guoluo* is now called *yinyong* in the world. It is a kind of slender-waisted wasp. This species only has males, no females. So they have neither copulation nor oviposition. They usually take the larvae of silkworms. While being cultivated, the larvae of silkworms all turn into the larvae of digger wasps.

[The Transformation of a Spirit at Gongting Shrine in Jiangnan during the Qin Dynasty]

When he was young, Zhou Fang of the Qin dynasty traveled along with some merchants upstream on the Yangzi River. One night they stayed at Gongting Shrine. His fellow travelers said to each other, "Who is willing to go into the shrine to sleep?" By nature Fang was brave, daring, and determined. Accordingly they went into the shrine to stay overnight, and throughout the long night it was comfortable. In the morning, when they woke up, they saw a gray-haired old man in the shrine. Fang captured him and [the old man] then transformed into a male duck. Fang caught [the duck] and returned to the boat, intending to cook it, but [the duck] promptly flew away. Somewhat surprisingly nothing else happened after this.

(This story appears in the *Shuyi ji* [*Records to Give Accounts of Extraordinary Things*].)

[The Mystery of the Luo People Whose Heads Could Fly in the South during the Qin Dynasty]

During the Qin dynasty there were the Luo people in the south. The heads of the people [of this tribe] could fly. The tribe practiced religious rites called *chongluo* ("insect falling"), and the name [of the tribe] was based on this.

In the time of Wu [of the Three Kingdoms], General Zhu Huan had a maid, and every night after going to bed her head flew away. [Her head] went out and in through a pet door sometimes, or a skylight at other times. [The head flew] using its ears as wings. It returned as daybreak approached. Since things like this happened frequently, the person who [slept] near her felt strange about it. At midnight this person shone a light on [the maid from the

Luo tribe] and saw that only her body was there, without the head. Her body was slightly cold, and the breath was weak. So the person covered the body with a coverlet. At daybreak the head returned, [but it] was obstructed by the coverlet and could not rejoin [the body]. It [tried to reconnect to the body] two or three times, but then it fell down on the ground. “Alas!” It shouted out sadly and breathed hard, seemingly about to die. The coverlet was then removed, and the head rose up and was reattached to the neck. Soon the maid went [to sleep] peacefully.

[Zhu] Huan thought [that the woman] was a great monster and was afraid of her. He dared not keep her [in his house], so he released her. He later investigated details about this and then found out that her oddity was natural [for the Luo people].

At that time the great generals who went to the south on expeditions often took [Luo people]. Once someone covered [the body of a Luo person] with a bronze bowl [when the head was away from the body]. The head could not enter [the bowl], and subsequently [that person] died.

[The Transformation of a Married Couple Who Were Brother and Sister in the Time of Emperor Gaoyang]

Formerly in the time of the Emperor Gaoyang (i.e., Zhuanxu) there was a married couple who were brother and his sister [from the same parents]. The emperor exiled them to the wilderness of Mount Kongtong where they died, tightly grasped in each other’s arms. A divine bird covered them with the grass
533a of immortality. Seven years later a hermaphrodite was born with two heads, four legs, and four arms. This is [the ancestor of] the Mengshuang clan.

(These two stories are found in the *Soushen ji* [*Records of Inquiries of the Spirits*].)

[The Transformation of the Occult Arts Practiced by a Barbarian of the Northern Mountain of Xunyang County during the Wei Kingdom]

During the Wei kingdom some barbarians who lived in the northern mountains of Xunyang county (in present-day Hubei province) practiced occult arts. They could transform a person into a tiger, and the color of the fur as well as the body [of the transformed tiger] were exactly like those of a real tiger.

Zhou Zhen, from a neighboring village, had a male servant. He ordered [the servant] to go into the mountains to cut firewood. The servant had a wife and a younger sister, and they also accompanied him. After they arrived in the mountains, the servant said to the two [women], "Climb up into a tall tree and observe what I am doing." [The two women] did as he said. In the meantime [the man] went into the grass.

Soon a large yellow-spotted tiger came out of the grass. [The tiger] braced itself up and roared. It was very terrifying. The two [women] were very afraid. After awhile [the tiger] returned into the grass. A little later [the man] came back, having transformed back into a human being [from his tiger form], and said to the two [women], "When you return home be careful not to speak of [this to others]."

Later [the two women] spoke about it to their fellow workers, and Zhou soon knew of it, too. [Offering] him strong wine [Zhou Zhen] caused [the servant] to become dead drunk and then had someone take off the servant's clothes. [Zhou] completely inspected the servant's body, but there was nothing unusual. He found only a piece of paper in the [servant's] topknot on which a large tiger was drawn, and beside [the drawing of] the tiger there was a written spell. Zhou secretly copied it. After the servant sobered up, [Zhou] summoned him and asked him [about the incident]. The servant then knew that the [secret] had been found out, so he fully explained the whole story. He said, "Formerly, when I bought grain from the barbarians, there was a barbarian teacher who said that he possessed this occult art. I received and attained this art by exchanging three *chi* of textiles, a *sheng* of polished rice, a red capon, and a *sheng* of wine for it."

[The Transformation of Song Shi[zong]'s Mother Who Bathed in Qinghe during the Wei Kingdom]

During the Wei kingdom in Qinghe (in present-day Hebei province) there was Song Shizong. On a summer day during the Huangchu era (220–226) his mother went to bathe in the bathroom. She sent all the sons and daughters of her family out of the room and remained alone in the bathroom. After a while the family members, having not understood her intention, peeped through a crevice in the wall, but they did not see anyone. In the water in the wooden tub there was a large snapping turtle.

Ultimately they opened the door, and all the adults and children went into the bathroom. They realized that [the turtle] could not communicate with people. A silver ornamental hairpin the mother had formerly worn still remained on its head. [The family members,] each and all, prevented [the turtle from going out]. They all wailed, but no one could do anything about it.

[The turtle] was looking for a chance to escape. It could not stay there a long time. The people saw that [the turtle] moved about from one place to another for days. It then went out of the door and left. Even though the people chased it, they could not catch up to it because it ran fast. Then [the turtle] went into water. Several days later it abruptly came back and walked around in the house as usual. Saying nothing, it left [again].

The people of that time said [Song] Shizong should perform a funeral service for [his mother] and observe mourning. Shizong thought that although his mother's form had changed her bodily functions still remained, so in the end he did not have a funeral for her. [This story] is similar to that of Huang's mother of Jiangxia prefecture.[188]

(These two stories appear in the *Xu Soushen ji* [*Second Series of Records of Inquiries of the Spirits*].)

[The Mystery of the Remarriage of Née Liang, Wife of Layman Wei Ying during the Liang Dynasty]

During the Liang dynasty, [the present-day] Kaishan Temple was the house of Wei Ying, a man from Jingzhao. Ying died at an early age. His wife, née Liang, did not take proper care of the funeral rites [for him] and then
533b remarried. Xiang Ziji, a man from Henei, was her new husband. **Even** though she had remarried, she continued to live in Ying's house.

[The spirit of] Ying heard that [his wife,] née Liang, had remarried. He returned [to this world] in daytime on horseback and attended by several subordinates. When he came to the yard, he called out, "My dear née Liang! Have you forgotten me?" Ziji was amazed and puzzled. He raised a bow and shot [Ying]. [Ying] was hit by the arrow, fell down, and immediately turned into a peach in the form of a human figure. The horse he had ridden also changed into a horse doll made out of thatch, and his subordinates all became dolls made of various kinds of rush. Née Liang was afraid and later donated the house, which became [Kaishan] Temple.

(This story is found in the *Luoyang si jizhuan* [*Records of Buddhist Temples in Luoyang*].)

Chapter Twenty-six

Dreams

(This chapter consists of five parts:) (1) Introduction, (2) The Three Types of Moral Nature, (3) Wholesome Nature, (4) Unwholesome Nature, and (5) Neutral Nature.

1. Introduction

Originally this one mind accumulates and becomes the three realms of existence. Ignorant people are in the flux [of the transmigration of birth and death]. Those with haughty minds fall into evil ways. Those of lazy mind are low in spirit. Even if one wished to examine this matter to its end, it is difficult to survey its basis.

Therefore, from remote, beginningless time to our current existence we are subject to the transmigration of birth and death. Even a wheel track is no match for [transmigration in terms of its length and continuance]. Brightness and darkness alternate. A torch passed from one piece of wood to another is not comparable to this. Running water may not be swift [yet it never ceases, day or night]. It is difficult to contain the moon in a vessel.

Moreover, the way of rising and falling and time pull against each other. The path of dreams moves in accordance with one's mind. Movement from within is cognition and the external object impregnates [the cognition]. Through cognition one is impregnated with wholesomeness or unwholesomeness.

A dream commonly has three types of moral nature. If people possessed wholesomeness or unwholesomeness in their previous existence, they will have either auspiciousness or inauspiciousness in their dreams. This is morally good or evil (Skt. *vyākṛta*). If they practiced nothing of good or evil and extensively saw things equally, this is morally neutral (Skt. *avyākṛta*). If one perceives blue and yellow colors by day and dreams of the same colors [at night], this is a conceptual dream. If one dreams of rising and falling or of water and fire that encroach upon each other, this is a morbid dream.

Even though a dream commonly has three types of moral nature, there is retribution and no retribution. If you wish to know about these matters, see the following statements from sutras.

2. The Three Types of Moral Nature

Just as the *Shanjianlü piposha* says:[189]

> There are four kinds of dreams. First is the dream of the disharmony of the four great elements (i.e., earth, water, fire, and wind); second is the dream of things previously seen; third is the dream of heavenly beings; last is the dream of what one conceives.
>
> [Question:] What is the dream of the disharmony of the four great elements?
>
> Answer: When you are asleep, if you dream of a landslide, of flying high in the sky, or of being chased by a tiger, wolf, lion, or burglar, this is the dream of the disharmony of the four great elements. It is groundless and unreal.
>
> [Question:] What is the dream of things previously seen?
>
> Answer: During the daytime if you see white or black color, or a man or woman, and at night you dream of it, this is called the dream of things previously seen. This is also unreal.
>
> [Question:] What is the dream of heavenly beings?
>
> Answer: If a heavenly being good friend appears [in your dream], this is a good dream that causes you to attain wholesomeness; if an evil friend appears, it is a nightmare. This [kind of dream] is precisely real.
>
> [Question:] What is the dream of what one conceives?
>
> Answer: Those [who have this kind of dream] created meritorious virtue or sin in a former existence; if they created meritorious virtue, they
> 533c have a good dream; but if they created a sin, they have a nightmare. It is just as when the Bodhisattva was about to enter his mother's womb, [his mother] dreamed that a white elephant descended from Trāyastriṃśa Heaven and entered her from her right side. This is the dream of what one conceives. If you dream of worshiping the Buddha, reciting sutras, observing the precepts, making a donation, or doing various meritorious things, these are dreams of what one conceives too.

Question: Is a dream morally good, bad, or neutral?

Answer: It can be either morally good, bad, or neutral. If you dream of worshiping the Buddha, listening to the Dharma, or preaching the Dharma, these are wholesome, meritorious [dreams]. If you dream of destroying life, stealing, or committing adultery, these are unwholesome dreams. If you dream of a color such as blue, yellow, red, or white, these are morally neutral dreams.

Question: If this is so, those [who dream] should receive reward or retribution [according to what they have dreamed].

Answer: No, they do not. Why? Since their mental function is fatigued and weak [while dreaming], they cannot perceive reward or retribution. Therefore, the Vinaya says, "It (i.e., reward and retribution) is excluded while one dreams. This is not violation of the precepts."

Furthermore, the *Jiayan lun* (i.e., *Apitan bajiandu lun;* T. 1543) says:

Question: Do all types of mental inactivity (*shui;* Skt. *śayita*) and sleep (*mian;* Skt. *middha*) correspond to each other?[190]

Answer: Some types of mental inactivity do not correspond to sleep. It is just as before you fall asleep your body has not yet relaxed and neither has your mind; your body feels heavy and so does your mind; you physically open your eyes wide yet you cannot see clearly, and you open your mind wide yet your mind is obscure; you are physically and mentally confused; you are physically and mentally inactive; and you are bound with inactivity. This case refers to mental inactivity that does not correspond to sleep.

Question: Does sleep not correspond to mental inactivity?

Answer: A dream of the undefiled mind is designated to be sleep that does not correspond to mental inactivity.

Question: Do mental inactivity and sleep correspond to each other?

Answer: A dream of the defiled mind is designated to be that mental inactivity and sleep correspond to each other.

Question: What is not mental inactivity as well as not sleep?

Answer: That except for the abovementioned cases.

Question: Is sleep said to be wholesome, unwholesome, or morally neutral?

Answer: Sleep is wholesome in some cases, unwholesome in some cases, and morally neutral in some cases.

Question: In what case is [sleep] wholesome?

Answer: Sleeping and dreaming with a wholesome mind.

Question: In what case is [sleep] unwholesome?

Answer: Sleeping and dreaming with an unwholesome mind.

Question: In what case is [sleep] morally neutral?

Answer: That except for the abovementioned cases.

[Question: Can it be said that merit made during sleep increases?]

[Answer:] This is just like when in a dream one makes a donation, does meritorious conduct, observes the precepts, or abides by purification. If while one is asleep the wholesome mind created a meritorious act, it can be said that surplus merit increases. This is called wholesomeness.

Question: Can it be said that nonmerit made during sleep increases?

Answer: This is just like when in a dream one commits evils such as destroying life or stealing. If one has an unwholesome mind while sleeping, it can be said that the nonmeritorious mind excessively increases. This is called unwholesomeness.

Question: Cannot it be said that merit and nonmerit made during sleep increase?

Answer: This is just as while sleeping the mind of wrong merit (*feifuxin*) and the mind of wrong nonmerit (*feibufuxin*) [do not] increase.[191] It is just like sleeping with a morally neutral mind. It cannot be said that merit and wrong merit increase during sleep. This is called morally neutral.

Question: What is a dream?

Answer: It is the hindrance of ignorance (Pāli *avijjā*) among the five hindrances (Skt. *pañca-nivaraṇāni*).

3. Wholesome Nature

Just as the *Chusheng Putixin jing* (T. 837) says:

534a At that time the World-honored One said to the brahman Kāśyapa, "You, good man! There are four types of wholesome dreams to attain the superior teaching. What are the four types? They are dreaming of lotus flowers, of a canopy, or of a halo around the moon and the Buddha's figure while

250

one is asleep. After having such a dream you should congratulate yourself on your encounter with the superior teaching."

Then the World-honored One said in verse:

If you have a dream of lotus flowers,
Of a canopy,
Or of a halo around the moon,
You should attain a great benefit.
If there is a dream of the Buddha's image,
The body completely adorned with all marks of physical excellence,
Sentient beings who see this should be happy,
And pray that they will become *puruṣa-damya-sārathi* ("tamers of humans") without fail.

Furthermore, the *Za baozang jing* says:

In former times King Caṇḍapradyota did cruel and heartless things. He had no sympathy, only a wrong view. The Tathāgata sent Kātyāyana to his home country (i.e., Avanti) to edify [King Caṇḍapradyota and his people]. King Caṇḍapradyota and his lady were all able to give rise to faith. The king's great lady was called Śivakośā, and she later gave birth to the crown prince called Gopāla.

At that time the king dreamed of eight things in his sleep. First, a fire burned over his head; second, two snakes enwrapped his waist tightly; third, a fine iron net bound his body; fourth, two red fishes swallowed his feet; fifth, four white cranes flew toward him; sixth, he was walking in blood-stained mud that rose beyond his armpits; seventh, he ascended a great white mountain; and eighth, he received a stork's droppings on his head.

After awakening from the dream he considered it to be inauspicious, and felt anxious about it and very sad. He promptly went to various non-Buddhists and brahmans. The non-Buddhists listened to the king's [description of his] dream. They usually detested the king and also were jealous of Venerable Kātyāyana. Regarding these dreams of the king, they said, "O Great King![192] It is ill-omened. If you do not perform an exorcism, serious trouble will befall you." The king heard these words and believed them. The king's anxiety and annoyance increased more and more. Then [the king] asked, "At the time of exorcism what things will I need?" All the brahmans said, "What is necessary is whatever you treasure. If we explain it to you, you will certainly be unable to [understand our words]."

At that time the king replied, "This dream was very fierce. I am simply afraid that a serious misfortune will befall me. I grudge nothing except myself. I beg you to explain to me about the things I will need." All the brahmans saw that he was polite and understood that his mind was sincere. They immediately said to the king, "As for what should be necessary, there are eight things in this dream. You will need eight kinds of things to be able to exorcise the disaster. First, kill Śivakośā, the lady whom you, the king, honor. Second, kill Gopāla, the crown prince whom you, the king, love. Third, kill the prime minister and the cabinet ministers. Fourth, kill all your black vassals. Fifth, kill your elephants that can travel three thousand *li* a day. Sixth, kill your camels that can travel three thousand *li* a day. Seventh, kill your fine horses. Eighth, kill Kātyāyana, the bald-
534b pated one you revere. If in seven days you kill all these eight groups, collect their blood, and walk in [a pool of their blood], you will be able to prevent the disaster." The king heard their words. Since he valued his life, he immediately approved of [the plan].

[The king] returned to the palace, but he felt anxious and remorseful. His lady asked him, "Why are you like this?" The king replied to her, fully explaining his inauspicious dream as stated above. At the same time he told her what the brahmans had said was necessary in order to exorcise [the disaster that might befall him because of] the dream. After hearing this, the lady said, "If I only cause you to be safe and have no troubles, how worthy is my humble body?" She addressed the king, "In seven days I should die. Please let me go to the place of the venerable one, Kātyāyana, where I will receive purification and hear the Dharma for six days." The king said, "No, you cannot. When you arrive at his place you will probably tell him the truth. If he knows of this, he will give up on me and fly away." The lady, however, [asked] him earnestly and the king could not make an excuse. So he allowed her to go.

The lady arrived at the venerable one's place. She worshiped him and asked questions. Consequently three days passed. The venerable one felt strange and asked her, "O king's lady! You have never before come here to stay for two nights. Why aren't you doing the same thing as usual this time?' The lady then spoke to him about the king's nightmare in detail. [She said,] "After seven days [from that time] the king must kill us in order to exorcise the disaster. My days are numbered. So I came to hear the Dharma." Accordingly, facing the venerable one, she explained about the king's dream.

Venerable Kātyāyana said, "This dream is very auspicious. [The king] will certainly have happy occasions. It is not worth being worried about. First, regarding the fire that burned over [the king's] head, the country of Treasure Owner [located to the west of the Snowcapped Mountains] possesses a beautiful crown valued at a hundred thousand taels of gold, and it will be brought to offer to the king. That is the exact meaning of this dream." The lady felt agitated. Toward the end of the seven-day period she was to be killed by the king, and she was afraid that [the offering] would come too late. So she asked the venerable one, "When is it coming?" The venerable one replied, "It will arrive in the late afternoon today."

[The venerable one continued,] "Second, regarding the two snakes that enwrapped [the king's] waist tightly, the king of Yuezhi will present a pair of swords worth a hundred thousand taels of gold. They will arrive today.

"Third, regarding the fine iron net that bound [the king's] body, the emperor of the Roman Empire will present pearl necklaces worth a hundred thousand taels of gold. They will arrive in the morning of the day after tomorrow.

"Fourth, regarding the [two] red fishes that swallowed [the king's] feet, the king of Siṃhala (present-day Sri Lanka) will present footwear made of lapis lazuli (Skt. *vaiḍūrya*) worth a hundred thousand taels of gold. They will arrive at mealtime of the day after tomorrow.

"Fifth, regarding the four white cranes that flew [toward the king], the king of Vṛji will present a golden vehicle decorated with various gems,[193] which will come at high noon on the day after tomorrow.

"Sixth, regarding [the king's walking] in the bloodstained mud, the king of Parthia will present *kambala*s (fine woven fabrics) of deer hide worth a hundred thousand taels of gold. They will come at sunset on the day after tomorrow.

"Seventh, regarding [the king's] ascending the great white mountain, the king of Aṭavī ("Wild Plain") will present a large elephant, which will arrive late afternoon on the day after tomorrow.

"Eighth, regarding [the king's receiving] a stork's droppings on his head, [this means that] the king and you, lady, must have a private, secret matter. The matter will come up [another day] when you must deal with it in person."

534c Indeed, just as the venerable one had said, the stipulated time soon passed. All the presents and offerings from various countries arrived. The king was very happy. Previously Lady Śivakośā had a crown. She put the beautiful crown presented by the county of Treasure Owner over it. Then the king playfully took off the crown that Lady Śivakośā had put over hers and put it on Lady Jinman's head. At that moment Lady [Śivakośā] said angrily, "When you had an undesirable matter, I first undertook it. Now that you have obtained this beautiful crown, you [took it from me and] put it on her!" Subsequently she threw a container of milk onto the king's head, and the king's head was entirely covered in it. The king, extremely enraged, drew his sword, intending to attack Lady Śivakośā. Afraid of the king, she ran into her room and promptly shut the door. The king could not advance further. The king soon realized by himself that the venerable one had divined his dream and said that [the king and the lady] would have a private, secret matter; this was exactly [what the venerable one had meant].

The king and the lady subsequently went to Venerable Kātyāyana's place and discussed what had happened in detail. [The king said,] "I used to believe in unlawful evil words, and I was almost about to do heinous things to you, Venerable One, my family, ministers, and those I love. Now, indebted to you, I have left behind evil matters. Therefore I came to visit you, Venerable One, and will respectfully serve you and make offerings to you. I will drive the non-Buddhists and brahmans far away from the national borders."

Then [the king] asked the venerable one, "Through what causes and conditions do I come to receive the valuables from each of the various countries presented to me in this way?" The venerable one replied, "In the past, ninety-one *kalpa*s ago, there was a buddha called Vipaśyin. When that buddha appeared, there was a country called Bandhumatī. The crown prince [of Bandhumatī] had serene faith and was diligent. He came to that buddha's place and made offerings to and worshiped [him]. He thereupon presented to that buddha a beautiful crown, a treasured sword, and a necklace, which [the crown prince] put on, and also a large elephant, a vehicle decorated with various gems, and *kambala* (woven fabrics). Being associated with this meritorious blessing, he is reborn as a noble in every life. Whatever jewels and valuables he wants spontaneously come to him without seeking."

After hearing this, the king gave rise to deep respect and faith before the Three Treasures. He made a bow and returned to his palace.

4. Unwholesome Nature

Just as the *Fajue jingxin jing* (T. 327; Skt. *Adhyāśaya-sañcodana*) says:

The Buddha said to Maitreya Bodhisattva, "Bodhisattvas should observe twenty kinds of various troubles due to torpor of the mind. What are the twenty kinds? First, those who take delight in torpor of the mind have laziness. Second, their bodies are listless and heavy. Third, their skin is impure. Fourth, their skin and flesh are rough and harsh. Fifth, all their elements are wicked and corrupt, and they have scant dignity and virtue. Sixth, they do not digest well what they eat and drink. Seventh, they have boils and pimples on the body. Eighth, they are often negligent. Ninth, they grow a net of ignorance. Tenth, their intelligence is feeble and weak. Eleventh, their wholesomeness is about to become exhausted. Twelfth, they will certainly go into darkness. Thirteenth, [people] are disrespectful to them. Fourteenth, their natural disposition is ignorant. Fifteenth, they often have various defilements, and therefore they focus their minds on the various defilements. Sixteenth, they do not give rise to hope even in 535a
the matter of the wholesome Dharma. Seventeenth, all pure things can be caused to diminish. Eighteenth, they continually conduct themselves in fearfulness. Nineteenth, when they see a diligent person they slander and disgrace him. Twentieth, they end in being despised by others when in a crowd of people."

Moreover, the *Guowang Bulixianni shimeng jing* (T. 148) says:

When the Buddha resided in the world, at that time there was a king called Prasenajit. One night he dreamed of ten things. First, he dreamed that three pots were placed side by side; the pots at each end were full; and steam rose out of them and commingled, but it did not go into the empty pot in the middle. Second, he dreamed that a horse ate from its mouth as well as from its rump. Third, he dreamed that a small tree produced flowers. Fourth, he dreamed that a small tree produced fruit. Fifth, he dreamed that a person held a rope; behind him there was a sheep; and the sheep's owner ate the rope. Sixth, he dreamed that a fox sat on a golden couch and ate from a golden vessel. Seventh, he dreamed that a large cow also suckled milk from a calf. Eighth, he dreamed that four bulls came from four directions while lowing; they chased each other and intended to fight, but just before they came together their whereabouts were lost. Ninth, he dreamed that the water in the center of a pond was muddy while the water in the rest of the pond was clean. Tenth, he dreamed that a stream in a great gorge was very red. After dreaming of these things, the king woke up. He felt great fear; he was afraid to lose his country, his life, and his family.

The next day the king summoned those who could explain [the meaning of] dreams from among the court nobles, ministers, and people of various religions. He said, "Last night I dreamed of ten things. I woke up and felt fearful. I am unhappy. Who can explain my dream?" A brahman said, "I will explain it for you, king. But I am afraid that if you hear [my explanation] you will be sad and unhappy." The king said, "Explain it just as you see! Do not hide anything!" The brahman said, "Your dream is entirely bad. You must summon your wives and the crown prince whom you seriously love as well as attendants and servants who are close to you, and kill all of them in order to worship heaven. O king! [If you do this] you will have no misadventure. You possess bedding, jewels and valuable clothing that you wear, and other good things. They all must be completely burned in order to worship heaven. If you do this, you will have no misfortune." The king, having heard that his dream was bad, felt sad and unhappy. So he went into a sanctuary and thought about these things.

The king's formal wife was called Mallikā. She came to the king and asked him, "Why are you staying in a sanctuary, sad and unhappy? Have I committed any fault against you, king?' The king replied, "No, you have committed no fault against me. I am just spontaneously sad." His wife again asked him. The king said, "You! Do not ask me! If you hear about

it, it will make you unhappy." His wife again said, "I am the king's better half. If there is something good or evil, you should tell me about it. Why don't we talk to each other?" So, the king fully explained for his wife the ten things of which he had dreamed last night. His wife said, "O king! Do not be sad! It is just as when a person buys gold, if he grinds it with a stone its beauty or ugliness, goodness or badness, or its color spontaneously appears on the stone. The Buddha is now staying in a monastery near here, 535b
not far from your country. Why don't you go and ask him? If [you receive] what the Buddha clarifies, you, king, must follow it." The king promptly ordered the whole staff of officials to arrange a carriage and went out.

[The king] arrived at the Buddha's place. He worshiped by bowing his head to the Buddha's feet, withdrew, and sat down. He addressed the Buddha, "Last night I dreamed of ten things" and explained in detail just as mentioned above. [He continued,] "What I dreamed of was like this. I woke up and felt fearful. I was afraid to lose my country, my life, and my family. I pray that you, O Buddha, will explain about the ten things of which I dreamed for my sake. I wish to hear your teaching and guidance." The Buddha said, "O king! Do not be afraid [of your dream]! Your dream is free from misadventure. These are about matters of a later age, the future, not about evils in this age. The people of the future will not be afraid of the prohibitions of the law. They will be dissipated and licentious, greedy for profit, envious, and insatiable. They will have little righteousness and no mercy. They will be emotional and shameless."

The Buddha continued, "Regarding the first thing of which the king dreamed, that three pots were placed side by side; the pots at each end were full; and steam rose out of them and commingled, but it did not go into the empty pot in the middle, this means that all of the wealthy people and nobles of later ages will follow each other, and they will not be kind to the poor. The king dreaming that pots were placed side by side precisely means this. O king! Do not be afraid [of your dream]! Your country, the crown prince, and your wives are all free from misadventure."

The Buddha continued, "Regarding the second thing of which the king dreamed, that a horse ate from its mouth as well as from its rump, this means that those of later ages who become sovereigns or ministers will receive an allowance from the government, and those who become a county magistrate will receive a government salary; further, they will insatiably exploit all the people. The king's dream exactly means this. O king! Do not be afraid [of your dream]!"

The Buddha continued, "Regarding the third thing of which the king dreamed, that a small tree produced flowers, this means that the people of later ages will become gray-haired before they are thirty years old. They will be greedy for sensual pleasure and too rapacious, and the younger will extort the older. The king's dream exactly means this. O king! Do not be afraid [of your dream]!"

The Buddha continued, "Regarding the fourth thing of which the king dreamed, that a small tree produced fruits, this means that women of later ages will marry before they are fifteen years old. They will bring their babies back [to their parents' house] without compunction. The king's dream exactly means this. O king! Do not be afraid [of your dream]!"

The Buddha continued, "Regarding the fifth thing of which the king dreamed, that a person held a rope; behind him there was a sheep; and the sheep's owner ate the rope, this means that in later ages, when a husband goes out to conduct business, his wife will be left behind and she will have an affair with a man from another family, and they will eat from her husband's stores. The king's dream exactly means this. O king! Do not be afraid [of your dream]!"

The Buddha continued, "Regarding the sixth thing of which the king dreamed, that a fox sat on a golden couch and ate from a golden vessel, this means that in later ages a person of humble origin will become noble and acquire property. The people will stand in awe of him, and the descendants of princes and marquises will experience poverty, be placed in lower
535c seats, and eat later [after the noble person has eaten]. The king's dream exactly means this. O king! Do not be afraid [of your dream]!"

Buddha continued, "Regarding the seventh thing of which the king dreamed, that a large cow also suckled milk from a calf, this means that the people of later ages will have no propriety. A mother will become a procuress for her own daughter rebelling against [social custom]. She will lead and help a man from another family to have an affair with her daughter. She will ask him for money in order to support herself. She will have no shame. The king's dream exactly means this. O king! Do not be afraid [of your dream]!"

The Buddha continued, "Regarding the eighth thing of which the king dreamed, that four bulls came from four directions while lowing; they chased each other, intending to fight, but just before they came together their whereabouts were lost, this means that in later ages the sovereign, the senior subalterns, and all the people will have no utmost sincerity. They will swindle each other, be ignorant and excitable, and they will not respect heaven and earth. For these reasons, untimely rain will occur. The senior subalterns and the people will pray for rain. Heaven will certainly raise clouds on all sides, and there will be thunderclaps. The senior subalterns and all the people will say it is going to rain, but soon the clouds scatter and there is not a single drop [of rain]. Why? This is because the sovereign, the senior subalterns, and all the people lack sincerity, righteousness, and benevolence. The king's dream exactly means this. O king! Do not be afraid [of your dream]!"

The Buddha continued, "Regarding the ninth thing of which the king dreamed, that the water in the center of a pond was muddy while the water in the rest of the pond was clean, this means that in later ages the central kingdom will be disturbed and the administration will be unjust. The people will be unfilial to their parents and not respect their elders. On the other hand, the surrounding countries will certainly be peaceful, and their people will be harmonious, respectful, and filial to their parents. The king's dream exactly means this. O king! Do not be afraid [of your dream]!"

The Buddha continued, "Regarding the tenth thing of which the king dreamed, that a stream in a great gorge was very red, this means that in later ages all countries will certainly fight in anger. They will raise armies, recruit soldiers, and send troops against each other. [The people] will become cart soldiers, foot soldiers, or cavalry soldiers, and they will all fight. They will kill and wound each other to an incalculable degree. On the roads the dead will shed blood that is deeply red. The king's dream exactly means this. O king! Do not be afraid [of your dream]! Your country, the crown prince, and your wives are also all free from misadventure."

The king heard this and knelt upright. He was delighted [and said,] "I have now received the Buddha's kindness, and it has caused me to attain peace." He made a bow and returned. He granted many gifts to court officials. [He said,] "From now on, I will not trust in various non-Buddhists and brahmans."

5. Neutral Nature

Just as the *Shisong lü* (T. 1435) says:

There was a *bhikṣu* who fell asleep in an assembly. The Buddha said [to all the *bhikṣus*], "I will allow you to go and rinse your head with water [to shake off sleepiness]." [The *bhikṣus* then sprinkled water on the *bhikṣu* who] was still asleep. [The *bhikṣu* complained about it, but the Buddha said,] "I cannot accept your words."

The Buddha instructed the *bhikṣus* to employ five methods to wash
536a others' heads with water. First is to have compassion for them; second is to not annoy them; third is to let them sleep; fourth is to rest their heads against a wall; and fifth is to stretch their legs.

If [a *bhikṣu*] was still asleep consecutively while remaining sitting on his seat, [the Buddha] allowed [the other *bhikṣus*] to prop him up with their hands. If he was still asleep consecutively as before, the Buddha allowed [the other *bhikṣus*] to toss a ball to him. If he was still asleep consecutively as before, the Buddha allowed [the other *bhikṣus*] to use the meditation stick.[194] [The Buddha said,] "When you take up the meditation stick, you should give rise to a respectful mind. Hold the stick with both hands and place and balance it on the crown of your head. If while sitting [in meditation] you fall asleep consecutively, you should stand up. When you see others sleeping, strike them with the meditation stick. After striking, return to your seat. Even if there is no one who is asleep, still take a seat after returning the meditation stick to its original place." If [a *bhikṣu*] was asleep consecutively as before, the Buddha allowed [the meditators] to use the meditation weight. A hole is properly made in it, and a cord is threaded through the hole. The top of the cord is knotted, and it is hung over an ear. Place the meditation weight as far as four fingerwidths away from the forehead so that it will touch the ground [if the meditator falls asleep and leans forward]. The Buddha said, "When the meditation weight falls down, you should stand up and walk composedly, in the same way as a goose walks."

Verses say:

Through the hindrance of torpor and drowsiness (Skt. *styāna-middha-āvaraṇa*),
A whimsical fancy appears.
Members of the same clan gather in vain,
And idly receive a good feast.
They have already awaken to emptiness,
But recklessly give rise to attachments.
Even though [a dream] has commonly three types of moral nature,
It turns into seven changes in the end.

Miracle Stories

(Six stories are briefly cited.)

[Wen Ying, Aide of Ganling Prefecture in the Han Dynasty]

In the Han dynasty, a man from Nanyang (in present-day Henan province) called Wen Ying, whose pseudonym was Shuliang, became the Aide of Ganling Prefecture (in present-day Gansu province) during the Jian'an era (196–220). [Traveling to take up his post] he passed by a border region, where he camped overnight.

When the night drum was beaten three times (i.e., at midnight), he had a dream in which a man knelt down in front of him and said, "Formerly my predecessors buried me in this place, but swift water flowed into my grave, and the bottom half of my wooden coffin was soaked. It cannot be dried by natural warmth. I heard that you are here, so I have come to rely on you. Please stay here for a short while tomorrow. I would be fortunate if you could move my coffin to high and dry land." The ghost spread out his garments to show Ying; they were all wet and damp. Ying woke up just as he felt broken-hearted.

After waking up, he told his attendants [about the dream]. His attendants said, "Dreams are just unreal. It is not worth concern." Ying then went back to sleep.

Toward the break of dawn he dreamed again. [The ghost] said to Ying, "I told you about my extreme suffering. Why do you not take pity on me and grieve for me?" Ying asked in the dream, "Who are you?" [The ghost] replied,

"I was originally a man of Zhao state. I am currently a subordinate of the deity of Wangmangshi state."[195] [Wen] Ying asked, "Where is your coffin now?" [The ghost] replied, "It is near your tent, ten plus several paces to the north,
536b under a withered willow tree at the water's edge. That is precisely mine. It is going to be light. I will not be able to see you again. Please keep this in mind without fail." Ying answered, "All right!" and suddenly woke up.

When dawn came and they were getting ready to depart, Ying said, "Even though you said that dreams are not worth concern, how greatly this stands to reason!" His attendants said, "In any case, why do we have to hurry? Why don't we certify it?" Ying promptly stood up, feeling happy about this, and leading a group of more than ten people he went up along the river. Just as he had been told, [Ying] found a withered willow tree. He said, "This is it!" [His attendants] dug the ground beneath the willow, and before digging very deep they discovered a coffin, just as [the ghost] had described. The coffin was decayed and half submerged in water. Ying said to his attendants, "As I heard previously from the people I thought [a dream] is unreal. Legends of the world cannot be said to be meaningless." They moved the coffin for [the ghost], poured wine over it [as an honorific act], and departed.

(This story is found in the *Soushen ji* [*Records of Inquiries of the Spirits*].)

[Chen Xiuyuan of the Song Dynasty]

Chen Xiuyuan of the Song dynasty, a man from Yingchuan (in present-day Henan province), was once Administrator of the Western Section in Xiang province and lived temporarily in Linxiang county. From his early life, he respectfully believed in the Three Treasures. Even after over the age of sixty years old, his sincere practice never lessened. One day in the seventh month of the second year of the Yuanhui era of the Song dynasty (474), he lay down on his bed at night but he did not fall asleep. He lamented that all beings transmigrate in the realms of birth and death; they are transient. He thought to himself, "Where did I come from?" He prayed wholeheartedly, hoping he would receive a mysterious response to his question.

At that time the evening dusk gathered, and there was no light in the room. Soon he saw something like the glow of a firefly close to his pillow. It brightly shone and smoothly flew away. Suddenly the room became completely bright, and accordingly even the space above him became as much light as in the daytime. Xiuyuan hurriedly sat up and joined hands, gasping for breath. Soon he saw a bridge structure that appeared four or five *zhang* high above the courtyard. The parapets were painted red, and it floated in the air. [Chen] Xiuyuan did not realize at all that he had moved when he saw himself sitting by the bridge. He observed that many people came and went on the bridge, filling the thoroughfare. Their clothes were no different from those of the people of this world.

There was a woman, whose age could be a little more than thirty, on the edge of the crowd. She wore a blue jacket and a white skirt. She came to Xiuyuan and stood to his left side. Soon another lady appeared. She wore white clothes, both top and bottom. Her hair was arranged into a topknot on one side. Holding flowers and incense in her hands, she stood just in front of [Xiuyuan] and said to him, "You want to see what you were in your previous existence. I am the one. I offer these flowers to the Buddha. Therefore I can be transformed and become you." She turned her head and said, pointing to the woman in the white [skirt], "Furthermore this is my former self." After she said this, she left, and the bridge began to gradually disappear, too. Suddenly Xiuyuan did not realize when he was back on the ground [away from the bridge]. Soon after, the light went out.

(This story is found in the *Mingxiang ji* [*Records of the Profound and Auspicious*].)

[Zhu Gefu, a Governor of the Song Dynasty]

Zhu Gefu from Langye (in present-day Shandong province) was appointed governor of Jiuzhen prefecture (in present-day Vietnam) during the Yuanjia era (424–453) in the Song dynasty,[196] but all his family dependents stayed in the capital city, Yanzhou. He only took his first son, Yuanchong, with him and proceeded to his post. Gefu died of illness in the prefecture [of his appointment]. Yuanchong, who had just attained the [Chinese] age of nineteen, intended to return to his hometown carrying [his father's body in] a coffin.

He Faseng, Gefu's follower, coveted [Yuanchong's] property. Along with 536c
his gang [he] pushed [Yuanchong] into a river, and [Yuanchong] died. [The gang] then divided [Zhu's] property between them.

That night Yuanchong's mother, née Chen, dreamed that Yuanchong had returned home and fully described his father's death and all the details of his own murder. [He said,] "My body is tossed about in the current. There is nothing more atrocious than this. I have disregarded serving you for years.

Today I will be parting from you forever. I harbor sorrow and resentment. How can I express it?" Between sobs he said that he was unable to overcome [his sorrow and resentment]. Moreover, he said, "I walked swiftly, and I am extremely tired." Accordingly he laid himself down on a bed at the side of a window, resting his head on the window frame. His mother saw the place her son had lain down and thoroughly knew that it was not false.

Née Chen was sad and grieving. She got up in surprise. Holding a torch she shone it on the place her son had lain down, which was all wet in the form of a human being. Then the whole family wept aloud. Thereupon, investigations started.

At that time Xu Senzhi was appointed for the first time [as governor of] Jiaozhou (in present-day Guangxi province), and Xu Daoli was a senior subaltern. Daoli was a son of née Chen's aunt on her father's side. [Née Chen] described her dream in detail and requested the two men of the Xu family (i.e., Senzhi and Daoli) to look into [the incident].

On their way the two men of the Xu family came across a boat that had the mark of Zhu Ge[fu]'s funeral and verified the death dates of the father and son; [the dates] were just as the ghost [of Yuanchong] had said. They subsequently arrested the two men who had committed murder, and who promptly submitted. In accordance with the law they were punished by death. Moreover, official messengers were dispatched to escort the coffins [of the father and son] to the capital city.

(This story is found in the *Yuanhunzhi* [*Records of Resentful Spirits of Those Who Died Unreasonably*].)

[Ma Qianbo of the Song Dynasty]

Ma Qianbo of the Song dynasty was from Langzhong county in Baxi (in present-day Sichuan province). He believed in the Buddhist Dharma from his early days. He was once the steward of Xuanhan county (in present-day Sichuan province). One night, in the seventh month of the twelfth year of the Yuanjia era (435), at his official residence he had a dream in which three figures appeared far in the distance in the sky. They were more than two *zhang* tall with a solemn and magnificent appearance. They looked down from the edge of a cloud. Music played by various heavenly female musicians resounded in the air. They said to [Qianbo], "You will have hardship in Jingchu (i.e., the area of present-day Hubei and Hunan provinces). On the fourth day of the eighth month of the *wu-yin* year, if you stay in the hills and valleys, you will be able to avert misfortune, or if you purify your mind and body, even if you are among people, you will be also able to avoid hardship. If you pass this period of time [in safety], you will certainly attain the Buddhist Way."

At that time, when [Ma Qianbo] looked down, he saw eight of his acquaintances including Yang Xian all bound with chains and shackled. Moreover, he saw the Buddhist Hu Liao, and the lower half of his body was buried in the earth. Supernatural beings in the center as well as at edges of heaven all recorded the last day of each of the eight men's lives. [The supernatural beings] said only to Liao, "If you can cultivate yourself and make merit, you will still be able to prolong your life span."

All [the eight] people including [Yang] Xian died, as had been expected. Liao felt more and more fearful. He believed in the Dharma, lived on a mountain, and exerted himself to practice the Dharma more diligently.

Qianbo later became an official of the Western Section in Liangzhou. The Regional Commander (General of the Liangzhou) was Xiao Sihua. When Xiao was transferred to the uncivilized southern area, [Qianbo] was appointed as Acting Administrator. Qianbo remembered the divine message "[You will have hardship] in Jingchu. . . ," and he was very frightened. So he asked Xiao to release him from his office and allow him to go to Mount Heng (in present-day Anhui province). Xiao earnestly discouraged [Qianbo] from resigning and did not approve his petition.

The fifteenth year [of the Yuanjia era] (438) was precisely the *wu-yin* year. [Qianbo] became ill at the end of the sixth month. On the fourth day of the eighth month, he fell into a critical condition and was barely alive. After dusk on that day it suddenly became bright, and he saw everything clearly. Far away in the western direction, three figures appeared; they were about two *zhang* tall. The one in front was nicely dressed, and his beard hung down. From the top of his head shone a halo. The two behind him possessed natural endowments that glistened with golden color and signs of good fortune in their demeanor. They stood abreast in the air several *ren* above the ground. 537a
Qianbo observed all of them in detail. They were the same beings that he had dreamed of previously. They soon disappeared. The fragrance lingered in the air for a while and then dissipated. People of all ages who roomed with him smelled the fragrance. After this, Qianbo was wet with perspiration and

soon came to a state of lull. [Ma] Qianbo's residence was squalid, but at that time he felt as if he was living in a [grand] palace, where the walls of the hallway glistened, and everything was made of jewels and valuables. He thus gradually recovered from his illness.

(This story is found in the *Mingxiang ji* [*Records of the Profound and Auspicious*].)

[Shi Senghu, a *Śramaṇa* of the (Northern) Qi Dynasty]

During the Qi dynasty of the Gao [royal family] (i.e., the Northern Qi dynasty, 550–577) there was Shi Senghu, who abided by the [Buddhist] Way, who was upright and honest, and who did not pursue the practices based on wisdom. His prayer was to create a stone image one *zhang* and eight *chi* tall. Everyone was surprised at his words. Later, in the valley north of the temple, he found a standing rock, which was estimated to be one *zhang* and eight *chi* long. [Senghu] then hired artisans to construct an image. They measured the circumference [of the rock] beforehand. The face and the front part [of the image] were roughly finished, but the back part [of the rock] was still attached to the ground. [The people] persistently tried to lift [the rock] using the six kinds of tools, but just as at the beginning it would not move. As daybreak came after that night, [the rock] suddenly turned over by itself. Accordingly the construction was completed, and the image was moved to the Buddha Hall.

On the day during the fall of Jinzhou (in present-day Shanxi province) the [rock] image was wet with perspiration that streamed onto the ground. When soldiers of the [Northern] Zhou dynasty (556–581) entered [the territory of] the [Northern] Qi dynasty and burned various Buddhist temples, this image alone did not change color. Moreover, [the soldiers] wanted to remove [the image], and people along with sixty oxen tried to pull it down. [The image,] however, did not move. Suddenly a strange monk appeared. He piled up tiles, wood, earth, and unbaked tiles around the image.[197] It was done in an instant, and then the monk disappeared.

The image later appeared in the dream of a faithful person and said,[198] "I suffer from pain in my fingers." The person woke up and inspected [the image] [and found that] a piece of wood had damaged two of its fingers. Consequently [the two fingers] were repaired immediately.

In the tenth year of the Kaihuang era (590) someone stole the streamers and canopy for the image. [That person] dreamed that a man who was one *zhang* and eight *chi* tall came into his room and upbraided him. The thief consequently felt ashamed and afraid, repented [of his fault], and apologized. The image remains today.

[Shi Zhixing, a *Śramaṇa* of the Tang Dynasty]

At Great Zhuangyan Temple in the metropolis of the Tang dynasty was Shi Zhixing (588–632), who had secular connections with the Song family. He was from Mingzhou (in present-day Hebei province) and he was humble, moderate, and accomplished his duties. He practiced with determination and was strong and bright. Relying on Vinaya Master [Zhi]shou (567–635), he recited sutras and observed the precepts. He received both the mind and oral trainings.[199] He never ceased performing [the practices], morning and evening.

In the second month of winter (i.e., the eleventh month of the year) in the fifth year of the Daye era (609) [Zhixing] assumed the position of Buddhist deacon (*weina;* Skt. *karmadāna*). He tolled the bell at the proper times so that the monks had no troubles.

In the same temple was a monk called Sanguo, whose elder brother attended Emperor Yang to the south, but he died on the way to Jiangdu (in present-day Yizheng prefecture in Jiangsu province). At first there was no announcement of his death, but he communicated with his wife in a dream. He said, "When I traveled and came to Pengcheng (in present-day Tongshan prefecture in Jiangsu province), unfortunately I died from an illness. Since I did not observe purification and the precepts, I have now fallen into hell. I have fully experienced the five kinds of suffering;[200] I am unable to explain all the hardships. Who could understand my suffering? I rely on being favored with the fact that at sunrise this month Zhixing, a monk of Zhuangyan Temple, tolls the bell and causes the sound to be emitted. The sound [of the bell] will shake up hell. Those who receive suffering in the same ways I do will immediately be delivered [from hell]. They will be reborn in a place of happiness and think to repay [Zhixing's] kindness. You should prepare ten rolls of silk fabric, immediately offer these to [Zhixing], and tell him of my intention. I hope you will be courteous, polite, and sincere."

The wife woke up in surprise, wondering why she had had such a dream. She talked with other people, but at first no one believed it. Subsequently she had the [same] dream again, and various sorcerers all told her the views of former people. After ten days passed, the announcement of her husband's 537b death abruptly reached her. [The announcement] was just the same as in her dream. [San]guo, therefore, received silk fabric with respect [from his brother's wife] and gave them to [Zhixing], but [Zhi]xing said that he had no virtue and [instead] bestowed them all on the masses.

The chief priest of the temple and Chan Master [Fa]gong together with great virtuous monks of the temple all asked [Zhi]xing, "What condition causes you to toll the bell and receive this response?" [Zhi]xing replied, "I have no other skill. I saw in the *Fufazang [yinyuan] zhuan* that when King Kaniṣka suffered hardships, he could stop them by tolling a bell. [I also read] the verse of tolling a bell in the *Zengyi ahan jing* (T. 125). I fortunately and respectfully follow this path, and I exert myself to practice it with determination. In the depth of winter I go up into the bell tower even as the [cold] wind cuts my skin and flesh [just like a knife]. A monk is given lambskin sleeves and holds a bell striker using them. I, [Zhi]xing, encourage myself and toll [the bell] holding the striker with my bare hands. The wounds in my hands break open, but I do not consider this to be painful. Also, at the beginning when I go to toll the bell, I first make wholesome vows. I pray that all virtuous people and sages will enter a seminar hall together and receive the Dharma meal together. Later I bow three times. I intend to strike [the bell] for a long time and pay respects as I said earlier: 'I pray that the beings in all the evil realms will hear the sound of this bell and together will be able to leave behind suffering and swiftly attain liberation.' I make a vow in this way and set my mind always to respectfully cultivate myself." Could it be only through his thorough sincerity that he was consequently able to perceive what is profound? The people submitted to his words. He doubled the efficacy correctly.

In the third month of the sixth year of the Zhenguan era (632) [Zhixing] became ill. After a short time he spontaneously recognized [what was coming] in his future. He gave up his body and his property and invited his teacher and all his friends. Then he had a meal with them and said goodbye. Soon after he passed away at Zhuangyan [Temple] at the age of forty-five.

(These two stories are found in the *Biographies of Eminent Monks* compiled in the Tang dynasty [*Tang Gaoseng zhuan*].)

[End of] Fascicle Thirty-two of *A Forest of Pearls from the Dharma Garden*

Fascicle 33

Chapter Twenty-seven

Establishing Merit

(This chapter consists of eight parts:) (1) Introduction, (2) Establishing Merit, (3) Giving Rise to Faith, (4) Conjecture through Comparison, (5) Repair and Creating, (6) Almsgiving, (7) Miscellaneous Merit, and (8) Bathing Monks.

1. Introduction

In ancient times Udayana for the first time carved sandalwood and Prasenajit for the first time melted gold [in order to make an image of the Buddha]. All these images actually represented [the Buddha's] real appearance, and his wonderful characteristics were skillfully portrayed. Therefore, [images of the Buddha] can emit light and create auspiciousness. People pay respect [to the images] by rising from their seats. Accordingly, everything up to the two stupas [containing] the [Buddha's] hair and fingernails [relics] as well as the two platforms [that held] his body and robe were already completed in their patterns at the time the Tathāgata resided in the world. After [the Buddha's] remains were collected at the riverside and cremated outside the grove, the kings of eight countries requested a share [of the Buddha's relics] and returned to their countries, where they erected stupas [in which to enshrine them].
There were also two more places: a stupa for the relics bottle and one for the 537c
cinders of charcoal [collected from the cremation site]. In this way the ten sites (Skt. *kṣetra*) [where the Buddha's relics were enshrined] came about. Stupas were erected and inscriptions were engraved at all places such as the Buddha's birthplace, the place where he attained the Buddhist Way, the places he expounded the Dharma, where he entered nirvana, [containing] his hair, the protuberance on his head, his skull, four of his teeth, a set of his footprints, his bowl and cane, his spittoon, and his *nivāsana* (waistrobe). The miracles of the Buddha were raised up high.

More than a hundred years later, King Aśoka dispatched messengers, who traveled on the sea, desroyed and removed all the stupas, and took the relics [from within the stupas]. On their way back they encountered a storm, and many of the relics were lost. To this day there are some among mariners who occasionally come across them. After this, eighty-four thousand [stupas] were erected [by the king] on account of this event.

All of King Aśoka's daughters also aspired to a pure mind, one after another. They also had stones engraved and metals smelted to depict the [Buddha's] image. [The images they had made] traveled by river and the sea and came to edify the people of the Eastern River (i.e., China). Even though the mysterious traces [of the Buddha] secretly reached [China], they had not manifested themselves visually or through sound. An image of Śākyamuni drawn on a piece of woolen cloth was introduced [into China] for the first time just as Cai Yin and Qin Jing returned from the Western Region. Thereafter, [the Buddha's] image was depicted on balconies and mausoleums. From that time on [buddha] images, stupas, and temples were made and proliferated as if competing with the passage of time. By the time of the Liang dynasty, the glorious traces of the Buddha flourished here.

There is, however, no fixed image for the Dharma body. It is formed by one's perception of it. Perception through sight varies [with each individual]. Therefore, there will be different forms [of the Dharma body]. If one's way of thinking is vast and endless, then even the appearance of [the Buddha's] true body (i.e., the Dharma body or the reward body) obstructs edification for him. If one's intention is contented and rigorous, even insentient beings open their minds. Therefore, Liu Yin was very filial and sincere.[201] He was very grateful that a small amount of aconite (rose of Sharon) grew for him. Ding Lan was temperate, pure, and wholehearted. The wooden mother [image engraved by him] changed color because of his good nature.[202] Duke Luyang turned around a spear and moved the sun.[203] Qi [Liang's] wife shed tears [for the death of her husband] and the city fell.[204] These are all cases where natural compassion entered the disposition [of heaven]. Therefore, auspicious signs shone upon the people's ears and eyes.

From this, we know that the Buddhist Way is propagated by people, and a spiritual being can be perceived by people. How can this be said to be false? Therefore, when you worship a spiritual being as if the spiritual being exists [right then and there], you will commune with the Way of the Spirit. When you pay respects to an image of the Buddha as if revering the actual Buddha, the Dharma body will respond to you. Therefore, in order to enter the [Buddhist] Way, you must take wisdom as the foundation, and wisdom must take merit as its foundation. It is just as a bird equipped with two wings swiftly flies unfathomably high into the sky, or a two-wheeled vehicle travels a thousand *li* in a moment. How could you not be diligent? How could you not be assiduous?

2. Establishing Merit

Just as the *Foshuo [zhude] futian jing* (T. 683) says:

> The Buddha said to Śakra-devendra, "Furthermore, there are seven issues. To give alms extensively is called the field of merit. Those who practice it attain merit; they will be precisely reborn in Brahma Heaven.
>
> "What are the seven issues? First is to establish stupas, residential quarters for monastics, halls, and pavilions in a monastery. Second is to [provide] fruit, a bathing pool, and a tree-shaded garden that are pleasant and cool. Third is to always dispense medicines and cure numerous diseases. Fourth is to make a secure and strong ship in order to save people and ferry them over [the sea of transmigration]. Fifth is to build a bridge so that emaciated and weak people can pass over. Sixth is to dig a well near the road so that thirsty people will be able to drink water. Seventh is to create a [public] latrine and provide a place for people to relieve themselves. These are the seven issues by which one may attain the merit [of rebirth 538a
> in] Brahma Heaven."
>
> At that time among all those present was a *bhikṣu* called Śroṇakoṭīviṃśa.[205] He was delighted to hear the Dharma. He readily addressed the Buddha, "I personally recall that at the time of my previous existence I was reborn in Vārāṇasī as a wealthy man's son. I built a monastery by the side of a main road and supplied bedding, food, and water to the sangha. Those who collapsed from exhaustion while traveling were also able to rest there. Due to this merit, after death I was reborn in [Trāyastriṃśa] Heaven as Śakra-devendra and then descended to be reborn in the world as a wheel-turning noble king. This process of rebirth was repeated thirty-six times. I ruled over and supervised heavenly beings. For ninety-one

*kalpa*s I grew hair under my feet and roamed around, treading lightly through the air. I was spontaneously blessed with food. Now I have met the World-honored One, who cares for and deals with sentient beings, who has removed my stupidity, who calms me with pure wisdom, who [clarifies] birth and death and arising and being extinguished, and who is called the Perfected One. Regarding this, a reward for a good act is true, it is right!"

There was another *bhikṣu* called Bakula. He addressed the Buddha, "I remember that I was formerly reborn in Kuśinagara as a wealthy man's son. In the world at that time there was no buddha. The sangha edified the people and preached the Dharma in a great assembly. I went and heard the Dharma there. I was delighted to hear the Dharma. I had a medicinal fruit called *harītakī,* which I offered to the sangha. Due to this reward, I was reborn in heaven after death. I descended to be reborn in the world, where I was always placed in a noble status surpassing the common people. For ninety-one *kalpa*s I have never been ill. Due to the extra merit, I have met the Buddha and came to attain arhatship."

There was another *bhikṣu* called Sudāya. He addressed the World-honored One, "I think of my previous existence in which I was reborn in Vaiśāli as a son of an insignificant family. In the world at that time there was no buddha. The sangha edified the people. On one occasion I brought milk to a marketplace, intending to sell it. I came across a Dharma talk given by the sangha in a great assembly. As I passed by, I listened to it while standing. I was delighted to hear the Dharma. I promptly donated the whole bottle of milk to the sangha. The sangha said a prayer, and I felt like dancing with joy even more. Due to this meritorious act, after death I was reborn in heaven and then descended to be reborn in the world where I was always placed in a noble status. After the end of ninety-one *kalpa*s, I had a remaining fault and descended to be reborn in the world. My mother was pregnant for several months and then died from an illness. In the grave in which my mother was buried, I was reborn in the fullness of time. In the grave I took my dead mother's milk for seven years in order to save myself [from hunger] and keep myself alive. For my small merit I have met the Buddha and came to attain arhatship."

There was another *bhikṣu* called Ānanda. He addressed the World-honored One, "I remember that I was formerly reborn in Rājagṛha as a commoner's son. I had a malignant boil on my body and tried to cure it, but I could not. A friend who was a Buddhist monk came to me and said, 'You should offer a bath for the sangha then collect the bathwater and cleanse the boil with it. You will be able to recover from [the boil], and also you will attain merit.' I was happy [to hear this]. I went to a monastery and sincerely paid my respects to the sangha, more and more. Then I dug a new well. With aromatic oil and bathing supplies I offered a bath for the sangha and then collected the bathwater, with which I washed the boil. I soon recovered [from the boil]. Due to this merit, wherever I was reborn 538b
I had regular features, [my form is] dazzlingly golden-colored, and I am not covered by dust and dirt. For ninety-one *kalpa*s I have always attained the merit of purity and increased virtue extensively and profoundly. Now furthermore I have met the Buddha. My defilements have been extinguished and I have attained arhatship."

At that time, among all those present there was a *bhikṣuṇī* called Āmrapālī. She addressed the Buddha, "I recollect that in my previous existence I was reborn in Vārāṇasī as a poor woman. In the world at that time there was a buddha called Kāśyapa. On one occasion he expounded the Dharma, surrounded by a crowd of people. I was then among all those present and heard the teaching, and I was happy. I wanted to give a donation to him, but I had nothing to give. Thinking of my humble and destitute circumstances, I felt sad. I went to someone's orchard, where I begged for fruit to offer to [Kāśyapa] Buddha. I obtained a large and fragrant apple, and along with a basin of water I offered the apple to Kāśyapa Buddha and all the sangha. The Buddha understood my utmost intention. Making a prayer he received them. He distributed the water and the apple to all the people. Due to this meritorious blessing, after death I was reborn in heaven where I became the Empress of Heaven. I descended to be reborn in the world without going through the placenta. For ninety-one *kalpa*s I was reborn among apple blossoms, and I was regular-featured, fresh, and pure. I always know of my previous existences. Now I have met the Buddha, who explains and shows the eyes of the [Buddhist] Way."

At that time Śakra-devendra rose from his seat and bowed to the Buddha. Kneeling upright and with folded hands he addressed the Buddha, "O World-honored One! I personally remember that at the time of my previous existence I was reborn in the great country of Kuru as a wealthy man's son. A female servant carried me in her arms, and we went to a city for sightseeing. Coincidentally we came across sangha members alms-begging in the streets. On that occasion I saw that very many people gave alms to them. I thought to myself, 'I wish to obtain money and jewels and donate them to the sangha. Wouldn't I be happy?' I promptly took off my pearl necklace and donated it to the sangha members, who said a prayer for me, being one in mind. I delightedly left there. Due to this cause and condition, after death I was reborn in [Trāyastriṃśa] Heaven and was able to become Śakra-devendra. For ninety-one *kalpa*s, a long time, I have left behind the eight difficulties."

The Buddha said to Śakra-devendra and all people, "Listen to my explanation of what I did in my previous existence! Formerly, in my previous existence, I installed [public] latrines near the side of a main road in Vārāṇasī. People all over the county attained ease and peace; everyone appreciated my integrity. Due to this merit, I attain purity, generation after generation, I have practiced the [Buddhist] Way for *kalpa*s, I am not defiled by filth and pollution, I am dazzlingly golden-colored, and I am not covered by dust and dirt. The food I ingest is spontaneously digested, and I have no trouble with excretion."

The Buddha said to Śakra-devendra, "Among the ninety-six kinds of paths the Buddhist Way is the most honorable. Among the ninety-six kinds of teachings the Buddhist Dharma is the most genuine. Among the ninety-six kinds of monks Buddhist monks are the most honest and virtuous. What is the reason for this? It is because incalculable *kalpa*s ago the Tathāgata made a vow to achieve truth, strove after virtue while undergoing transmigration in birth and death, and took an oath for the sake of sentient
538c beings. He universally possesses the six *pāramitā*s and the four kinds of immeasurable minds (Skt. *catur-apramāṇa*), and all wholesomeness.[206] His virtue and wisdom are fully completed. In the three realms of existence no one can equal the Bhagavat (i.e., the World-honored One). Among sentient beings, those who give rise to a respectful mind and who come before

the Tathāgata are better than those who obtain jewels and valuables in a trichiliocosm.[207] [The Tathāgata explains] the thirty-seven kinds of practices to attain enlightenment (Skt. *bodhipākṣika*) and the twelve kinds of scriptures. He discriminates evil acts from meritorious deeds. His words are all of the greatest sincerity. When he explains the three kinds of teachings applicable to bodhisattvas, *pratyekabuddha*s, and *śrāvaka*s, they are all able to uphold and practice them. Those who hear [the teachings] are delighted, wish to become *śramaṇa*s, believe in the Buddha, practice the Dharma, and esteem to make up their minds to pursue moral uprightness. To abandon worldly avarice and dispute, to direct [the people of] the world to make merit, and to lead [sentient beings] on the road to heavenly and human beings are the sangha's practices. This is the most honorable, supreme way."

3. Giving Rise to Faith

Just as the *Jiu zapiyu jing* says:

In ancient times, outside of Śrāvastī there was a laywoman who practiced in compliance with the precepts and was completely sincere.

The Buddha came to her gate in person and begged for alms. The woman put food in the Buddha's almsbowl, then withdrew and bowed. The Buddha said, "Planting one produces ten, planting ten produces a hundred, planting a hundred produces a thousand, planting a thousand produces ten thousand, planting ten thousand produces a hundred million." [The woman] was able to understand the way of truth (Skt. *satya-mārga*), but her husband did not trust it and kept silent.

Afterward, they heard the Buddha say a prayer. The husband said, "*Śramaṇa* Gautama, why did you exaggerate? She gave a bowl of food, so she attained merit. Further, she understood the way of truth." The Buddha asked him, "Where did you come from?" He answered, "I came from the city." The Buddha asked, "How tall is the *nyagrodha* tree you see?" He answered, "It is four or five *li* tall. The harvest is several tens of thousands *hu* of fruit. Their stones are as small as a mustard seed." The Buddha said, "You exaggerate. How can there be a case where [a seed as small as] a mustard seed is planted yet grows four or five *li* tall and it yields several hundreds of thousands *hu* [of fruit]?" The man answered, "The people of the world all see its reality in this way." The Buddha said, "The earth is ignorant of its power of reward just like this, not to speak of human beings who are sentient beings." [The couple] was delighted and held out a bowl with a food offering to the Buddha. The merit of this was exceedingly great and incalculable. The husband and wife were fascinated by this, and their minds were liberated. Immediately they attained the path of the *srota-āpatti-phala.*

Moreover, the [*Da*] *zhidu lun* says:

In ancient times when the Buddha resided in the world, accompanied by Ānanda the Buddha headed toward the brahman city from Śrāvastī. At that time the king of the brahman city was affiliated with a non-Buddhist teaching. When he heard that the Buddha was coming there, he immediately imposed restrictions: those who give food to the Buddha or spoke with him would be punished with a fine of five hundred *wen* of coins.

Later, the Buddha arrived, entered the city, and begged for alms. All the people [in the city] closed their gates. The Buddha and Ānanda, holding empty bowls, came out of [the city]. They saw an old maidservant holding a cracked earthenware vessel that contained the smelly water in which rice had been washed. She came out of the gate to dump [out the water] and saw the Buddha, who had the marks of physical excellence, approaching with an empty bowl. She wished to give alms to him. The Buddha was aware of her intention. So he extended [his hand] holding the almsbowl to receive the rice water that she was throwing out. With a pure mind the
539a maidservant held [the rice water] and came to give it to the Buddha. After receiving the alms, the Buddha said to Ānanda, "Due to this act of almsgiving, for fifteen *kalpa*s this maidservant will receive merit and be happy in heaven and in the realm of human beings, and she will not fall into evil realms. Afterward she will obtain a male body, renounce the world, learn the [Buddhist] Way, and become a *pratyekabuddha.*"

At that time a brahman near the Buddha overheard the Buddha's words. He said to the Buddha, "You are the crown prince of King Śuddhodana. Why do you say such a falsehood about food?" At that moment the Buddha put out his tongue, whichcovered his [entire] face up to the hairline, and said to [the brahman], "Have you ever seen a case where someone who has a tongue like this states a falsehood?" The brahman answered, "If one's tongue can cover his nose, he does not make a falsehood, not to mention the case where [the tongue] covers [the entire face] up to the hairline." [The brahman] promptly gave rise to faith and addressed the Buddha, "I do not understand why such meager alms are now so greatly rewarded." The Buddha asked, "Have you ever seen an uncommon occurrence?" The brahman answered, "Yes. Once while traveling I saw that the shade of a single *nyagrodha* tree covered over five hundred vehicles." The Buddha asked him, "Is the seed of that tree large or small?" He answered, "It is one-third the size of a mustard seed." The Buddha further asked, "Who would believe your words?" The brahman answered, "It is truly so. O World-honored One! I saw it with my own eyes. It is not a lie." The Buddha said, "I see that because this woman gave alms to the Buddha with a pure mind she attains a great reward, and this is just the same as with the tree, where the cause is small yet the result is great."

On that occasion the brahman was fascinated by this and his mind was liberated. Facing the Buddha, he repented of his faults. The Buddha expounded the Dharma for him. He attained the *srota-āpatti-phala*. He immediately raised his hands and cried out loudly, "All you people! The gate of nectar (i.e., the Buddhist teaching) has opened! Why do you not come out?" The people, on hearing this, offered money in the amount of five hundred [*wen*] to the king. They entreated the Buddha [to give the teaching] and made offerings to him. Immediately [the king's] restrictions [on making offerings to the Buddha] ended, and together with his entire body of ministers the king also took refuge in the Buddha. The Buddha expounded the Dharma for them and they all attained fruition of the [Buddhist] Way. Due to this cause and condition, whatever the Tathāgata speaks has no falsehood. The reward and retribution for good and bad acts are precisely received, not an iota less or more. All sentient beings must believe and receive them.

Furthermore, the *Piyu jing* says:[208]

In old times there were two *bhikṣus* who had attained the *srota-āpatti-phala* together. One of them always practiced edification and almsbegging.

Using the merit he had acquired, he offered food to other monks. The other [*bhikṣu*] simply sat in meditation; he maintained himself without wishing to gain merit.

On one occasion the meditation monk said to the almsbegging monk, "Why do you not sit in meditation but instead work assiduously, defying hardships in vain?" The one who cultivated merit answered, "The Buddha always said to the *bhikṣu*s, 'You must cultivate almsgiving.'"

Later both *bhikṣu*s died and were reborn in a wealthy man's house. The one who had made merit through almsbegging was the son of the wealthy man and part of his family. Servants waited on him, and clothes and food were spontaneously given to him. He was inexhaustibly happy. The one who had sat in meditation was reborn as a maidservant's son. He sat alone on the ground, wailing with hunger and thirst. Both of them were aware of their previous existence. One time the wealthy man's son
539b said to the maidservant's son, "I originally told you that you must practice almsgiving, but you were unwilling to accept my words. This is your fault. Why do you cry?"

After the wealthy man's son had grown up he rode a horse and went out sightseeing. All the servants as well as the maidservant's son accompanied him. Afterward both [the wealthy man's son and the maidservant's son] together sought to renounce the world. After their renunciation they attained the fruit of arhatship. The wealthy man's son always sat up straight. All the people vied with each other to make offerings to him; they brought clothes and food to give to him. The maidservant's son begged for alms outside but no one gave [him alms], so he always suffered from hunger and thirst. Due to this cause and condition, practitioners of the [Buddhist] Way should not only observe the precepts, meditate, and chant sutras, they must also make various merits through giving alms.

Therefore in the *Daaidao* [*biqiuni*] *jing* (T. 1478), the Buddha says in verse:

If you do not study day and night,
There is no end for a day,
And as you act, you will go into evil.
You will whirl around deeper and deeper.

And by yourself you will submerge your own body.
This is also adversity.
You go, but you do not come back.
You give up your life on Mount Tai.
Suffering in hell is
Difficult to endure.
If you do not study while you are living,
You must enter an abyss at death.
If you cannot stop lewdness in your old age,
In the world where sensual pleasures are exhausted,
Breathe and die.
It is not worth treasuring yourself.
You can repent of your faults by yourself.
Protecting yourself from evils is truly genuine.
If you extinguish your sins in this world,
You will be able to feel exhilaration after death.
If you have wealth and yet do not give alms,
You will suffer from poverty generation after generation.

4. Conjecture through Comparison

Just as the *Xuda jing* (T. 73) says:

> The World-honored One said to the wealthy man Sudatta, "There is a layman who practices almsgiving. If he gives alms without faith, not at a proper time, not with his own hands, or without going personally [to a receiver of the alms], or if he practices almsgiving unconsciously, without faith, or without knowing that there is a cause and a condition in his acting for reward, you must know that even if he receives a reward, his intention is not wonderful. (The case opposite to the above is wonderful.)
>
> "Formerly, in times past, the great brahman Vailāma had great wealth. He made great almsgiving with eighty-four thousand golden bowls filled with small silver coins. He practiced great almsgiving with eighty-four thousand silver bowls filled with small gold coins, with eighty-four thousand golden bowls filled with small gold coins, with eighty-four thousand silver bowls filled with small silver coins, with eighty-four thousand elephants

as white as snow, with eighty-four thousand horses decorated with gold and caparisoned in a pearl net, with eighty-four thousand containers filled with cow's milk, and with eighty-four thousand young and beautiful girls who were particularly well featured and adorned with various ornamental fringes on their garments. In this way he practiced almsgiving with other incalculable things. The layman Vailāma, the great wealthy one, practiced great almsgiving like this.

"One who gives alms to ordinary people in Jambudvīpa would attain
539c more merit when he gives alms to a hermit. Even if he gives alms to a hermit, it is not as good as giving alms to one who has attained the *srota-āpatti-phala.* By this conduct he attains more merit. Even if someone gives alms to one who has attained the *srota-āpatti-phala,* it is not as good as giving alms to one who has attained the *sakṛdāgāmi-phala.* Even if someone gives alms to one who has attained the *sakṛdāgāmi-phala,* it is not as good as giving alms to one who has attained the *anāgāmi-phala.* Even if someone gives alms to one who has attained the *anāgāmi-phala,* it is not as good as giving alms to an arhat. [Giving alms to] a hundred people who have attained the *srota-āpatti-phala* and a hundred people who have attained the *sakṛdāgāmi-phala* is not as good as giving alms to a single person who has attained the *anāgāmi-phala.* Even if someone gives alms to a hundred people who have attained the *anāgāmi-phala,* it is not as good as giving alms to a single arhat. Even if someone gives alms to a hundred arhats, it is not as good as giving alms to a single *pratyekabuddha.* Even if someone gives alms to a hundred *pratyekabuddha*s, it is not as good as giving alms to a tathāgata, one who has no attachment (*wusuozhe*),[209] a fully-enlightened one (Skt. *samyak-saṃbuddha*). By this conduct the almsgiver attains many merits.

"That layman practiced almsgiving in this way. Even if he gives alms to the ordinary people of Jambudvīpa, up to a hundred *pratyekabuddha*s, if he constructs residential buildings and gives them to monks from all over the world, he attains much more merit. Even if he gives [the buildings] to monks from all over the world, it is not as good as taking refuge in the Three Treasures, the Buddha, Dharma, and Sangha, with a pure intention and receiving the precepts. By this conduct that person attains many merits. Even if someone takes refuge in the Three Treasures and receives the precepts, it is not as good as practicing compassion for all sentient beings for even as brief a time as it takes to milk a cow.[210] By this conduct that person attains many merits. Even if someone prudently practices compassion for all sentient beings for even as brief a time as it takes to milk a cow, this is considered not as good as to contemplate for even as brief a moment as it takes to snap one's fingers that all conduct is impermanence, suffering, emptiness, and non-self. By this conduct that person attains many merits."

Furthermore, the *Zengyi ahan jing* says:

At that time the World-honored One said to all the *bhikṣu*s, "There are four kinds of merits possessed by the great Brahma King (Skt. *brāhma-puṇyatva*). What are the four kinds? If there is a believer who builds a stupa (*toupo;* a syonym for *ta*) in a place where no stupa has yet been built, by this conduct he receives the first merit possessed by the Brahma King. If there is a believer who repairs an old temple, by this conduct he is considered to receive the second merit possessed by the Brahma King. If there is a believer who harmonizes the Buddha's disciples, by this conduct he is considered to receive the third merit possessed by the Brahma King. Just as the time when the Buddha turned the Dharma wheel for the first time, if all heavenly beings and human beings sincerely request [the Buddha] to turn the Dharma wheel, by this conduct they are considered to receive the fourth merit possessed by the Brahma King."

At that time a foreign monk addressed the Buddha, "How great is all the merit possessed by the Brahma King?" The World-honored One said, "All merits possessed by the sentient beings of Jambudvīpa turn around and around in this way. Merits from the four continents surrounding Mount Sumeru up to Paranirmitavaśavartin Heaven (i.e., the sixth heaven of the realm of desire) are still not equal to a single merit possessed by the Brahma King. If you seek the merit [possessed by the Brahma King], this is its scope."

Moreover, the *Sapoduo lun* says:

A donor gave Channa Bhikṣu three hundred thousand in cash to build a large building. [The building] was completed in one day and then collapsed on the same day. The effort was large-scale and the donor was dispirited.

All the *bhikṣu*s preached the Dharma for the donor. [They said,] "Even though the building has collapsed, your merit has been accomplished.
540a Before the building collapsed the Buddha already came into this building and enjoyed being there. The Buddha is the supreme field of merit. Since the Buddha enjoyed being [in the building when it stood], your merit is deep and immeasurably extensive."

[They continued,] "When the building was first completed, a young *bhikṣu* who had newly received the precepts and whose merit of observing the precepts was pure entered this building. So, you, our donor, have already completed the merit of faithful almsgiving. Even if you were to establish a huge number of various buildings and adornments and adorn all things to the edge of the diamond land below as loftily and extensively as Mount Sumeru, if there is a single *bhikṣu* who observes the pure precepts and who enjoys himself there temporarily, you have already completed giving favors to others. The reason is the precepts are not worldly things, they are the gate to nirvana. They are not the same as a house, bedding, food and drink, or decoctions of medicine that are worldly things and not things that are difficult to obtain in order to leave the world."

5. Repair and Creating

If you want to repair [a Buddhist object] or create one, your reason must be in accordance with the Dharma. Making [or repairing an object] is a minor matter, yet the merit one attains is immeasurable. If you do not rely on the Dharma, even if you make many [objects] there is no benefit.

Therefore, the *Fo zai jin'guan jingfu jing* says:[211]

> [The Buddha said,] "One who donates a sutra or a [buddha] image (i.e., a benefactor) should not argue about the [Buddhist] Way with his employee craftsman. The craftsman who makes a copy of sutras or a [buddha] image should not talk about [the Way] to his client. Both the one who crafts an image of the Buddha and the one who donates it attain immeasurable merit. If you were to try to explain this merit, you would not finish even by the end of a *kalpa.* If you receive instruction and admonition, this is the Buddha's true disciple. If you are pure and sincere in this way, even if your creation is meager your merit is great."

Someone asked, "When craftspeople make a copy of sutras or a [buddha] image, do they obtain things or receive payment for their work?"

The Buddha replied, "They must not receive any remuneration. If you were to sell your parents for money, this is a deadly sin in the trichiliocosm. You are truly the heavenly devil (i.e., the king of Paranirmitavaśavartin Heaven). [If you do so,] leave my Buddhist Dharma quickly! You are not my followers. A group of people who drink wine and eat meat and the five kinds of pungent vegetables (i.e., leeks, onions, garlic, scallions, and ginger) do not rely on the sacred teaching. Even though they make as many copies of sutras or [buddha] images as there are particles of dust and sand, their merit is very little and probably of no consequence. At the time of the fire at the end of a *kalpa* when the universe is destroyed they will not be able to enter the Sea Dragon King's palace. They labor and yet receive little merit. Due to the sin of disrespect [for the Buddha] they enter hell after death. [In that case] if both the donor and the craftsman [make a copy of sutras or a buddha image] it will have no benefit. No heavenly beings can help them. It would have been better never to have made [a copy of a sutra or a buddha image]. If you worship with an upright and honest mind, you attain immeasurable merit. If you do what has been described above, even if you were to work on many [sutras and buddha images] your merit is little. If a craftsman creates a [buddha] image that is incomplete in the physical characteristics, all the sense organs of that person will be disabled for five million generations. First, it is superior to exert your mind to the utmost. The wonderful fruition ascends in advance."

Moreover, the *Zuofu jueyi jing* (*Sutra on Dispelling Doubts about Sin and Merit*) says:[212]

Monks, nuns, and laypeople! Some of you, by donating your own wealth or by soliciting other people for a contribution, obtain resources and plan to make a buddha image. If one who receives these things and manages them [instead] creates an image of a bird or an animal and places it on a wooden offering tray for the Buddha, or if he claims a loss or deceives [the donors even to as small an amount as] five *qian,* then he has commited a rebellious sin and cannot return to the human realm after all; he will fall into Avīci Hell for a *kalpa.* Those who buy aromatic oil and a lamp and offer them [to the Buddha] have no offense. The Buddha does not seek profit, but no one can bear it if [the lamp] dies out.

At the time of making offerings to the Buddha, all monks of the upper, middle, and lower seats must teach the laypeople to admire the Buddha
540b and the sangha. After offering to the Buddha, [the laypeople] serve a meal to the sangha and eat together. Do not violate this! If you do not do so, [this means that the sangha] will have eaten the Buddha's belongings. Therefore [violaters] will fall into Avīci Hell for ten billion years. Donors who do not receive the teaching explained earlier will also receive the retribution mentioned earlier. If they are reborn in the human realm, they will fall into a lower rebirth for nine million years. Why? It is because no one can assess the Buddha's belongings.

I will further explain. This means that donors who bear the expenses of a Buddhist service definitely take the buddha [image] into the main hall and [offerings] are received and used; therefore [the donors] need to buy things to offer. Just like today, in every Buddhist service food and drink are served on an offering tray for the Buddha, and there is a tacit understanding [between the sangha and the donors]. Those who do not limit their thoughts (i.e., broad-minded people) return to [the main hall] after the meal, and the donors do not trouble themselves to buy [things to offer]. On the fifteenth day of the seventh month, when offerings are made to the buddha [image] as well as to the sangha, if there is nothing for the buddha [image] and the sangha to receive and use, then [donors] must provide what is needed for [the sangha's] use.

Furthermore, the *Guanfo sanmei[hai] jing* (T. 643) says:

> Once King Udayana longed for the World-honored One and had an image [of the Buddha] cast in gold. He heard that the Buddha was just then descending the treasure stairs. Carrying the gold image on an elephant he welcomed the World-honored One. At that time the gold image came down from the back of the elephant and walked in the air, just as the living Buddha did. Under its feet flowers fell and it also emitted light. [The image] welcomed the World-honored One. With joined palms and hands folded in salute, it made a bow to the Buddha.
>
> At that time the World-honored One kneeled upright with his hands joined in prayer and faced the image. In the air all one hundred thousand

transformed buddhas also knelt upright with hands clasped in prayer and faced the image. At that time the World-honored One said to the image, "You will greatly perform Buddhist activities in the life to come. After I enter nirvana I will entrust all my disciples to you." All the transformed buddhas in the air intoned these words in one voice, "After the Buddha's nirvana, if there are sentient beings who create [buddha statues], uphold them, and make offerings to them, these people will certainly attain the pure *samādhi* of mindfulness of the Buddha in the next life."

The *Waiguo ji* (*Records of Foreign Countries*) further says:[213]

The Buddha expounded the Dharma for his mother in Trāyastriṃśa Heaven. Ninety days passed. King Prasenajit wished to see the Buddha, so he carved an image of the Tathāgata out of oxhead sandalwood (Skt. *gośīrṣa-candana*) and placed it on the Buddha's seat.

Later, when the Buddha returned into the monastery, the image came out to meet the Buddha on arrival. The Buddha said, "Go back to the seat! After my *parinirvāṇa* you should make various rules of etiquette for the four kinds of my disciples." The image promptly returned to the seat. This image is the origin of all [Buddhist] images.

The Buddha moved to a small monastery on the south side,[214] twenty paces away from the place where the image was located. Jeta Grove Monastery was originally seven stories tall. All countries competed with one another to make offerings ceaselessly. In the main hall there was a long, bright lamp. A rat bit the lamp wick, and it burned all the streamers and canopies. [The fire] then reached [Jeta Grove] Monastery; the entire seven-storied building was burned. The kings and the people of all countries were greatly sad and troubled. They thought that the buddha image made of sandalwood had been burned.[215] In fact, four or five days later, when 540c
they opened a door of a small monastery on the east side, they unexpectedly found the original image, which had moved to that room. All the people were greatly happy. They all together repaired the monastery and were able to make it a two-storied [building], and moved the image back to the present place.

Moreover, the *Youtianwang zuo foxingxiang jing* (T. 692) says:

Formerly, when the Buddha resided in the world, the king of Vṛji, called Udayana, came to the Buddha's place. He worshiped the Buddha by bowing his head to the Buddha's feet. With his hands joined in prayer he addressed the Buddha, "O World-honored One! If after the Buddha's nirvana his sentient beings make a buddha image, what merit will they attain?"

The Buddha said to the king, "If someone makes an image of the Buddha, the merit is immeasurable and incalculable. That person will not fall into evil realms in any rebirth, generation after generation. In heaven and the realm of human beings the person will receive bliss. His body will always be purplish-gold in color. His eyes are pure; his face is well featured; and his body and limbs are rare and excellent. He will always be loved and respected by the people. If such a person is reborn in the human realm, he is always reborn as a son of a sovereign, a ranking official, a wealthy person, or to a family of virtue. The family in which he is reborn will be highly influential, wealthy, and distinguished. His property and valuables are incalculable. He will always be loved and valued by his parents, siblings, and members of the same clan. If that person becomes a sovereign, he will be particularly noble among sovereigns, relied upon and looked up to by the sovereigns of all countries. Consequently he will become a wheel-turning noble king who reigns over the four continents surrounding Mount Sumeru. He will spontaneously possess the seven treasures and have a thousand children altogether. He will soar up to heaven and go everywhere. If that person is reborn in heaven, he will be the most distinctive in heaven. Consequently he is able to become king of the six heavens of the realm of desire, the most honorable in the six heavens. If he is reborn in Brahma Heaven, he will become the great king of Brahma Heaven, who is matchlessly well featured, who surpasses all heavenly beings of Brahma Heaven, and who is always respected by all heavenly beings of Brahma Heaven. Later all such people will attain rebirth in the Land of Infinite Life, where they will become the great bodhisattva who is the most esteemed. They will certainly attain buddhahood after the passage of numberless *kalpa*s and enter the path of nirvana. Anyone who makes an image of the Buddha will attain merits like these."

The *Lotus Sutra* further says in verse:

If a person, for the Buddha's sake,
Makes various buddha images,
Or even if a child, for fun,
With a blade of grass, a brush, or a fingernail,
Draws an image of the Buddha,
All such people have already
Achieved the Buddhist Way.

Moreover, the *Zaoli xingxiang fubao jing* (T. 693; Skt. *Tathāgata-pratibimba-pratiṣṭānuśaṃsā-saṃvadanti nāma dharma-paryāya*) says:

The Buddha came to Kauśāmbī. The king of that time was called Udayana. He had just turned fourteen years old. When he heard that the Buddha was coming, he ordered all his vassals and attendants to welcome the Buddha. When the Buddha arrived, the king worshiped the Buddha by bowing his head to the Buddha's feet. Kneeling upright and with palms joined, the king addressed the Buddha, "You are the Buddha whom no one in heaven and the realm of human beings can match. You are bright, majestic, and capable. After the Buddha leaves us, I am afraid we will no longer see you. 541a
I now wish to make an image of the Buddha, and I will respectfully follow and serve it. What reward for this good conduct will I attain? I pray that you, O Buddha, will feel pity for me and explain it for me."

At that time the World-honored One replied to him in verse:

O King! Listen to my explanation attentively!
A temple is inherent in bodhisattvas,[216]
Those whom no one surpasses in merit.
The reward for making an image of the Buddha is
To be continually reborn in a wealthy family of high position,
To be noble and limitlessly valuable,
And to be always respected by your dependents.
The reward for making an image of the Buddha is
To always attain the reward of the heavenly eyes,
Which are an incomparably deep blue color.
The reward for making an image of the Buddha is
That your parents see you with joy,

That your features are regular and your dignity and virtue are notable,
And that your insatiable attachment comes to an end.
The reward for making an image of the Buddha is
To have a golden-colored body with brilliant light,
Just like an image of a wonderful lion,
Which sentient beings see with joy.
The reward for making an image of the Buddha is
To be reborn in a longstanding influential family,
In the *kṣatriya* caste, or in the brahman caste
Among the well-off people of Jambudvīpa.
The reward for making an image of the Buddha is
To not be reborn in a remote country,
To not be blind and to not be bad-looking,
And to always be completely possessed of the six sense organs.
The reward for making an image of the the Buddha is
To know your own former existences at the moment of death,
To see the Buddha before you,
And to not feel pain at the time of death.
The reward for making an image of the the Buddha is
To become a great renowned king,
The golden-wheel flying emperor,[217]
Who rules over the four continents surrounding Mount Sumeru.
The reward for making an image of the the Buddha is
To become Śakra-devendra, called Indra,
Who governs the second [heaven] with supernatural powers,[218]
And who is served by thirty-three heavenly gods.
The reward for making an image of the the Buddha is
To transcend the realm of desire,
To become the king of Brahma Heaven,
Who is respected by all the brahmans in the state of Kāśi.
The reward for making an image of the Buddha is
To receive merits just like these.
If you can make [an image of the Buddha] by carving or drawing,
Heaven and earth still can praise.
This merit is incalculable.

Therefore, make an offering to [an image of] the Buddha,
And apply flowers, incense, and perfume to it.
Those who make an offering to *mahāsattva*s
Attain exhaustion of defilements as well as *wuwei* (i.e., nirvana). 541b

Furthermore, the *Fu fazing jing* (i.e., *Fu fazang yinyuan zhuan,* T. 2058) says:

In ancient times, ninety-one *kalpa*s ago, after Vipaśyin Buddha entered nirvana, the four kinds of his disciples erected a seven-treasured stupa. At one time, there was a buddha image in that stupa, and a small patch of the golden color on its face fell off. A poor woman who traveled around begging for alms had obtained a drop of gold. She saw that the face of the image [of the Buddha] was damaged and wished to repair it. Kāśyapa was at that time a metalsmith. The woman brought [the gold to him] and asked him to repair [the image]. The metalsmith recognized this as a meritorious matter and was happy to repair it for her. Using [the gold] he repaired the face of the image. Both [the woman and the metalsmith] accordingly made a vow together: "We pray that we will both continually be a married couple, possess a real golden-colored body, and always receive excellent pleasures." For ninety-one *kalpa*s since that time, [they both possessed] real golden-colored bodies, were reborn in the realms of heavenly beings or human beings, limitlessly enjoyed pleasures, and at last were reborn in the *brahma-loka* (i.e., the first meditation heaven in the realm of desire).

At that time in Magadha there was a brahman called Nyagrodha, who had cultivated merit in the past. He was bright and knowledgeable and possessed an immeasurable, colossal fortune of gold, silver, seven treasures, cows, sheep, farmlands, houses, slaves, and vehicles. He was a thousand times more wealthy than King Bimbisāra. King Bimbisāra had a thousand metal plows. The brahman [Nyagrodha] was concerned that if [the number of metal plows] he had was equal to the king's he might invite punishment upon himself. So, his household made just nine hundred and ninety-nine metal plows, one plow less than [what the king had]. In his house there were fine woolen fabrics. The least expensive one cost a hundred thousand taels of gold. There were sixty bamboo boxes containing gold and grain. One bamboo box contained three hundred and forty *hu*.

Even though his family was wealthy, [Nyagrodha] had no son. There was a tree deity at the side of his house, and he and his wife often went there to entreat and worship. They prayed for [a son], but there was no response for many years. He said angrily, "Now for seven more days we will serve you, devoting all our energies. If there is still no effect, I will certainly burn this tree down." Distressed and terrified, the tree deity reported this to the four heavenly kings, who reported it to Śakra-devendra. Śakra-devendra looked around Jambudvīpa, but there was no one suitable to become [Nyagrodha's] son. He immediately visited the king of Brahma Heaven and extensively spoke of this matter. The king of Brahma Heaven looked everywhere with his heavenly eyes and found a Brahma heavenly being who was just at the moment of death. He quickly went and spoke with [the Brahma heavenly being], exhorting him to be reborn [as Nyagrodha's son]. The Brahma heavenly being accepted the instruction and was reincarnated. After ten months, the fullness of her term, [Nyagrodha's wife] gave birth to a boy. He had regular features and a golden-colored body. The light [that emitted from his body] shone brightly over an area as far as forty *li* away.

A physiognomist divined and said, "This boy had merit in his former existences. Surely he will renounce the world." When the boy's parents heard this they felt very sad and distressed. Husband and wife discussed the matter, saying, "We must devise some measures to cause him to give up his intention [to renounce the world]. We should not allow any chance for him to reflect. What infatuates [males] in general are only attractive women. We should arrange for a good and well-featured girl to become his wife, and with her we will break his inclination [to renounce the world]."

When the boy turned fifteen years old [his parents] intended to arrange for a girl to become his wife. He said to his parents, "My purpose is pure.
541c I do not need a wife." His parents would not listen to him. The boy understood that [his wish] was difficult to accept, so he made an expedient plan. He said to his parents, "If you can arrange for me a purplish gold-colored girl whose regular features are otherworldly, I will surely accept her."

His parents promptly summoned all the brahmans and instructed them to travel everywhere to seek such a girl for their son's wife. The brahmans cast [the figure of] a girl in gold, particularly and rarely well featured.

They carried it on a carriage around the villages, reciting loudly, "Any woman who can see this golden goddess and worship it, later when she is married, she will certainly get a good husband whose body is purely golden-colored and who is exceedingly well featured." [The village] women who heard this all came out.

There was only one girl whose body was golden-colored and who was extremely well featured. This was the same woman who had donated the gold [to repair the image of the Buddha] in her former existence. Because of this excellent condition she had made in the past she had obtained this wonderful body. Her purpose was contented and pure and she was the only woman who was not willing to go out. All the other women pushed her [to go out] to see the golden goddess with them. [So] the girl then went out. Her golden light was more dazzling than that of the golden goddess. When the brahmans saw her they promptly [asked her to become] the boy's wife.

She soon arrived at her husband-to-be's house. The married couple faced each other, and they were both entirely pure-hearted with no desirous intentions at all. They made an agreement that they would each live in their own rooms. After learning about this, the man's parents destroyed and removed one of the rooms, forcing them to stay together in the same room, which was furnished with one bed.

Kāśyapa said to his wife, "When I sleep, you should walk about, and when you sleep, I will walk about." Later, when his wife lay down her hand hung down in front of the bed. A poisonous snake entered the room and was about to bite her hand. Seeing this, Kāśyapa reached out his hand from within his garments, lifted up [her hand], and placed it on the bed. His wife started from her sleep and said, accusing him, "We made a vow together to not be close to each other. Why did you now stealthily touch my hand?' Kāśyapa replied, "There was a snake coming into [the room] and I was afraid it would bite your hand. Therefore, I simply lifted it," and quickly pointed to the snake. His wife then understood.

Husband and wife kept their integrity unsullied. They felt deep revulsion toward the world. They said goodbye to their parents, seeking and wishing to renounce the world. After seeing [their resolve] the parents consequently acceded to their request. Thereupon, the couple together renounced the world and came to the Buddha's place.

The Buddha shared seats with them and expounded the Dharma for them. [Kāśyapa] immediately attained arhatship on his seat. Later his wife also attained arhatship.

When Kāśyapa resided in the world, he often sat face-to-face with the Tathāgata while [the Tathāgata] expounded the Dharma. After the Buddha's nirvana, all the Buddhist teachings were completely entrusted to Kāśyapa. Later he compiled the Tripiṭaka. After that he went to Mount Kukkuṭapādagiri and entered *parinirvāṇa.* His body did not break apart [after death]. Later, when Maitreya Buddha appears in the world, he will emerge from the mountain, make eighteen miraculous manifestations among the people, deliver immeasurable human beings, and later his body will be extinguished. In the future he will attain buddhahood and will be called Light.

(The story of the sixty bamboo boxes containing gold and grain appears in the *Sapoduo zhuan* [*Exposition of the Sarvāstivāda*].[219] The story of the attainment of buddhahood in the future appears in the *Lotus Sutra.*)

Again, the [*Da*] *zhidu lun* says:

In ancient times, when the Buddha resided in the world, in Kapilavastu there was Nanda, King Śuddhodana's son and the Buddha's younger brother. He had a regular figure and the thirty[-two] marks of physical excellence.
542a The king arranged for a girl called Sundarī to become his wife. Her features were well formed and matchless in the world. Nanda loved and respected his wife day and night, and so he did not wish to renounce the world.

Through expedient means the Buddha edified [Nanda] and caused him to [wish to] renounce the world. Soon thereafter he renounced the world and attained arhatship. After seeing this, the *bhikṣu*s addressed the Buddha, "What merit did the *bhikṣu* Nanda create in his previous existences in order to be reborn in the same family with the Buddha, to have the thirty[-two] marks of physical excellence, to possess a regular figure that is matchless in the world, to give up his great noble status and renounce the world, and to attain the [Buddhist] Way?"

The Buddha said to the *bhikṣu*s, "In the past, ninety-one *kalpa*s ago, after Vipaśyin Buddha had entered nirvana, at that time Nanda was an extremely wealthy person. He painted the walls of the *pratyekabuddha's* stupa dark blue and drew an image of that *pratyekabuddha.* Accordingly, he vowed, 'I pray that I will be reborn in a noble family generation after generation, continually attain regular features, have a golden-colored body, meet the Buddha, and attain the [Buddhist] Way.' Due to the merit of this good act and vow, for ninety-one *kalpa*s since that time he has not fallen into evil realms. In heaven and in the realm of human beings he has a regular figure, possesses the thirty[-two] marks of physical excellence, and is outstandingly noble, wealthy, high-ranking, and limitlessly happy. In the present existence he was reborn in the same family with me, renounced the world, and attained the [Buddhist] Way."

6. Almsgiving

Just as the *Lunzhuan wudao* [*zuifu baoying*] *jing* (T. 747B) says:

> The Buddha said, "Generally, making merit is one's natural conduct. By offering incense and lighting a lamp you will attain much merit. By offering incense you will make merit. With regard to reading a sutra, you cannot hire a person or offer anything to someone else [to recite for you]. When you wish [to eat], if you instead make someone else eat, how will you satisfy your appetite? By offering incense you will be cleansed. By lighting a lamp you will extend brightness. Burning incense, serving a meal in a Buddhist service, reading a sutra, and giving alms are all regarded as common practices. By giving alms you will attain merit. All heavenly beings will draw near you and help you, all myriad evils will be turned away, and numerous devils will surrender to you. Negligent people cannot be diligent. Once they fall ill, they are even more unhappy. They will soon wish to offer incense and only then start making merit. All heavenly beings have not yet descended for them, while all devils remain before their eyes, competing with each other to trouble and offend them, and make various monstrous transformations. For these reasons, you must always be diligent. Sin and happiness follow people just as a shadow follows the form. Plant well in the field of merit. Just like a *nyagrodha* tree, the kernel of the original seed is very small but it gradually grows big, and you can collect seeds limitlessly." The Buddha continued, "Ānanda! If you give once, you will receive ten thousand times. My words are not groundless."

On that occasion, the Buddha said in verse:

The wise are fond of almsgiving.
Heavenly gods spontaneously help them.
If you give one, you will obtain ten thousand times more.
You will be comfortable and live long.
As for virtuous people who give alms today,
Their merits are incalculable.
They will surely all attain the Buddhist Way,
And liberate all beings in the ten directions.

542b

7. Miscellaneous Merit

Just as the *Sapoduo lun* says:

If someone constructs a monks' residence as well as a stupa and a [buddha] image, digs a well near a high road, or builds a bridge,[220] that person's merit arises continuously. He will always be a donor who bears the expenses of the necessities of monks' lives, but three kinds of causes and conditions are excluded. First is if the project is abrogated beforehand, second is on the death of that person, and third is if the person gives rise to evil. If these three kinds of causes and conditions do not occur, [that person's] merit will always arise.

Furthermore, the *Zengyi ahan jing* says:

At that time the World-honored One said to the *bhikṣu*s, "There are five kinds of almsgiving by which you do not attain merit. What are the five kinds? First is to give a sword to others, second is to give poison to others, third is to give a wild ox to others, fourth is to give a prostitute to others, and fifth is to make a shrine to worship a deity. These are the five kinds of almsgiving for which one does not attain merit. In addition there are five kinds of almsgiving by which people attain great merit. What are the five kinds? First is to make a garden and a watchtower, second is to plant trees, third is to construct a bridge, fourth is to build a large ship, and fifth is to build a residential building for the sake of the past and future. These five kinds of things cause one to attain merit."

At that time the World-honored One further said in verse:

By providing clean and cool [environment] at a watchtower in a garden,
By consructing a good bridge
Or making a ferry to help people cross over a river,
And by constructing a good residential building,
That person will always,
Day and night, receive merit.
Through accomplishing the precepts and meditation
That person will certainly be reborn in heaven.

Moreover, the [*Mohe*] *sengqi lü* (T. 1425) [says]:

All gods asked the Buddha in verse:

Which people go to wholesomeness?
Which people are reborn in heaven?
Which people, day and night,
Cultivate virtuous merits?

At that time the World-honored One replied in verse:

If one digs a good well near a high road,
Plants fruit trees in a garden and gives the fruit to others,
Provides a clean and cool [environment] by planting trees,
Helps people cross over [a river] by a bridge or by ferryboat,
Gives alms, cultivates the pure precepts,
And gives up stinginess and covetousness through wisdom,
This person's merit increases day and night,
And [all such people] will be always reborn in the realms of heavenly or human beings.

Furthermore, the *Zheng fanian*[*chu*] *jing* (T. 721) says:

If a sentient being gives others delicious water, or covers over a well in case a poisonous snake may fall into the well and then passers-by who drink water [from the well] will suffer in misery, [that sentient being] will be reborn in the Heaven of Three Harps (Skt. *vīṇā*) after death where he will receive pleasures of the five desires (Skt. *pañca kāma-guṇah*). After the end of this existence [in the Heaven of Three Harps], if [such people] obtain a human body they will be loved and honored by a sovereign.

When [a sentient being] sees that someone suffers from illness, cries
542c as if squeezing sounds from his throat, and has not yet died, if they give the ill person a starch solution and some money in order to keep the [ill] person alive, [all such people] will be reborn in the Heaven of Deep Water (*shenshui tian*) after death, where they will be as happy as Śakra-devendra. Following their death [in this heaven] they will transmigrate according to their karma. They will not fall into the three evil realms and will be able to receive a human body. From one existence to another they will not encounter the torment of illness and will have no troubles.

When a sentient being who observes the precepts sees *bhikṣu*s and offers fans to them, which help them stay nice and cool, and causes them to read and recite the teaching [in such a comfortable condition], after their death [in this existence] [such people] will be reborn in the Wind Blowing Heaven (*fengxing tian*), where fragrant winds blow and they will be incomparably happy.

If a sentient being consructs a bridge or a ship on the riverbank near a ferry, or with goodwill ferries those who observe the precepts along with others over [to the yonder shore], and does not do any evil, [such people] will be reborn in Mālādhara Heaven after death, where they will receive the pleasures of the five desires. After death [in that heaven] they will become Assistant Supply Commissioner for a sovereign in the human realm.

The *Piyu jing* further says:[221]

In the past there was a mother who had [two] children. These three people always performed three services. First was to build a large ferryboat and to place it in a river so that people could cross over the river. Second was to dig a good well in a metropolis in order to offer [water] to all the people. Third was to construct a latrine at each of four [city] gates for the people's benefit in attending to their needs. Due to the merit of this they were all reborn in heaven after death, where they received happiness spontaneously. When they descended to be reborn in the human realm, they were in wealthy and high-ranked [families] and enjoyed long life spans. Whenever they were reborn, they never experienced the three evil realms.

Even in the case of having little merit people still attain a majestic immeasurable reward, not to mention a case of someone who extensively cultivates merit. If one erects a stupa, gives alms, and makes all meritorious acts, the reward is ten billion times greater than this; it is incalculable.

Therefore, the *Chengshi lun* (T. 1646) quotes a verse from a sutra:

If one plants trees in a park,
And creates a well, a bridge, and other [things],
The merit made by this person
Continually grows day and night.

Furthermore, the *Huashou jing* (T. 657; Skt. *Kuśalamūla-saṃgraha*) says:

The Buddha said to Śāriputra, "Bodhisattvas have four methods by which they do not retrogress [from proceeding to] highest enlightenment in the end. What are the four methods? First, if they see that a stupa is damaged, they [straightaway] repair it with a lump of earth, clay, or even a brick. Second, if they erect a stupa and make a [buddha] image near a crossroads where many people see it, this is a condition of the virtuous merit of mindfulness of the Buddha. In the stupa are depicted events such as [the Buddha's] preaching the Dharma, renouncing the world, and entering nirvana under the twin [*śāla*] trees. Third, if they see two groups of *bhikṣus* disputing and fighting with each other, they diligently seek an expedient way and reconcile them. Fourth, if they see that the Buddhist Dharma is about to be destroyed, they read, recite, and preach it well or recite even a single verse to cause the Dharma to not be cut off. Due to protecting the Dharma [in this way] they respectfully support a Dharma exponent and wholeheartedly protect the Dharma without regard fortheir own lives.

"If bodhisattvas accomplish these four methods, [they] will become wheel-turning noble kings (Skt. *cakravartins*) generation after generation and obtain physical power as great as that of Nārāyaṇa. They will give up the four continents surrounding Mount Sumeru and renounce the world. They will be able to cultivate freely the four kinds of pure mind (Skt. *catvāry apramāṇāni*). They will be reborn in heaven after death and 543a
become King Mahābrahman. Consequently they will achieve highest enlightenment at the end."

For this reason a wise person who wishes to seek the Buddhist Way must concentrate on learning this.

Moreover, the *Fangniu jing* (T. 123), or a separate chapter in the *Zengyi ahan jing,* the Chinese translation [of the Pāli text *Gopāla-sutta,*] says:

> The Buddha said to the *bhikṣu*s, "There are eleven issues that a herdsman may not know. [By improving them] he will gain advantage in grazing cattle, and yet he does not understand [eleven things] about raising cattle. What are these? First, a herdsman does not distinguish the forms [of cattle]. Second, he does not understand the characteristics [of cattle]. Third, he does not know how to groom and brush them. Fourth, he does not know how to care for wounds [on cattle]. Fifth, he does not know when he has to create smoke [to smudge and drive off insects]. Sixth, he does not know how to choose the [best] path for them to take. Seventh, he does not know where to raise the cattle. Eighth, he does not know where to ford a river. Ninth, he does not know how to seek good water plants. Tenth, he does not know how to completely milk a cow. Finally, he does not know how to discern which [cattle] are usable or not.
>
> "If a herdsman does not know these eleven issues in raising and protecting his herd, the cattle will not calve; [their numbers] will decrease day by day.
>
> "This can be compared to *bhikṣu*s. They have eleven kinds of merits and demerits, too. These cannot be fully explained."
>
> The Buddha thereupon said in verse:
>
> If a herdsman fully knows [these eleven issues],
> The owner of cattle will have good fortune.
> In six years six cows will become
> Sixty cows, without decrease.
> Such a herdsman is bright.
> He knows how to discern all characteristics.
> A herdsman like this was praised
> By the Buddha in his previous existence.

8. Bathing Monks

Just as the *Piyu jing* says:[222]

On the eighth day of the twelfth month the Buddha subdued six [non-Buddhist] masters through supernatural powers. The six masters could not best [the Buddha] and drowned themselves in the water. [The Buddha] thereafter extensively expounded the Dharma and liberated all non-Buddhists. The non-Buddhists were subdued and edified. They addressed the Buddha, "O Buddha! You washed away our mental defilements with the Dharma water. We now invite the monks to bathe in order to cleanse the filth from their bodies."

Thereupon, [the act of offering bathing for the monks] became a regular condition. Today, [the event of offering] bathing for the monks on the eighth day of the twelfth month appears only in this sutra.

Moreover, the *Mohechatou jing* (T. 696), also called the *Guan*[*xi*] *fo xing-xiang jing* (T. 695), says:

The Buddha said to the people of the world, "All buddhas in the ten directions were reborn at midnight on the eighth day of the fourth month.

"They all left home and [began to] study the [Buddhist] Way at midnight on the eighth day of the fourth month. They all attained the Buddhist Way at midnight on the eighth day of the fourth month. They all entered *parinirvāṇa* at midnight on the eighth day of the fourth month."

The Buddha continued, "The reasons why [key events take place on] the eighth day of the fourth month are because it is the time between spring and summer, when disasters and sins completely come to an end, all things are regenerated everywhere, the poisonous vapor has not yet spread, it is neither cold nor hot, the climate is harmonious and comfortable, and now it is [celebrated as] the Buddha's birthday. Therefore, all the people of the world together recall the Buddha's merits and offer a bath to images of Buddha, just as when the Buddha resided [in the world]. Therefore, the people of the world are thus notified."

The Buddha continued, "When I was a bodhisattva, I became Śakra- 543b
devendra thirty-six times, a golden-wheel king thirty-six times, and a flying emperor (i.e., a wheel-turning noble king) thirty six-times.

"Today, among all wise people, anyone with goodwill thinks of Śākyamuni Buddha's benevolent virtue and bathes buddha images with fragrant flowers. Those who seek this primary merit are testified by all heavenly beings and spiritual beings.[223]

"On the eighth day of the fourth month when a buddha image is bathed, you must use three kinds of scents. First is *arethusa,* second is wrinkled giant hyssop (i.e., *Agastache rugosa*), and third is *aina.*[224] Mix the three kinds of fragrant grass in water and press and soak them, which turns the water blue-colored. If the fragrance is too subtle, you can substitute the bark of the Chinese medicine *gandaiqin.* Additionally, use saffron. Press [the aromatics] with your hands and soak them in water. Crush them up to make red-colored water. Pour the water over the buddha image to cleanse it, then wipe it with white silk. After concluding [this rite], if you make a personal wish and wash [the image] again, this is called pure [washing]. The merit for this is the greatest."

Furthermore, the *Wenshi [xiyu zhongseng] jing* (T. 701) says:

The Buddha said to the wealthy man Jīvaka, "In the way to bathe you must use seven things and get rid of seven types of diseases. You will then attain seven good rewards. What are the seven things? First is blazing fire, second is pure water, third is a ground-bean bag for bathing, fourth is *ghṛta,*[225] fifth are clean ashes, sixth is a toothbrush made from a willow branch, and seventh is *antarvāsa.* This is the [proper] way to take a bath.

"What does it mean to get rid of the seven types of diseases? First is to pacify your body, second is to get rid of a cold, third is to get rid of rheumatism, fourth is to remove [suffering from] a cold wind and freezing, fifth is to remove heat, sixth is to wash off dirt, and seventh is to have a light feeling in your body and clear and bright eyes. This is what is meant to get rid of the seven types of diseases.

"Regarding attainment of the seven rewards, these are, first, [your body that consists of] the four great elements is healthy and wherever you are reborn it is always peaceful; second, wherever you are reborn, [your birthplace] is clean and you have regular features; third, your body is always fragrant and your clothes are clean; fourth, your skin is smooth and you possess great power and virtue; a fifth, numerous people follow you and cleanse the dust and dirt from [your body]; sixth, your mouth and teeth smell good and your speech is seriously regarded and followed; and seventh, wherever you are reborn clothes are spontaneously provided for you."

The *Shisong lü* furthermore says:

By bathing you obtain five advantages. First is to remove dust and dirt, second is to regulate the skin of your body and even out its tone, third is to remove cold and heat, fourth is to get rid of diseases like paralysis, and fifth is to diminish the pain of disease.

[The *Foshuo zazang jing* (T. 745) says:]

At the hottest time in summer Śāriputra [came to an *āmra* fruit garden] where a hired laborer was drawing water [from a well] in the garden to water the trees. When [this person] saw Śāriputra he slightly gave rise to faith. He called out to Śāriputra and [bade him] to take off his robe under a tree so that [the laborer] could wash him by pouring water on him. [Śāriputra] then felt light and cool. This laborer was reborn in Trāyastriṃśa Heaven immediately after death, where he possessed great awesome power. [He thought to himself,] "Even though [my act] made only a small merit, because I met a good field [of merit] I attained a very great reward." He immediately went to visit Śāriputra, scattered flowers, and made an offering. On the basis of this man's faith, Śāriputra preached the essentials 543c
of the Dharma for him and caused him to attain the *srota-āpatti-phala*.

Moreover, the *Xianyu jing* (T. 202) says:

At that time Śuddhāvāsa descended to Jambudvīpa, came to the Buddha's place, and asked the Buddha and the sangha to allow him make an offering of a bath for them. The World-honored One silently gave his permission.

[Śuddhāvāsa] arranged food and drink and purchased supplies for bathing. In a bathroom the water was warmed and adjusted to be comfortable. *Ghṛta* and the herb *huancao* were all provided.[226] Thereupon the Buddha and all the *bhikṣus* accepted his offering. They bathed themselves and afterward received ample food and drink. The meal was delicious; it was a very rare meal in the world. After the meal they washed their hands and rinsed their mouths. Everyone returned to his original place.

At that moment Ānanda addressed the Buddha, "What merit did this heavenly being make in the past in order to have an excellent body, an outstandingly dignified countenance, and to be as gloriously bright as a large treasure mountain?" The Buddha said to Ānanda, "In the past, at the time of Vipaśyin Buddha, this heavenly being was the child of a poor family in that world. He always worked as a laborer to support himself. He once heard that [Vipaśyin] Buddha spoke of the virtue of providing a bath to the sangha, and he felt joyful in his mind. He thereupon diligently worked and earned a small amount of money and grain, with which he provided the supplies for bathing as well as food and drink [for the monks]. He invited [Vipaśyin] Buddha and the sangha and offered all [these things] to them. Due to this meritorious act he was reborn in Śuddhāvāsa Heaven after death and possesses such a glorious countenance. The [past] seven buddhas have already appeared, and a thousand buddhas will subsequently appear in the world. He offered a bath to each of the buddhas and the sangha, and he will also do the same for the future buddhas, exactly in this way." The Buddha then gave a prediction to [that heavenly being] of his future attainment of buddhahood, [saying,] "In the future world, two *asaṃkhya*s and a hundred *kalpa*s from now, you will certainly attain buddhahood and be called Jingshen ("Pure Body") and completely possess the ten epithets [for a buddha]."

Furthermore, the *Zapiyu jing* (T. 204) says:

Formerly there was Nanda, the Buddha's younger brother, who in ancient times had lived at the time of Vipaśyin Buddha. For the merit he earned by offering a bath to the sangha one time, he was spontaneously reborn as a member of the Śākya clan. [Nanda] possessed the thirty[-two] marks of physical excellence, and his appearance was bright and golden-colored. Due to the advantage of the merit he made in his former existence, he lived during the same generation as the Buddha. He closely studied and investigated [the Dharma] in a Buddhist seminary. He then attained the six supernatural powers.

This ancient one who had just once offered [a bath to the sangha] received a great reward, not to mention the case where donors of today can offer much more. Through universal and common practices you will certainly attain an honorific title, your joy will increase, and you will extensively deliver all sentient beings.

Moreover, the [*Foshuo zhude*] *futian jing* says:

There was another *bhikṣu* called Ānanda. He addressed the World-honored One, "I remember that in my previous existence I was reborn in Rājagṛha as a commoner's son. I had a malignant boil on my body and tried to cure it but I could not. A friend who was a Buddhist monk came to me and said, 'You should offer a bath for the sangha then collect the bath water and cleanse the boil with it. You will be able to recover from [the boil] and also you will attain merit.' I was happy [to hear this]. I went to a monastery and sincerely paid my respects to the sangha, more and more. Then I dug a new well. With aromatic oil and bath supplies I offered a bath for the sangha and then collected the bath water, with which I washed the boil. I soon recovered [from the boil]. Due to this cause and condition, wherever I was 544a
reborn I had regular features, [my form is] dazzlingly golden-colored, and I am not covered by dust and dirt. For ninety-one *kalpa*s I have always attained the merit of purity and been extensively and profoundly blessed with divine help. Now furthermore I have met the Buddha. My defilements have been extinguished and I have attained arhatship."[227]

The *Shisong lü* further says:[228]

The bathing rooms in a foreign country are round, just like a round cabin. The door is opened to let out [steam and] smoke. An underground ditch is made to drain the water. Inside [the structure] are three supported shelves evenly spaced; this is the place where the people [bathe]. Water is put in long-necked pots on the three shelves. The heat from the fire rises, so that the water on the top shelf is hot, that on the middle shelf is warm, and that on the bottom shelf is cold. At one's own discretion, everyone takes [some of the variously heated] water and uses it. No one separately makes [their own supply of] hot water. Therefore, it is simply called pure water.

Again, the *Zengyi ahan jing* says:

At that time the World-honored One said to all the *bhikṣu*s, "In making a bathing room there are five merits. What are the five [merits]? First is to cure a cold. Second is to be able to cure disease. Third is to remove dust and dirt. Fourth is to cause the body to feel light. Fifth is to gain weight and attain fair skin. If among the four kinds of the Buddha's disciples there are those who wish for these five merits, they must seek [an expedient way] and create a bathing room."

Furthermore, the [*Mohe*] *sengqi lü* says:

When [the sangha members] intend to bathe, [the monks in charge of bathing] should have the workers of the monastery gardens sweep and wash [the bathing room] to make it clean and prepare firewood and charcoal. When [the temperature of the bath water] becomes warm, they should toll a bell (Skt. *ghaṇṭā*) to let [all the monks] know that the bath is ready.

Each person ties up his robes in the waistband and places [the bundle] on the clothes rack, marking it. When entering [the bathing room], they cannot swing their arms about freely; when they enter they must cover their private parts with [at least] one hand. If they want to help bathe their teacher, they must first state [their intention] so that there will be no fault. [When a disciple bathes the teacher,] they cannot use both arms at the same time; while using one arm to wash, the other hand should cover their private parts. After [washing one arm] the other arm, hands, and other parts of the body should all be washed.

After the [hot] water is put into [the tub],[229] close the door, be seated, and allow the body to sweat. Estimate how much water is needed. Do not use too much.

If you freely bathe in a pond, there is no fault. It is not permissable to be naked while washing one's body at an open outside place. If the water is as deep as the waist or [comes up to] the armpits and is suitable for bathing, there is no fault. If when sitting in water it reaches the navel, you can also [wash yourself outside].

After coming out of the water, put on your clothes, adjust [the robes] properly, and leave.

I will further explain this. The reasons and clarifications for bathing among the sangha have been successfully stated. I praise and am grateful for this. I am, however, concerned that monks and laymen in the borderlands are not accustomed to this teaching. Therefore, I will briefly clarify the matter in order to present their essence.

I think personally that in the Nairañjanā River there is no dirt to be removed and in Lumbinī (i.e., the birthplace of Śākyamuni Buddha) there is truly no dust to wash away. Therefore, we know that bathing is the foundation to purely ascend (i.e., to reach nirvana) and cleansing oneself is the origin of purity. It may be said that these are beautiful examples from previous cultivation, and they give rise to a virtuous path in one's future acts. Consequently, countries to the east [of India] were replete with the water of the seven flowers (i.e., the seven factors of enlightenment or the seven kinds of purity) and cleansed by the followers of the One Vehicle path to enlightenment. The pure pond of eight virtues in the west is used to cleanse aspirants of the nine grades. Therefore, this causes the King of Physicians (i.e., the Buddha) to give rise in every moment to the idea of creating a bathing room. One morning a wealthy man respectfully made a vow to offer a bath to the sangha. This 544b
was fulfilled through the Tathāgata's skillful expedient method.

I will explain familiar matters of seven things. The Great Awakened One bestows benevolence. In the remote past he gave an account of the rewards of rebirth in the five heavens. Now suppose there is a certain government official who is a great donor, who makes use of his immense mind and performs the supreme act. Lifetime after lifetime he always cultivates the Buddha's altruistic activity, and generation after generation he always turns the Dharma wheel. Therefore, he fully believes in the true Dharma more than all evils and respects monks even in the last period of the semblance Dharma. He deeply knows that to explain and propagate verses is as valuable as the pearl of Marquis Sui. He makes offerings of meals and baths to all members of the sangha, which are loftier than those of non-Buddhist traditions. Consequently [donors and the sangha] all [undertake to] lead and encourage each other and exhort and assign roles to their mates. Each [donor] gives alms [to the sangha], and all equally honor this meritorious act.

Thereupon I will clarify seven things. Cleanse the Three Revered Ones at the proper time. On that day, you may bow and invite a certain Dharma master of eminent virtue to explain and propagate the *Wenshi xiyu zhongseng jing*. The Dharma master lately praised as the sea of learning and called the great master of letters in the world brings forth the profound meaning like clouds gathering [in the sky], and he breaks numerous difficulties just as water gushes out from a spring. He can cause secular people to understand the truth just as a clear day dispels heavy darkness. Those who study the Buddhist Dharma have their doubts removed. [The Dharma master] is like a severe frost that controls fallen leaves. After he has completed [expounding] a scroll [of the sutra] with the chapter on abstruseness in the thunderous pure and clean voice of eight superior qualities, he remains on his seat. Now it is time for bathing.

Next, I will praise the seven things for bathing the sangha. The first thing is to build a fire that burns fiercely in a huge stove and generates steam vigorously from a large cauldron. The bathing room is closed up tightly and already keeps out the cold. The dragon spring (*longquan*) is spontaneously extremely hot. The second thing [is pure water]. The soft clean water of virtue flows and brims over the golden pond. When you wash away the dirt you are clean, just like rosy lotus flowers. Your torso and head are moistened and become fresh and beautiful. The third thing [is the ground-bean bag for scrubbing,] filled with fine and smooth soybean flour that glitters like silver. [Using this, your skin] becomes [light in color] like white cotton (Skt. *tūla*); after removing the dirty grease, your clean body is revealed just like when clouds spread out. The fourth thing is *ghṛta* of the eight kinds of flavors, along with the five kinds of fragrant incense. [Using these,] you can expel a cold and get rid of rheumatism. You do not have to appreciate the miraculous medicine *maghī*. You will have a constitution like the precious stone *ying* and a lustrous countenance. Why are you ashamed of miraculous medicines? The fifth thing [is clean ash]. Wind instruments made of jade, wondrous ash, snowflakes, and frost are immaculate. They cause you to give rise to confused thoughts when encountering an evil wind. Rely on yourself peacefully in an upright manner. The sixth thing [is the toothbrush made from a willow branch]. Purple willow and young fine willow have green trunks and light branches. When you cool down [after a bath] your mouth releases [the scent of] an orchid. When you purify your teeth your breath gives off [the scent of] a blue lotus flower (Skt. *utpala*). The seventh thing is *antarvāsa* made from Qi raw silk, which is magnificent and pure white. It protects you from troubles and keeps your body safe. As a reward for washing it, it becomes adorned with natural light. All these seven things are entirely provided and wholeheartedly presented. Thinking of the people's benevolence, offer a prayer for them.

If you wish to transcend and live in the pure land, you must wash an image of one who possesses the ten powers (i.e., a buddha or bodhisattva) beforehand and entrust yourself to the Celestial Palace from far away. First, you must offer a bath to the sangha members who live with the six kinds of harmony and respect. It is just as when a voice is well tuned it sounds smooth, or when a form is straight its shadow is upright. The law of cause and effect is inevitable and is not concerned with what spiritual beings grant. Now donors respectfully follow the King of Medicine and build a bathing room, manage the seven things, and bathe the Three Revered Ones. They encourage and lead the people who are related to a buddha or a bodhisattva in the past (*youyuan*) to propagate the wondrous text. On this account they are remarkable and outstanding. These are the most wholesome acts.

First, make everything dignified. Today a certain group of Dharma masters 544c
have great influence. Lifetime after lifetime, they continually turn the Dharma wheel and attain great supernatural powers. Generation after generation, they always cultivate the Buddha's altruistic activity. Both young and old receive boundless knowledge [from them]. Their dependents will reach the age at which their deaths would not considered to be untimely. Hindrances and nuisances all vanish along with the morning mist. Auspicious things line up, as numerous as stars.

All donors make a vow to loftily attend to the eightfold holy path, to proceed on the Great Way to enlightenment, to be wealthy and possess the seven treasures, and to benefit ordinary people limitlessly. Moreover, they wish that those who manage and assist [in bathing the Three Revered Ones] will be free of seven kinds of diseases without remainder and those who offer a modicum of help will obtain the seven kinds of happiness without exhaustion. They feel happy about what they see and hear. They all go to the city of the Dharma. They bow their heads to the ground and in as brief an instant as the time it takes to snap one's fingers they simultaneously ascend to the fruition of buddhahood. They have already completed propagating and praising the profound teaching in their own areas. With a dignified manner the equipment for bathing has been prepared again. The people invite the Three Treasures respectfully and wholeheartedly.

Bow your head to the ground and take refuge in [the Buddhist saints]. First, invite all the buddhas in the ten directions and the great compassionate saints of the three periods of existence! They are the ones whose bodies are one-half the Dharma body (Skt. *dharmakāya*) and other half the true body (i.e., reward body; Skt. *saṃbhogakāya*) and the corresponding body (Skt. *nirmāṇakāya*). They have already exhausted the ninety-eight kinds of defilements. Their thirty-two marks of physical excellence are subtle and glorious. [For them] the four kinds of attachments that do not truly exist are tentatively equal to the four [necessities for the monks' daily use]. For sentient beings' sakes, therefore, if they receive a request they will come. We wish only that they all ascend to the palace of *maṇi,* sit upon the clouds of agate, emit ten billion rays of light, and shine throughout the trichiliocosm. The Brahma King holds a canopy, and Śakra-devendra scatters flowers. They descend to this Buddhist seminary, enter the bathing room, and take a bath.

Next, invite those above the stage of awakening the aspiration for enlightenment, those who have already taken up a buddha's place, those who are happy to leave behind defilement, bodhisattvas in the stages of wondrous wisdom and the Dharma cloud (i.e., the ninth and tenth stages of the ten bodhisattva stages), high-ranking bodhisattvas (i.e., those from the eleventh to the fiftieth ranks of the fifty-two ranks), and all other bodhisattvas. We wish only that they will transport heavenly beings in the palms of their hands, place the Dharma realm at the tip of one hair, and drive the four-legged mysterious birds called *peng,* accompanied by the swift spiritual horses of the six supernatural powers. They appear without the intention to appear. They come without the intention to come. They descend to this Buddhist seminary, enter the bathing room, and take a bath.

Next, invite great *pratyekabuddha*s who sit in meditation in the mountains, eminent people who promptly testify to the truth and the four fruits of sainthood, and monks who proceed to sainthood such as Piṇḍolabhāradvāja and senior monks. We wish only that they will shake the metal rings attached to the top of their staffs through the air, play with the six supernatural powers, hold a bottle amid the clouds, possess the eighteen transformations, give rise
545a to faith just like that of Prasenajit, and subdue the non-Buddhist Raudrākṣa's evil mind. They come and manifest themselves here before harmonious

people. Those in the religious age from a hundred to zero all enter a bathing room and take a bath.[230]

Next, invite those who have made the great benevolent original vow to liberate all living beings who undergo the four modes of birth, those who are good at skillful means (Skt. *upāya-kauśalya*) by which they expediently manifest in the six realms [of existence], those who promptly come complying with the voice, just as a shadow follows the form, and friends who manifest themselves without being recalled and who help others without being asked to do so.[231] They all enter a bathing room and take a bath.

Next, invite heavenly beings of the three realms of existence, the dragon kings of the four seas, the eight kinds of spiritual beings, and all sentient beings such as material species and vermicular animals. They all enter a bathing room and take a bath.

Praise and invitation have been completed. A row of people harmoniously chant hymns to praise [the Buddha], carry incense with them, and proceed in order.

Verses say:

The Three Treasures profoundly flourish.
The four modes of birth are forms to mark.
Benevolence protects the ten directions.
[The Buddha's] favor flows as do a myriad of his virtues.
His wisdom embraces the eight Dharma storehouses.
He edifies ten billion beings completely.
Rewarding his favor is important.
This is due to the power of merit.
Through painting or carving an image
Or propagating a sutra, you can establish merit.
Make a ship or a bridge to help people cross over the stream.
Initiate purification and bathing.
Have no concern for your life.
Why do you repress purity and sincerity?
How prosperous excellent acts are!
It is difficult to surmise how one can accomplish merit.

Miracle Stories[232]

(Eleven stories are briefly cited.)

[Huan Wen, Commander-in-Chief of the Jin Dynasty]

Huan Wen (312–373), Commander-in-Chief of the Jin dynasty, greatly believed in the Dharma in his later years and offered meals to monks and nuns.

A nun whose name is unknown had come from far away and lived under Wen's roof. Wen became her donor (Skt. *dānapati*). The nun's intelligence and moral conduct were extraordinary. So Wen treated her with great respect and had her live inside of the gate of his residence. Every time the nun took a bath, she took a long time without fail. Suspicious, Wen had spied on her [while she was taking a bath]. He saw that the nun who was naked cut her belly with a sword, took her intestines, severed her head from her body, and chopped everything into pieces. Wen was very surprised and returned [to his residence]. After a while, the nun came out of the bathroom with her body restored to its original state. Wen sincerely asked [the nun] about [what he had seen]. She answered, "If you realize your will to go above your sovereign, the punishment will be like that." Just at that time, Wen had been scheming to become the ruler of the country. When he heard this he felt disappointed. Accordingly he became prudent and abided by the principle to remain a loyal subject until the end of his life. The nun [later] left. It is unknown where she went.

[Née Xie, Wife of Wang Ningzhi of the Jin Dynasty]

545b Née Xie, the wife of Wang Ningzhi in Langye (in present-day Shandong province) during the Jin dynasty, namely the lady of the Left General of the Jin dynasty, was the daughter of [Xie] Yi. She had formerly lost two sons in succession and heartrendingly deplored [the death of her two sons]. She was drowned in tears for year after year and seemed to live an extremely difficult life. Later, her two sons suddenly returned together, but they were both bound in chains and shackled. They consoled their mother, "You should be magnanimous. We, your sons, both accept the guilt ourselves. If you have sympathy for us, you should do virtuous deeds for us." Thereafter, [the mother's] painful feelings of grief lessened and she became diligent in performing meritorious acts.

(These two stories are found in the *Mingxiang ji* [*Records of the Profound and Auspicious*].)

[Shi Huida, a *Śramaṇa* of the Sui Dynasty]

In the Sui dynasty there was Shi Huida (524–610) at Pubu Temple on Mount Tiantai. His [secular] family name was Wang, and he was from Xiangyang (in present-day Hubei province). He renounced the world when he was a child. He performed repairing as his task. He climbed mountains, crossed rivers, or traveled about towns and villages. When up at a vantage point, however, he entirely gave his mind over to thinking of the construction of temple buildings in a quiet place for monks to practice the [Buddhist] Way.

In the middle years of the Renshou era (601–604), at Baita Temple in Yangzhou (in present-day Jiangsu province), [Huida] built a seven-storied wooden stupa. There were sufficient construction materials, and he gave others [the task of] managing the building. [Huida] then crossed a large river and went to the west. He reached various prefectures, such as Poyang (in present-day Shanxi province) and Yuzhang (in present-day Jiangxi province), where he went around to inspect [how he could make] merit and prayed to share with sentient beings the conditions in which they would have happiness. Therefore, when he arrived in a village or town and found a Buddhist temple, a meditation building, a stupa, or a shrine for deities, regardless of the materials [it was constructed with], such as metal, wood, earth, or stone, he led and edified [the people] to complete its construction. [He was involved with constructing] a large number [of buildings].

Afterward, responding to the *śramaṇa* Huiyun's invitation, [Huida] went to Mount Lu (in present-day Jiangxi province) and arrived at Xilin Temple. He later constructed a pavilion consisting of seven sections, the ancones of which were stacked up high, one upon another.[233] [The pavilion] was bright, attractive, and splendid.

On the day [Huida] first reached [the temple] he pledged to use yellow *nanmu* wood [for its concstruction]. He sought to obtain [yellow *nanmu*] in all areas but finally understood that there was not even a single [*nanmu*] tree [in the region]. Everyone wanted him to change [his plan] and use [wood from] other kinds of trees. [Hui]da said, "My sincerity lies in this [tree, *nanmu*]. How can I instead seek for other [kinds of wood]? There must be a respondent sign [to my sincerity]. Then pine trees will change and become *nanmu* trees. Even if there is no mysterious response [to my sincerity], the pavilion will be completed soon." The people, frightened at his words, went out in every direction to look for [*nanmu* trees]. [Huida] then perceived that a valley near Mount Chao, below the precincts [of the temple and the valley], was completely covered by yellow *nanmu* trees. [The valley], however, was located in an extremely damp, dark, and steep area, and there was no way to bring [logged *nanmu* trees] out from there. [Hui]da went looking around along a precipice. Suddenly he saw a spot where there was a bright light. He looked inside and ascertained a path that led to [the valley of the *nanmu* trees]. [The path] was only five *chi* wide, surrounded by large precipices reaching up toward the sky. [The people] moved the construction materials to the headwaters of a large river. In the middle [of the river] there were rapids and a whirlpool, and all their rafts were broken. When they arrived at Lufu (i.e., Mount Lu), however, not a single piece [of wood] was missing.

The pavilion was thus successfully completed, and it was larger than the previous building. [The pavilion] later abruptly shifted three *chi* toward the south. The builders wished to devise a way [to restore the building], but they could not come up with an effective method. The Shimen mountain stream was just south of the pavilion. Suddenly a windstorm arose and blew to the north, thus shifting [the pavilion] back to its previous position. [The pavilion] still remains today.

[Hui]da's clothes were so coarse and threadbare that they were almost transparent. When he assumed the attitude of an onlooker, he was dull and slow and appeared to be unable to speak, but when he instructed [others] and dealt with matters, he immediately successfully accomplished them. This means precisely that [Huida] was a person who can adapt to various changes and who does not submit to a superior force.

On the last day of the seventh month of the sixth year of the Daye era (610) [Huida's] chronic disease abruptly became serious. He lay in his sickbed for seven days. A rare fragrant smell came into his room and floated around
545c like a cloud. Venerable images in the pavilion were [seen to] perspire without exception, and their sweat [trickled down and] ran onto the ground. When [the people] saw this good omen they knew that [Hui]da was about to die. Government officials inspected and fully reported [what they had found] to the emperor. [Hui]da's consciousness was as usual, and he was still thinking intently of unfinished tasks. He suddenly passed away at the Chinese age of eighty-seven.

[Shi Zhuli, a *Śramaṇa* of the Tang Dynasty]

In the Tang dynasty there was Shi Zhuli (544–623) at Changle Temple in Yangzhou (in present-day Jiangsu province). His [secular] family name was Chu, and he was from Yangdi County in Henan. He possessed an upright and lofty character. He was openminded and attained awakening. His high reputation was known to both monks and laypeople.

At his original temple (i.e., Changle Temple), along with the four kinds of Buddhist followers and princes he built high pavilions that completely encompassed two towers.[234] They were wonderfully complete and remarkable works. [The construction] was completed within a year. All three hundred people of the temple were greatly delighted.

In the tenth year of the Daye era (614) [Zhuli] used his own money to copy an auspicious buddha image and two bodhisattva images using fragrant sandalwood. Within a short time [the images] were completed and placed in a pavilion.

In the fourteenth year (618) the Sui dynasty suffered a downfall and fell into disorder. Monks and laypeople all became wandering refugees. Corpses and bones filled the streets and marketplaces, just like withered [trees] and rotten [stumps]. [Zhuli] pledged to protect the temple buildings without concern for his own life. He lived in the temple along with foxes and rabbits, and when he saw his own shadow he considered it to be his companion. He had [only meager portions of] bean [soup] and water and passed through a winter and a summer. Even though he was aged, his mental power was even more vigorous. The mud fell away from the walls, and the surrounding area [of the temple] was burned. He, however, never stopped reciting [sutras] and carrying out repairs with his own hands. Even the rebels [were affected by seeing Huida's acts and] cried out with tears as loudly as a thunderclap,[235] and those who saw [how Zhuli was living] lamented. They frequently repented [of their faults] and helped [Zhuli] repair [the temple buildings].

When the Tang dynasty (618–907) received the mandate of heaven and broadly declared the constitution of a nation, the former [resident] monks and the other people all returned [to the temple] to live there. Even though the houses in the town had been burned down, the temple still stood.

In the sixth year of the Wude era (623) Fu Gongyou, Commander-in-Chief of the rebels of Jiangbiao (i.e., the area south of the Yangzi River), took advantage of the precarious situation, raised an army without authorization, and secretly plotted treason [against the central government]. A hundred Buddhist and Daoist temples altogether were evacuated and relocated to Jiangnan (i.e., southern Jiangsu). Then [Zhu]li sent a letter and petitioned once again. [He wrote,] "I wish to burn my body in front of the pavilion in order to remain in the temple building." [Fu Gong]you held an honorable title illegally and was determined only to overthrow [the Tang dynasty]. So when he received the letter he did not take it into consideration at all.

[Zhu]li said to his disciples, "I have had a deep-rooted habit of greedy attachment from immeasurable *kalpa*s ago. I have been unable even to give up my life in order to requite the kindness of the Dharma. Now I wish to receive my death personally before the buddha [image]. I certainly do not have the heart to see the images crossing over the large river. You should pile up dried firewood, with which I will burn myself as an offering to [the images]. After my death the images will certainly be taken to the south. My clothing, money, and miscellaneous goods should all be placed inside venerable images. The laws of mourning and the rites for the repose of the dead should be reformed." Thereupon, [Zhuli] bathed in fragrant hot water and sat cross-legged. Facing west, he ignited a fire and commited self-immolation, and died in a pile of charcoal at the age of eighty Chinese years old. This took place precisely on the eighth day of the tenth month of the sixth year of the Wude era (623). When his life ended and the fire burned out, his body [was seen to] have settled with his hands joined in prayer. [His body] was further cremated, and it changed [into relics] all at once.

When [Zhu]li first began to burn [himself] before the buddha [image], a flock of magpies cried out mournfully, making a very pathetic sound. They circled in a clockwise direction seven times and then began to fly away. After [Zhuli's] death, the images were moved to the south, just as [Zhuli] had predicted. [The temple] building complex was saved from turning into ashes. The Dharma treasures (i.e., the Buddha's teachings) and the sangha were
546a just as they had been in the past. [Zhuli's] disciples Huian and Zhize valued the significance of the relationship between teacher and disciple, which is deeper than a husband's debt to his father-in-law. A high stone tablet was established for [Zhuli] within the temple. The son of the crown prince and

his concubine, Yu Shinan, composed a text [for the tablet]. The images have been returned to the pavilion [of the temple] and still remain there today.

[Shi Zhichao, a *Śramaṇa* of the Tang Dynasty]

In the Tang dynasty there was Shi Zhichao at Guangyan Temple in Fenzhou (in present-day Shanxi province). His secular family name was Tian, and he was from Fengyi in Tongzhou (in present-day Shaanxi province). He exerted himself with diligence and was far superior to others; he had a graceful manner and was lofty and profound.

In the seventh year of the Wude era (624) [Zhichao] stayed on Mount Baofu in Fenzhou. There were only a hundred monks, solely supported by meals served in a great Buddhist service. There were only six *dan* of wheat stored in the granary. Five *sheng* of ground [wheat] per day were needed to supply for regular use. From spring to summer, the consumption [of wheat] was calculated at an extremely high rate. [The people] were suspicious about this and investigated. Only a couple of *dan* [of wheat from the granary] had been used. Measuring from this fact, it was thinkable that [Zhichao] had secretly offered [the extra wheat].

Furthermore, [people] often perceived a strange monk coming and going in the sky. Even though there was no information [about the monk], his dignified appearance verified [that he was Zhichao]. If those who lived with [Zhichao] indulged in evil ways, they received supernatural warnings [from him]. As to calling the people, a bell would toll by itself at the time [when he needed to summon the people]. A fountain gushed out from some rocks, and [the water] was sufficient for the people's use. Mysterious and auspicious signs were frequently perceived. They truly derived from [Zhichao's excellent] merit.

On the eleventh day of the third month of the fifteenth year of the Zhenguan era (641), after [Zhichao] had suddenly fallen ill, he died at Cheng Temple. He was seventy-one Chinese years old.

[Shi Huizhen, a *Śramaṇa* of the Tang Dynasty]

In the Tang dynasty there was Shi Huizhen at Tongquan Temple in Zizhou (in present-day Sichuan province). His secular family name was Pang, and he was eight *chi* tall. When he heard Master [Jing]gao's [exposition of] the three discourses his profound awakening became greater. In the first month every year [the ritual of] turning the pages of sutras (*zhuanjing*) was performed[236] and enough *kaṣāya* robes for a thousand monks were respectfully offered, without deficiency. [Huizhen] always promulgated the three discourses to an audience of over a hundred monks. [Huizhen], sitting upon the raised seat, suddenly looked sorrowful. Regarding all the people, he said, "It would be good to build a great image of the Buddha on top of Mount Xi." He then regained consciousness and descended the seat. Guiding the people, he made an inspection round [of the area]. The middle part [of a certain site] was suitable for building an image [of Buddha].[237] Spring[water] flowed on both sides. Immediately [Huizhen] ordered stonemasons to carve the seated body [of the image], which was a hundred and thirty *chi* tall. In the eighth year of the Zhenguan era (634) [the image], equipped with everything necessary, was completed. People from all directions gathered, and thirty thousand monks and laypeople celebrated the venerable image. The image emitted the great bright light from its mouth, and people from far and near all saw it.

Previously there was a horse that could go five hundred *li* a day. [This horse] had once before gone to war. All the other warhorses died [on the battlefield]; only this [horse] survived. In the seventh month of the fourteenth year (640) [the horse] suddenly neighed and then would not eat for three days. When [Hui]zhen heard about this his hair stood on end. A strange monk whose name was Shili ("Ten Powers") said to [Hui]zhen, "The horse is separating from you. You must go first. On the fifteenth day of the first month of next year, precisely at noon, you should enter nirvana. Dharma teacher, you have to give away your property so that nothing is left after [you are gone].[238] There is no advantage for you [to keep any goods]." After he had spoken, he disappeared. No one knew his whereabouts.

First [Huizhen] compiled the Buddhist canon, [and after it was completed] he asked the other monks to continually chant it. The gate of great almsgiving was opened. People from all over respectfully lamented, and [Huizhen's property] was given away to whomever came to receive it. At the beginning of his last year, he again asked the sangha to recite the sutras. [A group of monks] chanted the sutras while circumambulating [an image of the Buddha], and they performed [this rite] for twenty-one days. His worldly relations, brothers and sisters, as well as [all the people] inside and outside [the temple] gathered together.

On the eighth day [fragrance filled the temple] and was not yet dissipated even on [the fifteenth day].[239] From dawn to noon, all the trees and land within 546b the temple precincts produced lotus flowers. When the people saw the wonderful and auspicious sign they knew that [Huizhen] was leaving the world.

[Hui]zhen said, "A good aspect has already been revealed. I will not allow myself to wait for the fullness [of time]." Thereupon, he performed monetary almsgiving [to the masses] and finished his early meal.[240] Holding an incense burner in his hand, he circumambulated [an image of] Vairocana Buddha three times, returned to the front of [image of] the Buddha, and knelt in mindfulness. A crowd of people had filled the hall. [Huizhen] passed away before they realized it. He was sixty-six Chinese years old.

[The people] stayed in mourning, waiting for the fullness [of time]. The fragrance still remained. [Huizhen's] three brothers each donated five hundred thousand in cash. At [Huizhen's] grave they performed almsgiving to the monk's virtue and the field of compassion. They built a tombstone, five *zhang* tall. In a niche a rope bed was arranged, and [Huizhen's] corpse was placed upon it. Even after more than a hundred days, [his corpse] had not yet decayed. More than ten thousand people, from monks to laypeople, mournfully wept one after another.

[Shi Huiyun, a *Śramaṇa* of the Tang Dynasty]

In the Tang dynasty there was Shi Huiyun at Hongfu Temple in the metropolis. His [secular] family name was Wang, and he was from Taiyuan (in present-day Shanxi province). His remote ancestors had fled from their original homeland and stayed in Jiujiang (in present-day Jiangxi province). At the Chinese age of twenty he became delighted in the [Buddhist] Way, and when he was twenty-five years old he joined Dalin Temple in Mount Kuang (i.e., Mount Lu in present-day Jiangxi province).

Chan Master Da was engaged in construction in the areas around the Yangzi River and the Huai River (i.e., the area of present-day Jiangsu and Anhui provinces).[241] Because [Huiyun's] temple buildings were damaged, [Hui]yun requested [Chan Master] Da to rebuild them. [Da was struck with Huiyun's sincerity, and the temple buildings] were completed.

In the last year of the declining period of the Sui dynasty (618), the Central Plains (i.e., the downstream regions of the Yellow River) were entirely in disorder. A man called Lin Shihong gathered the people in Yuzhang (in present-day Jiangxi province) and falsely assumed the title of emperor of Chu. Hu Xiucai in Poyang (in present-day Jiangxi province), Director of the Department of State Affairs of the false state, personally led the people and temporarily occupied Jiujiang. Due to receiving [spiritual power], he awakened the aspiration for [*bodhi*] and wished to copy the auspicious image of Mañjuśrī in Donglin Temple on Mount Lu. Since [Hui]yun had outstanding and rare [skills], [Xiucai] ordered him to study how to cast [the image].

[The image] was completed, glorious in appearance. It had holes only in two places, on the neck and the side of the body. At that time the people were not aware of [the reason for this]. In that year Xiucai was expelled by a false imperial decree. A hundred and twenty *liang* of gold to coat the [Mañjuśrī] image were contained in a bamboo tube. When the rebels rose up against [the central government] [Hui]yun had no way to protect [the gold] from them, so he consigned it all to [Hu Xiu]cai. Furthermore, [Huiyun] sent [Xiucai] a string of bronze beads to use for reciting [a sutra or the buddhas' names] as a token of faith. [Xiucai] went to [Lake] Gongting (in present-day Jiangxi province) and humbly prayed for good luck for his soldiers. [Xiu]cai obtained a favorable wind, the sails were hoisted, and he led [his troops] from the front. They encountered [high] waves midway on the water, and their boat sank. Their belongings were completely washed away. Only the people were able to reach the riverbank. [Xiucai] had no resentment at all, but he regretted the loss of the gold that was to be used to decorate the image. He was worried and cried with regret ceaselessly on the riverbank. He had not fulfilled his vow and deeply [believed] that he had done a [sinful] act.

Instanteously, the [bamboo] tube with the gold rose up on the waves and flowed back [to Xiucai]. In addition, the string of bronze beads [sent by Huiyun] also returned to him almost simultaneously. Floating up and down [with the waves, the tube and the beads] headed toward the bank and then came to [rest on the shore near Xiu]cai. When the people retrieved the gold for the image, they all shouted in great joy and immeasurably rejoiced. [The people] estimated [the distance between] where [the bamboo tube and the beads] sank and the riverbank they had reached to be more than thirty *li*. [These items] were heavy, yet they rose to the surface, went against the current [of the river], and successively returned to [the people]. The soldiers and civilians were all surprised at this and amazed at the supernatural responsive activity in conjunction with human receptivity.

When [Xiu]cai was murdered, the sword cut into his neck and the side of his body. [These wounds] tallied exactly with [the holes in the Mañjuśrī] image. At the beginning [of the uprising], when [Xiu]cai intended to attack the rebels, he entrusted [Chan Master Xiao],[242] the younger brother of his father, with the gold. [Chan Master Xiao] shouldered it and fled for safety, but he could not escape from being robbed. He had already lost the gold for 546c
the image and had no plan to get it back. Subsequently one of the robbers who had stolen the gold presented it to [Chan Master] Xiao as a gift. Neither of them knew that this was the same gold [Xiao] had carried away [for safety]. [Chan Master] Xiao thus obtained the original gold that [Hui]yin had entrusted to him. [The image] was completed, and its glorious appearance was outstanding. Even today [the image] remains in the pavilion on the mountain.

At the outset of casting metal for the image, Li Sijie personally made a vow, "On the day when the gold is melted I take an oath that I will burn one of my arms. I wish that [Hui]yun's work on the image will soon be accomplished and [the image] will be completed ahead of schedule." [Sijie] of the Li did not know that a metal image had already been cast. Thereupon, he dreamed about the image, which said, "You previously took an oath to burn your arm. Why have you gone against your faith?" When [Sijie of] the Li woke up from the dream he accordingly knew [that the image had been completed] for the first time. He immediately went before the image and cut apart his arm. He wrapped the bone [of his arm] in a wax-coated cloth, burned it, and offered it to [the image]. Fragrance wafted down from heaven and the image emitted rays of light. The various kinds of unusual, wonderful, and auspicious happenings cannot be completely described.

Early in the Zhenguan era (627–649), due to an engagement [Hui]yun entered the capital city. He met Vinaya Master [Zhi]shou (567–635) and treasured the vinaya practices in his mind. The prime minister and the nobles regarded his virtue to be lofty. They petitioned the throne, and [Huiyun] was requested to reside in Hongfu [Temple].

In the twentieth year of the Zhenguan era (646) [Huiyun] yearned for his 547a
native village and returned to the temple in his native place, Jiujiang. He presently lives there.

[Shi Daoying, a *Śramaṇa* of the Tang Dynasty]

In the Tang dynasty there was Shi Daoying (560–637) at Puji Temple in Puzhou (in present-day Shanxi province). His [secular] family name was Chen, and he was from Yishi in Puzhou. When [Daoying] was eighteen Chinese years old, Vinaya Master Shuxiu edified him and guided him to renounce the world. [Daoying's] parents loved him and compelled him to take a wife. [Dao]ying reluctantly gave up parting from his parents. [He stayed in the secular world for several more years], and after obtaining his parents' consent [regarding his leaving home] he abandoned [everything] unsparingly. In his secular life he had never indulged in sensual pleasures.

[Daoying] renounced the world and understood clearly the sutras and discourses. Thereupon, he said, "We should know the characteristics of elements. We must understand our mental delusions."

In the nineteenth year of the Kaihuang era (599), he entered Baiti Temple on Mount Taixing in Jie county (in present-day Shanxi province), where he studied the practice of tranquility and contemplation (*zhiguan;* Skt. *śamatha* and *vipaśyanā*). He suddenly attained the understanding of the emptiness of both human beings and elements and deeply awakened to the foundation of the mind. Sitting under trees, he projected himself into the four directions. At the same time he managed services for the sangha and through the services he studied the mind.

Later [Daoying] lived in Shengguang Temple located in the metropolis, followed Chan Master Tanqian, and heard the *Mahāyāna-saṃgraha* (*She dasheng lun*). There were five hundred students. [Dao]ying was bright so only he understood [the essence of the text]. Chan Master [Tanqian] said in wonderment, "My students are extremely numerous. Although they understand the meaning of the text thoroughly, the only one who attains its principle is Daoying."

Relying on the *Garland Sutra,* [Dao]ying always made vows and offered services to the monks. In accordance with a matter he showed reason, controlling his mind and actions. Due to his nature he did not observe the written rules regarding ceremonial dress and drinking and eating, and this caused those who observed him to think that he was somewhat strange and disobedient. Other than managing the sangha, he meditated and recited [sutras] unceasingly. He made a thorough search on the noumenal principle and exhaustively clarified it with his mind's eye.

In the ninth year of the Daye era (613) he found that [the temple] he resided was contending with secular people for a piece of land. [Daoying] was concerned that the loss of the monks' profit was against the secular people's interests. He gave them a bitter-pill admonition, but [they] did not listen to him. Thereupon, [Daoying] said to them, "I will die for your sake." He suddenly collapsed and became as rigid as a corpse. All the secular people persisted and said, "This Buddhist monk is very deceitful. If we pierce the back of his hand with a needle we can find out whether or not [he really has died]." They pierced [Daoying] deeply with a needle, but he paled in color like a corpse and his body as well as mind remained motionless. [His body] was on the point of becoming swollen and decaying. At his side there was a wise man who instructed [the people], ordering them to take refuge in [Buddhism], repent of their sins, and pledge that they would not continue to dispute [against Daoying and the temple]. [After the people] followed [the wise man's] admonitions, [Daoying] aroused, sat up, talked, and smiled as usual.

Furthermore, [Daoying] went to the marsh in [Long]tai (in present-day Shaanxi province) and saw fish swimming around in a pond. He said, "I will compete with you [in swimming]. You or I, who will win a victory?" Then he took off his clothes and entered the water. Six nights passed. His disciple kept watch over his clothes. Afterward, [Daoying] emerged from [the water] and said, "While I was in the water, only bad soil covered [over my body]. I was not conscious of any wetness."

Then a very cold winter arrived. Thick ice [covered the earth], and snow heavily [fell from] the sky as well. [Daoying] said, "In a peaceful and pure place like this, how can I not sleep?" Consequently he took off all his clothes, lay on his back, and spent three nights [in the open]. Then he got up and said, smiling, "I wish that I will not be burned and killed by fire." In this way, whenever he followed situations he dealt with them by using the Dharma. He had his own way in everything; he was free from resistance. He did not think about anything difficult. This is truly because through the doctrine of consciousness-only (*weishi;* Skt. *vijñapti-mātratā*) he thoroughly knew about the mind. How could he have any hindrances from the substance of external matters?

Later, [Daoying] returned to Puzhou and lived at Puji Temple. Manors were established in three places, all located in deep and hidden sites on Mount Dong in Xia county (in present-day Shanxi province). He did not cause 547b trouble or fight with secular people. Therefore, he caused the four categories of Buddhists from all directions to gather together, just like [trees in] a forest. In the daytime he administrated the affairs of the sangha, and at night he gave talks on meditation and contemplation for [the people]. There were those who were exhausted by their labor, but [when they heard the Dharma preached by Daoying][242] they forgot their weariness. [Daoying] always relied on the *Mahāyāna-saṃgraha* and the *Awakening of Faith in the Mahayana* (*Dasheng qixin lun*) to support the mind. As to this fact, one day he gave a talk on the *Awakening of Faith.* When he reached the section on the essential gate of true thusness (i.e., ultimate reality), he suddenly stopped speaking. His audience was surprised and saw that his breath had stopped and his body was cold. They understood he was in [the meditation in which mental functions are] completely exhausted. So they left him alone and did not feel strange about it. After successive nights he just got up from the meditation. His physical appearance was calm as he testified to the first meditation [stage of the four meditation stages in the realm of form].

Daosun, a *śramaṇa* of Hedong (presently the southwestern part of Shanxi province), was a highly virtuous and distinguished monk. He was originally a fellow student [of Daoying]. He learned the way of the mind as his foundation. [Daoying and Daosun] were intimate friends. [Daosun] first lived in Jie county (in present-day Shanxi province).[244] Leading his followers, he actively gave talks. When [Dao]sun gave up his life he was a hundred and fifty *li* away from [Dao]ying. Although the report of [Daosun's death] had not not yet reached [Daoying], he knew of it the same evening [that Daosun] died. [Daoying] told the people, "Eminent [Dao]sun has already passed away. Let him make a journey to the [other] world beyond!" Someone asked him why [he had said] this. [Daoying replied,] "This is a secular matter, but communication from mind to mind is beyond comprehension." When [Daoying] had traveled halfway to [Daosun's place] he met the messenger coming with the report [of Daosun's death]. Other stories that [Daoying] secretly knew of future events are all like this.

Prior to the time of [Daoying's own] death, he gathered the people and told them, "Today we must quickly gather the harvest. I am afraid that tomorrow numerous people and beasts will come and consume the grains and grasses." [Dao]ying also carried the crops himself and was strongly urged by the other people. The people then understood that they had to help him even though they did not fathom his intention. By nightfall everything was finished. [Daoying] asked for water and took a bath. He returned to the place where he had originally been seated. Covering himself with a *saṃghāṭī,* he told the people, "All people call me Chan Master [Dao]ying. A Chan master's bearing should not go against the secular people's [expectations]." He asked his disciple Zhibao, "Do you, Chan Master, know how many more times I will draw breath?" [Zhi]bao responded to him through serving him. [Dao]ying's words were just like this. Accordingly [Daoying] spoke of the essence of the Dharma and said, "Impermanence is permanence. You cannot deceive yourself. You must not die in vain." He ordered [his disciples] to recite Xianshou's verses on the *Garland Sutra.* At the moment of his death he exhorted them to think of a good realm (i.e., the realms of heavenly and human beings). The clear seal [of death] had already appeared on his face. He said, "I will give up my old body," and suddenly passed away. The people wondered why he was no longer moving. [Someone] touched [Daoying's body] with his hand, [and felt that the body] was [gradually] growing cold from the lower part. [The people] then verified [his death].

Even ordinary people surely ascend to a good realm; moreover, Daoying had good signs like these. How could [Daoying] be the same as ordinary monks? This ocurred in the middle of the ninth month of the seventh year of the Zhenguan era (633).[245] [Daoying] was seventy-seven Chinese years old.

Before this, on the day [Daoying] was to die, people asked him about matters after his death. He replied, "The Buddha has excellent teachings. Just rely on them and practice them. Then numerous nuisances will be exhausted." On the very last day a flock of birds gathered in the resident monks' quarters; they were counted to be more than a thousand. [The birds] mournfully cried incessantly and caused the people to grieve excessively. Intelligent [Zhi]bao sat by [Daoying's] side and saw two boys in blue clothes came into [the room] holding flowers. A purple vapor-like light came out from [Dao]ying's body, and a flame rose and went around the beams [of the room]. At daybreak on the following day, there was fog throughout the area within twenty *li* [of the temple]. The people [in this area] had no light. [This condition] lasted three days and then stopped.

[People] in the area where the Pu and Jin [Rivers] meet each other (i.e., present-day Taiyuan prefecture in Shanxi province) heard the sad [news].
547c They gathered and went in procession as if they had lost their parents or grandparents. Moreover, it was realized that the howls of the temple cows resounded from several *li* away. [They] howled in choked voices, weeping, and would not take water or grass. Seven days passed. When [Daoying's body] was about to be placed in a coffin, the monks and laypeople contended with each other [to place his body in the coffin]. They thought that since [Dao]ying was originally not fond of loud noises and just kept to the activities of the [Buddhist] Way,[246] they dug up the earth on the south side of the manor, which is east of Xiayu City and south of the high mound of Yannian, and enshrined him there. When they began to put the cauldron down, the earth suddenly heavily quaked. Eveyone grabbed onto some grass for self-protection, fearing that they would fall. The surrounding region within fifteen *li* was entirely shaken, and all [the people] were greatly terrified.

Furthermore, [people] realized that two rainbows rose, bestriding the place where [Daoying's] coffin was laid, and two white birds soared [above Daoying's coffin], crying. They circled around, gazing at [the small shrine], hovered around [for a little while], and giving mournful cries they were gone.

[Daoy]ing edified the people and benefited all the living and the dead. Except for those equal in position to his spiritual affinity, could anyone perceive such good and auspicious phenomena? Overall, he did not bear glory for himself. The sincerity of the world refers to such a person.

[Shi Chade, a *Śramaṇa* of the Tang Dynasty]

In the Tang dynasty there was Shi Chade (d. 638) on Mount Liang in Yongzhou (in present-day Shaanxi province). He was from Liquan county [in Yongzhou]. Regarding his physical appearance, he was tall and large, good-looking, and had a slender face. His actions following [the Buddhist Way] were clean. He wore coarse and simple clothes. He was fond of traveling to edify secular people and engaged himself in making meritorious acts. He spoke freely about things of the future. There were many things he greatly encouraged [others to do].

There was a year of misfortunes. Among those who suffered from poisonous vapor or the plague, [Chade] first persuaded the four classes of people (i.e., scholars, farmers, artisans, and merchants) and brought them to believe in the Three Treasures, to worship the Buddha, to practice purification rituals, to chant the buddhas' names, or to think intently of a buddha and recite [a sutra]. All those who accepted his words had no misfortunes. Disasters and calamities, one after the other, visited those who did not believe in [his words].

He made a prediction, nearly equivalent to seeing with one's own eyes. Once a drought occurred and people fearfully asked [Chade about it]. Cha[de] gestured with his hands [and said], "It will rain on a certain day, but the rain will fall in a certain area." At the predicted time the rain certainly fell just as [Chade] had said. Moreover [Chade] could perceive how large or small an area would be affected by a plague of locusts, or how far or near and how deep or shallow heaven would bestow favor with a long rain. Every event tallied with [his words] as clearly as a mirror; [his predictions] did not miss even a small detail.

Moreover [Chade] upheld his determination and was honest and prudent. He did not recklessly punish beyond the proper laws. He did not take teachings for anything above his ability. Formerly when he was in the prime of his life, he pursued the [Buddhist] Way and only observed the ten wholesome precepts. He, however, took and studied many miscellaneous things from books.

Later he created Lake Anavatapta to the south of Mount Jiujun.[247] At the same time he carved a bowl from stone, then placed it on the shore of the lake in order to relieve sentient beings.

In the twelfth year of the Zhenguan era (638) [Chade] passed away in his mountain retreat. The common people missed him and built a white stupa for him, which stood loftily on the mountain.

[Shi Tongda, a *Śramaṇa* of the Tang Dynasty]

In the Tang dynasty there was Shi Tongda at Lüzang Temple in the metropolis. He was a man from Jingyang in Yongzhou (in present-day Chang'an prefecture in Shaanxi province). He renounced the world at the Chinese age of thirty and had no permanent abode. Then he entered Mount Taibo [near Chang'an], but he was not offered provisions. When he was hungry he ate grass, and when thirsty he drank water. To rest he leaned on a tree and whenever he sat down he meditated. For a span of more than five years, he remained busy without taking a rest. Incidentally he struck a clod of earth with a piece of wood and the dirt clod broke apart, losing [its original] shape. On seeing this transformation he was boundlessly and greatly awakened; he realized the path of the mind (i.e., the way to think).

Later, [Tongda] resided in Lüzang [Temple]. He traveled about and heard the Mahayana [teachings]. He possessed vast and open emotional capacity.
548a His lower garment, outergarment, and Buddhist surplice made from rags were repeatedly patched and repaired, [as he led a frugal life]. The hemp-fiber sandals he wore were thirty years old. He had never worn silk fabrics or miscellaneous ornaments. He spent a winter and a summer with only one robe and never withdrew from the [wintry] cold or the heat [of summer]. Whenever lectures were given he frequently commented and talked about the profound teachings. He never engaged in music. There was no one like him. At first his sayings contradicted [his actions]. When he ate [there was no difference from the food of secular people].[248] It is difficult to carry out such things. All the world obeyed him.

When Left Vice Director Fang Xuanling heard what [Tongda] had said, he felt that [Tongda was] extraordinary. [Tongda] was welcomed at [Fang Xuanling's] mansion. [Fang Xuanling] revered [Tongda] as much as he did his own father. Nevertheless, [Tong]da had mastered the [Buddhist] Way and was not restricted by a physical body. The words that came out [of Tongda's mouth] were not simple; he spoke freely what he cherished in his mind. [Fang] Xuanling dealt with him according to the manners shown by him. [Tongda] did not keep others away based on their appearance and what they said. He engaged even with a noble in this way. The whole nation obeyed him.

[Tongda] did not eat grain of any sort, only vegetables. If he was able to find mugwort and wild spinach, he picked and ate them, and [these wild herbs] served him as well as delicious food. If he obtained a variety of stone fruits such as peaches and apricots, he ate [the whole fruit], even the pits. He did not think this was difficult. Someone thought this was odd and asked him [the reason]. He answered, "It is hard to throw away gifts from believers."

During the Zhenguan era (627–649) [Tongda] began revealing miracles. He frequently visited people in their houses; if he was greatly joyful, it was fortunate, and if he was unhappy, it was certainly unfortunate. Once he sought money or manpower. In accordance with whatever amount he ordered, the people immediately had to provide it for him. If anyone went against his request, that person would later encounter a terrible disaster. One time a man riding a donkey passed through [the precincts of Lüzang] Temple, seeing the sights. [Tong]da begged him [for alms], but the man was stingy and did not donate. The man's donkey soon died. There are numerous examples like this.

Accordingly, the royal family and the people, both eminent and humble, completely served him with faith. Fortune and misfortune derived from a single word of his. In leading the people by expounding, [Tongda] simply kept [the tenet of] leaving behind attachments.[249] Any wealth he obtained was used mainly to manage the temple.

When Great General Xue Wanjun first heard of [Tongda's] extraordinary conduct he invited [Tongda] to his house and made an offering to him. For more than a hundred days [Tongda] followed the monastic rules [in regard to the proper times for taking meals] without fail. Suddenly, one night he demanded food and wanted to eat. At first no one would give him [food], but he would not stop pleading for [food]. Some [food] was tentatively given to him and then he ate it. From that time on, [Tongda] gradually switched back to his former conduct. He exclusively manifested his flexibility in responding to circumstances. His acts were very unusual. He intended to go to Xue Wanjun's house [to stay overnight]. The Great General's brothers were crude and ferocious in nature. They did not know about [the Buddhist] secret practice (i.e., observing the precepts very strictly). They were very angry with [Tongda] and beat him almost to death. [Tongda] looked up and told them, "You have already beaten me, and my entire body and flesh are injured, stained by blood, and no longer pure. You must wash me with hot water." He waited until the water was at a boil, then removed his clothes and entered into the cauldron. His body was neither wounded nor burned; he looked like he had just been in a freezing pond. The bystanders were frightened by this, but [Tongda] urged them to replenish the fire, saying, "It does not warm my body." The whole family was amazed and admired him. [So Tongda] could stay overnight [at their house] at will. Because of this, thereafter if there was anyone who was suffering from a disease, [Tongda] ordered [that person or his family] to heat water until boiling hot, then he first went [into the hot water] and washed [his body] and then instructed the [ill] person to go into [the hot water after him]. There was no disease that was not cured this way.

[Tong]da once owed a person more than a hundred *guan.* He later got the money but had no one to send to return [the money back to the person]. So [Tongda] brought the money out to the temple gate where he saw some passers-by. Because of a large amount of money he owed, [Tongda] went to the western market to employ someone to find the creditor and return [the money to him]. [Everyone tried to stop him from doing so but Tongda] insisted on consigning the money. It was later counted and not even a single penny was missing. [This is] because [Tong]da carried out virtuous conduct and was openminded, so the people did not lose their faith in him.

548b Furthermore, at one time the price of rice was very high, so [Tongda] intended to set up a great [assembly] for serving meals. He ordered the sangha to release a great quantity [of rice from the temple storehouse] and submitted a petition [to the emperor requesting aid]. The next morning those who came [to the meal assembly] numbered fully a thousand. The monks in charge of the meal offering remained calm even though they had no idea what to do. The crowd of people felt ashamed and blamed [the temple]; it was deeply shameful for the guests who were not close to the temple. [Tong]da said, "[The meal] offering was sent to another place. The plan is true!" At [meal] time the monks and nuns who were afraid of their faults were about to leave. Suddenly they saw that carts and carriages loaded with cooked food and beautiful meals were lined up one after another, filling the road, coming swiftly. Everything was plentiful. The surplus was offered to the [temple] storehouse and further provided to many people. After the meal, the people and carriages all disappeared in an instant. They investigated from where [the people and carriages] had come, but in the end it remained unknown. Truly because it is difficult for either wise or ignorant people to clarify the reasons for such events, the salvific activity from the unseen world revealed mysterious offerings. The government and the people all revered [Tongda]. It would be endless to narrate all the stories [about Tongda].

(The eight stories above are found in the *Biographies of Eminent Monks* compiled in the Tang dynasty [*Tang Gaoseng zhuan*].)

[Wang Huaizhi, Supreme Pillar of State of the Tang Dynasty]

Wang Huaizhi, Supreme Pillar of State of the Tang Dynasty, was from Fangzhou (in present-day Shaanxi province) and died at the beginning of the Xianqing era (656). His mother, née Sun, and his brothers Huaishan and Huaibiao all survived.

In the sixth month of the fourth year [of the Xianqing era] (659), in Gaoling county in Yongzhou (in present-day Shaanxi province), a person, whose name is unknown, died. After seven days had passed the back of his body was already decaying, yet he revived. This person had met Huaizhi underground [in the netherworld].

[Huaizhi] said [to him], "My present post is Office Manager of Mount Tai." [Huaizhi] released him in order to write down what he said in a letter. [Huaizhi] said to the man, "Even though you have truly died, I will now let you return home as an expedient. Take this letter, go to Fangzhou, visit all the people of my house for my sake, and give [the letter to my mother,] which reads, 'I, Huaizhi, am currently Administrative Supervisor of Mount Tai. I am fortunately placed under safety. My family, however, once borrowed a tree from a monastery to make a gate for the house. Since the [tree] was a thing of merit, I must ask you to reciprocate and compensate for it quickly. Otherwise, Huaishan will die. It is improper to remain for a long time. Copy a sutra and make a [buddha] image promptly to relieve [Huaishan], or I am afraid there is no other law that can help him.'"

After the man had completely revived, he took the letter and delivered it to [Huaizhi's] house. The household incident discussed [in the letter] entirely agreed with [the facts]. Three days later Huaishan suddenly died.

Every Buddhist and layperson in [Fang]zhou and [Yong]zhou who heard of this increased their cultivation for merit. Hou Zhichun, a man from a good family for distinguished service in Fuzhou (in present-day Shaanxi province), spoke of this.

(This story is found in the *Gleanings of Anecdotes of Rewards and Retributions from the Unseen World* [*Mingbao shiyiji*].)

[End of] Fascicle Thirty-three of *A Forest of Pearls from the Dharma Garden*

Fascicle 34

548c

Chapter Twenty-eight

Contemplation

(This chapter consists of two parts:) (1) Introduction, and (2) Quoted Testimonies.

1. Introduction

I think that it is difficult to suppress worldly feelings, which can be compared to wild monkeys that always follow the external world or similar to violent elephants. The three kinds of acts [of body, speech, and mind] throb, and a condition brings the manifestation [of worldly feelings]. Therefore, the Buddha established the teaching that causes people to always control themselves. Consequently, [the *Nirvana*] *Sutra* says:

> You must be the master of your own mind and not allow your mind to master you. Do not keep company with evil in bodily, verbal, and mental acts. Observe the precepts bodily! Be wise mentally! Be immovable like a mountain!

Furthermore, the sutra (i.e., the *Fochui banniepan lüeshuo jiaojie jing,* T. 389) says, "If you control [the mind] in one place, everything can be discerned." The nature of the mind, however, is deluded and perverted. Ego comes first.

It is difficult to regulate the defilements. Confusion causes one to act even in ordinary occasions. At all times excitement should be allayed. Other than relying on the tranquil world and placing yourself there, [you should] break and subdue the three poisons. Do not bodily wander about! Maintain silence! Take less sleep! Be more awake! Sit continually and reduce your consumption during meals! Contemplate the true Dharma and know that [phenomena are] neither existence nor nonexistence. Hold yourself upright! Rectify your mind!

Concentrate your thoughts! Then [what you seek] will be in front of you. Teachings like these are called contemplation.

2. Quoted Testimonies

Just as the *Zengyi ahan jing* says:

> At that time the World-honored One said to all the *bhikṣu*s, "You must cultivate the ten thoughts. You will then achieve supernatural powers, leave behind all confused thoughts, and attain nirvana. The first refers to recollection of the Buddha (Pāli *buddhānussati*); the second refers to recollection of the Dharma (Pāli *dhammānussati*); the third refers to recollection of the Sangha (Pāli *saṅghānussati*); the fourth refers to recollection of the precepts (Pāli *sīlānussati*); the fifth refers to recollection of almsgiving (Pāli *cāgānussati*); the sixth refers to recollection of heavenly beings (Pāli *devatānussati*); the seventh refers to recollection of cessation (Pāli *upassamānussati*); the eighth refers to recollection of the counting-breath meditation (Pāli *ānāpānasati*); the ninth refers to recollection of the impermanence of the physical body (Pāli *kāyagatāsati*); and the tenth refers to recollection of death (Pāli *maraṇasati*).
>
> "You must thoroughly cultivate:
>
> Recollection of the Buddha, Dharma, and Sangha,
> Recollection of the precepts, almsgiving, and heavenly beings,
> Recollection of cessation and the counting-breath meditation,
> And recollection of the physical body and death that come later."
>
> [The *Zengyi ahan jing* continues,]
>
> First, regarding recollection of the Buddha, exclusively think of the Buddha, the Tathāgata's features, the completeness of his merits, the limitlessness of his body and wisdom, and his omniscience about the transmigration of birth and death. If you cultivate this teaching you will spontaneously attain nirvana. Do not neglect recollection of the Buddha and you will attain merits. This is called recollection of the Buddha.
>
> Second, regarding recollection of the Dharma, if you devotedly think of the Dharma you will remove all defilements of the realm of desire and
> 549a have no evil passions, and further you will not give rise to the mind of

deluded attachment like thirst (Skt. *tṛṣṇā*). You will have no desire in [the realm of] desire and leave behind diseases of all defilements (Skt. *bandhana* and *nivaraṇa*). [This teaching] is just like various fragrances. There is no defective or confused thought. [If you cultivate this teaching,] you will then achieve supernatural powers and spontaneously attain nirvana. Ponder this, do not go against [recollection of the Dharma], and you will attain merits. This is called recollection of the Dharma.

Third, regarding recollection of the Sangha, this refers to devotedly thinking of the Tathāgata's sangha, which accomplishes [wholesome acts]. The nature [of the members of the sangha] is upright; they have no evil or perversion in their nature. They make peace between the upper and lower ranks. The Tathāgata's sangha consists of those of the eight stages of sainthood [of the Hinayana]. You must respect and serve them. [If you cultivate this teaching] you will remove all confused thoughts and spontaneously attain nirvana. Do not go against recollection of the Sangha and you will attain merits. This is called recollection of the Sangha.

Fourth, regarding recollection of the precepts, what are called the precepts put an end to all evils. Therefore, the precepts enable people to attain buddhahood and cause them to be happy. The precepts adorn the body and reveal many good points. Therefore, [the precepts] are just like the bottle of good fortune (*jixiang ping*). What you wish can easily be accomplished. [If you cultivate this teaching] you will remove all confused thoughts and spontaneously attain nirvana. Do not go against recollection of the precepts and you will attain merits. This is called recollection of the precepts.

Fifth, regarding recollection of almsgiving, this refers to devotedly thinking of almsgiving. [You should think,] "What I now give is the utmost in almsgiving." If you do not feel regret [for your almsgiving] eternally and if you do not expect a reward [for almsgiving], you will pleasantly attain great benefit. Even if someone scolds and slanders you, or even if [a mob] raises swords or sticks against you, you must give rise to benevolence. Do not become angry! [Think,] "Whatever I give, the intention for almsgiving will not come to an end." [If you cultivate this teaching] you will remove all confused thoughts and spontaneously attain nirvana. Do not go against recollection of almsgiving and you will attain merits. This is called recollection of almsgiving.

Sixth, regarding recollection of heavenly beings, this refers to devotedly thinking of heavenly beings, whose acts of body, speech, and mind are pure, who do not make filthy acts, who observe the precepts and fulfill themselves, who emit light from their bodies and shine everywhere. Achieve the body of such a heavenly being! Good acts bring rewards. Achieve the body of a heavenly being and completely possess numerous practices! [If you cultivate this teaching] you will remove all confused thoughts and spontaneously attain nirvana. Do not neglect recollection of heavenly beings and you will attain merits. This is called recollection of heavenly beings.

Seventh, regarding recollection of cessation, this refers to the cessation of mental functions. If you ascertain the determination and temperament to attain buddhahood (Skt. *āśaya-saṃpadā*) and also are not short-tempered, if you always concentrate your mind and are delighted with a quiet life, if you seek an expedient way at all times and enter *samādhi,* and if you keep in mind the avoidance of greed, then the superb light will reach the higher authorities. You will remove all confused thoughts and spontaneously attain nirvana. Do not neglect recollection of cessation and you will attain merits. This is called recollection of cessation.

Eighth, regarding recollection of the counting-breath meditation, this refers to devotedly thinking of the counting-breath meditation. When you take a long breath, you should observe it and know, "I now breathe for a long time." When you take a short breath, you should also observe it and know, "I now breathe for a short time."' If your breath is extremely cold or extremely hot, you should also observe that and know, "My breath is now cold or hot." If you discern the exhalation and inhalation of the breath and count the length and brevity of your breaths, you will remove all confused thoughts and spontaneously attain nirvana. Do not neglect recol-
549b lection of the counting-breath meditation and you will attain merits. This is called recollection of the counting-breath meditation.

Ninth, regarding recollection of the physical body, this refers to devotedly thinking of the physical body, such as the hair, nails, teeth, skin, flesh, bones, muscles, the gall, the liver, the lungs, the heart, the spleen, the kidneys, the colon, the small intestine, the chest, the bladder, bodily waste, the stomach, the movement of the bowels, diarrhea, urine, tears, spit, nasal mucus, pus, blood, the fat, saliva, the skull, and the brain. What comprises the physical body? It consists of the earth seed, the water seed, the fire seed, and the wind seed. Is it entirely what one's parents created? From where did it come? Who created it? Where will the six sense organs of the body be produced after [one's life] comes to an end? [If you cultivate this teaching] you will remove all confused thoughts and spontaneously attain nirvana. Do not neglect recollection of the physical body and you will attain merits. This is called recollection of the physical body.

Tenth, regarding recollection of death, this refers to devotedly thinking of death. You die here and will be reborn over there, transmigrating through all the paths. Your life departs and never stays [in one place]. All the sense organs break apart and decay, just like decomposing wood. Life is cut off and the eighteen elements for human existence (Skt. *gotra*) separate. There is no form and no sound. There is no countenance, either. [If you cultivate this teaching] you will remove all confused thoughts and spontaneously attain nirvana. Do not neglect recollection of death and you will attain merits. This is called recollection of death.

Then, [the Buddha] also spoke in verse,

Starting with [recollection of] the Buddha, Dharma, and Sangha,
It continues to recollection of death at the end.
Even though [each one] is the same term in its beginning,
Their meaning differs from the others.

Furthermore, the *Fenbie gongde lun* (T. 1507) says:

First, what matter is recollection of the Buddha? The Buddha's body is as hard as diamond and has no defilement at all. When he steps, his feet are at four *cun* above the ground. The footprint with a thousand-wheel pattern appears on the ground. All insects under his footsteps are peaceful for seven days. If they die, they will attain rebirth in heaven.

In ancient times there was an evil *bhikṣu* who was originally a heretic. Taking advantage of a [monk's] robe he tried to slander [the Buddha] and followed after the Tathāgata wherever he went. He killed flying insects, put them on the Buddha's footprints, and said that the Buddha had trampled on them. Even though the insects died, since they had met with the sites where the Buddha left his footprints they could soon revive. When [the Buddha] entered a city and stepped through the doorsill of a city gate, heaven and earth greatly shook, and all kinds of music spontaneously sounded without any players. All those who were deaf, blind, dumb, or had numerous diseases were naturally restored to health. Those who saw the Buddha's major and minor marks of physical excellence attained liberation in accordance with their practices. It is impossible to enumerate points delivered by [the Buddha's] merits. Generally speaking, [the Buddha] comprehends myriad acts and takes ferrying [beings to the yonder shore] as the primary act. This is what is called recollection of the Buddha. Its significance is just like this.

Second, regarding recollection of the Dharma, the Dharma is the path of no defilement, the transcendent state (*wuwei;* Skt. *asaṃskṛta*), and no desire. The Buddha is the lord of all phenomenal things, and the Dharma is the lord of defilements.

The Dharma brings out all buddhas. The Dharma produced the Buddhist Way. [Question:] "If this is so, why doesn't recollection of the Dharma come first? Why does it come after recollection of the Buddha?" Answer: "[Because] the Dharma is subtle; there is no one who can understand it.
549c It is just like valuables that are hidden in the earth everywhere, but one must rely on an experienced person who can indicate the place [they are hidden], who can obtain them and spontaneously save one from destitution. The Dharma is also like this. Even though the truth is profound, only the Tathāgata can explicate it. Therefore, recollection of the Buddha comes first. The Dharma in accord with reason comes after it.

Third, regarding recollection of the Sangha, [the sangha] refers to those of the eight stages of sainthood [in the Hinayana] and the twelve men of high moral standing,[250] who forsake greed and the disputes of the world, who edify and guide [sentient beings] to the paths of heavenly and human beings. This is because they are precisely a good, helpful field of merit for sentient beings.

In ancient times there was a *bhikṣu* of little merit called Brahmadatta (Fanmoda; in vinaya texts he is called Luoxunyu Bhikṣu.) He was in a group of one thousand two hundred fifty monks, and he caused all the monks to be unable to eat. No one knew whose fault it was. The Buddha divided the sangha into two groups. One group was provided food but the other was not. Again the group that did not get any food was divided into two groups, and one of these groups obtained food while the other did not. In this way, after repeated division it came down to two monks, one of whom obtained food but the other (i.e., Brahmadatta) did not. [Brahmadatta] then realized he had no merit. Even if he could take up a bowl, [all the food in the bowl] spontaneously dispersed. The Buddha had compassion for his hardship, and with his own hands placed food in the bowl. Due to [the Buddha's] supernatural powers, [the food] did not disappear. The Buddha wished to cause [Brahmadatta's] current body to attain merit. Therefore, he ordered two *bhikṣu*s who had destroyed defilements [to stay by his side], and [Brahmadatta] was to feed these [two *bhikṣu*s] to the full. [Brahmadatta] promptly attained merit.

At that time King Prasenajit heard that this [*bhikṣu*] was of little merit and that the Buddha had taken pity on him and given him food. [The king thought,] "I should also now provide merit for him." He immediately sent [a messenger] to polish rice [to offer to the monk]. At that point a crow flew in, took a grain of rice in its beak, and flew off. The messenger scolded it in a loud voice, "The king has [given this rice to] provide merit for Brahmadatta. Why did you take it away?" The crow promptly returned [the rice] to its original place. The reason for that is this *bhikṣu* was placed under the power of the sangha's merit and [therefore] birds and beasts could not infringe on him.

Because of this testimony we know that [the sangha] is a good field of merit. They have already liberated themselves, liberate other people, and come to the paths of the three vehicles. Regarding the Dharma of recollection of the Sangha, its significance is just like this.

Fourth, regarding recollection of the precepts, everything from the five precepts, the ten wholesome precepts, and the two hundred and fifty precepts to the five hundred precepts prohibits bodily and verbal acts, restrains all evils, controls the six sense organs, and cuts off all desires. If you are clean within and without you will comply with the nature of the precepts.

In ancient times there were two *bhikṣu*s who were coming together to the Buddha's place. On their way they came to a broad marsh. Suddenly [they found] they were short of drinkables. Then there was a small pond, but the water of the pond was full of numerous insects. One of the *bhikṣu*s deeply thought of the precepts and took nonviolation to them to be primary. [He thought,] "If I drink this water I will destroy very many lives. I would rather accomplish [the observance of] the precepts and die." Thereupon, he died and was reborn in heaven. The other *bhikṣu* thought to himself, "If I drink water and stay alive, I can arrive at the Buddha's place. How can I know in what realm I will be reborn after death?" He drank the water with insects, and [numerous insects] were killed [in this way]. Even though he was then able to go and see the Buddha, he was far away from [the Buddha's] teaching.[251]

Facing the Buddha, [the *bhikṣu*] wailed in grief and said, "My companion died!" The Buddha said, pointing to a heavenly being, "Do you know this heavenly being? This is your [former] companion. For the merit
550a of his accomplishment of observing the precepts, he was reborn in heaven and now came and stays here. Although you see me, you are very far away from me. Even though he lost his life, he is always at my place. You now see me, but actually you only see my physical body. How could you know the true precepts?"

For this reason, a sutra says:[252]

The code of the precepts (Skt. *prātimokṣa*) are your great teacher. If you can observe the precepts and practice them over and over again, then the Dharma body of the Tathāgata permanently dwells and it is eternal.

There are three kinds of precepts. The first is the precepts for the eight kinds of beings (Skt. *pratimokṣa-saṃvara;* i.e., *kṣatriyā,* brahman, lay believers, *śramaṇa*s, the four heavenly kings, beings in Trāyastriṃśa, demons, and beings in Brahma Heaven), the second is the undefiled precepts (Skt. *anāsrava-saṃvara*), and the last is the meditation precepts (Skt. *dhyāna-saṃvara*). The precepts that comprise the five precepts, the eight precepts, and the ten wholesome precepts are for the eight kinds of beings. Purity and the fourfold noble truths are the undefiled precepts. *Samādhi* and *dhyāna* are the meditation precepts.

[The *Fenbie gongde lun* says:]

If you manage the precepts with wisdom and achieve purity, then it suits the undefiled precepts. The *śrāvaka*'s precepts are compared to flowers resting on one's knee; when [the knee] moves they disperse. The precepts *mahāsattva*s observe are compared to flowers fixed onto one's hair; when that person moves or stops, they are stable. The Hinayana [precepts] restrict one's form. When one moves, he transgresses a rule. *Mahāsattva*s understand the mind and are not concerned about the rules for external matters, because the Mahayana rules and the Hinayana rules differ from each other. The form and the mind differ from each other. Even though the inside and the outside differ from each other, both attain nirvana. Therefore, this is called recollection of the precepts.

Moreover, the *Fo banniyuan jing* (T. 6) says:

Furthermore, if you want a shorter way, you must have the four kinds of happiness that you should keep in mind and practice well. The first is to think of the Buddha, to be happy, and to not leave behind [this happiness]. The second is to think of the Dharma, to be happy, and to not leave behind [this happiness]. The third is to think of the sangha, to be happy, and to not leave behind [this happiness]. The fourth is to think of the precepts, to be happy, and to not leave behind [this happiness]. If you think of these four kinds of happiness, you will certainly come to completely possess them and spontaneously have clear views. You must wish for right liberation and seek emancipation. Surely you can remove and cut off [rebirth in] hell and the realms of animals and hungry ghosts. Even if you transmigrate in heaven and the realm of human beings, you will attain the termination of suffering (i.e., liberation) in less than seven existences.

The [*Da biqiu*] *sanqian weiyi* (T. 1470) further says:

There are five matters that you must think about. First, you must think of the Buddha's merits. Second, you must think of the Buddha's Dharma and Vinaya. Third, you must think of the Buddha's wisdom. Fourth, you must think that the Buddha's favor is great and hardly requited. Fifth, you must think of the Buddha's diligence leading to nirvana. Additionally there are five more matters. First, you must think of the *bhikṣu* sangha. Second, you must think of your teacher's favor. Third, you must think of your parents' favor. Fourth, you must think of your fellow students' favor.

Fifth, you must think to liberate all people and cause them to leave behind all suffering.

Moreover, the [*Foshuo*] *Chuchu jing* (T. 730) says:

[The Buddha said to Ānanda,] "For instance, it is just as you cannot count and know how many grains of sand there are in an ocean. It is again impossible to enumerate the good and evil or fortune and misfortune that people create from beginning to end. It is necessary to exhaust [all that they make] while you are alive. If you commit evil deeds, you will encounter evil realms. If you perform good acts, you will meet good realms. All fortune and misfortune have their grounds in advance. Similarly, if beforehand you have parents, brothers, wife, children, and dependents, they may hinder your attainment of enlightenment. If you do not attain enlightenment, then you will not sever [good and evil acts]."

The Buddha said to *bhikṣu*s, "You must think that your body is imper-
550b manent." A *bhikṣu* immediately responded to the Buddha,, "I think that impermance is namely the human life span, which can be at most fifty years." The Buddha said, "Do not say that!" Another *bhikṣu* said, "It could be thirty years!" The Buddha said, "Do not say that!" There was another *bhikṣu* who said, "It could be ten years." The Buddha said, "Do not say that!" Yet another *bhikṣu* said, "It could be a year." The Buddha said, "Do not say that!" Again a *bhikṣu* said, "It could be a month." The Buddha said, "Do not say that!" Another *bhikṣu* said, "It could be a day." The Buddha said, "Do not say that!" Furthermore another *bhikṣu* said, "It could be a moment." The Buddha said, "Do not say that!" Then a *bhikṣu* said, "It could be as brief as taking a breath." The Buddha said, "Correct!" The Buddha said, "Before the breath you just exhaled returns, you belong to your next life. Human life goes as swiftly as the brief time of taking a breath."

The *Pinimu jing* furthermore says:

Similarly, a *bhikṣu* who preaches the Dharma should also always think and contemplate that the physical body is of suffering, impermanence, nonself, and impurity. He should not discontinue [this practice]. Why? Because he must attain the twelve thoughts and accomplish the sacred Dharma. What are the twelve thoughts? The first is to think to fulfill yourself. The second is to think to complete others. The third is to think and pray to obtain a human body. The fourth is to think to be reborn in a family of good lineage. The fifth is to think to be able to give rise to faith in the Buddhist Dharma. The sixth is to think to attain enlightenment without attaining more merits in the place where you are reborn. The seventh is to think to completely possess all the sense organs in the place where you are reborn. The eighth is to think to meet the Buddha, the World-honored One, when he appears in the world. The ninth is to think to be able to preach the true Dharma always in the place where you are reborn. The tenth is to think and pray that the Dharma you preach is able to continually exist forever. The eleventh is to think and pray that the Dharma exists eternally and you are able to cultivate yourself by following it. The twelfth is to think to always attain the mind of compassion for all sentient beings. If you are able to completely possess these twelve thoughts with intent, you will certainly attain the sacred Dharma.

Moreover, the *Za ahan jing* says:

At that time the World-honored One said to all the *bhikṣu*s, "In a past world, there was some grass in a river where a turtle lived. On one occasion, a fox (*yegan*) was roaming about with an empty stomach and looking for food. [The fox] saw the turtle from a distance and swiftly came to catch it. The turtle saw [the fox] coming and promptly retracted its six body parts (i.e., head, tail, and four limbs) [into its shell]. The fox waited and watched, hoping that [the turtle] would put out its head and feet, as it wanted to catch and eat [the turtle]. [The fox] watched the turtle for a long time, but [the turtle] did not put out its head and feet during that time. The fox, starving, left in a fury.

"All *bhikṣu*s! Today you are just like that [turtle]. Be aware that Māra-pāpīyān always watches your doings. He hopes that your eyes will catch color and form, your ears will hear sounds, your nose will smell odors, your tongue will taste with relish, your body will contact external objects, and that you will think of phenomenal things in your mind. He wants to cause you to give rise to attachment to the objects of the six sense organs (i.e., color and form, sound, odor, taste, tangible objects, and mental objects). For this reason, *bhikṣu*s, today you must always hold fast to the 550c precepts regarding the eyes and abide by them. If you hold fast to the precepts regarding the faculty of sight, the devil cannot take advantage of you. Follow [the precepts] and come out! Follow [the precepts and] be conditioned! [The precepts regarding] the ears, nose, tongue, tactile body, and mind are also like this. [If you hold fast to the precepts] regarding the six sense organs, even if you come out or you are conditioned, [the devil] cannot take advantage of you, just as the fox was not able to take advantage of the turtle."

At that time the World-honored One said in verse:

A turtle was afraid of a fox
And retracted its six body parts into its shell.
If a *bhikṣu* is skillful in concentrating the mind,
He will secretly hide all thoughts (Skt. *tarka*).
Do not rely on that [devil]!
Do not be afraid of him!
Hide the mind and do not make a statement!

[The *Za ahan jing* says:]

At that time the World-honored One said to all the *bhikṣu*s, "For instance, it is just as when a learned person walks up and down a vacant house he obtains six kinds of sentient beings. First, he obtains a dog and then keeps it tied up at a place. Next, he obtains a bird. Next, he obtains a poisonous snake. Next, he obtains a fox (*yegan*). Next, he obtains a *śiśumāra*.[253] Next, he obtains a rhesus monkey. He obtains these sentient beings and keeps all of them tied up at one place.

The dog wishes to go into a village. The bird always wants to fly in the sky. The snake always wants to go into a hole. The fox wishes to go to a graveyard. The *śiśumāra* wants to be in the sea for a long time. The rhesus monkey wants to be in a forest on a mountain. These six sentient beings are all tied at one place, but each desires to go to a place where they may be content. None [of the animals] is happy since they are tied elsewhere. Each employs their own power to go in the direction of the place they seek, but they cannot escape. Just in this way, among the various objects of the six sense organs, each [sense organ] seeks an object that it wishes for and does not seek other objects. The eyes always seek pleasing color and form; they give rise to aversion toward the color and form to which they cannot incline. The ears, nose, tongue, tactile body, and mind are also like this. In the various spheres of activities of these six kinds of sense organs, none seeks the objects of the other sense organs. The powerful one [among these six kinds of sense organs] is capable of freely perceiving objects, just as the learned person tied the six sentient beings [at one place]. For this reason, you must diligently study and learn the contemplation on the physical body as defiled (Skt. *kāya-smṛty-upasthāna*)."

At that time, the World-honored One said to all the *bhikṣu*s, "For instance, suppose four atrocious and extremely poisonous pit vipers are contained in a box. On one occsion there is a learned person who is bright, seeks happiness, detests suffering, seeks existence, and detests death. Another learned person says to him, "If you were to take the vipers out of this box, rub them, wipe them, bathe them, treat them tenderly and intimately, raise them, and feed them, then you need the proper timing to take them out of [the box] and return them to it. If these four poisonous vipers escape and cause trouble, they might kill you or cause you to nearly die. You must protect yourself." [This person adds, "Five enemies will draw their swords, chase you, and want to kill you. You must protect yourself."] At that time, the first learned person becomes afraid of the four poisonous vipers and the five enemies who [chase after him] with drawn swords [in their hands] and quickly runs away.

"Someone further tells the learned person, 'You have six internal rebels that follow you and wait for a chance; if they get a chance, they will kill you. You should protect yourself.' At that time the learned person is afraid 551a
of the four poisonous vipers, the five enemies who [chase after him] with drawn swords [in their hands], and the six internal rebels. He swiftly runs away in fear and returns to a deserted village, where he sees that his vacant house is dangerously in decay and ruined. There are various ferocious things. He grasps for them, but everything is precarious and fragile; nothing is firm.

"The man again says to the learned man, 'This is a deserted village. Six thieves will come and certainly attack you by surprise.' At that time, the learned person is afraid of the four poisonous vipers, the five enemies who [chase after him] with drawn swords [in their hands], the six evil internal rebels, and the group of thieves in the deserted village. He again swiftly runs away.

"Suddenly the road comes to a large river. Its water is deep and flows rapidly. He only sees that there are various fears on this shore, but he sees peace, happiness, purity, and no fear on the yonder shore. There is, however, no bridge and no boat by which he can cross over and reach the yonder shore. He thinks, 'I will gather grass and tree [branches], bind them, and make a raft. Resorting to the expedient of using my hands and feet [to paddle], I will cross over to the yonder shore.' After thinking this, he collects grass and tree [branches] and on the shore [of the river] he binds them to make a raft. Using his hands and feet as an expedient means he crosses the swiftly running river to the other side. In this way the learned person avoids the four poisonous vipers, the five enemies who [chase after him] with drawn swords [in their hands], and the six evil internal rebels. Also he is able to escape from the group of thieves in the deserted village. He crosses over the rapid stream and leaves behind the various fears on this shore. He is able to reach peace and happiness on the yonder shore.

"I have spoken this simile. You must understand its meaning. O *bhikṣu*s! The box is compared to the coarse four great elements of this physical body. The body of pure blood made from the four great elements is filthy; it grows and is nourished by food, bathes, and wears clothes. It is an impermanent, deteriorating, and fragile thing.

"The poisonous vipers are compared to the four great elements of earth, water, fire, and wind. If you are at variance with the earth element, it can cause your body to die or to nearly die. If you are at variance with the water, fire, or wind elements, they can also act like this.

"The five enemies who [chase after him] with drawn swords [in their hands] are compared to the five *skandha*s. The six internal rebels are compared to the six [feelings], such as love and pleasure. The deserted village is compared to the six sense organs. When we observe, what meets our eyes are impermanent, deteriorating, and spurious things. The ears, nose, tongue, tactile body, and mind are also like this. The group of thieves in the deserted village is compared to objects of the six sense organs. The eyes are pleasantly or unpleasantly harmed by [perceiving] color and form. The ears and sounds, the nose and odors, the tongue and tastes, the tactile body and tangible objects, and the mind and its objects are also like this. The rapid stream is compared to the four rapid currents of the defilements (Skt. *catur-ogha*): the rapid current of defilements except views and ignorance in the realm of desire, the rapid current of defilements except views and ignorance in the realms of form and nonform, the rapid current of defilements in the three realms of existence, and the rapid current of defilements that washes away the wholesome Dharma. The river is compared to three kinds of cravings: craving in the realm of desire, craving in the realm of form, and craving in the realm of nonform. The numerous fears on this shore are compared to having a physical body. Being nice and cool and comfortable on the yonder shore is compared to complete nirvana. The raft is compared to the eightfold holy path. To cross the swiftly running river to the other side resorting to the expedient of using one's hands and feet is compared to being able to reach the yonder shore through heroic effort. The brahman's residence is compared to the Tathāgata, Arhat, Samyak-saṃbuddha."

Furthermore, the *Muhuanzi jing* (T. 786) says:[254] 551b

At one time there was a king, called Boliuli,[255] whose kingdom had many hardships. He said to the Buddha, "My kingdom is small and remote and it is invaded by bandits every year. The five staple grains soar in price. An epidemic prevails. The people are in great distress, and I am always uneasy. The store of the Dharma (i.e., all the Buddhist teachings) is profound and extensive, but I cannot cultivate it. I pray that you will have compassion for me and bestow the key points of the Dharma to me."

The Buddha said to the king, "If you want to exterminate defilements and hindrances, you must string a hundred and eight seeds from a *bodhi* tree on a thread [to make prayer beads (Skt. *japamālā*)], always keep [the beads] with you, follow your utmost mind, do not let [the beads] scatter, and chant, 'I take refuge in the Buddha, Dharma, and Sangha.' [With each recitation,] you pass one *bodhi* seed on the string. In this way you will count the *bodhi* seeds piece by piece, ten, twenty, a hundred, a thousand, up to ten million times. If you can fulfill [this practice] two hundred thousand times, if your body and mind do not fall into disorder, and you go against perverting your mind in order to flatter someone else, after death you will be able to be reborn in Yama Heaven, the third [of the six heavens in the realm of desire]. Clothes and food will be spontaneously provided, and you will have peaceful and easy practices there. If you can fulfill [this practice] a million times, you will remove the hundred and eight acts caused by defilement and attain highest fruition."

The king was happy to hear this [and said], "I will uphold the teaching and practice it." The Buddha said to the king, "Sātikaivartaputra Bhikṣu recited the names of the Three Treasures for ten years and attained the *sakṛdāgāmi-phala.* He studied step by step. Now he has become a *pratyeka-buddha* in the World of Universal Fragrance." On hearing this, the king redoubled his practice [of the teaching].

The *Xianyu jing* further says:

In Vārāṇasī there was a householder whose nickname was Gupta. This man had a son called Upagupta. When [Upagupta] grew up, his family was [still] in dire poverty. His father entrusted all his belongings to him and had him occupy a place to display and sell them. Then the arhat Sambhūta went to [Upagupta], preached the Dharma for him, taught him, and caused him to secure his thought. [Sambhūta said to Upagupta,] "Using white and black pebbles you should rate [your thoughts]. Put down a white [pebble] for a good thought and a black one for an evil thought." Upagupta respectfully received his instruction. Every time [Upagupta] had a good or evil thought, he placed a pebble. At first black [pebbles] dominated while white ones were very few in number. As he gradually studied and learned the number of white and black [pebbles] was the same. He did not stop securing his thought. Eventually there were no black pebbles, only white ones. His good state of mind was completely established and [Upagupta] came to attain the first of the four fruits (i.e., *srota-āpatti-phala*).

Moreover, the *Piyu jing* says:[256]

Formerly there was a man who neither believed in nor respected [the Buddha], while his wife cordially worshiped the Buddha. She said to her husband, "Human life is impermanent. You should cultivate good conduct." Her husband had no such intention and was lazy. The wife was afraid that he would fall into hell in the future. So she addressed him again, "I would like to hang a bell on the door. Whenever you go in and out, the hanging bell will make a sound. [At the sound,] chant 'I take refuge in the Buddha!'" Her husband said, "Very good!" [and practiced] in this way for a long time. [Eventually] he died [and fell into hell].

A hell warden, using a two-pronged weapon, threw him into a cauldron full of hot water. When the two-pronged weapon struck the cauldron it made a sound. The man thought it was the sound of the bell and chanted, "I take refuge in the Buddha!" An official of hell heard this [and said,] 551c
"This person respects the Buddha. Release him and let him go out of here!" [The husband then] attained rebirth in the human realm.

Furthermore, the *Za piyu jing* (T. 207) says:

Formerly there were five hundred merchants who boarded a ship and went to sea. They encountered a *makara* (a mythological huge fish). [The *makara*] stuck out its head and opened its mouth, wishing to eat the sentient beings.

On that day the wind had lulled, yet the ship went as fast as an arrow. The chief of the marine caravan said to all the people, "The ship is going too fast. We should lower a sail." Thereupon, just as he said, a sail was lowered. The ship then took a turn and continued to sail on; it could not be stopped. The chief of the marine caravan asked the man who was on lookout, "What do you see there?" [The lookout answered,] "I see two suns rising above, a white mountain below, and a black mountain in the middle." The chief of the marine caravan said, surprised, "That is a big fish. What should we do now? We have encountered dire straits. If we go into the fish's stomach there is no way for us to survive. Each of you, follow whatever you worship and pray wholeheartedly!" Then everyone followed whatever they respected, wholeheartedly took refuge in it, and prayed to escape from the hardship. The more seriously they prayed, the more swiftly the ship went, not stopping even for a moment. [The ship] then went toward the fish's [open] mouth.

At that moment the chief of the marine caravan said to all the people, "I serve a great deity whose name is Buddha. Each of you, give up the deity you worship and wholeheartedly recite his name!" At that time the five hundred people together cried out in a loud voice, "We take refuge in the Buddha!" The *makara* heard the name of the Buddha and thought, "Today the Buddha is again in the world. Why must I mercilessly harm sentient beings?" [The *makara*] immediately shut its mouth and all the water rushed backward. [The ship] turned around and sailed away from the fish. The five hundred merchants immediately gave rise to a wholesome mind. Everyone attained liberation.

Furthermore, the [*Dafangdeng*] *daji jing* says:

For instance, it is just as a *śramaṇa* on whose head naturally hair grows does not know how long it grows in a day. In this way, a bodhisattva who gives rise to a sin is unable to know it personally and claims, "I am an innocent man."

Moreover, the *Za ahan jing* [says]:

At that time the World-honored One said in verse:

To be good at protecting
All bodily, verbal, and mental acts,
To be ashamed of your sins, and to prevent yourself from making them,
These are called to be good at guarding.

[The *Za ahan jing* also says:]

At that time the World-honored One said to all the *bhikṣus*, "There are two pure teachings that can protect the world. What are the two? They are what are called *can* and *kui*.[257] If these two pure teachings are not in the world, the people of the world also do not know the order of importance between father and mother, elder brother and younger brother, elder sister and younger sister, husband and wife or children, or among members of the same clan or leaders of government officials. [The world] will be as perverted and confused as the realm of animals."

Accordingly, the World-honored One said in verse:

If in the world there are not
The two teachings *can* and *kui*,
552a [The people] will disobey and transgress against the pure path

And head toward [the suffering of] birth, aging, sickness, and death.
If the people of the world accomplish
The two teachings *can* and *kui,*
They will increase and advance the pure path
And shut the gate of birth and death eternally.

The *Weiwu sanmei jing* (*Sutra of Devotedly Attending to Samādhi*) further says:[258]

The Buddha said to Ānanda, "Good man! If a person seeks the [Buddhist] Way and quietly sits in meditation, first he must cut off thoughts. People are born in the world, and those who do not attain the [Buddhist] Way merely sit and think. Filthy thoughts are numerous. Surely one thought comes and another thought goes. In one day and night you will have eight hundred and forty million thoughts. A thought arises every moment, without cessation. Those who have a single wholesome thought attain a good reward while those who have one unwholesome thought attain an evil retribution. It is just as an echo arises responding to the voice or as a shadow follows the form. For this reason, wholesomeness and unwholesomeness, or evil acts and meritorious deeds, differ from each other."

Verses say:

In meditation you forget a thought.
Having a thought is not the way to highest truth.
Arising external objects are thrown into the empty sky.
Why is the empty sky the place where one has deep emotion?
Entrusting myself to shade, I wander about the manifold darkness.
When the darkness is gone, images disappear.
Those on the [path of the] four stages of sainthood all gladly seek.
The One Vehicle teaching alone quietly vanishes.

Chapter Twenty-nine

Making a Vow

(This chapter consists of two parts:) (1) Introduction, and (2) Quoted Testimonies.

1. Introduction

The fruition of buddhahood is peerless. There is a flight of steps to ascend to it. The Dharma clouds are extremely lofty. There is an order to arrive at it. Therefore, if you establish great sincerity, the profound merit will bring you to highest fruition.

If you make a great vow for the first time, that wonderful vow will pervade until the end of future time. Start practicing wholeheartedly, and you will find the *uḍumbara* [flower] that blooms [once every three thousand years] for an enormously long time. Prudently bend your body for a short time, and you will obtain the nectar of the trichiliocosm. Perhaps this is the foundation of the Mahayana and a ferry and thoroughfare to the Buddha's wisdom.

2. Quoted Testimonies

Just as the *Amituo jing* (T. 361, T. 362; Skt. *Sukhāvatīvyūha*) says:

> The Buddha said to Ānanda, "When Amitābha Buddha was a bodhisattva, he always upheld and practiced twenty-four vows. He treasured, loved, valued, sustained, and submitted to them. What are the twenty-four vows?
>
> "The first vow: 'If and when I become a buddha, I will cause my land to be free of hells, animals, hungry ghosts, and species of wriggling and flying creatures. If I can fulfill this vow, then I will become a buddha. If I cannot, I will not become a buddha.'
>
> "The second vow: 'If and when I become a buddha, I will cause my land to be free of women. Females who wish to be reborn in my land will 552b
> become male. All of an infinite number of heavenly and human beings and species of wriggling and flying creatures who are coming to be reborn

in my land will be reborn transformed among the lotus flowers in the pond of the water of seven treasures. When they grow up they will all become bodhisattvas and arhats limitlessly. If I can fulfill this vow, then I will become a buddha. If I cannot, I will not become a buddha.'

"The third vow: 'If and when I become a buddha, I will cause my land to naturally be composed of the seven treasures, to be very extensive in length and breadth, to be boundless and limitless, to be naturally mild and good, and all houses, clothes, food, and drink will be provided spontaneously. This is just like the king's residence of the sixth heaven [in the realm of desire]. If I can fulfill this vow, then I will become a buddha. If I cannot, I will not become a buddha.'

"The fourth vow: 'If and when I become a buddha, I will cause my name to be completely heard in an infinite number of buddha lands in the ten directions, and I will entirely cause all the buddhas to speak of my merits and the wholesomeness of my land in a great assembly of the *bhikṣu* sangha. When all heavenly and human beings and species of wriggling and flying creatures hear my name, every being will be compassionate and dance with joy, and I will then cause them all to come to be reborn in my land. If I can fulfill this vow, then I will become a buddha. If I cannot, I will not become a buddha.'

"The fifth vow: 'If and when I become a buddha, I will cause all of an infinite number of heavenly and human beings as well as all the species of wriggling and flying creatures in the ten directions, even if they made evils in their former existences, who hear my name and who wish to be reborn in my land to return to the right path, to repent their sins in person, to practice wholesomeness for the [Buddhist] Way, to hold fast to the Dharma and Vinaya, and to pray and desire to be reborn in my land without cessation. I will cause them all to not return to hell and the realms of animals and hungry ghosts after death. Their rebirth in my land is precisely what I vow. If I can fulfill this vow, then I will become a buddha. If I cannot, I will not become a buddha.'

"The sixth vow: 'If and when I become a buddha, I will cause all heavenly and human beings and good men and good women in an infinite number of buddha lands in the ten directions to wish to be reborn in my land. Because they listen to me, they will create more wholesomeness, such as almsgiving, circumambulating stupas, burning incense, scattering flowers, lighting lamps, hanging various colored silk fabrics, offering food for *śramaṇa*s, erecting stupas, building monasteries, cutting off attachments and desires, purifying mind and body, and thinking of me purely and singleheartedly for a whole day and night without cessation. I will cause them all to come to be reborn in my land and to become bodhisattvas. If I can fulfill this vow, then I will become a buddha. If I cannot, I will not become a buddha.'

"The seventh vow: 'If and when I become a buddha, I will cause all heavenly and human beings and good men and women in an infinite number of buddha lands in the ten directions to be able to practice the bodhisattva way and to respectfully practice the six *pāramitā*s. If they become *śramaṇa*s, they will not give up the Dharma and Vinaya, will cut off attachment and desire, purify mind and body cleanly and singleheartedly, and think and wish to be reborn in my land day and night without cessation. When such people are about to die, I will fly to them and welcome them together with all the bodhisattvas and arhats. They will immediately come to be reborn in my land and become a bodhisattva in the stage of nonretrogression for realizing highest enlightenment (Skt. *avaivartya*), who is wise and brave. If I can fulfill this vow, then I will become a buddha. If I cannot, I will not become a buddha.' 552c

"The eighth vow: 'If and when I become a buddha, I will cause all the bodhisattvas in my land, if they wish to go to other buddha lands to be reborn, to not experience hell or the realms of animals and hungry ghosts. I will cause them all to attain the Buddhist Way. If I can fulfill this vow, then I will become a buddha. If I cannot, I will not become a buddha.'

"The ninth vow: If and when I become a buddha, I will cause all the bodhisattvas and arhats in my land to have regular features and to be clean and comely. They will all be of the same color and the same kind, just like beings of the sixth heaven [of the realm of desire]. If I can fulfill this vow, then I will become a buddha. If I cannot, I will not become a buddha.'

"The tenth vow: 'If and when I become a buddha, I will cause all the bodhisattvas and arhats in my land to have entirely the same mind. Whatever they think and whatever they are about to say, their intention will be mutually understood in advance. If I can fulfill this vow, then I will become a buddha. If I cannot, I will not become a buddha.'

"The eleventh vow: If and when I become a buddha, I will cause all the bodhisattvas and arhats in my land to never give rise to a licentious mind, to have no intention to think of women ultimately, and to have no anger and stupidity in the end. If I can fulfill this vow, then I will become a buddha. If I cannot, I will not become a buddha.'

"The twelfth vow: 'If and when I become a buddha, I will cause all the bodhisattvas and arhats in my land to have a wholesome mind, to mutually respect and love and to never hate one another ultimately. If I can fulfill this vow, then I will become a buddha. If I cannot, I will not become a buddha.'

"The thirteenth vow: 'If and when I become a buddha, I will cause all the bodhisattvas in my land to wish to make offerings together to an infinite number of buddhas in the ten directions. I will cause them all to promptly come flying, to desire and obtain all kinds of things spontaneously before them, to hold, use, and offer [these things] to all buddhas, to obtain all [the things for the buddhas] throughout, and to fly back to my land after-
553a ward before noon on the same day. If I can fulfill this vow, then I will become a buddha. If I cannot, I will not become a buddha.'

"The fourteenth vow: 'If and when I become a buddha, I will cause all the bodhisattvas and arhats in my land to spontaneously receive a meal of all flavors in their almsbowls made of the seven treasures before them just at the moment they are about to eat, and [the bowls] to naturally disappear after the meal. If I can fulfill this vow, then I will become a buddha. If I cannot, I will not become a buddha.'

"The fifteenth vow: 'If and when I become a buddha, I will cause all the bodhisattvas in my land to have a purplish gold-colored body and the thirty-two major and the eighty minor marks of physical excellence. I will cause them all to look like a buddha. If I can fulfill this vow, then I will become a buddha. If I cannot, I will not become a buddha.'

"The sixteenth vow: 'If and when I become a buddha, I will cause all the bodhisattvas and arhats in my land, when they speak, to sound just as if three hundred bells were tolling, to explain a sutra and chant a sutra while walking around, just as a buddha does. If I can fulfill this vow, then I will become a buddha. If I cannot, I will not become a buddha.'

"The seventeenth vow: 'If and when I become a buddha, I will cause myself to be ten times more skilled than all other buddhas in clairvoyance, hearing thoroughly, and flying. If I can fulfill this vow, then I will become a buddha. If I cannot, I will not become a buddha.'

"The eighteenth vow: 'If and when I become a buddha, I will cause myself to be ten times more skilled than all other buddhas in wisdom, explaining a sutra, and chanting a sutra while walking around. If I can fulfill this vow, then I will become a buddha. If I cannot, I will not become a buddha.'

"The nineteenth vow: 'If and when I become a buddha, I will cause all the heavenly and human beings and all the species of wriggling and flying creatures in an infinite number of buddha lands in the ten directions to entirely attain the path of human beings, to completely become *pratyekabuddha*s and arhats, and to practice meditation wholeheartedly. They may all wish to count and measure how many *kalpa*s my life span is. I will cause them all to know that no one can determine my life span. If I can fulfill this vow, then I will become a buddha. If I cannot, I will not become a buddha.'

"The twentieth vow: 'If and when I become a buddha, I will cause all the heavenly and human beings and all the species of wriggling and flying creatures in a hundred billion buddha lands in each of the ten directions to entirely become *pratyekabuddha*s and arhats and to practice meditation wholeheartedly. They may all wish to count all the bodhisattvas and arhats in my land and know how numerous they are. I will cause them all to know that no one can determine the number. If I can fulfill this vow, then I will become a buddha. If I cannot, I will not become a buddha.'

"The twenty-first vow: 'If and when I become a buddha, I will cause 553b
the life span of all the bodhisattvas and arhats in my land to be an infinite number of *kalpa*s. If I can fulfill this vow, then I will become a buddha. If I cannot, I will not become a buddha.'

"The twenty-second vow: 'If and when I become a buddha, I will cause all the bodhisattvas and arhats in my land to be entirely wise and brave, to know spontaneously their former lives, to limitlessly know of the wholesomeness and unwholesomeness they had in their past existence a trillion *kalpa*s ago, to be clairvoyant, to hear thoroughly, and to know of matters in the past, future, and present times in the ten directions. If I can fulfill this vow, then I will become a buddha. If I cannot, I will not become a buddha.'

"The twenty-third vow: 'If and when I become a buddha, I will cause all the bodhisattvas and arhats in my land to be entirely wise and brave and to have light emitting from the crown of their heads. If I can fulfill this vow, then I will become a buddha. If I cannot, I will not become a buddha.'

"The twenty-fourth vow: 'If and when I become a buddha, I will cause myself to emit light, extremely bright, from the crown of my head. [The light] will be a hundred trillion times brighter than that of the sun and moon and absolutely more brilliant than the light of all buddhas. Its brightness will shine on the lower regions of an infinite number of worlds, and everywhere will be greatly lightened. If all heavenly and human beings and all the species of wriggling and flying creatures, when they see my light, are compassionate and have wholesomeness, I will cause them all to come to be reborn in my land. If I can fulfill this vow, then I will become a buddha. If I cannot, I will not become a buddha.'"

The Buddha said to Ānanda, "When Amitābha Buddha was a bodhisattva he certainly upheld and practiced these twenty-four vows. He did not violate the path to enlightenment and completely abandoned property and sensual pleasures. He keenly sought the achievement of the vows. He accumulated merit and piled up virtue for an infinite number of *kalpa*s, and now he has become a buddha. He has completely fulfilled [these vows]. Do not forget his merit."

Moreover, the *Foshuo mie shifang ming jing* (T. 435; Skt. *Daśadhigandhakāravidhvaṃsana*) says:

At one time there was a boy of the Śākya clan called Mianshanyue.[259] He came and addressed the Buddha, "O Supreme Heavenly Being (Skt. *devātideva*)! Currently my parents are not peaceful [because] they are unjustly invaded and confused by a nonhuman being. Day and night they tried to sleep, but they are unable to rest peacefully. When they go in and out or go on a walk, they are annoyed and troubled. They often encounter the wicked nonhuman being who bewitches them with seductive charm. There is nothing to protect them. I simply pray that you, World-honored One, will tell me and show me the way to relieve them according to circumstances and cause them to be free of annoyance and harm." The Buddha said to Mianshanyue, "I will speak of the way to protect them for you."

The Buddha said, "Beyond eight thousand *nayuta*s of buddha lands east of here is the world called Bazhong-chenlao.[260] The buddha there is 553c
called Dengxing Tathāgata, and he expounds the Dharma at the present time.[261] If someone goes to the east, he must first bow his head to the ground, take refuge in, and make an offering to the buddha of the eastern direction. Then he will have no fear; nothing will dare aggress and confuse him. If there is something he wants to make, everything will be done as he wishes."

The Buddha said to the boy, "Beyond a billion hundred thousand buddha lands in the south from here is the world called Xiaomingdengyaotuo.[262] The buddha there is called Chufaxin nianlikongwei guiyichaoshou Tathāgata,[263] and he expounds the Dharma at the present time. If someone intends to go to the south, he must bow his head to the ground from a distance, take refuge in that buddha singlemindedly, and not leave [that buddha]. Then he will have no fear, and he will not encounter any distress."

The Buddha said to the boy, "Beyond all buddha lands as numerous as grains of sand in the Ganges River in the west from here is the world called Shanxuanze.[264] The buddha there is called Jingangbuji Tathāgata,[265] and he expounds the Dharma at the present time. If someone intends to go to the west, he must first bow his head to the ground and worship that buddha, and singleheartedly take refuge in [that buddha]. Then he will have no fear, and he will not encounter distress."

The Buddha said to the boy, "Beyond twenty thousand buddha lands in the north from here is the world called Juebian.[266] The buddha there is called Baozhishou Tathāgata,[267] and he expounds the Dharma at the present time. If someone intends to go to the north, [he must] set up a house and live there, bow his head to the ground, worship, and take refuge in that buddha. Then he will have no fear, and he will not encounter distress."

The Buddha said to the boy, "Beyond a hundred trillion buddha lands in the northeast from here is the world called Chisuonian.[268] The buddha there is called Huaimomandubu Tathāgata,[269] and he expounds the Dharma at the present time. If someone goes to the northeast, he must bow his head to the ground from a distance and take refuge in that buddha. If he attains peace in the place where he is, he will have no fear."

The Buddha said the boy, "Beyond as many buddha lands as twice the number of grains of sand in the Ganges River in the southeast from here is the world called Changzhaoyao.[270] The buddha there is called Chufaxin butui zhuanlun chengshou Tathāgata,[271] and he expounds the Dharma at the present time. If someone goes to the southeast, he must first bow his head to the ground, prostrate his body in worship, and wholeheartedly take refuge in [that buddha]. Later, if he continues, he will have no fear."

The Buddha said to the boy, "Beyond eighty thousand buddha lands in the southwest from here is the world called Fubaijiaolu.[272] The buddha there is called Baogai zhaokong Tathāgata,[273] and he expounds the Dharma at the present time. If someone goes to the southwest, he must first bow his head to the ground [to worship] the tathāgata of that direction, scatter flowers from a distance, and think of the noncharacteristics [of all phenomena]. Later, if he continues [traveling], he will have no fear."

554a The Buddha said to the boy, "Beyond as many buddha lands as six times the number of grains of sand in the Ganges River in the northwest from here is the world called Zhuqingjing.[274] The buddha there is called Kaihua Bodhisattva Tathāgata,[275] and he expounds the Dharma at the present time. If someone goes to the northwest, [he must] first worship that buddha, personally take refuge in [that buddha], repent his sins, and cultivate pure conduct. Later, if he renounces the world, he will have no fear."

The Buddha said to the boy, 'Beyond ninety-two *gai* buddha lands downward from here is the world called Nianwudao.[276] The buddha there is called Nian chufayi duanyi bayu Tathāgata,[277] and he expounds the Dharma at the present time. When someone intends to sit down or goes to bed at night, he must think of this tathāgata, bow his head to the ground, and personally take refuge in [this tathāgata]. If he always saves other sentient beings with a universal compassion, later whenever he sits down or sleeps, he will have no fear."

The Buddha said to the boy, "Beyond as many buddha lands as sixty times the number of grains of sand in the Ganges River upward from here is the world called Lizhukongju wuyouchusuo.[278] The buddha there is called Xiaoming dengchao wang Tathāgata,[279] and he expounds the Dharma at the present time. If someone rises from his seat, he must always worship that buddha. If he personally takes refuge in and makes an offering to [that buddha], he will have no fear and attain peace wherever he goes."

The Buddha said to the boy, "Whoever receives this sutra must hold, chant, read, recite, and explain it for others. [This sutra] completely possesses everything. It causes nothing to be deficient and diminish and everyone to promptly achieve whatever they have made a vow for. They will have no fear in the end. If they go before a county magistrate their rights will not be violated wrongly. Even if they encounter bandits they will not be harmed. Even if they enter into a big fire, it will be promptly extinguished. Even if they are caught in a flood they will not be drowned after all. [That person] is one whom no heavenly beings, dragons, spiritual beings, or harmful and evil spirits dare to offend, none among all evil animals dare to approach, and none among the mischievous spirits and monsters can annoy. Even if [such people] lead a quiet, solitary life, they are protected by the Tathāgata."

The Buddha spoke in this way. Śakra-devendra, the boy Shanmianyue, and others heard the sutra and were delighted. They bowed to [the Buddha] and withdrew.

The [*Pusa*] *dichi lun* (i.e., *Pusa dichi jing,* T. 1581; Skt. *Bodhisattva-bhūmi*) says:

> Regarding the vows made by bodhisattvas, it is briefly said that there are five kinds. First is the vow for awakening the aspiration for enlightenment. Second is the vow for rebirth. Third is the vow for the objective world. Fourth is the vow for equality. Fifth is the great vow.
>
> These bodhisattvas first resolve to attain supreme enlightenment. This is called the vow for awakening the aspiration for enlightenment. They make vows for the sake of sentient beings in the future. Therefore, in conformity with wholesomeness [bodhisattvas] come to be reborn. This is called the vow for rebirth. They make vows to correctly observe that all phenomenal things are immeasurably equal to the root of wholesomeness and to ponder the objective world. This is called the vow for the objective world. They make vows that in the future all bodhisattvas will regulate matters well. This is called the bodhisattvas' vow for equality. The great vow is precisely the vow for equality.

Bodhisattvas furthermore elucidate ten kinds of great vows:

554b First is the vow to offer all kinds of things immeasurably to all buddhas.

Second is the vow to protect and hold the true Dharma of all buddhas.

Third is the vow to clearly understand the true Dharma of all buddhas.

Fourth is the vow to be reborn in Tuṣita Heaven leading up to *parinirvāṇa.*

Fifth is the vow to perform all kinds of bodhisattvas' right practices.

Sixth is the vow to mature sentient beings.

Seventh is the vow to be able to manifest themselves in all worlds.

Eighth is the vow that all bodhisattvas wholeheartedly use expedient means and liberate [sentient beings] by means of the Mahayana.

Ninth is the vow for all right practices, expedient means, and non-hindrance.

Tenth is the vow to achieve highest, perfect enlightenment.

These bodhisattvas abide in the first stage. Having expedient means and pure faith they currently train themselves. They give rise to the ten great vows regarding future matters.

First, with a pure mind they continually vow to make offerings to all buddhas.

Second, they hold fast to and protect the true Dharma of all buddhas.

Third, they urge and request all buddhas to preach unprecedented matters (Skt. *adbhuta-dharma*).

Fourth, they perform bodhisattvas' right practices in order.

Fifth, they are complete and mature in the physical environment of sentient beings (Skt. *bhājana-loka*).

Sixth, they can manifest themselves in all worlds.

Seventh, they spontaneously purify buddha lands.

Eighth, all bodhisattvas use expedient means in the same way and edify [sentient beings] by means of the Mahayana.

Ninth, they benefit sentient beings by all kinds of nonemptiness (Skt. *aśūnya*).

Tenth, they attain highest, perfect enlightenment in all worlds and conduct all the altruistic activities of a buddha.

With great vows like these, [bodhisattavas] can give rise immeasurably to a hundred thousand great vows. Staying in the realm of sentient beings and the secular world, together with all these vows they are reborn over and over again and continually practice them, never forgetting them.

Moreover, the *Garland Sutra* says:

All disciples of the Buddha! When bodhisattvas abide in the stage of joy (Skt. *kamalaśīla*), they consider the ten vows as primary and give rise to a million *asaṃkhya* great vows like these. They make these vows by means of inexhaustible matters. In order to fulfill these vows they assiduously practice diligence. What are the ten [inexhaustible matters]? First, sentient beings are inexhaustible. Second, the world is inexhaustible. Third, the sky is inexhaustible. Fourth, the Dharma realm is inexhaustible. Fifth, nirvana is inexhaustible. Sixth, buddhas' appearances in the world are inexhaustible. Seventh, all buddhas' wisdom is inexhaustible. Eighth, 554c
objects of perception possessed in the mind are inexhaustible. Ninth, arising wisdom is inexhaustible. Tenth, the changes of the secular world, all phenomenal things, and wisdom are inexhaustible.[280]

If sentient beings are exhausted, then my vows will be exhausted. If [everything from the world] up to arising wisdom and the changes of [the secular world, all phenomenal things, and wisdom] are exhausted, then my vows will be exhausted. [Everything from] sentient beings up to arising wisdom and the changes of [the secular world, all phenomenal things, and wisdom] are, however, inexhaustible in fact. [Therefore,] the wholesome root of all my vows is also inexhaustible.

Furthermore, the *Wenshushili wen puti jing* (T. 464; Skt. *Gayāśīrṣa*) says:

At that time a sovereign asked Mañjuśrī, "How many aspirations does a bodhisattva have in order to be able to regulate cause and effect?" Mañjuśrī replied, "All bodhisattvas have four aspirations by which they can regulate cause and effect. What are the four [aspirations]? The first is the original aspiration for enlightenment. The second is the aspiration for practicing the [Buddhist] Way. The third is the aspiration for nonretrogression in proceeding to highest, perfect enlightenment. The fourth is the aspiration for taking up a buddha's place in the next life.

"The original aspiration for enlightenment becomes the cause and condition for the aspiration for practicing the [Buddhist] Way. The aspiration for practicing the [Buddhist] Way becomes the cause and condition for the aspiration for nonretrogression in proceeding to highest, perfect enlightenment. The aspiration for nonretrogression in proceeding to highest, perfect enlightenment becomes the cause and condition for the aspiration for taking up a buddha's place in the next life.

"Moreover, the original aspiration for enlightenment can be compared to [one's wish] to plant grains in farm land. The aspiration for practicing the [Buddhist] Way is like [his wish] for the [planted] grain to grow. The aspiration for nonretrogression in proceeding to highest, perfect enlightenment is like [his wish] that the flowers and fruits [of the grain] begin to be produced. The aspiration for taking up a buddha's place in the next life is like [his wish] that the flowers and the fruits become consumable.

"Furthermore, the original aspiration for enlightenment is just like a cartmaker's [wish] to collect wood. The aspiration for practicing the [Buddhist] Way is just like [his wish] to cut and plane the wood. The aspiration for nonretrogression in proceeding to highest, perfect enlightenment is like [his wish] to install the wood [to create a vehicle]. The aspiration for taking up a buddha's place in the next life is just like [his wish] that the vehicle is completed and delivered.

"Moreover, the original aspiration for enlightenment can be compared to the new moon. The aspiration for practicing the [Buddhist] Way is like a five-day-old moon. The aspiration for nonretrogression in proceeding to highest, perfect enlightenment is like a ten-day-old moon. The aspiration for taking up a buddha's place in the next life is like a fourteen-day-old moon. The wisdom of the Tathāgata is like a full moon.

"In addition, the original aspiration for enlightenment enables people to get to the *śrāvaka* stage. The aspiration for practicing the [Buddhist] Way enables them to get to the *pratyekabuddha* stage. The aspiration for nonretrogression in proceeding to highest, perfect enlightenment enables them to get to the stage of nonmeditation (Skt. *asamāhita*). The aspiration for taking up a buddha's place in the next life enables them to peacefully abide in the stage of meditation (Skt. *dhyāna-bhūmi*).

"Again, the original aspiration for enlightenment is just like when an ill person seeks medicine. The aspiration for practicing the [Buddhist] Way is just like when the ill person decides what medicine to take. The aspiration for nonretrogression in proceeding to highest, perfect enlightenment is just like when the ill person takes medicine. The aspiration for taking up a buddha's place in the next life is just like when the ill person is restored to health."

Furthermore, the [*Da fangdeng*] *Daji jing* (T. 397) says:

At that time Śāriputra said to the Buddha, "O World-honored One! When bodhisattvas awaken the aspiration for highest, perfect enlightenment for the first time, they hear that all sentient beings have a practice like this and yet they are neither surprised nor afraid. This fact is really difficult to understand and it is mysterious."

The Buddha said, "Śāriputra! What do you think about this? They are just like a [baby] lion. At the beginning when [the lion cub] was born, when it hears a lion's roar, does it have fear?" 555a

"No, World-honored One!"

"When bodhisattva *mahāsattva*s awaken the aspiration for highest, perfect enlightenment for the first time, they hear that all sentient beings' practice is also like this. O Śāriputra! What do you think about this? Even if the force of a fire is weak, is [the fire] afraid of dried firewood?"

"No, World-honored One!"

"After a bodhisattva originally awakens the aspiration for highest, perfect enlightenment, they attain the fire of wisdom just in this way. O Śāriputra! I will now take non-allegory as an allegory. Śāriputra! For instance, it is as if a raging fire and all dried firewood must fight a major battle against each other, over a seven-day time period. In that time, all the dried trees, grasses, plants, and various kinds of branches and leaves are completely collected and [piled up as high as] Mount Sumeru. At that time the raging fire has a good friend that says to it, 'Why do you now not make yourself magnificent, and why do you not seek reinforcement? Helpers for [the firewood] are numerous while you are alone. How can you engage them?' On that occasion, the fire replies, 'Even though my enemies are numerous, my power can match them and does not need any company.'

"O Śāriputra! Bodhisattva *mahāsattva*s are also like this. Even though all the defilements may completely unite and their force is vigorous, the power of the bodhisattvas' wisdom is able to remove and subdue them. It is just like [swallowing] a pill of an antidote (Skt. *agada*) can destroy serious poisons. The power of the bodhisattvas' wisdom is also like this. Even a small amount of their wisdom medicine can counteract an immeasurable amount of the poisons of defilement."

The *Fo benxing[ji] jing* (T. 190) says:[281]

At that time, the Buddha said to the *bhikṣu* sangha in this way, "All you *bhikṣu*s! I remember that in the remotest past there was a poor man who supported himself by means of begging for alms. He came to Vārāṇasī from another city. After he arrived in the city [of Vārāṇasī], all the beggars of that city saw him and questioned him, scolding and blaming him, 'From where did you come here?' Then they blocked him and did not allow him to wander about to appeal and beg for alms. At that time he saw this obstruction, he thought in this manner, 'I am free from fault against these people. Why do they hinder me from appealing and begging for alms?'

"On that occasion, there was a wealthy man in Vārāṇasī who had lost a copper bowl. Then he looked for the copper bowl, but he could not find where it was. Looking for the bowl, he came to another village.

"At that time that beggar found the [wealthy man's] copper bowl in a manure pit and placed it on the top of a staff. Carrying [the staff], he entered Vārāṇasī. From street to street, from lane to lane, from this crossroads to that crossroads, and from this corner to that corner he chanted these words, 'Whose copper bowl is this? The one who recognizes it should take it.' Accordingly, he traveled about here and there, from east to west, looking for its owner, but he could not find [the owner] after all. Since he was not able to find [the owner], he went to King Brahmadatta and entrusted [the bowl] to the king.

"Consequently, the wealthy man later learned that a man had found a
555b copper bowl in a manure pit, placed it on the top of a staff, entered Vārāṇasī
carrying it, traveled about here and there, not knowing the owner's place,

and then entrusted [the bowl] to King Brahmadatta since he had not found the owner. On hearing this, [the wealthy man] approached King Brahmadatta and then addressed [the king], 'O Great King! You must know that the copper bowl a beggar previously offered to you is mine.' King Brahmadatta then sent a messenger to summon the beggar [who had given him the bowl]. Accordingly, the king said to [the beggar], 'Now this wealthy man claims that the copper bowl you previously gave me is from his place. What do you think about this?' The beggar immediately addressed King Brahmadatta, 'It is just like this. O Great King! I originally did not know whose copper bowl it was. I found it in a manure pit. I placed it on the top of my staff and came into the city carrying it. I visited here and there but I could not find out who was its owner. Consequently, I offered it to you, Great King, and left it with you for your use.'

"At that time, on hearing his words, Brahmadatta was greatly delighted and said [to the beggar], 'O kind man! You are at my side now. What do you wish to beg from me? I will bestow anything on you.' Accordingly, the copper bowl was returned to the wealthy man.

"The beggar then addressed King Brahmadatta in this way, 'O great king! If you want to joyfully bestow what I wish for on me now, I wish you, king, will make me king of all beggars of Vārāṇasī.' At that time, King Brahmadatta again asked him, 'Why do you now need to be king of the beggars? You should just beg, instead, for various other good things that you wish for, gold or silver, or ask for the best village in the country in order to make it your manor estate. I will then bestow it on you.' At that time the beggar again addressed the king, 'O king! If you joyfully bestow what I wish upon me, I now only want to obtain what I earlier wished for.' The king thereupon replied to him, 'I will leave it to your choice and simply follow your decision.'

"At that time, there were altogether five hundred beggars who depended on and dwelled in Vārāṇasī. The one who had begged [to be king of the beggars] summoned them all to gather and he said to them, 'I was now able to become the king of you. You must certainly listen to my discretion.' All the beggars then asked the [beggar] king, 'How will you now take action against us? What services will you cause us to perform?' At that moment, [the beggar king] said, 'You must all serve me together. Some of you will carry me on your shoulders. Some of you will carry me on your backs. All others will become my servants and walk closely around me.' Accordingly the five hundred beggars, after hearing this, followed his measures. Some carried him [on their shoulders], and some carried him on their backs. They traveled around everywhere, going to all places that had seats for eating and drinking, where [the beggar king] begged for [food and drink]. After begging, he brought the [food and drink] to a place where he distributed them and ate with [all the other beggars]. Through such expedient means he lived for a long time.

"One time someone was eating a cake called *modaka* (*mohutujia,* which is called *huanxi wan,* "small ball of joy," in the Sui dynasty) by himself
555c in a hiding place. The beggar king then took that food by force from the person and ran away with it. The king's followers, the five hundred beggars, ran after him and came to a remote place. Everyone was completely exhausted. Therefore they all spun round and round. The beggar king had strong physical powers; he ran, yet he was not tired. After going further, he turned around and gazed back into the distance. The five hundred beggars could not be seen at all. Since he did not see them [coming afer him], he then entered a garden, took some water and washed his hands, sat to one side, and was about to eat the food.

"Just before eating he gave rise to penitence. 'I am not proper now. Why did I take that person's food by force and further deceive the people who follow me? There is plenty of this food so even if I eat some it will not be exhausted. If there are various sages in the world, I pray that they will know my intention, and if they come here I will share [this food] with them.'

"After [the beggar king] gave rise to this thought, a *pratyekabuddha* called Subhadra came flying high in the sky. Before the [beggar king's] eyes, [Subhadra] descended straight from the sky and [alighted] not far from [the beggar king]. [The beggar king] saw from a distance that the *pratyekabuddha* had a dignified manner, his steps were uniform and upright, and his deportment was ideal, neither slow nor hurried. After seeing this, [the beggar king] attained pure faith in the *pratyekabuddha.* On attaining pure faith, he thought in this way, 'The torment of poverty I received in the past and experience even now in the present time is entirely due to the fact that I have not before met a field of merit like this and have not practiced almsgiving and offering with respect to such a person.

"'If I had formerly met a field of merit like this, I would not have to experience the financial straits today, and also I would not have to be incessantly harassed by others and I could have lived [peacefully]. I will now offer this food to the hermit (i.e., the *pratyekabuddha*). I do not know whether or not he will accept it. If I receive his favor and he accepts it, I will pray that in the future I will avoid having a body that experiences the torment of poverty and dire straits.' After thinking this, he brought the food and offered it to the hermit.

"There is, however, a law for *pratyekabuddha*s that is to say that they can edify sentient beings only through revealing supernatural powers. There is no other law. When the *pratyekabuddha* received that food he left the earth, soaring up to the sky.

"[The beggar king] saw this and danced in joy, which filled his entire body. He could not control himself. In his great joy he placed the palms of his hands on top of his head and from a distance worshiped at the feet of that venerable *pratyekabuddha*. After worshiping in this way, he vowed, 'I pray that in my future life I will always meet the World-honored One in this way or one who is even greater than this [*pratyekabuddha*]. I pray that on hearing the Dharma spoken by the World-honored One just once I will be able to testify and understand it promptly. Again, I pray that in my future life I will be in a greatly virtuous, influential, and powerful clan and become a king who governs and edifies the people, and further that I will never [again] be among poor people.' He moreover made this vow, 'I will not fall into the evil realms eternally.'"

The Buddha said to all the *bhikṣu*s in this way, "All you *bhikṣu*s! If you 556a
have a question regarding who was the king of beggars in Vārāṇasī of that time, who offered the *modaka* cake to the *pratyekabuddha,* do not entertain a different view! He was Bhadrika Bhikṣu. On that occasion, the beggar king offered food to the *pratyekabuddha.* In accordance with the result of his conduct, he has presently been reborn in the Śākya clan, a great, powerful, noble clan. His [vast] wealth cannot be exhausted. Due to the vow he made in the past, he has now ascended the throne. Furthermore, due to

the vows he made in the past he does not fall into evil realms, is always reborn in the human realm or in heaven, and receives much happiness. In addition, due to the vows he made in the past he has now met me and was able to renounce the world, receive a complete set of [two hundred and fifty] precepts, and attain arhatship. I furthermore give him this prediction: 'Among my *śrāvaka* disciples, the superlative, the number one of those from powerful clans who have renounced the world is Bhadrika Bhikṣu.'"

Verses say:

A wise person admires lofty principles.
Aspiration is the cause for enlightenment.
Coaching a crane, he soars over the Yi River.
Whipping up his horse, he goes out of the imperial field.
With the original prayer he makes a great vow.
He receives Amitābha's body as a reward.
Śākyamuni cultivated the eightfold holy path.
He jumped over nine *kalpa*s to former times.
His voice flows all over the three realms of existence.
He benevolently educates throughout the trichiliocosm.
He conceals defilements and puts an end to delusions.
Ordinary people and sages are completely happy.
Sentient beings have the same resolution and path.
Their minds are protected, benefited, and enlightened.
The transmigration of birth and death is certainly exhausted eternally.
How could he be the same as the transcendents in the philosophy of
 Laozi and Zhuangzi?

[End of] Fascicle Thirty-four of *A Forest of Pearls from the Dharma Garden*

Notes

Translator's Introduction

1 See Genmyō Ono, *Bussho kaisetsu daijiten* (Tokyo: Daitō Shuppansha, 1967), vol. 10, p. 5; Gajin Nagao, Seizan Yanagida, and Yūichi Kajiyama, eds., *Daijō Butten,* Chūgoku Nihon-hen, 3, *Shutsusanzōki shū Hōon jurin* (Tokyo: Chūō Kōronsha, 1993), p. 299; and Fumio Ōuchi, "Hōon jurin Chūgoku no mono to natta Bukkyō no sekai," *Gekkan Shinika* 9/3 (1998): 23–24.

2 *Chusanzang jiji,* T.2145:38b2–3. Sengyou of the Liang dynasty notes that this scripture is no longer extant.

3 The compilation of the *Neidian boyao* is explained in two Buddhist catalogues: the *Lidai sanbao ji* (T.2034:100a20–24) and the *Da Tang neidian lu* (T.2149:267b17–21).

4 See Li Yan's preface to the *Fayuan zhulin,* T.2122:269b5–6, and the *Guang hongming ji,* T.2103:246c11–12.

5 *Fayuan zhulin,* T.2122:269b10–11. The English translation of the quoted section is from Koichi Shinohara, trans., *A Forest of Pearls from the Dharma Garden* (Moraga CA: BDK America, Inc., 2019), Vol. I, p. 5.

6 *Guang hongming ji,* T.2103:246c15–16.

7 See Ono, *Bussho kaisetsu daijiten,* vol. 10, p. 5; Shinkō Mochizuki, *Mochizuki Bukkyō Daijiten* (Tokyo: Sekai Seiten Kankō Kyōkai, 1974), vol. 5, p. 4556.

8 Nagao, Yanagida, and Kajiyama, eds., *Daijō Butten,* p. 304.

9 *Song gaoseng zhuan,* T.2061:726c6–727a3.

10 Not all chapters have miracle stories. For example, among the twenty-eight chapters from Chapter Ten to Chapter Thirty-seven there are no miracle stories in Chapters Ten, Twelve, Fourteen, Twenty-one, Twenty-two, Twenty-eight, and Twenty-nine.

11 Yoshiteru Kawaguchi, "Hōon jurin ni mirareru itsuzon betsuzon kyō ni tsuite," *Nanto Bukkyō* 37 (1976): 83–102.

12 Nagao, Yanagida, and Kajiyama, eds., *Daijō Butten,* p. 307.

13 Ōuchi, "Hōon jurin Chūgoku no mono to natta Bukkyō no sekai," pp. 22–26.

Fascicle 28
Chapter Twenty

14 The *Dafangdeng daji nianfo sanmei jing* 大方等大集念佛三昧經 refers to the *Dafangdeng dajijing pusa nianfo sanmei fen* 大方等大集經菩薩念佛三昧分 (T. 415; Skt. *Mahāvaipulya-mahāsaṃnipāta-sūtra*).

15 In a *hāni-kalpa* the human life span decreases by a year every hundred years, going from eighty thousand years to ten years.

16 The Chinese character *xia* 下 ("to put down") is replaced with the character *bu* 不 ("not"), according to the *Dafangdeng dajijing pusa nianfo sanmei fen,* T.415:840a27.

17 The Sanskrit name of this buddha, Nansheng 難勝, is unknown. His Chinese name is Nanshengwei 難勝威 in the relevant passage in the *Dafangdeng dajijing pusa nianfo sanmei fen,* T.415842a13–14, 18.

18 *Ayuwang jing* refers to the *Ayuwang zhuan* (T. 2042).

19 The Chinese character *zhu* 住 ("to live") is replaced with the character *wang* 往 ("to go"), according to the *Za baozang jing,* T.203:452c5.

20 The Chinese character *man* 縵 ("plain silk" or "slow") is replaced with the character *man* 瞞 ("to hide the truth"), according to the *Za baozang jing,* T.203:452c23.

21 The following citation is not found in the *Piyu jing* 譬喻經 (T. 217) but it is found in the *Jinglü yixiang,* T.2121:237c6–18, in a citation from the tenth fascicle of the *Piyu jing.*

22 The following citation is not found in the *Piyu jing* but it is found in the *Jinglü yixiang,* T.2121:257c25–258a14, in a citation from the second fascicle of the *Piyu jing* and also in the *Zhiguan fuxingchuan hongjue,* T.1912:268b8–20.

23 The Chinese term *hu* 斛 is a unit of measurement for volume. In the Tang dynasty there were two kinds of *hu:* large, 60 liters, and small, 20 liters.

24 The text has two Chinese characters, *niu* 牛 ("cow") and *ju* 筥 (meaning either taro or a round bamboo basket for holding rice), but the compound of these characters does not fit the context. Following the *Zhiguan fuxingchuan hongjue,* T.1912:268b9–10, which also has this story, I translated only the character *niu* 牛.

25 The following citation is not found in the *Piyu jing* but it is found in the *Jinglü yixiang,* T.2121:258a155–258b8, in a citation from the fourth fascicle of the *Piyu jing* and also in the *Cibei daochang chanfa,* T.1909:938a22–b7.

26 The *Shanxin jing* 善信經 is not found in *Taishō shinshū daizōkyō.* The following section is found in the *Jinglü yixiang,* T.2121:12c7–13a5, in a citation from the second fascicle of the *Shanxin jing.*

27 The Chinese name of the *madana* tree is read *motuoluo* 摩陀羅 instead of *moluotuo* 摩羅陀.

28 The following description is probably cited from the *Jinglü yixiang,* T.2121:14a21–b6, and not from of the *Garland Sutra*, T.278:622c4–623a3.

29 The Chinese character *su* 蘇 (purple perilla) is replaced with the character *su* 酥 (*koumiss*), according to the *Garland Sutra,* T.278:623a1.

30 See *Gaoseng zhuan,* T.2059:406b26–c7.

31 According to the *Gaoseng zhuan,* T.2059:346b29–c1, and the *Chu sanzang jiji,* T.2145: 7b10–11, 97b8, the sutras were delivered to Chenliu 陳留, Shuinan 水南, and Cangheng 倉恒 temples.

32 *Gaoseng zhuan,* T.2059:346c5–6.

33 Master Shi might refer to Daoan 道安 (312–385).

34 Yue Guang 樂廣 was well known for his skill in discussion. His biography is found in the forty-third fascicle of the *Jin shu* 晉書.

35 "Six times a day" refers to three times in the daytime and three times at night during which Buddhist rites are performed.

36 The Chinese term *dou* 斗 is a unit of measurement of volume. In the Tang dynasty there were two kinds of *dou:* large, six liters, and small, two liters.

37 The Chinese term *dan* 石 is a unit of measurement for dry goods, such as grain, or a measure of weight. In the Tang dynasty one *dan* is 79,320 grams.

38 The Chinese character *xiao* 効 ("to imitate," "effect") is replaced with the character *jiao* 郊 ("suburbs"), according to the *Xu Goaseng zhuan,* T.2060:682a26.

39 The Chinese character *bie* 別 ("to part") is replaced with the character *dao* 到 ("to reach"), according to the *Xu Gaoseng zhuan,* T.2060:651c29, n. 37.

40 The seasonal day called *hanshi* 寒食 is designated as the one hundred and fifth day after the winter solstice. On this day the use of fire was prohibited, and food was supposed to be consumed cold.

41 The Chinese character *qian* 前 ("front") is replaced with the character *bian* 邊 ("edge"), according to the *Xu Gaoseng zhuan,* T.2060:652a24.

42 *Xu Gaoseng zhuan,* T.2060:652b12.

43 The Chinese character *tang* 唐 ("abrupt") between the characters *huang* 皇 and *tai* 泰 is deleted, according to the *Xu Gaoseng zhuan,* T.2060:652c22.

44 The phrase "Zhuanming said" is added here according to the *Xu Gaoseng zhuan,* T.2060:653a2.

45 The Chinese character *chang* 常 ("often") is replaced with the character *chang* 嘗 ("once"), according to the *Xu Gaoseng zhuan,* T.2060:653b29. The three Chinese characters *zhang* 張 ("to stretch"), *he* 河 ("river"), and *jiang* 江 ("river") are replaced

with the two characters *qing* 清 ("clean") and *he* 河 ("river"), according to the *Xu Gaoseng zhuan,* T.2060:653b29–c1.

46 The Chinese character *deng* 等 ("equal") is read as the character *zhe* 者 ("he who"), according to the *Xu Gaoseng zhuan,* T.2060:653c10.

47 The Chinese character *bei* 北 ("north") before the character *jing* 景 ("scenery") is read as the character *bi* 比 ("to compare").

48 The Deng Grove (Denglin 鄧林) was made from the cane of Kuafu, an overconfident person who engaged in a race with the sun. This story is found in the *Haiwai bei jing* 海外北經 of the *Shanhai jing* 山海經.

Fascicle 29

Chapter Twenty-one

49 There are several different theories regarding the unit of measure for distance, a *li* 里, used by Xuanzang 玄奘 in the *Da Tang xiyuji* 大唐西域記. Shinjō Mizutani, *Daitō saiiki ki* (Tokyo: Heibonsha, 1999), vol. 1, pp. 264–265, concludes that Xuanzang's estimation of a *li* is roughly 400–440 meters.

50 The state called in Chinese Damo Tiexidi 達摩鐵悉 (Skt. Dharmasthiti) is unknown. Mochizuki, *Bukkyō Daijiten,* p. 3123, indicates that this state was located near present-day Wakhan. According to Daoxuan's *Shijia fangzhi,* T.2088:951c22, the state of Damo Tiexi is a former territory of the state of Tukhāra.

51 The Iron Gate is a mountain pass about three kilometers long located west of present-day Derbent (or Darband).

52 Usually the rainy retreat is from the sixteenth day of the fourth month to the fifteenth day of the seventh month.

53 The Chinese terms *cun* 寸 and *fen* 分 are units of length. In the Tang dynasty there were two kinds of *cun* and *fen:* a large *cun* is 3.6 centimeters and a small *cun* is 3 centimeters; a *fen* is one-tenth of a *cun.*

54 Mount Beiluipolu 北羅婆路 is given as Mount Biluosuoluo 比羅娑洛 in the *Da Tang xiyuji,* with the note, "called Xiangjian 象堅 (Skt. Pīlusāra)"; T.2087:875a24.

55 Mizutani, *Daitō saiikiki,* vol. 1, p. 205, suggests Nagarahāra should be Nagarahar.

56 See *Da Tang xiyuji,* T.2087:881a24 for the original sentence. To donate one's eyes to restore or confer eyesight to other people is one of the bodhisattva practices and is mentioned in various sutras. For example, see the story of King Śibi in the *Zhuanji Baiyuan jing,* T.200:218a22–c14.

57 This story is found in sutras such as the *Za baozang jing,* T.203:492a12–29 and the *Guizimu jing,* T.1262:290c6–291c8.

58 This story is found in various sutras. For instance, see the *Pusa Shanzi jing,* T.174:436b1–438b4.

59 For example, see the *Taizi Xudana jing,* T.171:418c19–424a24.

60 See the story of the "one-horn hermit" in the *Da zhidu lun,* T.1509:183b1–c16.

61 See the *Xianyu jing,* T.202:359c8–360b7, for this story.

62 See the *Xianyu jing,* T.202:351b12c1, for this story.

63 This is a well-known *jātaka* story. See, for example, the *Xianyu jing,* T.202:351c26–352a25.

64 See the *Xianyu jing,* T.202:360b9–c13, for this story.

65 See the *Zengyi ahan jing,* T.125:818c5–819a21.

66 See the *Xianyu jing,* T.202:387b3–390b12, for this story.

67 In the *Da Tang xiyuji,* T.2087:885a3–4, the one whose eyes were gouged out is not Candraprabha but Kuṇāla, King Aśoka's son.

68 *Xianyu jing,* T.202:352b19–353b16.

69 The text mentioned here, the *Da zhi lun,* is not the *Da zhidu lun* 大智度論 composed by Nāgārjuna. It may refer to the *Fazhi lun* 發智論 (Skt. *Abhidharma-jñāna-prasthāna*) composed by Kātyāna; see the *Da Tang xiyuji,* T.2087:889c4.

70 The Chinese character *li* 釐 in the first mention of the name Youpoli means "to revise," while it is the character *li* 離,"to leave," in the latter reference.

71 Mizutani, *Daitō saiiki ki,* vol. 2, p. 155, n. 1, suggests that the origin of the Ganges River mentioned here is not the headwaters in the Himalayas but the area of present-day Hardwār, where the Bhāgīrathi River and the Alaknanda River join and form tributaries of the Ganges River.

72 *Da Tang xiyuji,* T.2087:893a20–21.

73 The Chinese term *bu* 步 is a unit of length. The definition of one *bu* varies as equivalent either to a step, two steps, six *chi,* six *chi* and four *cun,* or eight *chi.* I translate *bu* as "pace."

74 The term "lion's seat" usually refers to a seat for the Buddha or an eminent monk, but in this case it probably means a royal throne.

75 A boy king (*tongzi wang* 童子王) appears as a king of the state of Jiamolouduo 迦摩縷多國 in Xuanzang's biography in the *Xu Gaoseng zhuan,* T.2060:453a22–b12.

76 See the *Guang Bai lun ben* 廣百論本 (T. 1570) for Xuanzang's translation of this treatise.

77 Each of the four Śākya men became the kings of Uḍḍiyāna, Bāmiyān, Hīmatala, and Śami respectively. See *Da Tang xiyuji,* T.2087:901c2–16.

78 *Da Tang xiyuji,* T.2087:902a13–14.

79 For Cunda see the *Chang Ahan jing,* T.1:18a23–c29.

80 For Subhadra see the *Chang Ahan jing,* T.1:25a1–b26.

81 For the story of Vajiradhara see the *Foru niepan miji Jingang lishi ailian jing,* T.394: 1116a19–1118a6.

82 This *jātaka* tale is found in several Buddhist scriptures; for example, see the *Liuduji jing,* T.152:17a19–b29.

83 This *jātaka* tale is also found in several Buddhist scriptures; for example, see the *Sifen lü,* T.1428:940a7–25.

84 This *jātaka* tale is also found in several Buddhist scriptures; for example, see the *Liuduji jing,* T.152:12b29–13a4.

85 This *jātaka* tale is found in several Buddhist scriptures; for example, see the *Zhuanji Baiyuan jing,* T.200:221b27–c19.

86 See Mizutani, *Daitō saiiki ki,* vol. 2, p. 370.

87 For this story see the *Za baozang jing,* T.203:452b18–453c1.

88 The text titled *Pumenzhu* 普門住 cannot be identified. In the *Da Tang xiyuji,* T.2087: 909a21, the sutra expounded by the Buddha here is the *Pumen tuoluoni* 普門陀羅尼 (Skt. *Samantamukha-dhāraṇī*).

89 This is Xuanzang's misunderstanding. King Aśoka is the grandson of Candragupta, founder of the Maurya dynasty, and the son of Bindusāra and Subhadrāngī. See Mizutani, *Daitō saiiki ki,* vol. 3, p. 29, n. 2.

90 *Da Tang xiyuji,* T.2087:915a3–4.

91 *Da Tang xiyuji,* T.2087:915a16–b3.

92 According to ancient Indian cosmology, there are the three layers of different elements: the wind layer on the bottom, the water layer in the middle, and the gold layer on the top. The earth is included in the gold layer.

93 The months of *da shenbian* 大神變 refer to the first, fifth, and ninth months for purification. Here the term refers only to the fifteenth day of the first month in the Chinese calendar.

94 For the story of the *bodhi* tree see the *Da Tang xiyuji,* T.2087:915b27–c25.

95 Their Sanskrit names cannot be identified.

96 The Chinese character *di* 帝 ("emperor") is replaced with the character *di* 弟 ("younger brother").

97 Mount Tianyan 闐顔 is located in Central Asia.

98 A similar story is found in the *Fo bexingji jing,* T.190:803c6–804a18. A woman

donated an old robe to the Buddha, and the Buddha washed it in a river created by Śakra-devendra and dried it on rocks brought by the god for the Buddha's sake.

99 For this section, the *Da Tang xiyuji,* T.2087:917c, says that there is a stupa at the place where two wealthy persons offered a wheat-honey cake to the Buddha.

100 *Mishasaibu Hexi Wufenlü,* T.1421:103a24.

101 The three Kāśyapa brothers are Uruvilvā-kāśyapa, Nadī-kāśyapa, and Gayā-kāśyapa; see the *Da Tang xiyuji,* T.2087:917c22.

102 Mizutani, *Daitō saiiki ki,* vol. 3, p. 105, n. 3, suggests that Xuanzang might have here mixed up the days of completing the Buddha's "supernatural transformation" months with the date the Buddha entered *parinirvāṇa.*

103 Siṃhala is the Sanskrit translation of Laṅkādvīpa (present-day Sri Lanka).

104 The *jātaka* tale of the decorated elephant is found in the *Fo benxingji jing,* T.190: 910b5–911b23, and the *Za baozang jing,* T.203:456a2–b22.

105 *Za baozang jing,* T.203:488c25–489b10.

106 *Zengyi ahan jing,* T.125:773c20–775b28.

107 *Zengyi ahan jing,* T.125:803b11–20.

108 Mizutani, *Daitō saiiki ki,* vol. 3, p. 137, n. 1, points out that this description is not correct; Mount Vipula should be to the east of the north gate of the city, while Mount Baibhāra is on the west side.

109 The *Xu Gaoseng zhuan,* T.2060:451c6, says the top wall instead of the lowest wall.

110 The Chinese character *bo* 波 ("waves") is added after the character *yan* 沿 ("along"), according to the *Xu Gaoseng zhuan,* T.2060:452b21.

111 The Chinese character *zhuan* 傳 ("biography") is replaced with the character *fu* 縛 ("to bind"), referring to the relevant passage in the *Xu Gaoseng zhuan,* T.2060:452b24.

112 *Da Tang xiyuji,* T.2087:934b22–23.

Fascicle 30

Chapter Twenty-two

113 The following citation is from the *Sifen lü shanfan buque xingshi chao,* T.1804:21b29–c1.

114 The Sanskrit term *duṣkṛta* (*tujiluo*) refers to the least serious among the five categories of violations of the two hundred and fifty precepts for *bhikṣus*. The violator repents of his sin by himself or confesses to another monk.

115 The Sanskrit for the Chinese *jiemo* 羯磨 is *karman,* commonly translated into English as "deed" or "action" (karma). It generally refers to rites and proprieties in the sangha.

Here, all seven deeds are concerned with punishments for monks who commit an offense: (1) to move an offender from his current dwelling to another locale, (2) to reproach an offender who is given to disputing, who committed evil, and who criticized the Three Treasures, temporarily suspending his rights as a monk, (3) to decide to suspend an offender's rights, (4) to cause an offender who did something against the Dharma to a layperson to apologize to the layperson, (5) to expel from the sangha an offender who does not admit to having been in the wrong, (6) to disqualify an offender who does not repent of his sin to a monk and expel him from the sangha, and (7) to expel an offender who never gives up wrong views.

116 The Chinese character *dang* 當 ("ought to," "must") is replaced with the character *chang* 常 ("always"), according to the *Nirvana Sutra,* T.374:383c5.

117 The Sanskrit equivalent to the Chinese name Juede 覺德 is unknown.

118 The Sanskrit equivalent to the Chinese name Youde 有德 is unknown.

119 The offenders of the four grave offenses are exiled from the sangha. See note 114 for *duṣkṛta.*

120 The sentence "If, on the contrary, [*bhikṣu*s] learn these things" is not found in the *Nirvana Sutra.*

121 The Chinese character *xu* 麩 (a person's first or last name) is replaced with the character *yi* 麫 ("wheat husks"), according to the *Nirvana Sutra,* T.374:421c11.

122 The sentence "If one preaches the sutra under these wrong conditions" is added on the basis of the description found in the *Nirvana Sutra,* T.374:467c22–23.

123 *Fozang jing,* T.653:793b26.

124 The *Moheyan dabaoyan jing* 摩訶衍大寶嚴經 refers to the *Puming Pusa hui di sishisan* 普明菩薩會第四十三 of the *Da Baoji jing,* T.310:631c17–638c3.

125 The Sanskrit equivalents for the names of these *bhikṣu*s are unknown.

126 The Chinese name Yiqiexiang 一切相 is read as Yiqieming 一切明 according to the *Fozang jing,* T.653:795b23–28. The Sanskrit equivalent is unknown.

127 The *Jiashe jing* 迦葉經 refers to the *Mohe jiashe hui* in the *Da Baoji jing,* T.310: 501b12–514b7).

128 The Chinese characters *ershi* 爾時 ("at that time") are replaced with the character *jin* 今 ("now"), according to the *Da Baoji jing,* T.310:503c20.

129 The Chinese character *zheng* 正 ("right") is replaced with the character *wu* 五 ("five"), according to the *Dafangdeng daji jing,* T.397:381b28–29.

130 The Sanskrit equivalent of the Chinese name Wushengyi 無勝意 is unknown.

131 In the *Dafangdeng daji jing,* T.397:167b26, the Chinese character *chao* 潮 ("tide") is used instead of the character *hu* 湖 ("lake").

[132] There are several different Sanskrit equivalents for the Chinese name Wusheng 無勝, but there is no clue to identify which one is most suitable.

[133] The *Dafangdeng daji jing,* T.397:168a10, has the thirteenth day instead of the twelfth day.

[134] The following passage is directly quoted from the *Ji shenzhou sanbao gantong lu,* T.2106:431a5–7, not from the *Ru Dasheng lun* (T. 1634).

[135] Regarding the Sanskrit equivalents for the names of the sixteen arhats, there are some differences. For instance, the thirteenth arhat, in Chinese Yinjietuo 因揭陀, is shown as Aṅgaja (Mochizuki, *Mochizuki Bukkyō Daijiten,* vol. 1, p. 175), Iṅgata (Oda, *Bukkyō Daijiten,* p. 1775), Iṅgada (Ono, *Bussho kaisetsu daijiten,* vol. 7, p. 204), or Aṅgada (Ciyi, comp., *Foguang dacidian* [Gaoxiong: Foguan chubanshe, 1997], p. 2300). I follow the first source listed for all the arhat names. Moreover, I have indicated as many Sanskrit terms for the places they reside as possible, some of which are transliterations of Chinese terms.

[136] The Sanskrit term *pañca-vārṣika* refers to an assembly to provide alms to both sangha members and laypeople, which is held every five years.

[137] The Chinese character *chang* 長 ("long") is replaced with the character *duan* 短 ("short"), according to the *Da Aluohan Nantimiduoluo suoshuo fazhuji,* T.2030:13b26.

[138] The Chinese character *hua* 化 ("to change") is replaced with the character *bei* 北 ("north"), according to the *Youposai jie jing,* T.1488:1034b16.

[139] The Chinese character *fo* 佛 ("buddha") is added to *boji* 鉢記 ("records of the bowl"). The *Chu sanzang jiji,* T.2145:39a16, Sengyou's catalogue compiled around 515, lists the *Foboji* as a Chinese indigenous scripture, but the text is no longer extant. This section, however, was quoted in its entirety in the *Sifen lü mingyi biaoshi,* X.744:570b1–5, complied by Hongzan in 1630, and that quotation has *foboji* 佛鉢記 instead of *boji* 鉢記.

[140] The Sanskrit equivalent of the Chinese name Shuangtongmu 雙瞳目 is unknown.

Fascicle 31

Chapter Twenty-three

[141] The Chinese character *bai* 白 ("to state") is replaced with the character *qiu* 囚 ("to imprison"), according to the *Sheng jing,* T.154:78c29.

[142] The Chinese character *chi* 勅 ("to order") is replaced with the character *qian* 遣 ("to dispatch"), according to the *Sheng jing,* T.154:79a13.

[143] The Chinese character *xiang* 象 ("elephant") is replaced with the character *xiang* 像 ("image"), according to the *Xianyu jing,* T.202:432a27.

[144] The Chinese character *su* 蘇 (purple perilla) is replaced with the character *su* 酥 (*koumiss*), according to the *Za baozang jing,* T.203:493b5.

[145] The Chinese character *wei* 違 ("to go against") is replaced with the character *yuan* 遠 ("far"), according to a similar verse in the *Guang hongming ji,* T.2103:198c15.

[146] The Chinese characters *yuan xiang* 元象 ("original elephant") are replaced with the characters *wu xiang* 無像 ("no image"), according to a similar verse in the *Guang hongming ji,* T.2103:198c15.

[147] These province names are from Daoshi's time.

[148] The text says, "During the beginning of the Yongjia era he passed away," but there is a discrepancy: the Yongjia era is 307–313, but according to the *Gaoseng zhuan,* T.2059:392a11–12, Beidu died in the third year of the Yuanjia era (426). I follow the year given in the *Ji shenzhou sanbao gantong lu,* T.2106:433b27.

[149] The Chinese character *qie* 切 ("to cut") is replaced with the character *chu* 初 ("first, early"), according to Shaoshi's biography in the *Gaoseng zhuan,* T.2059:392c29–393a1.

[150] The Chinese character *jun* 郡 (prefecture) is replaced with the character *pi* 郫 (place name), according to Shaoshi's biography in the *Gaoseng zhuan,* T.2059:393, n. 2.

[151] The Chinese character *ling* 靈 ("the spirit") is replaced with the character *yun* 雲 ("cloud"), according to Shaoshi's biography in the *Gaoseng zhuan,* T.2059:393a16.

[152] The Chinese character *zai* 在 ("to be alive") is replaced with the character *li* 立 ("to build"), according to Senghui's biography in the *Gaoseng zhuan,* T.2059:393c4.

[153] The Chinese character *qu* 屈 ("to bend") is replaced with the character *ju* 居 ("to dwell").

[154] The Chinese character *qu* 屈 ("to bend") consists of the characters *shi* 尸 ("corpse") and *chu* 出 ("to come out").

[155] *Fahua jing,* T.262:56c12–13.

[156] Lai village in Ku county is east of present-day Luyin county in Henan province.

[157] There are two different theories regarding this pass: it is either Dasan Pass in present-day Shaanxi province or Hanyu Pass in present-day Henan province.

[158] The Chinese character *men* 門 ("gate") is replaced with the character *wen* 聞 ("to hear").

[159] The Chinese character *kang* 糠 ("rice bran") is replaced with the character *geng* 粳 ("nonglutinous rice").

Chapter Twenty-four

[160] The Chinese character *ju* 居 ("to dwell") is replaced with the character *jun* 君 ("sovereign"), according to the *Fo benxingji jing,* T.190:879a23.

[161] The *ke* shell is a kind of cowry. The exterior of the shell is yellowish-black, and the inside is pure white.

162 The Chinese character *kang* 糠 ("rice bran") is replaced with the character *geng* 粳 ("nonglutinous rice"), according to the *Fo benxingji jing,* T.190:881a5.

163 The Chinese character *zhu* 諸 ("all") is deleted.

164 The Chinese character *wo* 我 ("I") is replaced with the character *fu* 復 ("again"), according to the *Fo benxingji jing,* T.190:881b3.

165 Zhao is a region in the southern part of present-day Hebei province, the eastern part of Shandong province, and north of the Yellow River in Henan province.

166 This incident is known as Wuchong yu 巫蠱獄; Jiang Chong 江充 falsely accused Crown Prince Wei 衛 of causing his father, Emperor Wu, to fall ill through sorcery, which led him to rebel and commit suicide; the Crown Prince was later cleared of the charge.

167 The Chinese term *tongbo* 桐柏 literally means paulownia and cypress.

168 The *Funiao fu* 鵩鳥賦 is found in the thirteenth fascicle of the *Wenxuan* 文選.

169 The Chinese character *zhi* 治 ("to administer") is replaced with the character *ye* 冶 ("to smelt").

170 Ti Ying 緹縈 was a filial daughter who lived during the reign of Emperor Wen 文 of the Former Han dynasty. She tried to save her father who had been sentenced to corporeal punishment by offering herself as a slave.

171 This expression is found in the *Shiji* 史記, *juan* 47, *Kongzi shijia* 孔子世家, and in the *Kongzi jiayu* 孔子家語, *Bianwu* 辯物. See Hsien-yi Yang and Gladys Yang, trans., *Selections from Records of the Historian* (Peking: Foreign Languages Press, 1979), p. 5.

172 The Chinese term *sangeng* 三更 means the two-hour span between midnight and 2:00 A.M.

173 A more detailed narrative of the last story appears in the eighth fascicle of the *Yiyuan* 異苑.

174 *Kongzi jiayu* 孔子家語, *Bianwu* 辯物.

175 *Shiji* 史記, *Qin Shihuang benji* 秦始皇本紀; see Nienhauser, ed., *The Grand Scribe's Records,* vol. 1, p. 151.

Fascicle 32

Chapter Twenty-five

176 Following the *Da zhuangyan famen jing,* T.818:825b1, her name is read Sheng Jinse Guangming De 勝金色光明德 instead of Jinse Guangming Weide 金色光明威德. The Sanskrit equivalent for the name is unknown.

177 The Chinese character *zi* 子 ("son" or "child") is added after the characters *zhangzhe* 長者 ("wealthy man"), according to the *Da zhuangyan famen jing,* T.818:832b6.

178 The Chinese characters *puzou* 悑走 ("to be frightened and run away") are changed

to the characters *buwei* 怖畏 ("to be frightened"), according to the *Zhuanji Baiyuan jing,* T.200:253b24.

[179] Probably "male" and "female" are used in reverse order here.

[180] *Laozi Daode jing* 老子道德經, Chap. 13; Legge, trans., *The Dao de jing ji Zhuangzi quan ji*, p. 104.

[181] *Chunqiu Zuozhuan* 春秋左傳, Zhaogong's 昭公 seventh year; Legge, trans., *The Chinese Classics,* vol. 5, p. 617 (right column). The Chinese character *neng* 能 ("able to") is read as *xiong* 熊 ("bear").

[182] *Shiji* 史記, *juan* 9, *Lü Taihou benji* 呂太后本紀; Nienhauser, ed., *The Grand Scribe's Records,* vol. 2, pp. 125–126.

[183] The Revolt of the Seven States refers to the historical fact that seven states, including Wu 吳 and Chu 楚, rebelled against the Han dynasty in 154 B.C.E.

[184] See the *Lunyu* 論語, *Wei Linggong* 衛靈公 for Confucius's hardship in Chen state; Legge, trans., *The Chinese Classics,* vol. 1, p. 294, chap. 1, n. 2.

[185] *Qi Xie's Records* (*Qi Xie ji* 齊諧記) was compiled by Dongyang Wuyi 東陽無疑 of the Liu-Song dynasty. The term *qi xie* 齊諧 originally appears in the *Zhuangzi* 莊子, *Xiaoyaoyou* 逍遙遊. There are two different interpretations for the term: it is either the name of a book circulated in the state of Qi 齊 or the name of a person who was good at making jokes.

[186] The three Chinese characters *e* 惡 ("bad" or "evil"), *jia* 佳 ("good"), and *fan* 反 ("reverse") after the name Nüwa 女娃 indicate the pronounciation of the character *wa* 娃 by the rapid enunciation of the characters *e* and *jia.*

[187] See Cheng, Hsiao-Chieh, et al., trans., *Shan Hai Ching: Legendary Geography and Wonders of Ancient China* (Taibei: Committee for Compilation and Examination of the Series of Chinese Classics, National Institute for Compilation and Translation, 1985), pp. 60, 164.

[188] The story of Huang's 黃 mother in Jiangxia 江夏 prefecture is found at 531b18–21, above. This story is originally from the *Soushen ji* 搜神記.

Chapter Twenty-six

[189] The *Shanjianlü piposha* (T. 1462) is very similar to the Pāli *Samantapāsādikā.*

[190] The two Chinese characters *yun he* 云何 ("how is it that?") are not found in the *Apitan bajiandu lun,* T.1543:779c14.

[191] The Chinese character *bu* 不 ("not") is added before the character *hui* 迴 ("to turn"), according to the *Apitan bajiandu lun,* T.1543:780a7. "Wrong merit" (Skt. *apuṇya*) refers to unworthy acts in the realm of desire.

[192] The Chinese character *wang* 王 ("king") is added after the character *da* 大 ("great"), according to the *Za baozang jing,* T.203:490b6.

[193] The Chinese character *che* 車 ("vehicle") is added after the character *bao* 寶 ("gem"), according to the *Za baozang jing,* T.203:490c15.

[194] A meditation stick (staff or cane), *chanzhang* 禪杖, is a bamboo stick used to tap sleeping meditators on the shoulders to wake them up.

[195] According to the *Sōshinki,* the Chinese state name Zhusongmin 注送民 is replaced with Wangmangshi 汪芒氏, which existed during the dynasties of Xia 夏 or Shang 商. Its capital city was located in present-day Wukang 武康 county in Zhejiang 浙江 province. See *Sōshinki,* p. 301, n. 2.

[196] The Chinese character *yong* 永 ("eternal") is replaced with the character *yuan* 元 ("the beginning").

[197] The Chinese character *qian* 塹 ("trench") is replaced with the character *ji* 墼 ("unbaked tile"), according to the *Xu Gaoseng zhuan,* T.2060:693c23.

[198] The Chinese character *ri* 日 ("day") is replaced with the character *yue* 曰 ("to say"), according to the *Xu Gaoseng zhuan,* T.2060:693c24.

[199] The Chinese character *diao* 弔 ("to mourn") is replaced with the character *shi* 師 ("to teach"), according to the *Xu Gaoseng zhuan,* T.2060:5695b28.

[200] Usually the five kinds of suffering refers to birth, illness, aging, death, and separation from loved ones. Here, the term probably means suffering from various torments in hell.

Fascicle 33

Chapter Twenty-seven

[201] Liu Yin 劉殷 in the Jin 晉 dynasty was a man who wanted to give some aconite to his grandmother in midwinter, but it was impossible to find it. He cried out, and in response to his grief and filial piety, aconite grew. See the *Kokuyaku Issaikyō, Shidenbu* 7, p. 309, n. 37.

[202] *Kokuyaku Issaikyō, Shidenbu* 7, p. 309, n. 38.

[203] *Huainanzi* 淮南子, *Lanming xun* 覽冥訓; English translation in Charles Le Blanc, *Huai-nan Tzu: Philosophical Synthesis in Early Han Thought* (Hong Kong: Hong Kong University Press, 1985), p. 105, 2a6.

[204] *Kokuyaku Issaikyō, Shidenbu* 7, p. 310, n. 40.

[205] This *bhikṣu* is also called Śroṇaviṃśatikoṭi in Sanskrit.

[206] The Chinese character *de* 得 ("to attain") is replaced with the character *de* 德 ("virtue"), according to the *Foshuo zhude futian jing,* T.683:778c5.

[207] The Chinese character *shi* 施 ("to act" or "to bestow") is deleted after the characters

zhenbao 珍寶 ("jewels and valuables"), according to the *Foshuo zhude futian jing,* T.683:778c9.

208 The following citation is not found in the *Piyu jing* (T. 217).

209 The Chinese term *wusuozhe* 無所著 is one of the ten epithets for the Buddha, usually called *yinggong* 應供, arhat ("one worthy of almsgiving").

210 The Chinese character *qie* 切 ("to cut") is added after the character *yi* 一 ("one"), according to the *Xuda jing,* T.73:879c13.

211 The *Fo zai jin'guan jingfu jing* 佛在金棺敬福經 (*Sutra of Respect and Merit of the Golden Coffin in Which the Buddha Rests*) is a Chinese indigenous sutra listed in the *Da Zhou kanding zhongjing mulu,* T.2153:472c2, a catalogue of Buddhist scriptures compiled in 695. CBETA contains two different texts similar to this sutra: the *Fo zai jin'guan shang zhulei jing* 佛在金棺上囑累經 (ZW4n43a) and the *Rulai zai jin'guan zhulei qingjing zhuangyan jingfu jing* 如來在金棺囑累莊嚴敬福經 (ZW4n43b). The passages quoted here appear in both texts.

212 The *Zuofu jueyi jing* 罪福決疑經 is a Chinese indigenous sutra listed in the Buddhist catalogues compiled in the seventh century, such as the *Da Tang neidian lu,* T.2149:335c25, and the *Kaiyuan shijiao lu,* T.2154:677a7. The entire text is, however, no longer extant.

213 Information on the text titled *Waiguo ji* 外國記 cannot be found, but the citation comes from the *Gaoseng Faxian zhuan,* T.2085:860b18–c1. The *Jinglü yixiang,* T.2121:30a11–21, has a very similar passage and says that it is derived from the *Waiguo ji.*

214 The Chinese character *liang* 兩 ("two") is replaced with the character *nan* 南 ("south"), according to the *Gaoseng Faxian zhuan,* T.2085:860b23.

215 The Chinese character *jie* 界 ("boundary") is replaced with the character *wei* 謂 ("to think"), according to the *Gaoseng Faxian zhuan,* T.2085:860b27.

216 The Chinese characters *shang hui tu* 上灰土 ("on the dust") are read as *hui shang shi* 恢上士 ("inherent in bodhisattvas"), according to the *Zaoli xingxiang fubao jing,* T.693:789c6.

217 "Flying emperor" (*feixingdi* 飛行帝) is an old translation of the term "wheel-turning noble king" (*zhuanlun shengwang* 轉輪聖王; Skt. *cakravartin*). There are four kinds of wheel-turning kings according to the different qualities of the wheel, of which the golden-wheel flying emperor (or king) is one.

218 The second heaven refers to Trāyastriṃśa Heaven in the realm of desire.

219 The text called *Sapoduo zhuan* 薩婆多傳 is unknown. The *Chuyao jing,* T.212:674b24, mentions the story of sixty bamboo boxes containing gold and grain.

220 The Chinese character *chuan* 船 ("ship") is deleted, according to the *Sapoduo lun* (i.e., *Sapoduo pini piposha,* T.1440:545b27.

[221] The following citation is not found in the *Piyu jing.*

[222] The following citation is not found in the *Piyu jing.*

[223] The Chinese character *zhi* 知 ("to know") is deleted, according to the *Mohechatou jing,* T.696:797, n. 13.

[224] An English translation for the Chinese term *aina* 艾納 is unknown. It is a kind of scent produced in a region in the west of China derived from green moss that grows on the bark of pine trees.

[225] *Ghṛta* is a dairy product similar to yogurt.

[226] *Huancao* 浣草 refers to the plant *Asparagus cochinchinensis.*

[227] This citation from the *Foshuo zhude futian jing* 佛說諸德福田經 has appeared earlier in this fascicle, 538a25–b4.

[228] The following section is not found in the *Shisong lü* (T. 1435).

[229] The Chinese character *wai* 外 ("outside") is replaced with the character *shui* 水 ("water"), according to the *Mohe sengqi lü,* T.1425:509a29.

[230] The section from 544c27–545a2 is verbatim with this section from 544c2–26, and has been deleted from the translation.

[231] The Chinese term *bu qing zhi you* 不請之友 ("friends who help others without being asked to do so"; Skt. *anadhīṣṭa-kalyāṇamitra*) refers to bodhisattvas who approach and aid sentient beings as their friends.

[232] The Chinese compound *yinggan* 應感 ("responsiveness and receptivity") is read as *ganying* 感應 ("receptivity and responsiveness").

[233] The Chinese character *zhong* 重 ("to repeat") is replaced with the character *wan* 晚 ("later"), according to the *Xu Gaoseng zhuan,* T.2060:694a29.

[234] Following the *Xu Gaoseng zhuan,* T.2060:695a21, the passage *bing er xie lou* 并二挾樓 ("both embraced a tower,") is read as *bing xie er lou* 並夾二樓 ("completely embraced two towers.")

[235] The Chinese character *xue* 雪 ("snow") is replaced with the character *lei* 雷 ("thunder"), according the *Xu Gaoseng zhuan,* T.2060:695, n. 4.

[236] "Turning [the pages of] sutras" later became a ritual performance in which the first several lines of a sutra are chanted and the rest is skipped while the sutra text is held up and its pages/leaves are allowed to turn.

[237] The Chinese character *kan* 龕 ("a niche for an idol") is replaced with the character *kan* 堪 ("fit for"), according to the *Xu Gaoseng zhuan,* T.2060:698a28.

[238] The Chinese character *san* 散 ("to scatter") is added after the character *xu* 須 ("to have to"), according to the *Xu Gaoseng zhuan,* T.2060:698b6.

239 The passages in the square brackets have been added, according to the *Xu Gaoseng zhuan,* T.2060:698b11–12.

240 The Chinese character *ling* 令 ("to order") is deleted, according to the *Xu Gaoseng zhuan,* T.2060:698b15.

241 Chan Master Da 達 cannot be identified. *Kokuyaku Issaikyō, Shidenbu* 10, p. 217, n. 6, lists several monks as likely candidates, but his identity is still unknown.

242 *Xu Gaoseng zhuan,* T.2060:698c29.

243 The passage in the square brackets has been added, according to the *Xu Gaoseng zhuan,* T.2060:654b24–25.

244 The Chinese character *xia* 夏 ("summer") is replaced with the character *jie* 解 ("to unfasten"), according to the *Xu Gaoseng zhuan,* T.2060:654b28.

245 It is given as the tenth year (636), according to the *Xu Gaoseng zhuan,* T.2060:654c13.

246 The Chinese character *su* 素 ("plain") is replaced with the character *ye* 業 ("work"), according to the *Xu Gaoseng zhuan,* T.2060:654c23.

247 Lake Anavatapta was named after the lake in Buddhist cosmology that is believed to be located in the northern part of the Himalayas and is the origin of the four main rivers of Jambudvīpa.

248 The passage in the square brackets was added, according to the *Xu Gaoseng zhuan,* T.2060:655b16–17.

249 The Chinese characters *sui* 雖 ("although") and *za* 雜 ("miscellaneous") are replaced with the characters *wei* 唯 ("only") and *li* 離 ("to leave behind"), according to the *Xu Gaoseng zhuan,* T.2060:655c1.

Fascicle 34

Chapter Twenty-eight

250 The Chinese compound *sishuang babei shier xianshi* 四雙八輩十二賢士 ("those of the eight stages of sainthood [in the Hinayana] and the twelve people of high moral standing") appears in the *Zengyi ahan jing,* T.125:668a4–5; the *Dafangbian fo baoen jing,* T.156:141b24; the *Chuyao jing,* T.212:654c10, 691a21, 756a1–2; and additionally the *Fenbie gongde lun,* T.1507:36a10–11.

251 The Chinese character *wo* 我 ("I") is replaced with the character *jiao* 教 ("teaching"), according to the *Fenbie gongde lun,* T.1507:36b12.

252 *Fochui banniepan lüeshuo jiaojie jing,* T.389:1110c22, 1112b11–12.

253 A *śiśumāra* is a mugger or a type of shark that lives in the Ganges River.

254 The Chinese term *muhuan* 木槵 is the name of a tree (*Sapindus detergens roxb*), called in Sanskrit *ariṣṭa.* Its seeds are often used to make Buddhist prayer beads.

255 The king's name, Boliuli 波瑠璃, is the Chinese reading. The Sanskrit term is unknown.

256 This citation is not found in the *Piyu jing* but it is found in the *Jinglü yixiang,* T.2121:236a25–b2, in a citation from the *Piyu jing.*

257 See *A Forest of Pearls from the Dharma Garden,* Vol. IV, p. 292, n. 84. There is an extensive explanation for the Chinese terms *can* 慚 (Skt. *hrī*) and *kui* 愧 (Skt. *apatrāpya*) in fascicle 23, chap. 14, of the *Fayuan zhulin,* T.2122:453c8–457a3.

258 The *Weiwu sanmei jing* 惟無三昧經 is a Chinese indigenous scripture listed in Sengyou's catalogue, *Chusanzang jiji,* T.2145:38c1. The complete text has not yet been found.

Chapter Twenty-nine

259 The Sanskrit equivalent for the Chinese name Mianshanyue 面善悅 is unknown.

260 The Sanskrit equivalent for the Chinese name Bazhong-chenlao 拔眾塵勞 ("to uproot numerous defilements") is unknown.

261 The Sanskrit equivalent for the Chinese name Dengxing 等行 ("to practice equally") is unknown.

262 The Sanskrit equivalent for the Chinese name Xiaomingdengyaotuo 消冥等要脫 ("to disperse darkness is equally necessary to liberation") is unknown.

263 The Sanskrit equivalent for the Chinese name Chufaxin nianlikongwei guiyichaoshou 初發心念離恐畏歸依超首 ("with the first thought to awaken aspiration for *bodhi,* leave behind fear, take refuge in [the Buddha], and become outstanding") is unknown.

264 The Sanskrit equivalent for the Chinese name Shanxuanze 善選擇 ("good choice") is unknown.

265 The Sanskrit equivalent for the Chinese name Jingangbuji 金剛步迹 ("*vajra* footprint") is unknown.

266 The Sanskrit equivalent for the Chinese name Juebian 覺辯 ("awakening and debating") is unknown.

267 The Sanskrit equivalent for the Chinese name Baozhishou 寶智首 ("honorably intelligent head") is unknown.

268 The Sanskrit equivalent for the Chinese name Chisuonian 持所念 ("to hold to what one thinks") is unknown.

269 The Sanskrit equivalent for the Chinese name Huaimomandubu 壞魔慢獨步 ("to destroy a devil that is rude and unrivaled") is unknown.

270 The Sanskrit equivalent for the Chinese name Changzhaoyao 常照曜 ("continually shining") is unknown.

271 The Sanskrit equivalent for the Chinese name Chufaxin butui zhuanlun chengshou 初發心不退轉輪成首 ("to not retrogress in proceeding to highest enlightenment from

the original aspiration for enlightenment, turn the wheel, and achieve the top") is unknown.

[272] The Sanskrit equivalent for the Chinese name Fubaijiaolu 覆白交露 ("to cover with a white bead curtain") is unknown.

[273] The Sanskrit equivalent for the Chinese name Baogai zhaokong 寶蓋照空 ("the jeweled canopy shines upon the sky") is unknown.

[274] The Sanskrit equivalent for the Chinese name Zhuqingjing 住清淨 ("to dwell in purity") is unknown.

[275] The Sanskrit equivalent for the Chinese name Kaihua 開化 ("edification") is unknown.

[276] The Chinese term *gai* 垓 is a numerical unit for a large number, said to be a hundred million, a hundred billion, or 9.1 billion multiplied by ten million-billion. The Sanskrit equivalent for the Chinese name Nianwudao 念無倒 ("to think of no perversion") is unknown.

[277] The Sanskrit equivalent for the Chinese name Nian chufayi duanyi bayu 念初發意斷疑拔欲 ("to think that the original initiative cuts off doubts and uproots desires") is unknown.

[278] The Sanskrit equivalent for the Chinese name Lizhukongju wuyouchusuo 離諸恐懼無有處所 ("to leave behind fears and have no residence") is unknown.

[279] The Sanskrit equivalent for the Chinese name Xiaoming dengchao wang 消冥等超王 ("king who disperses darkness and equally jumps over it") is unknown.

[280] The Chinese character *lun* 輪 ("wheel") of *falun* 法輪 ("Dharma wheel") is replaced with the character *zhuan* 轉 ("to turn"), according to the *Garland Sutra,* T.278:546a23.

[281] According to Ono, *Bussho kaisetsu daijiten,* vol. 9, p. 337, the Sanskrit title of the *Fo benxingji jing* could be either **Śākyamuni-buddhacarita* or **Buddhacarita-saṃgraha.*

Glossary

ācārya (*asheli* 阿闍梨): A Buddhist teacher; a master or preceptor.

anāgāmin: Nonreturner. *See* four fruits.

arhat: One who has completed the four stages to the attainment of sainthood in the Hinayana. *See* four fruits; Hinayana.

asaṃkhya (*asengqi* 阿僧祇): A numerical unit. One *asaṃkhya* is ten to the fifty-ninth power, therefore it signifies a very large number.

auspicious *kalpa* (*xianjie* 賢劫): The present cosmic period (*kalpa*). *See also kalpa.*

bhikṣu (*biqiu* 比丘 or *bichu* 苾芻): A mendicant; a Buddhist monk.

bhikṣuṇī (*biqiuni* 比丘尼 or *bichuni* 苾芻尼): A Buddhist nun.

bodhisattva (*pusa* 菩薩): In Sanskrit, "enlightenment being," one who has generated the aspiration for highest enlightenment and is on the path to buddhahood. In the Mahayana bodhisattvas seek enlightenment not just for themselves but in order to compassionately aid others to attain liberation as well. *See also* Mahayana.

Cakravāḍaparvata (Tieweishan 鐵圍山): In Sanskrit, "Ring of Mountains," the proper name of the eight ranges of metallic mountains, of which this mountain is the farthest from Mount Sumeru, the central mountain, presumed in Buddhist cosmology to surround our world-system.

caṇḍāla (*zhantuoluo* 栴陀羅 or 旃陀羅): In the Indian caste system the lowest class of people, also sometimes called outcastes.

Dharma (*fa* 法): The Buddhist Law, truth, or the Buddha's teaching.

Dharma eye (*fayan* 法眼): The wisdom or insight to see the reality of things. *See also* five kinds of eyes.

Dharma of warmth (*nuanfa* 暖法): The first stage of the four wholesome roots (*kuśala-mūla*) for the attainment of sainthood.

dhūta (*toutuo* 頭陀): Ascetic practices, including mendicancy, undertaken by Buddhist monks; also refers to ascetic practitioners.

eight difficulties (*banan* 八難): The eight conditions in which one is unable to encounter a buddha or hear the Dharma: existence in the realms of hell, animals, hungry ghosts (*preta*s), in the heaven of long life, or in Uttarakuru, the continent to the north of Mount Sumeru, where people always enjoy great happiness and are therefore not motivated to seek the truth; being deaf, blind, and mute; being knowledgeable about worldly affairs and eloquent, which may impede one from following the true path; and living during a time before or after a buddha's appearance in the world.

eight superior qualities of the Buddha's voice (*ba*[*zhong*]*yin* 八[種]音): The Buddha is said to possess (1) a pleasant voice, (2) a soft voice, (3) a harmonious voice, (4) a dignified and wise voice, (5) a masculine voice, (6) an unerring voice, (7) a deep and far-reaching voice, and (8) an inexhaustible voice.

eighteen realms ([*shiba*]*jie* 十八界): The twelve sense fields (*āyatana*s) and the six sense consciousnesses (visual, auditory, olfactory, gustatory, tactile, and mental). *See also* six sense consciousnesses; twelve sense fields.

eightfold holy path (*bazhengdao* 八正道): The last of the fundamental Buddhist teaching of the Four Noble Truths is the cessation of suffering through the eightfold path to enlightenment or nirvana, consisting of (1) right view, (2) right thought, (3) right speech, (4) right action, (5) right livelihood, (6) right effort, (7) right mindfulness or recollection, and (8) right meditation. *See also* Four Noble Truths.

evil realms (*echu* 惡處, *edao* 惡道, or *equ* 惡趣): The hell realms and the realms of hungry ghosts, animals, and *asura*s (angry titans). *See also* three evil realms; samsara.

field of merit (*futian* 福田): (1) A buddha or monk; (2) the Three Treasures. *See also* Three Treasures.

five kinds of consciousnesses (*wushi* 五識): The consciousnesses that arise from the functioning of the five senses of sight, hearing, smell, taste, and touch (tactile sensation). *See also* six kinds of consciousness.

five kinds of eyes (*wuyan* 五眼): (1) The physical eye, (2) the divine eye, (3) the wisdom eye, (4) the Dharma eye, and (5) the Buddha eye. *See also* Dharma eye.

five obscurations (*wugai* 五蓋): Greed, anger, sloth and torpor, restlessness and anxiety, and doubt.

five precepts (*wujie* 五戒): The five basic moral and ethical behaviors undertaken by all Buddhists: (1) not to kill, (2) not to steal, (3) not to commit adultery (or, in the case of monastics, not to engage in sexual behavior), (4) not to lie, and (5) not to ingest intoxicants. *See also* six important precepts.

five realms (*wudao* 五道or *wuqu* 五趣): Rebirth in the realms of hell, hungry ghosts, animals, human beings, and heavenly beings (*deva*s). *See also* evil realms; four realms; good realms; samsara; three evil realms.

five *skandha*s (*wuyin* 五陰): The five constituent elements of existence that produce various kinds of suffering: matter or form, perception, conception, volition, and consciousness.

five transcendental faculties (*wutong* 五通): (1) The divine eye, the ability to see anything at any distance; (2) the divine ear, the ability to hear any sound at any distance; (3) the ability to know one's former lives and those of others; (4) the ability to know the thoughts of others; and (5) the ability to go anywhere and transform oneself at will. *See also* six transcendental faculties.

four categories of Buddhists/four kinds of disciples (*si*[*bu*]*zhong* 四[部]衆 or *sibudizi* 四部弟子): Monks *(bhikṣus*), nuns (*bhikṣuṇīs*), laymen (*upāsakas*), and laywomen (*upāsikās*).

four foundations for attaining supernatural powers (*sishenzu* 四神足): (1) Making the vow to attain excellent meditation; (2) exerting effort to attain excellent meditation; (3) controlling the mind to attain excellent meditation; and (4) observing with wisdom to attain excellent meditation.

four fruits (*siguo* 四果 or *sishamenguo* 四沙門果): The four stages of the path to sainthood in the Hinayana: (1) the fruit of entering the stream of the sacred Dharma (*srota-āpatti-phala*), (2) the fruit of one more rebirth in samsaric existence (*sakṛdāgāmi-phala*), (3) the fruit of nonreturning to samsaric existence (*anāgāmi-phala*), and (4) the fruit of arhatship or sainthood (*arhat-phala*). *See also* Hinayana; samsara.

four great elements (*sida* 四大): Earth, water, fire, and wind.

four kinds of favors (*sien* 四恩): Essential kinds of support that all people receive: (1) parents' favor; (2) sentient beings' favor; (3) sovereign's favor; and (4) the favor of the Three Treasures.

four kinds of necessities (*sishi* 四事): The four basic requisites for monastics, consisting of food and drink, clothing, bedding, and medicine. *See also* six kinds of necessities.

four kinds of unhindered speech (*si*[*wuai*]*bian* 四[無礙]辯): (1) Thorough knowledge of and the command of language to explain the Dharma, (2) thorough knowledge of the meanings of the teachings, (3) the absence of impediments to communicating in various dialects, and (4) the absence of impediments to preaching to people according to their capacities.

four modes of birth (*sisheng* 四生): The four ways beings may be born, i.e., from a womb, from an egg, from moisture, and through metamorphosis.

Four Noble Truths (*sidi* 四諦 or *sizhendi* 四真諦): The Buddha's fundamental teaching: (1) the truth of suffering, (2) the truth of the cause of suffering, (3) the truth of the cessation of suffering, and (4) the truth of the eightfold path to the cessation of suffering, i.e., nirvana (extinction). *See also* eightfold holy path; nirvana.

four past buddhas (*sifo* 四佛): Krakucchanda, Kanakamuni, Kāśapa, and Śākyamuni.

four realms (*siqu* 四趣): Rebirth in the realms of hells, hungry ghosts, animals, and *asuras*. *See also* evil realms; five realms; six realms; samsara; three evil realms.

four reliances (*siyi* 四依): (1) Leaving behind evils, (2) adopting wholesomeness, (3) abandoning greed, anger, and ignorance, and (4) being diligent without negligence.

good realms (*shanchu* 善處, *shandao* 善道, or *shanqu* 善趣): The realms of rebirth in heaven and in the realm of human beings. *See also* evil realms; five realms; four realms; six realms; three evil realms.

Hinayana (*xiaosheng* 小乘): In Sanskrit, "Lesser Vehicle," a pejorative term coined by the Mahayana tradition to refer to the doctrines and practices of the mainstream Buddhist tradition, the two vehicles of *śrāvaka*s (disciples) and *pratyekabuddha*s (self-enlightened ones). *See also* four fruits; Mahayana; *śrāvaka; pratyekabuddha.*

icchantika (*yichanti* 一闡提): One who has no possibility of attaining buddhahood because their nature completely lacks wholesomeness.

kalpa (*jie* 劫): In Sanskrit, "eon" or "age"; the unit of measurement for cosmological time. *See also auspicious kalpa.*

kaṣāya (*jiasha*袈裟): The Buddhist monastic robe. *See also saṃghāṭī;* three kinds of robes.

kṣatriya (*cha*[*di*]*li* 刹[帝]利): In the Indian caste system, the second-highest class of nobles and warriors.

mahāsattva (*dashi* 大士): "Great being," another term for a bodhisattva. *See also* bodhisattva.

Mahayana (*dasheng* 大乘): "Great Vehicle"; a term, originally of self-appellation, which is used historically to refer to a movement that began some four centuries after the Buddha's death, marked by the composition of texts that purported to be his words. Although ranging widely in content, these texts generally set forth the bodhisattva path to buddhahood as the ideal to which all should aspire and described bodhisattvas and buddhas as objects of devotion. The key doctrines of the Mahayana include the perfection of wisdom, the skillful methods of a buddha, the three bodies of a buddha, the inherency of buddha-nature, and pure lands or buddha lands. *See also* bodhisattva; Hinayana.

mūrdha-avasthā (*dingfa* 頂法): A Sankrit term that refers to the second of the four preparatory stages to the sacred state in the Sarvāstivāda school, one of the most influential Indian Buddhist schools.

nayuta (*nayouta* 那由他): An Indian numerical unit. One *nayuta* is ten million or a hundred billion, among various other definitions.

nirvana (*niepan* 涅槃): The ultimate goal of Buddhism, a state in which delusions are extinguished and the highest wisdom is attained; counterposed to samsara, cyclic existence. *See also* samsara.

nivāsana (*niyuanseng* 泥洹僧 or *qun* 裙): A monk's undergarment, worn beneath the outer robes. *See also kaṣāya; saṃghāṭī.*

parinirvāṇa (*panniepan* 般涅槃 or *panniyuan* 般泥洹): Complete, perfect nirvana; the term often refers to the nirvana of the Buddha. *See also* nirvana.

pratyekabuddha (*yuanjue* 緣覺, *dujue* 獨覺, or *bizhifo* 辟支佛): "Self-enlightened one," one who attains enlightenment and liberation without a teacher's guidance and who does not teach others.

rākṣasa (*luocha* 羅刹) and *rākṣasī* (*luochanü* 羅刹女): A male or female demon, respectively, that harms people; one of the eight classes of supernatural beings adopted into Buddhism as guardians and protectors.

sakṛdāgāmin: Once-returner. *See* four fruits.

saṃghāṭī (*sengqieli* 僧伽梨, *sengqiezhi* 僧伽胝, or *dayi* 大衣): A monk's formal robe made of nine to twenty-five pieces of cloth, worn when practicing mendicancy or when invited to a royal palace; one of the three kinds of monastic robes. *See also kaṣāya;* three kinds of robes.

saṃkakṣikā (*sengqizhi* 僧衹支, *sengjiaoqi* 僧脚崎, or *fubo* 覆膊): A monastic garment worn under the *kaṣāya* in order to cover the chest and the side of the body. *See also kaṣāya.*

samsara (*lunhui* 輪迴): In Sanskrit and Pāli, "wandering," i.e., the cycle of rebirth, the transmigration of birth and death in the various realms of existence. Nirvana is liberation from samsara. *See also* evil realms; five realms; four realms; good realms; nirvana; six realms; three evil realms; three realms of existence.

six important precepts (*liuzhongjie* 六重戒): (1) Not to kill, (2) not to steal, (3) not to lie, (4) not to commit adultery, (5) not to announce transgressions committed by the four kinds of disciples, and (6) not to sell or buy intoxicants. *See also* five precepts; four categories of Buddhists/four kinds of disciples.

six kinds of domestic animals (*liuchu* 六畜): Horses, cattle, sheep, chickens, dogs, and pigs/hogs.

six kinds of necessities (*liuwu* 六物): Another set of requisites for monastics: three kinds of robes, an almsbowl, a mat for sitting and sleeping, and a filter bag for water. *See also* four kinds of necessities.

six *pāramitā*s (*liudu* 六度 or *liu boluomi* 六波羅蜜): The perfection (*pāramitā*) of six qualities or attitudes undertaken by Buddhist practitioners: giving or generosity (*dāna*), observance of the precepts or moral and ethical behavior (*śīla*), forbearance or patience (*kṣānti*), diligence or effort (*vīrya*), meditation (*dhyāna*), and wisdom (*prajña*).

six purification days (*liuzhai* 六齋 or *liuzhairi* 六齋日): Six days each month on which purification rites and practices are undertaken, on the eighth, fourteenth, fifteenth, twenty-third, twenty-ninth, and thirtieth days.

six realms (*liudao* 六道 or *liuqu* 六趣): The six realms of rebirth in samsara: the realms of hell, hungry ghosts, animals, *asura*s, human beings, and heavenly beings (*deva*s). *See also* evil realms; five realms; four realms; good realms; samsara; three evil realms.

six sense consciousnesses (*liushi* 六識): The consciousnesses that arise from the functioning of the six sense organs with their objects, consisting of visual, auditory, olfactory, gustatory, and tactile senses and mental activity. *See also* six sense organs; twelve sense fields.

six sense organs (*liugen* 六根 or *liuqing* 六情): The eyes, ears, nose, tongue, body (tactile sense), and mind (thought or mental activity).

six transcendental faculties (*liutong* 六通): (1) the ability to go anywhere at will and to transform oneself or objects at will, (2) the ability to see anything at any distance, (3) the ability to hear any sound at any distance, (4) the ability to know the thoughts of others, (5) the ability to know one's former lives and those of others, and (6) the ability to destroy all evil passions. *See also* five transcendental faculties; three major evil passions/three poisons; three transcendental knowledges.

śrāvaka (*shengwen* 聲聞): Literally, "hearer," a follower of the Buddha who was present in his lifetime and heard his teachings directly. The term later came to mean a Buddhist disciple in general.

srota-āpanna: Stream-enterer. *See* four fruits.

ten wholesome acts (*shishan* 十善): (1) not killing, (2) not stealing, (3) not committing adultery, (4) not telling lies, (5) not speaking with harsh or abusive language, (6) not using language that causes enmity between people, (7) not engaging in idle talk, (8) not being greedy, (9) not being angry, and (10) not having wrong views.

ten wholesome precepts (*shi*[*shan*]*jie* 十[善]戒): Ten precepts undertaken by laypeople to perform the ten wholesome acts.

three discourses (*sanlun* 三論): Three important Mahayana Buddhist texts that formed the basis for a Chinese Buddhist school (Sanlun): Nāgārjuna's *Zhonglun* 中論 (*Mādhyamaka-śāstra*) and *Shiermen lun* 十二門論, and Āryadeva's *Bailun* 百論.

three evil realms (*san'edao* 三惡道, *san'equ* 三惡趣, or *santu* 三途): The three lowest realms of rebirth in samsara, the realms of hell, hungry ghosts, and animals. They are sometimes described as the realms of fire (i.e., hell), of blood (i.e., the realm of animals), and of the sword (i.e., the realm of hungry ghosts). *See also* evil realms; samsara.

three kinds of actions (*sanye* 三業): Acts of body, speech, and mind, i.e., physical actions, speech, and thought.

three kinds of robes (*sanyi* 三衣): The three monastic robes, consisting of (1) the formal robe (*saṃghāṭī*); (2) a robe made of seven pieces of cloth worn at services, lectures, and ceremonies (*uttara-āsaṅga*); and (3) the regular everyday robe (*antarvāsa*). *See also saṃghāṭī.*

three major evil passions/three poisons (*sangou* 三垢 or *sandu* 三毒): Greed or craving, anger or hatred, and ignorance or stupidity.

three periods of existence (*sanshi* 三世): Past, present, and future.

three purification months (*sanchangyue* 三長月 or *zhaiyue* 齋月): Three months in a year in which purification rites and practices are undertaken, the first, fifth, and ninth months.

three realms of existence (*sanjie* 三界): The realm of desire (*kāmadhātu*), the realm of form (*rūpadhātu*), and the formless realm (*ārūpyadhātu*).

Three Revered Ones (*sanzun* 三尊): (1) Buddhas, *pratyekabuddha*s, and arhats; (2) Buddha, Dharma, and Sangha, i.e., the Three Treasures; or (3) a buddha with his two attendant bodhisattvas. *See also* arhat; *pratyekabuddha;* Three Treasures.

three transcendental knowledges (*sanming* 三明 or *sanda* 三達): (1) The ability to know one's former lives and those of others, (2) the ability to know one's future destiny and that of others, and (3) the ability to know of all the suffering of the present life and remove its root cause. *See also* six transcendental faculties.

Three Treasures (*sanbao* 三寶): In the Buddhist tradition, the term Three Treasures refers to the three principal objects of veneration: Buddha, Dharma (the teaching), and Sangha (the order of Buddhist monks and nuns). One of the most common practices that defines a Buddhist is "taking refuge" in the Three Treasures. This formula, which accompanies many lay and monastic rituals, involves a formal declaration that the practitioner "goes to" each of the Three Treasures for refuge or protection and commits themself to the Buddhist path.

three vehicles (*sansheng* 三乘): The three paths of practice of bodhisattvas, *pratyekabuddha*s, and *śrāvaka*s; the three kinds of Buddhist teachings applicable to these three paths.

trichiliocosm (*sanqian daqian shijie* 三千大千世界): A designation of the universe comprised of worlds numbering a thousand to the third power.

Tripiṭaka (*sanzang* 三藏): The "three baskets" (*piṭaka*s) comprising the Buddhist canon, Sutra (the Buddha's teachings, delivered in discourses), Vinaya (the monastic code), and Abhidharma (commentaries on the teachings).

twelve causations (*shieryinyuan* 十二因緣): The fundamental Buddhist teaching on the twelve-part chain of causality that drives cyclic existence (samsara), also called dependent origination (*pratītyasamutpāda*): (1) spiritual ignorance (*avidyā*), (2) blind volition (*saṃskāra*), (3) consciousness (*vijñāna*), (4) mental functions and the formation of physical elements ("name-and-form," *nāmarūpa*); (5) the six sense fields (*āyatana*s), (6) contact with external objects (*sparśa*), (7) sensation or feeling (*vedanā*), (8) craving ("thirst," *tṛṣṇā*), (9) grasping or clinging (*upādāna*), (10) existence or the process of becoming (*bhava*), (11) birth (*jāti*), and (12) old age and death (*jarāmaraṇa*). *See also* samsara.

twelve kinds of scriptures (*shierbujing* 十二部經): (1) Sutras, the Buddha's exposition of the Dharma in prose; (2) *geya,* verses that repeat the ideas already expressed in prose; (3) *vyākaraṇa,* prophecies by the Buddha regarding his disciples' attainment of buddhahood; (4) *gāthā,* verses containing ideas not expressed in the prose section of a sutra; (5) *udāna,* an exposition of the Dharma by the Buddha without awaiting his disciples' questions or requests; (6) *nidāna,* narratives of one's past or events that explain their present state; (7) *avadāna*, an exposition of the Dharma through allegories; (8) *itivṛttaka,* narratives of past existences of the Buddha's disciples; (9) *jātaka,* narratives of the Buddha's past existences; (10) *vaipulya,* a detailed or extensive exposition of principles of truth; (11) *adbhuta-dharma,* accounts of miracles performed by the Buddha or other deities; and (12) *upadeśa*, doctrinal discussions.

twelve sense fields (*āyatana*s; [*shier*]*ru* [十二]入): The six sense organs of the eyes, ears, nose, tongue, body, and mind, and their corresponding objects of form/color, sound, odor, taste, tangible objects, and mental objects. *See also* six sense conciousnessess.

upādhyāya (*heshang* 和上 or 和尚): Originally, a preceptor; later used as a title of respect for a virtuous monk.

upāsaka (*youposai* 優婆塞 or *qingxinnan* 清信男): A Buddhist layman.

upāsikā (*youpoyi* 優婆夷 or *qingxinnü* 清信女): A Buddhist laywoman.

Way of the Spirit (*shendao* 神道): The unfathomable mysterious way, the transcendental religious world; also a synonym for a supreme spiritual being. The term *shendao* is found in the *Book of Changes* completed before the Han dynasty (206 B.C.E.–220 C.E.). After the introduction and adoption of Buddhism in China, the term began to appear in Buddhist texts.

yakṣa (*yuecha* 夜叉): A dangerous demon who harms people; one of the class of eight supernatural beings adopted into Buddhism as guardians and protectors.

yojana (*youxun* 由旬): An Indian unit of measuring distance, usually defined as the distance that can be covered by the royal army in one day. Modern estimates vary widely; eight miles is often given as an approximation, although other estimates varying from four to ten miles are also found.

Bibliography

Beal, Samuel, trans. *Si-Yu-Ki: Buddhist Records of the Western World,* 2 vols. London: Routledge, 2000.

Cheng, Hsiao-Chieh, et al., trans. *Shan Hai Ching: Legendary Geography and Wonders of Ancient China.* Taibei: Committee for Compilation and Examination of the Series of Chinese Classics, National Institute for Compilation and Translation, 1985.

Kanaoka, Shōkō. *Kan'yaku Butten.* Tokyo: Gakushū kenkyūsha,1992.

Kawaguchi, Yoshiteru. "Hōon jurin ni mirareru itsuzon betsuzon kyō nit suite," *Nanto Bukkyō* 37 (1976): 83–102.

Kawamura, Kōshō. *Shin Kokuyaku Daizōkyō,* Hon'enbu 2 and Monju kyōtenbu 1 and 2. Tokyo: Daizō Shuppan, 1993–1996.

Kokuyaku Issaikyō. Indo senjutsu bu, Hon'enbu 1 and 7 and Bidonbu 12. Tokyo: Daitō Shuppansha, 1930–1932.

Kokuyaku Issaikyō. Wa-Kan senjutsu bu, Gokyōbu 5 and Shidenbu 6, 7, and 10. Tokyo: Daitō Shuppansha, 1959–1964.

Le Blanc, Charles. *Huai-nan Tzu: Philosophical Synthesis in Early Han Thought.* Hong Kong: Hong Kong University Press, 1985.

Legge, James, trans. *Dao de jing ji Zhuangzi quan ji.* Taibei: Wen xing shu ju, 1963.

—. *I ching: Book of Changes.* Ch'u Chai with Winberg Chai, eds. With Introduction and Study Guide. New Hyde Park, NY: University Books, 1964.

—. *The Chinese Classics: With a Translation, Critical and Exegetical Notes, Prolegomena, and Copious Indexes,* vols. 1 and 3. Taipei: Wen shih che ch'u pan she, 1972, second revised ed.

—. *The Chinese Classics: With a Translation, Critical and Exegetical Notes, Prolegomena, and Copious Indexes,* vol. 5. Hong Kong: Hong Kong University Press, 1960.

Makita, Tairyō. *Gikyō kenkyū.* Kyoto: Kyōto Daigaku Jinbun Kagaku Kenkyūjo, 1976.

Makita, Tairyō, and Toshinori Ochiai, eds. *Nanatsudera koitsu kyōten kenkyū sōsho,* vol. 2. *Chūgoku senjutsu kyōten* (*sono* 2). Tokyo: Daitō Shuppansha, 1996.

Mizutani, Shinjō, trans. *Daitō saiiki ki,* vols. 1–3. Tokyo: Heibonsha, 1999.

Mochizuki, Shinkō. *Mochizuki Bukkyō Daijiten,* vols. 1–10. Tokyo: Sekai Seiten Kankō Kyōkai, 1954–1958.

Nagao, Gajin, Seizan Yanagida, and Yūichi Kajiyama, eds. *Daijō Butten,* Chūgoku Nihon-hen, 3, *Shutsusanzōki shū Hōon jurin.* Tokyo: Chūō Kōronsha, 1993.

Nienhauser, William H., Jr., ed. *The Grand Scribe's Records,* vols. 1–2. Bloomington, IN: Indiana University Press, 1994–2002.

Ōchō, Enichi. "Jiku Dōshō sen Hokkekyōsho no kenkyū," *Ōtani Daigaku kenkyū nenpō* 5 (1952): 167–276.

Oda, Tokunō. *Bukkyō Daijiten.* Tokyo: Daizō Shuppan, 1980, fifth printing.

Ono, Genmyō. *Bussho kaisetsu daijiten,* vols. 1–15. Tokyo: Daitō Shuppansha, 1967–1991.

Ōuchi, Fumio. "Hōon jurin Chūgoku no mono to natta Bukkyō no sekai," *Gekkan Shinika* 9/3 (1998): 22–26.

Sadakata, Akira. "Jari futo no na ni tsuite," *Indogaku Bukkyōgaku kenkyū* 29/1 (1980): 31–36.
—. *Shumisen to gokuraku: Bukkyō no uchūkan.* Tokyo: Kōdansha, 1973.

Takakusu, Junjiro, and Kaigyoku Watanabe, eds. *Taishō shinshū daizōkyō,* vols. 1–85. Tokyo: Taishō Issaikyō Kankōkai (Society for the Publication of the Taishō Edition of the Tripitaka), 1924–1932.

Takeda, Akira, trans. *Sōshinki.* Tokyo: Heibonsha, 1982.

Wakatsuki, Toshihide, et al., eds. "Hōon jurin no sōgōteki kenkyū," *Shinshū Sōgō Kenkyūjo kenkyū kiyō* 25 (2007): 1–224.

Ware, James R., trans. *Alchemy, Medicine, Religion in the China of A.D. 320: The Nei P'ien of Ko Hung (Pao-p'u Tzu).* Cambridge, MA: M.I.T. Press, 1966.

Watson, Burton, trans. *Chuang Tzu: Basic Writings.* New York: Columbia University Press, 1964.

Willemen, Charles, trans. *The Storehouse of Sundry Valuables.* Berkeley, CA: Numata Center for Buddhist Translation and Research, 1994.

Xingyun dashi, et al., eds. *Fo guang da ci dian,* vols. 1–8. Taiwan Gaoxiong Shi: Fo guang chu ban she: Fa xing zhe Fo guang da zang jing bian xiu wei yuan hui, 1988.

Yang, Hsien-yi, and Gladys Yang, trans. *Selections from Records of the Historian.* Peking: Foreign Languages Press, 1979.

Ziegler, Harumi Hirano. "The Sinification of Buddhism as Found in an Early Chinese Indigenous Sūtra: A Study and Translation of the *Fo-shuo Ching-tu San-mei Ching* (*The Samādhi-Sūtra on Liberation through Purification Spoken by the Buddha*)," Ph.D. dissertation, University of California, Los Angeles, 2001.

Index

A

Abhidharma, 68
Abhidharma-jñāna-prasthāna. See Fazhi lun
Abhidharma-mahāvibhāṣā, 66, 68
Abode of Neither Thought nor Non-thought, 20, 119
Acala, 106
ācārya, 8, 9, 10
adbhuta-dharma, 360
Adhyāśaya-sañcodana. See Fajue jingxin jing
afflictions, 21, 127, 130, 189
Agni, 102, 144
Ai, Emperor, 236, 237
Ajātaśatru, King, 101, 155, 222
Ajita, 141
Ājñāta-kauṇḍinya, 96
alms, 14, 17, 74, 110, 144, 271, 274, 275, 276, 277, 278, 279, 280, 289, 293, 294, 295, 297, 305, 327, 364, 377n136
almsbegging, 32, 277, 278
almsbowl(s), 37, 61, 83, 96, 106, 146, 275, 276, 354
almsgiving, 73, 112, 118, 119, 121, 126, 141, 269, 276, 278, 279, 280, 282, 293–294, 316, 317, 332, 333, 352, 367, 382n209
Amitābha, 351, 356, 368
Amituo jing, 351
Āmrapālī, 84, 273
anāgāmi-phala, 227, 280
Ānanda, 4, 5, 6, 17, 61, 68, 69, 84, 101, 138, 224, 226, 273, 276, 293, 302, 303, 340, 349, 351, 356
Āndhra, 104
Anding, 37, 212
Anfeng prefecture, 237
Aṅgaja, 140, 377n135
Aṅgulimāla, 75
Anhui province, 185, 209, 232, 233, 265, 317
animal(s)/beast(s)/creature(s), 12, 22, 32, 36, 52, 53, 67, 73, 82, 85, 121, 128, 129, 136, 137–138, 155, 194, 200, 201, 206, 208, 219, 227, 231, 232, 235, 236, 238, 239, 283, 309, 322, 337, 342, 351, 352, 355, 356, 359
ape(s), 73, 212
bear, 236, 380n181
boar/hogs/pig, 36, 37, 137, 201
bulls, 256, 259
camels, 26, 170, 252
carp, 185, 200
catfish, 50, 239
cattle/cow(s), 16, 54, 89, 114, 119, 123, 137, 164, 193, 203, 241–242, 256, 258, 280, 281, 289, 298, 324, 370n24
chicken(s)/hen/rooster, 37, 98, 137, 203, 208, 210, 238, 240
crab(s)/mud crabs, 214–215, 238
deer/doe, 11, 12, 13, 14, 73, 81, 82, 94, 179, 183, 217, 231, 253
dog(s), 4, 44, 74, 106, 137, 183, 201, 204, 210–211, 236, 342

Changzhaoyao, 358, 385n270
Channa, 281
Chen and Zhao, 181, 182
Chen Feng, 236
Cheng, 169
Cheng, Emperor, 200
Cheng Dedu, 29
Chengdu, 167
Chengguo village, 34
Cheng Huihe, 34
Chengnan, 172
Chengshi lun, 297
Chenliu, 23, 208, 232, 371n31
Chenna. *See* Dignāga
Chen prefecture, 213
Chen state, 239, 380n184
Chen Xianda, 174
Chen Xiuyuan, 262–263
Chen Zhenglu, 176
Che Tan, 171
China, xiii, xiv, 23, 55, 59, 61, 62, 66, 67, 68, 70, 71, 75, 76, 77, 81, 83, 88, 89, 90, 91, 94, 96, 97, 99, 100, 103, 105, 138, 147, 179, 230, 270, 383n224
Chinese, xiv, 29, 55, 56, 86, 91, 92, 146, 147, 148, 163, 170, 183, 237, 242, 263, 300, 312, 314, 315, 317, 320, 323, 325, 370n17,
  calendar, 79, 87, 93, 94, 97, 165, 374n93
  character(s)/language, 48, 56, 69, 170, 213, 214, 242, 298, 370nn16, 19, 20, 23, 24, 27; 371nn29, 36–39, 41, 43; 371–372n45, 372nn46, 47, 50, 53; 373nn70, 73; 374n96, 375nn110, 111; 375–376n115, 376nn116–118, 121, 126–132; 377nn135, 137–145; 378nn146, 149–154, 158–160, 162; 379nn163, 164, 167, 169, 172, 177, 178; 380nn181, 186, 190–192; 381nn193, 195–199, 206, 207; 382nn209, 210, 214–216, 220; 383nn223, 224, 229, 231–233, 235, 237, 238; 384nn240, 244, 246, 249–251, 254; 385nn255, 259–270; 385–386n271, 386nn272–280
  indigenous sutra/literature/translation, xiii, 298, 382nn211, 212; 385n258
  music/musical instruments/zither, 183, 185, 186, 206
Chisuonian, 357, 385n268
Chu, emperor of. *See* Lin Shihong
Chuchu jing, 219, 220, 340
Chufaxin butui zhuanlun chengshou, 358, 385n271
Chufaxin nianlikongwei guiyichaoshou, 357, 385n263
Chungu, 37
Chunqiu Zuozhuan, 380n181
Chun Yujin, 211
Chunyu Yi, 199
Chusanzang jiji, 369n2, 385n258
  See also Fayuan jing
Chusheng Putixin jing, 250
Chuyao jing, 382n219, 384n250
Cibei daochang chanfa, 370n25
Cīnabhukti, 68
Ciñcā, 76
Ci province, 158, 159
clergy, 22, 34, 109, 111
  See also monk(s)
compassion, 35, 112, 113, 133, 135, 136, 137, 138, 191, 195, 220, 224, 260, 270, 281, 308, 317, 337, 341, 345, 352, 356, 358
Confucius, 206, 214, 239, 243, 380n184
consciousness-only, 321
contemplation, 94, 131, 134, 320, 322, 331–332, 343
  See also meditation
corpse(s), 18, 19, 34, 43, 47, 106, 151, 152, 168, 174, 210, 222, 223, 226, 313, 317, 321, 378n154

G

K

L

M

N

O

P

S

T

Z

BDK English Tripiṭaka (First Series)

Abbreviations

Ch.: Chinese
Skt.: Sanskrit
Jp.: Japanese
Eng.: Published title

Title		Taishō No.
Ch.	Faju piyu jing (法句譬喻經)	211
Eng.	*The Scriptural Text: Verses of the Doctrine, with Parables* (1999)	
Ch.	Xiaopin banruo boluomi jing (小品般若波羅蜜經)	227
Skt.	Aṣṭasāhasrikā-prajñāpāramitā-sūtra	
Ch.	Jingang banruo boluomi jing (金剛般若波羅蜜經)	235
Skt.	Vajracchedikā-prajñāpāramitā-sūtra	
Ch.	Daluo jingang bukong zhenshi sanmoye jing (大樂金剛不空眞實三麼耶經)	243
Skt.	Adhyardhaśatikā-prajñāpāramitā-sūtra	
Eng.	*The Sutra of the Vow of Fulfilling the Great Perpetual Enjoyment and Benefiting All Sentient Beings Without Exception* (in *Esoteric Texts,* 2015)	
Ch.	Renwang banruo boluomi jing (仁王般若波羅蜜經)	245
Skt.	*Kāruṇikārājā-prajñāpāramitā-sūtra	
Ch.	Banruo boluomiduo xin jing (般若波羅蜜多心經)	251
Skt.	Prajñāpāramitāhṛdaya-sūtra	
Ch.	Miaofa lianhua jing (妙法蓮華經)	262
Skt.	Saddharmapuṇḍarīka-sūtra	
Eng.	*The Lotus Sutra* (Revised Second Edition, 2007)	
Ch.	Wuliangyi jing (無量義經)	276
Eng.	*The Infinite Meanings Sutra* (in *Tiantai Lotus Texts,* 2013)	
Ch.	Guan Puxian pusa xingfa jing (觀普賢菩薩行法經)	277
Eng.	*The Sutra Expounded by the Buddha on Practice of the Way through Contemplation of the Bodhisattva All-embracing Goodness* (in *Tiantai Lotus Texts,* 2013)	
Ch.	Dafangguang fo huayan jing (大方廣佛華嚴經)	279
Skt.	Avataṃsaka-sūtra	
Ch.	Shengman shizihou yisheng defang bianfang guang jing (勝鬘師子吼一乘大方便方廣經)	353
Skt.	Śrīmālādevīsiṃhanāda-sūtra	
Eng.	*The Sutra of Queen Śrīmālā of the Lion's Roar* (2004)	
Ch.	Wuliangshou jing (無量壽經)	360
Skt.	Sukhāvatīvyūha	
Eng.	*The Larger Sutra on Amitāyus* (in *The Three Pure Land Sutras,* Revised Second Edition, 2003)	

Title		Taishō No.
Ch.	Guan wuliangshou fo jing (觀無量壽佛經)	365
Skt.	*Amitāyurdhyāna-sūtra	
Eng.	*The Sutra on Contemplation of Amitāyus* (in *The Three Pure Land Sutras,* Revised Second Edition, 2003)	
Ch.	Amituo jing (阿彌陀經)	366
Skt.	Sukhāvatīvyūha	
Eng.	*The Smaller Sutra on Amitāyus* (in *The Three Pure Land Sutras,* Revised Second Edition, 2003)	
Ch.	Da banniepan jing (大般涅槃經)	374
Skt.	Mahāparinirvāṇa-sūtra	
Eng.	*The Nirvana Sutra* (Volume I, 2013)	
Ch.	Fochuibo niepan lüeshuo jiaojie jing (佛垂般涅槃略説教誡經)	389
Eng.	*The Bequeathed Teaching Sutra* (in *Apocryphal Scriptures,* 2005)	
Ch.	Dizang pusa benyuan jing (地藏菩薩本願經)	412
Skt.	*Kṣitigarbhapraṇidhāna-sūtra	
Ch.	Banzhou sanmei jing (般舟三昧經)	418
Skt.	Pratyutpanna-buddhasammukhāvasthita-samādhi-sūtra	
Eng.	*The Pratyutpanna Samādhi Sutra* (1998)	
Ch.	Yaoshi liuli guang rulai benyuan gongde jing (藥師琉璃光如來本願功德經)	450
Skt.	Bhaiṣajyaguru-vaiḍūrya-prabhāsa-pūrvapraṇidhāna-viśeṣavistara	
Eng.	*The Scripture of Master of Medicine, Beryl Radiance Tathāgata* (2018)	
Ch.	Mile xiasheng chengfo jing (彌勒下生成佛經)	454
Skt.	*Maitreyavyākaraṇa	
Eng.	*The Sutra That Expounds the Descent of Maitreya Buddha and His Enlightenment* (2016)	
Ch.	Wenshushili wen jing (文殊師利問經)	468
Skt.	*Mañjuśrīparipṛcchā	
Eng.	*The Sutra of Mañjuśrī's Questions* (2016)	
Ch.	Weimojie suoshuo jing (維摩詰所說經)	475
Skt.	Vimalakīrtinirdeśa-sūtra	
Eng.	*The Vimalakīrti Sutra* (2004)	

Title	Taishō No.
Ch. Yueshangnü jing (月上女經) Skt. Candrottarādārikā-paripṛcchā Eng. *The Sutra of the Girl Candrottarā* (2018)	480
Ch. Zuochan sanmei jing (坐禪三昧經) Eng. *The Sutra on the Concentration of Sitting Meditation* (2009)	614
Ch. Damoduoluo chan jing (達磨多羅禪經)	618
Ch. Yuedeng sanmei jing (月燈三昧經) Skt. Samādhirāja-candrapradīpa-sūtra	639
Ch. Shoulengyan sanmei jing (首楞嚴三昧經) Skt. Śūraṅgamasamādhi-sūtra Eng. *The Śūraṅgama Samādhi Sutra* (1998)	642
Ch. Jinguang ming zuishengwang jing (金光明最勝王經) Skt. Suvarṇaprabhāsa-sūtra	665
Ch. Dasheng rulengqie jing (大乘入楞伽經) Skt. Laṅkāvatāra-sūtra	672
Ch. Jie shenmi jing (解深密經) Skt. Saṃdhinirmocana-sūtra Eng. *The Scripture on the Explication of Underlying Meaning* (2000)	676
Ch. Yulanpen jing (盂蘭盆經) Skt. *Ullambana-sūtra Eng. *The Ullambana Sutra* (in *Apocryphal Scriptures,* 2005)	685
Ch. Sishierzhang jing (四十二章經) Eng. *The Sutra of Forty-two Sections* (in *Apocryphal Scriptures,* 2005)	784
Ch. Dafangguang yuanjue xiuduoluo liaoyi jing (大方廣圓覺修多羅了義經) Eng. *The Sutra of Perfect Enlightenment* (in *Apocryphal Scriptures,* 2005)	842
Ch. Da Biluzhena chengfo shenbian jiachi jing (大毘盧遮那成佛神變加持經) Skt. Mahāvairocanābhisambodhi-vikurvitādhiṣṭhāna-vaipulyasūtrendra-rājanāma-dharmaparyāya Eng. *The Vairocanābhisaṃbodhi Sutra* (2005)	848

Title		Taishō No.
Ch.	Jinggangding yiqie rulai zhenshi she dasheng xianzheng dajiao wang jing (金剛頂一切如來眞實攝大乘現證大教王經)	865
Skt.	Sarvatathāgata-tattvasaṃgraha-mahāyānābhisamaya-mahākalparāja	
Eng.	*The Adamantine Pinnacle Sutra* (in *Two Esoteric Sutras,* 2001)	
Ch.	Suxidi jieluo jing (蘇悉地羯囉經)	893
Skt.	Susiddhikara-mahātantra-sādhanopāyika-paṭala	
Eng.	*The Susiddhikara Sutra* (in *Two Esoteric Sutras,* 2001)	
Ch.	Modengqie jing (摩登伽經)	1300
Skt.	*Mātaṅgī-sūtra	
Eng.	*The Mātaṅga Sutra* (in *Esoteric Texts,* 2015)	
Ch.	Mohe sengqi lü (摩訶僧祇律)	1425
Skt.	*Mahāsāṃghika-vinaya	
Ch.	Sifen lü (四分律)	1428
Skt.	*Dharmaguptaka-vinaya	
Ch.	Shanjianlü piposha (善見律毘婆沙)	1462
Pāli	Samantapāsādikā	
Ch.	Fanwang jing (梵網經)	1484
Skt.	*Brahmajāla-sūtra	
	The Brahmā's Net Sutra (2017)	
Ch.	Youposaijie jing (優婆塞戒經)	1488
Skt.	Upāsakaśīla-sūtra	
Eng.	*The Sutra on Upāsaka Precepts* (1994)	
Ch.	Miaofa lianhua jing youbotishe (妙法蓮華經憂波提舍)	1519
Skt.	Saddharmapuṇḍarīka-upadeśa	
Eng.	*The Commentary on the Lotus Sutra* (in *Tiantai Lotus Texts,* 2013)	
Ch.	Shizha biposha lun (十住毘婆沙論)	1521
Skt.	*Daśabhūmika-vibhāṣā	
Ch.	Fodijing lun (佛地經論)	1530
Skt.	*Buddhabhūmisūtra-śāstra	
Eng.	*The Interpretation of the Buddha Land* (2002)	
Ch.	Apidamojushe lun (阿毘達磨俱舍論)	1558
Skt.	Abhidharmakośa-bhāṣya	

Title		Taishō No.
Ch.	Zhonglun (中論)	1564
Skt.	Madhyamaka-śāstra	
Ch.	Yüqie shidilun (瑜伽師地論)	1579
Skt.	Yogācārabhūmi-śāstra	
Ch.	Cheng weishi lun (成唯識論)	1585
Eng.	*Demonstration of Consciousness Only* (in *Three Texts on Consciousness Only,* 1999)	
Ch.	Weishi sanshilun song (唯識三十論頌)	1586
Skt.	Triṃśikā	
Eng.	*The Thirty Verses on Consciousness Only* (in *Three Texts on Consciousness Only,* 1999)	
Ch.	Weishi ershi lun (唯識二十論)	1590
Skt.	Viṃśatikā	
Eng.	*The Treatise in Twenty Verses on Consciousness Only* (in *Three Texts on Consciousness Only,* 1999)	
Ch.	She dasheng lun (攝大乘論)	1593
Skt.	Mahāyānasaṃgraha	
Eng.	*The Summary of the Great Vehicle* (Revised Second Edition, 2003)	
Ch.	Bian zhongbian lun (辯中邊論)	1600
Skt.	Madhyāntavibhāga	
Eng.	*Analysis of the Middle and Extremes* (2021)	
Ch.	Dasheng zhuangyanjing lun (大乘莊嚴經論)	1604
Skt.	Mahāyānasūtrālaṃkāra	
Ch.	Dasheng chengye lun (大乘成業論)	1609
Skt.	Karmasiddhiprakaraṇa	
Eng.	*A Mahayana Demonstration on the Theme of Action* (in *Three Short Treatises by Vasubandhu, Sengzhao, and Zongmi,* 2017)	
Ch.	Jiujing yisheng baoxing lun (究竟一乘寶性論)	1611
Skt.	Ratnagotravibhāga-mahāyānottaratantra-śāstra	
Ch.	Yinming ruzheng li lun (因明入正理論)	1630
Skt.	Nyāyapraveśa	
Ch.	Dasheng ji pusa xue lun (大乘集菩薩學論)	1636
Skt.	Śikṣāsamuccaya	

Title		Taishō No.
Ch.	Jingangzhen lun (金剛針論)	1642
Skt.	Vajrasūcī	
Ch.	Zhang suozhi lun (彰所知論)	1645
Eng.	*The Treatise on the Elucidation of the Knowable* (2004)	
Ch.	Putixing jing (菩提行經)	1662
Skt.	Bodhicaryāvatāra	
Ch.	Jingangding yuqie zhongfa anouduoluo sanmiao sanputi xin lun (金剛頂瑜伽中發阿耨多羅三藐三菩提心論)	1665
Eng.	*The Bodhicitta Śāstra* (in *Esoteric Texts,* 2015)	
Ch.	Dasheng qixin lun (大乘起信論)	1666
Skt.	*Mahāyānaśraddhotpāda-śāstra	
Eng.	*The Awakening of Faith* (2005)	
Ch.	Shimoheyan lun (釋摩訶衍論)	1668
Ch.	Naxian biqiu jing (那先比丘經)	1670B
Pāli	Milindapañhā	
Eng.	*The Scripture on the Monk Nāgasena* (2021)	
Ch.	Banruo boluomiduo xin jing yuzan (般若波羅蜜多心經幽賛)	1710
Eng.	*A Comprehensive Commentary on the Heart Sutra* (*Prajñāpāramitā-hṛdaya-sūtra*) (2001)	
Ch.	Miaofalianhua jing xuanyi (妙法蓮華經玄義)	1716
Ch.	Guan wuliangshou fo jing shu (觀無量壽佛經疏)	1753
Ch.	Sanlun xuanyi (三論玄義)	1852
Ch.	Dasheng xuan lun (大乘玄論)	1853
Ch.	Zhao lun (肇論)	1858
Eng.	*Essays of Sengzhao* (in *Three Short Treatises by Vasubandhu, Sengzhao, and Zongmi,* 2017)	
Ch.	Huayan yisheng jiaoyi fenqi zhang (華嚴一乘教義分齊章)	1866
Ch.	Yuanren lun (原人論)	1886
Eng.	*Treatise on the Origin of Humanity* (in *Three Short Treatises by Vasubandhu, Sengzhao, and Zongmi,* 2017)	
Ch.	Mohe zhiguan (摩訶止觀)	1911

Title		Taishō No.
Ch.	Xiuxi zhiguan zuochan fayao (修習止觀坐禪法要)	1915
Ch.	Tiantai sijiao yi (天台四教儀)	1931
Eng.	*A Guide to the Tiantai Fourfold Teachings* (in *Tiantai Lotus Texts,* 2013)	
Ch.	Guoqing bai lu (國清百録)	1934
Ch.	Zhenzhou Linji Huizhao chanshi wulu (鎭州臨濟慧照禪師語録)	1985
Eng.	*The Recorded Sayings of Linji* (in *Three Chan Classics,* 1999)	
Ch.	Foguo Yuanwu chanshi biyan lu (佛果圜悟禪師碧巖録)	2003
Eng.	*The Blue Cliff Record* (1998)	
Ch.	Wumen guan (無門關)	2005
Eng.	*Wumen's Gate* (in *Three Chan Classics,* 1999)	
Ch.	Liuzu dashi fabao tan jing (六祖大師法寶壇經)	2008
Eng.	*The Platform Sutra of the Sixth Patriarch* (2000)	
Ch.	Xinxin ming (信心銘)	2010
Eng.	*The Faith-Mind Maxim* (in *Three Chan Classics,* 1999)	
Ch.	Huangboshan Duanji chanshi chuanxin fayao (黃檗山斷際禪師傳心法要)	2012A
Eng.	*Essentials of the Transmission of Mind* (in *Zen Texts,* 2005)	
Ch.	Yongjia Zhengdao ge (永嘉證道歌)	2014
Eng.	*Yongjia's Song of Actualizing the Way* (2021)	
Ch.	Chixiu Baizhang qinggui (勅修百丈清規)	2025
Eng.	*The Baizhang Zen Monastic Regulations* (2007)	
Ch.	Yibuzonglun lun (異部宗輪論)	2031
Skt.	Samayabhedoparacanacakra	
Eng.	*The Cycle of the Formation of the Schismatic Doctrines* (2004)	
Ch.	Ayuwang jing (阿育王經)	2043
Skt.	Aśokāvadāna	
Eng.	*The Biographical Scripture of King Aśoka* (1993)	
Ch.	Maming pusa zhuan (馬鳴菩薩傳)	2046
Eng.	*The Life of Aśvaghoṣa Bodhisattva* (in *Lives of Great Monks and Nuns,* 2002)	

Title	Taishō No.
Ch. Longshu pusa zhuan (龍樹菩薩傳) Eng. *The Life of Nāgārjuna Bodhisattva* (in *Lives of Great Monks and Nuns,* 2002)	2047
Ch. Posoupandou fashi zhuan (婆藪槃豆法師傳) Eng. *Biography of Dharma Master Vasubandhu* (in *Lives of Great Monks and Nuns,* 2002)	2049
Ch. Datang Daciensi Zanzang fashi zhuan (大唐大慈恩寺三藏法師傳) Eng. *A Biography of the Tripiṭaka Master of the Great Ci'en Monastery of the Great Tang Dynasty* (1995)	2053
Ch. Gaoseng zhuan (高僧傳)	2059
Ch. Biqiuni zhuan (比丘尼傳) Eng. *Biographies of Buddhist Nuns* (in *Lives of Great Monks and Nuns,* 2002)	2063
Ch. Gaoseng Faxian zhuan (高僧法顯傳) Eng. *The Journey of the Eminent Monk Faxian* (in *Lives of Great Monks and Nuns,* 2002)	2085
Ch. Datang xiyu ji (大唐西域記) Eng. *The Great Tang Dynasty Record of the Western Regions* (1996)	2087
Ch. Youfangjichao: Tangdaheshangdongzheng zhuan (遊方記抄: 唐大和上東征傳)	2089-(7)
Ch. Hongming ji (弘明集) Eng. *The Collection for the Propagation and Clarification of Buddhism* (Volume I, 2015) *The Collection for the Propagation and Clarification of Buddhism* (Volume II, 2017)	2102
Ch. Fayuan zhulin (法苑珠林) Eng. *A Forest of Pearls from the Dharma Garden* (Volume I, 2019) Eng. *A Forest of Pearls from the Dharma Garden* (Volume II, 2019) Eng. *A Forest of Pearls from the Dharma Garden* (Volume III, 2020) Eng. *A Forest of Pearls from the Dharma Garden* (Volume IV, 2020) Eng. *A Forest of Pearls from the Dharma Garden* (Volume V, 2022)	2122
Ch. Nanhai jigui neifa zhuan (南海寄歸內法傳) Eng. *Buddhist Monastic Traditions of Southern Asia* (2000)	2125

Title		Taishō No.
Ch.	Fanyu zaming (梵語雜名)	2135
Jp. Eng.	Shōmangyō gisho (勝鬘經義疏) *Prince Shōtoku's Commentary on the Śrīmālā Sutra* (2011)	2185
Jp. Eng.	Yuimakyō gisho (維摩經義疏) *The Expository Commentary on the Vimalakīrti Sutra* (2012)	2186
Jp.	Hokke gisho (法華義疏)	2187
Jp.	Hannya shingyō hiken (般若心經秘鍵)	2203
Jp.	Daijō hossō kenjin shō (大乘法相研神章)	2309
Jp. Eng.	Kanjin kakumu shō (觀心覺夢鈔) *Oberving the Mind, Awakening from a Dream* (2021)	2312
Jp. Eng.	Risshū kōyō (律宗綱要) *The Essentials of the Vinaya Tradition* (1995)	2348
Jp. Eng.	Tendai hokke shūgi shū (天台法華宗義集) *The Collected Teachings of the Tendai Lotus School* (1995)	2366
Jp.	Kenkairon (顯戒論)	2376
Jp.	Sange gakushō shiki (山家學生式)	2377
Jp. Eng.	Hizōhōyaku (秘藏寶鑰) *The Precious Key to the Secret Treasury* (in *Shingon Texts*, 2004)	2426
Jp. Eng.	Benkenmitsu nikyō ron (辨顯密二教論) *On the Differences between the Exoteric and Esoteric Teachings* (in *Shingon Texts*, 2004)	2427
Jp. Eng.	Sokushin jōbutsu gi (即身成佛義) *The Meaning of Becoming a Buddha in This Very Body* (in *Shingon Texts*, 2004)	2428
Jp. Eng.	Shōji jissōgi (聲字實相義) *The Meanings of Sound, Sign, and Reality* (in *Shingon Texts*, 2004)	2429
Jp. Eng.	Unjigi (吽字義) *The Meanings of the Word Hūṃ* (in *Shingon Texts*, 2004)	2430
Jp. Eng.	Gorin kuji myōhimitsu shaku (五輪九字明秘密釋) *The Illuminating Secret Commentary on the Five Cakras and the Nine Syllables* (in *Shingon Texts*, 2004)	2514

Title		Taishō No.
Jp.	Mitsugonin hotsuro sange mon (密嚴院發露懺悔文)	2527
Eng.	*The Mitsugonin Confession* (in *Shingon Texts,* 2004)	
Jp.	Kōzen gokoku ron (興禪護國論)	2543
Eng.	*A Treatise on Letting Zen Flourish to Protect the State* (in *Zen Texts,* 2005)	
Jp.	Fukan zazengi (普勧坐禪儀)	2580
Eng.	*A Universal Recommendation for True Zazen* (in *Zen Texts,* 2005)	
Jp.	Shōbōgenzō (正法眼藏)	2582
Eng.	*Shōbōgenzō: The True Dharma-eye Treasury* (Volume I, 2007) *Shōbōgenzō: The True Dharma-eye Treasury* (Volume II, 2008) *Shōbōgenzō: The True Dharma-eye Treasury* (Volume III, 2008) *Shōbōgenzō: The True Dharma-eye Treasury* (Volume IV, 2008)	
Jp.	Zazen yōjin ki (坐禪用心記)	2586
Eng.	*Advice on the Practice of Zazen* (in *Zen Texts,* 2005)	
Jp.	Senchaku hongan nembutsu shū (選擇本願念佛集)	2608
Eng.	*Senchaku Hongan Nembutsu Shū: A Collection of Passages on the Nembutsu Chosen in the Original Vow* (1997)	
Jp.	Kenjōdo shinjitsu kyōgyō shōmon rui (顯淨土眞實教行証文類)	2646
Eng.	*Kyōgyōshinshō: On Teaching, Practice, Faith, and Enlightenment* (2003)	
Jp.	Tannishō (歎異抄)	2661
Eng.	*Tannishō: Passages Deploring Deviations of Faith* (1996)	
Jp.	Rennyo shōnin ofumi (蓮如上人御文)	2668
Eng.	*Rennyo Shōnin Ofumi: The Letters of Rennyo* (1996)	
Jp.	Ōjōyōshū (往生要集)	2682
Jp.	Risshō ankoku ron (立正安國論)	2688
Eng.	*Risshōankokuron or The Treatise on the Establishment of the Orthodox Teaching and the Peace of the Nation* (in *Two Nichiren Texts,* 2003)	
Jp.	Kaimokushō (開目抄)	2689
Eng.	*Kaimokushō or Liberation from Blindness* (2000)	

Title		Taishō No.
Jp.	Kanjin honzon shō (觀心本尊抄)	2692
Eng.	*Kanjinhonzonshō or The Most Venerable One Revealed by Introspecting Our Minds for the First Time at the Beginning of the Fifth of the Five Five Hundred-year Ages* (in *Two Nichiren Texts,* 2003)	
Ch.	Fumu enzhong jing (父母恩重經)	2887
Eng.	*The Sutra on the Profundity of Filial Love* (in *Apocryphal Scriptures,* 2005)	
Jp.	Hasshūkōyō (八宗綱要)	extracanonical
Eng.	*The Essentials of the Eight Traditions* (1994)	
Jp.	Sangō shīki (三教指帰)	extracanonical
Jp.	Mappō tōmyō ki (末法燈明記)	extracanonical
Eng.	*The Candle of the Latter Dharma* (1994)	
Jp.	Jūshichijō kenpō (十七條憲法)	extracanonical